AMERICAN FICTIONS: 1980-2000

AMERICAN FICTIONS: 1980-2000

Whose America Is It Anyway?

Frederick R. Karl

Copyright © 2001 by Frederick R Karl.

Library of Congress Number: 2001117546
ISBN #: Hardcover 1-4010-1659-6
Softcover 1-4010-1658-8

All rights reserved. No part of this book may be reproduced or transmitted in any form or by any means, electronic or mechanical, including photocopying, recording, or by any information storage and retrieval system, without permission in writing from the copyright owner.

This book was printed in the United States of America.

To order additional copies of this book, contact:
Xlibris Corporation
1-888-7-XLIBRIS
www.Xlibris.com
Orders@Xlibris.com

CONTENTS

ACKNOWLEDGMENT 9
INTRODUCTION 11

CHAPTER ONE 27
    GROWING UP OR DOWN IN AMERICA

CHAPTER TWO 80
    THE RESURGENT NEW

CHAPTER THREE 155
    THE MEGA-NOVEL: DO WE DESERVE It?

CHAPTER FOUR 226
    THE NEW REALISM-HOW NEW IS IT?

CHAPTER FIVE 269
    THE SHORT STORY-WHERE IS IT TAKING US
    AND WHOSE LANGUAGE IS IT?

CHAPTER SIX 300
    SECOND WORLD WAR AND VIETNAM WAR
    FICTION: CONTRAST AS CULTURAL DIFFER-
    ENCE

CHAPTER SEVEN ... 337
BLACKS-WOMEN-JEWISH WRITERS: RACIAL, ETHNIC, AND GENDER SEPARATION— A LOOK BACK AND FORWARD

CHAPTER EIGHT ... 377
ROTH AND UPDIKE, ZUCKERMAN AND RABBIT— JEWISH AND GENTILE PERSPECTIVES OF AMERICA

CHAPTER NINE ... 408
THE FICTIONAL NINETIES: GOING WHERE?

NOTES ... 485

INDEX ... 523

To the Six:

Channa, Christopher, Nora, Sophia, Tepi

And

Bella

ACKNOWLEDGMENT

My wife, Dolores, has been involved in nearly every aspect of this book, and without her constant and supportive help, this project would not have been completed. She has been indispensable.

INTRODUCTION

A defining moment for me came when I completed *American Fictions: 1940-1980* more than 20 years ago. I was fearful that the novel as a meaningful explanation of who and what we are, were, or would be was no longer viable. By this, I did not ignore the many talented writers who were just beginning to appear; as we shall see, they are of many kinds, and with them we must include the still active older generation. What I saw then was not paucity of talent, but the condition of the country, which made any whole vision impossible, and a situation in which a general or universal language was being jeopardized. Once again, it was not a lack of language-in fact, language had been enshrined by so many linguistic subcultures flowing into it-but the fact that language had ceased to mean anything. It was not only political double talk; it was that language was being subdivided into small segments by groups who increasingly insisted on "their language" and none other.

Each subculture and division within-while perhaps a plus for democracy and free expression-was also creating a kind of fundamentalism in which only its vision or position mattered. Language was sundered not by its lessening or flattening but by its ineffectiveness as a tool for resolution or even argument. Dialogue became almost impossible: the commonalities of language had given way to an angry din. The multiculturalism which seemed a natural outgrowth of our system did not mean more dialogue and more well-defined discourse, but less; not an addition to, but a loss of vision, creativity, imaginative fare. The novelists, I feared, would become bystanders of sorts, swept away by historians, biographers, memoirists. They would continue to write novels, since that is what novelists do, but their books would increasingly lose a common language, or a common purpose. Their very advocacy would become a minor tale in a minor key, or else a voice no one cared to listen to.

My fears, however, were not realized and I decided to go ahead with a kind of "sequel" to the earlier book. But my sequel has within it a cautionary tale: that the very democratic processes which led to such a proliferation of voices has made it increasingly difficult for the writer to grab hold of the country. It is not chance, I believe, that so much good writing has gone into what I call "Growing Up" nonfiction novels: these memoirs, with their strong autobiographical and biographical dimension, appear as a wave of the present-although whether they will continue past the decades of the 80s and 90s is hard to judge. In the meanwhile, they have served a useful function, since they have chewed off that part of the country the writer can surely understand, his or her part, his or her experiences. Although most of these memoirs, coming as they do in the 80s, have striking social and political vibrations, they are also personalized, their languages individualized. "Vision" is not a major issue.

Similarly, the avalanche of shorter fiction, while heartening in one respect and a reflector of considerable talent, serves as an indicator: that the shorter form is a refuge; that a holistic view is increasingly difficult; that the "story" is a way of getting in and out without grappling with tougher questions of subject, form, language, creativity itself. The short story becomes in this post 80s period an art form in itself, but small, tidy, manageable. It only partially answers who we are and where we are going.

I have been forced to make other adjustments between this book and the former study, which ended with 1980. Decades in American life are like centuries elsewhere, so rapid is change. In the earlier volume, I attempted a literary history of the period after the Second World War, and within that historical record a critical evaluation. My thesis was that the main hope for American fiction was an innovative and experimental streak. American literature could be meaningful only if its writers attempted to expand the frontiers of their craft, while also reflecting their "Americanism." There seemed little point in repeating what had already been done in forms exhausted by Hemingway or Fitzgerald, and, more notably, Faulkner, the three abiding presences. My major proponents of novelty were William Gaddis, Thomas Pynchon, Joseph McElroy, Donald Barthelme, John Barth, the early work of John Hawkes and Joseph Heller, some of Robert Coover, William Gass, and Ralph Ellison, with intimations of Flannery O'Connor. I felt there, and continue to feel, that this body of work opened up American fiction, or at the least provided a lead for other novelists to follow.

Many in that group I brought together as "Mega-Novelists": writers of extremely long books which encompassed the country in terms of complex, unbounded space, and creative language; those who thought in terms of openness, not closure, and attempted new forms for fiction. By vaunting this group, I did not denigrate those who followed more traditional paths, Bellow, Baldwin, Updike, Roth, Walker, Malamud, Mailer, Oates, Morrison, Styron, Reed, Vonnegut, and Doctorow. Although their fiction is often uneven and they have frequently repeated themselves in successive works, they have established their own voices. But most (not all) have received the lion's share of the public's attention to serious fiction, the lion's share of the serious fictional market, and, for nearly the entire group, the plaudits of journalists and critics no matter what they write. Many of them have turned writing careers into celebrity careers, with the latter carrying them well past what their fictional skills can support. A serious effort to redress this was needed and *American Fictions: 1940-1980* intended to do this.

The present book has a different agenda. Not wishing to repeat myself, I have used the 1980s and thereafter as a kind of battleground for American fiction, a cultural mosaic of so many conflicting ideas and efforts that any statement about direction, or even achievement, is difficult to make. While the 1950s and 60s, and even the 70s, were clear, the 80s and 90s so far are enigmatic, paradoxical, uncertain. New, interesting, accomplished writers have emerged, from the mid-70s-there is little question of that as we survey Don DeLillo, Paul Auster, T. Coraghessan Boyle, Toni Morrison (a continuing story), among others. This study attempts to present that mosaic, with the basic theme that the uncertainty, the tentativeness, the shiftiness, the sense of conspiratorial forces and exhaustion in the serious fictional scene are reflections of the extreme uncertainty of American life in general in the 80s and after, despite ostensible prosperity for perhaps two-thirds of the population. There are few heart-warming stories, no more straight narratives, little that can be resolved. Irony, paradox, ambiguity dominate. Even harsh realism, one of our staples, has run aground, unless in the detective story minor mode. The undertones of the fictional world reveal a loss of direction and purpose, which is what may be writ large in the broader American world. Whether this is altogether true or not, it *is* perception. At perhaps no other time in our history has our fiction so illuminated the larger culture, not only in themes but as a confusing kaleidoscope of American life. Roth's *Operation Shylock*, in 1993, reinforces uncertainty in the use of conspiracy, doubling, hallucinatory experience. We are not bipolar, but multipolar. The issue is no longer between innovative, modernistic writers and those who use more conventional means; it is between those who insist on disorder, even anarchy, in our life and those who still see or yearn for some forms of order. It is between those who insist on identifying the false and those who think fabrications are real.

William Gaddis's *J R*, in 1975, is both unique and representative in its revelation of a changing, self-consuming America. It reaches back into 1960s egalitarianism and looks ahead to 70s and 80s belief in upward mobility through shaky financial deal, scams, fabrications. As an acoustical novel, dependent on spoken dialogue, *J R* borrows from and parodies communications systems. That other representative novel of the 70s, Thomas Pynchon's *Gravity's Rainbow*, is also deeply concerned with information, mis-or disinformation, disruptive communication. Both novels assimilated the enormous growth of television since the 1960s, a development which in its use of visual and auditory effects to convey incomplete information has influenced nearly every aspect of American fiction, along with all other forms of the printed word. Made up of small bytes, *J R* has within it the compactness television demands, the shifting and brevity of attention that medium has accustomed us to. Some of this same sense of foreshortened, disrupted language and attention span occurs in Mailer's *Why Are We in Vietnam?*, in Joseph Heller's *Catch 22* (itself a large presence in 1960s and early 70s fiction), in John Barth's acoustical shorter pieces, in Joseph McElroy's saga-like *Women and Men*, in somewhat more narrowly-based work like Barry Hannah's *Ray*. This list is not exhaustive.

One key to what has occurred in American fiction since the 1960s, as suggested before, is found in the proliferation of languages, voices, often just sounds. Innovation in this area cuts across all gender, racial, ethnic groups, from effervescent Ishmael Reed and Kathy Acker to more studied Donald Barthelme and Paul Auster. William Burroughs, especially his *Naked Lunch*, has been a large presence in this development; and then in writers as seemingly distinct as Barth (*Giles Goat-Boy, Lost in the Funhouse*), Pynchon (from *V.* through *Vineland*), and Joseph McElroy (the metaphysical excursions of *Hind's Kidnap* and *Lookout Cartridge*.

In Barth and Barthelme, we find the ambiguities of language, voice, tone; in Pynchon, language is infinite possibility, as if an act of vengeance on previous fiction, but always distinguished by attention to the American vernacular.[1] The groups succeeding or paralleling these writers in the 70s and 80s offer fewer pure forms of innovative language and more of a bottoming-out, such as we find in the so-called neo-realists (factualists who bleed over into fantasy: Raymond Carver in the short story and Paul Auster in his deliberately flattened-out novels, or in the lyrical-realistic narratives of Richard Ford. Yet not all is flatness, since in 1981, running against the realistic trend, the stories by Guy Davenport, in *Eclogue*, made fiction an assemblage, a verbal, nonrepresentational collage.

In T. Coraghessan Boyle (especially *Water Music* and *East Is East*), we encounter a riot of words, a variety of tongues that parallels a Robin Williams riff. And in Don DeLillo, language can be both soft and gentle and rapier-like and incisive. We find, also, the continuation of the Mega-Novel, with Harold Brodkey's *The Runaway Soul*, Gaddis's *A Frolic of His Own*, Wallace's *Infinite Jest*, books in which language swamps the subject, offers unlimited extension, and disallows closure or even narrowing down.

In those novels whose structures are more nearly disrupted, such as Toni Morrison's *Beloved* or Barry Hannah's *The Tennis Handsome*, we discover a lyricism which pushes against hip-hop narrative to create unique zones of meaning. While there is a general diminution of innovative work-with both modernism and postmodernism seemingly almost mined out-there are still the broad possibilities of the American language as it rediscovers itself and absorbs foreign words into English. While remaining intensely American, the language of the last two decades has also reached out to the world-we need note only the witty use of Japanese words and phrases in Boyle's *East Is East*. Yet, on a note of caution, that very proliferation of languages, voices and sounds signals that the possibilities of wholeness have ended; the richness of the languages may be the harbinger of breakup.

In another, but related, area, the re-emergence of the short story as a meaningful force indicates a concern not only with design, shaping, patterns, but once again with language. This literary development in the 70s and 80s is complex, but in part must be related not only to the brief segments of television but also to the growth of gossip magazines like *People*, as well as to the proliferation of university-based writing courses and the emergence of almost innumerable small literary magazines. These story writers-Raymond Carver, Ann Beattie, Frederick Barthelme, Bobbie Ann Mason, Barry Hannah, Tobias Wolff, Guy Davenport-although often grouped, are not homogeneous. They are not the same person writing the same story. Some reveal almost negative resonances, a throwback to planes of abstraction in nonrepresentational art or to the anomie we recall from French existentialism. Donald Barthelme is a large, creative presence here. But others have attempted ornamentation, an imposing rhetorical intrusion, as in the aforementioned Guy Davenport or in Barry Hannah's exuberant *Airship* stories.

The divisions here in the short story, although not cast in stone, fit well into the larger split between those who have rejected innovation and those who feel there is still some mileage in experimentation. As America has shaped itself in the 1980s and 90s, it takes a hardy soul, a true believer, to insist on innovation. The entire era calls for more direct social, political, economic, cultural response, little of which is conducive to large-scale formalistic experimentation, which assumes an anarchic, even surreal world.[2] The tendency, as we see in Don DeLillo's work, up to *Underworld*, is to *reflect* political and cultural events: the Kennedy assassination in *Libra*, terrorism in *Mao II*, toxic pollution in *White Noise*, social anomie in *Players*, the rock scene in *Great Jones Street*.

In screening the 80s and 90s, the serious reader must continue to wonder how a fiction writer can deal with a period of such contradictions. For it has been the period in our postwar history which, despite prosperity, has made the least sense, undermining both idealism and hope. It was (is) an age of incoherence: not least because of governmental incompetence running parallel with the proliferation of ideological groupings and increasing divisions within already existing groupings; not least, further, because all explanations of human behavior appear to cancel each other and all the old coalitions have fallen apart-political, social, ideological, economic, even those associated with class and ethnicity. That the national parties realigned dramatically was not a cause of the anarchy, but itself only a symptom. The felt sense was that the country was escaping; that boundaries no longer counted. The name *America* belonged to the historical entity which was still worshipped as a mythical place; but, in reality, was a place which existed as memory, in part as language, in another part as nostalgia. Only new immigrants could consistently think of it as hope, and here disillusionment was often not distant. Behind the superficial good cheer and official deception, people began, finally, to perceive rot. The Vietnam War was one revelation of how rot entered the system, as we shall see in our canvass of Vietnam War literature, by the veterans themselves.

If we measure the dropoff in voting at presidential as well as at lower levels (50% is considered a bonanza), we see it not solely as a failure in candidates-note Bush and Gore in 2000-but as a recognition the country no longer wishes to choose among *any* candidates. Not only were the ones who offered themselves unacceptable, the very idea of voting, of choice, of favoring one point of view over the other had become burdensome or irrelevant. The myth of voting remained, nevertheless: a free choice in a free country, the vote as the backbone of democracy, change as something brought about by the ballot box. While the myth was there, the actuality had vanished. The election process was a metonymy: the country, for many-perhaps for a third to half-was becoming unrecognizable. Such is the perception.

It has not been a period of alienation. The latter suggests that once the right formula or resolution is found, there may be a chance for elements eventually to cohere. Ours is not alienation; it is incoherence of another kind. People drifted off to the margins. California, as we observe it in Pynchon's *The Crying of Lot 49* and *Vineland*, is a state of mind and, then later, the state of the country. Yet if our writers were correct in one prediction, it was in their almost unanimous belief that to fill the holes language itself must rise to the occasion. The glory of American fiction has been and still is its varied use of vernaculars, colloquialisms, tongues; but that very use paradoxically revealed how precarious language had become.

An example: the ten-or fifteen-year period when minimalism seemed to reign in the literary marketplace was part not only of a disbelief in the reality of America but in the reality of a language which could possibly delineate the country. It seemed that not only was the country a self-consuming artifact, language had itself become jeopardized. It might slip away. Minimalism became more than a weapon or response, it was part of a negative prediction; and not unexpectedly, its nihilism turned off reviewers and critics, who seemed only too happy to observe its demise. But in its implications for language, minimalism would not go away; for in its use of words it predicated pauses, silences, omissions, ellipses, and incompleteness: something very striking about American life, American memory and history, American nostalgia. In *its* language, it penetrated the myths, refused to partake in the celebration of fabrication (clichés, stereotyping, deception) and insisted on understatement as a means of achieving some balance. It stressed a language based on denial of language as usual. It took the sound byte into fiction, turned it on its end, as it were, so that once fictionalized, the sound byte became credible. In DeLillo's *White Noise*, Murray Jay Siskind, who plans a university department centering on Elvis Presley, catches the presence of the tube as language:

> You have to learn how to look. You have to open yourself to the data. TV offers incredible amounts of psychic data. It opens ancient memories of world birth, it welcomes us into the grid, the network of little buzzing dots that make up the picture pattern. There is light, there is sound. I ask my students, what more do you want? Look at the wealth concealed in the grid, in the bright packaging, the jingles, the slice-of-life commercials, the products hurtling out of darkness, the coded messages and endless repetitions, like chants, like mantras. "*Coke is it, Coke is it, Coke is it.*" The medium practically overflows with sacred formulas if we can remember how to respond innocently and get past our irritation, weariness and disgust.

Yet even as minimalism echoes this, it recognizes the shallowness and falsity of it. In its time, minimalism insisted on a kind of honesty, even as it destabilized language, in fact endangered it.

Because so much has been destabilized, writers from the 1970s, 80s, and early 90s-with markedly uneven results-are attempting to work out whether they live in a real or mirrored world; whether there is substance-whether, in fact, *anything* is worthwhile-or whether they are merely going through the motions from birth through death. A heavy overlay of Kafka and the Kafkaesque is upon this literature, but lacking the Czech writer's witty, bemused belief that through pain and suffering (his!) one gains a point of view akin to survival. Kafka fought against the beast of the apocalypse, the real as well as the imagined ones; whereas American writers are waiting out the uncertainties. Their depression or despondency is such that even sexual energy is depleted or pro forma. The trenchant, prophetic New York trilogy of Paul Auster is typical, in that his protagonists work hard at accomplishing geometric patterns: activity without accomplishment, energy expended without either fulfillment or even comprehension. Repeatedly, in our fiction, there is seemingly no way out of the labyrinth; repeatedly, the image is of conspiracies, tunnels, abbreviated spaces (hotel rooms, closets, basements, attics, cars), ever tighter deceptions which preclude open movement, no less resolution.

Perceptions having become so minimal, the serious reader may well wonder what in American life, so reduced into subcultures within subcultures, can generate larger fictions. Toni Morrison, Alice Walker, John Edgar Wideman, and Ishmael Reed have found subjects in Afro-American life, but that segment is crumbling, also, into ever smaller units; so that there is hardly a large entity such as "Afro-American life" anymore: only isolated subcultures, some of which speak different languages. Where does the Afro-American writer seeking the broader world, like Ralph Ellison in *Invisible Man*, go or fit? Similarly, for the Latino novelist. So, too, the impetus which gave energy to the so-called "Jewish novel" is no longer there. If ever a particular vein has been exhausted that one, distinctly linked to the fortunes of Jews after the war, has been. Only Philip Roth still mines it. There remains female or feminist fiction, but women writers as much as men are caught up by American life, and if male writers are confused or frustrated, so are women. Distinct female-oriented novels may particularize that experience, but it is doubtful if the subject *alone* of the female experience will move outside traditional and conventional forms. We must say the same for any other minority or ethnic writers; only the subcultures remain.

While there is still enormous variety and great adeptness in American fiction, any theory for the 80s and 90s must deal mainly with cultural negatives. The larger themes of course still remain out there for the clairvoyant writer able to perceive what is important and to muster the techniques needed to contain it. Wallace's *Infinite Jest* suggests that only functional strategies can capture the incoherence. But these large themes are difficult to see whole: American decline or deterioration (both real and perceived), decay of the social structure (real, not only perceived), desecration of cultural values amidst depreciation of rational discourse itself (undeniable), social, economic, racial, and class divisions which seem unbridgeable (undeniable). With the country having broken up into ever smaller units, each unit or group calls for satisfaction on its terms. All such claims seem valid, whether gay rights, female equality in the workplace or in the military, or racial justice. And yet egalitarianism divides us culturally; greater democracy leads to breakup, not unity. The sense of a country with a common destiny or calling hardly exists-and this was true long before we had insipid debates over what is politically correct. Those debates, which usually depend on first amendment questions, are simply another dimension of the larger question of what the country is, what it stands for, what it might do in the future.

Part of the blame for the disintegration of a national vision or destiny lies in the appalling leadership the country has experienced, going back to the end of the Second World War. No country, despite its powerful economy and democratically-protected freedoms, can withstand long-term second-and third-rate leaders. This is not a matter of conservative or liberal, Republican or Democrat, northerner or southerner, or any other binary division. Too many leaders have suffered ignominy, been proven liars and deceivers of Congress and the American public, been discovered on the take, directly or indirectly, or, more apparently, revealed themselves as intellectually incapable of handling their position. Foreigners speaking English as their second or third languages articulate better and more succinctly than American presidents.

Several of the large novels of the 60s and 70s reflected that overall failure of leadership or direction, *The Recognitions, J R, Giles Goat-Boy, V., Catch-22,* as well as shorter works of more traditional novelists, Bellow (in *Henderson the Rain King, Herzog*), Roth (in the Zuckerman series), Mailer (in *Why Are We in Vietnam?*) and others. Now that the disintegration of social purpose has further intensified and it has become clear no leader, however well-meaning, can be effective, the novelist is also forced toward fragmentation. We can look forward to sniping actions: an attack on this, an exposé of that, a marginalization of significant issues, an emphasis on the kinkiness of American life. Don DeLillo's impressive ten novels, to date, for example, can be viewed as pieces in an American puzzle, each novel a segment which must be linked to other segments seeking to find a whole. In form, they are like a television miniseries, each part dependent on the other. Clearly, the influence of television comes not only from the more immediate effect of deceptive visuals or sound bytes, or from its subversion of language, but from its excerpting of life, its squeezing of elements into marginal comments, its avoidance of wholes in favor of parts, and, of course, its sensationalism as a substitute for analysis or the longer haul. It has made introspection too heavy to bear, too boring to tolerate. The major networks have become the K-Marts of broadcasting. Words no longer mean. Language lies in shadows, cool, hip, ungrammatical, groovy, insubstantial: a mutant language reflecting a fabricated world.

In another area, the new critical theories, whether deconstruction or hermeneutics, however effective in academe, have not proven a positive development for fiction writers who look to critical language for support. Films, another language, do little better, nor should more be expected of them; their interaction with books has not proven positive for literature. The novelist is left to pick up the pieces and to try to fit them together into larger elements, even while barraged by the other media. What, then, can the serious writer assume his material to be? What can he or she believe in? Where does the writer find suitable material, when all elements of contemporary life seem to be layered by official lies, unofficial deceptions, a process which does not add up to an "experience"? What is language itself? The quest for literary illumination becomes incredibly difficult.

The era of the novel will not end, but fiction as an adventurous testing out of boundaries and frontiers has become an endangered species. That will be a constant in this study. If we take the present level of social and political discourse as some revelation of the 90s decade, then we see blandness, lack of innovation, mere holding on: in all, a depreciation of language, history, memory, comprehension. Both public and private discourse have shrunk, or become shrill and self-serving. These are bound to influence novel-writing; and even if fiction writers work antagonistically to subvert the political or social vision, or lack of it, we should not expect the surge following World War Two. One hopeful sign, although with quite uneven results: Brodkey's *The Runaway Soul*, Helprin's *A Soldier of the Great War*, David Bradley's *The Chaneysville Incident*, Gaddis's *A Frolic of His Own*, on an even larger scale, McElroy's *Women and Men*, Wallace's *Infinite Jest* and Pynchon's *Mason & Dixon*. Another sign, although not of mega-size, is the rich outpouring of autobiographical memoirs, part fiction, part biography, part history of the self, a mutant form capable of giving the novel serious competition. Our hope: a large movement in satire, such as we saw in *Catch 22* in the 60s, or some of Barth, Gaddis, Pynchon, and Barthelme; but the satire must have breadth as well as pungency. It cannot particularize, or *only* particularize, but should spread, venomously, across the entire land, Rabelasian, Swiftian, or Dickens-like: and it must somehow recapitulate all the tools of the novelist. Washington D. C. calls out for its own *Bleak House*. The writer, however, cannot simply rework old territory-we have the older generation doing that. We need nasty books to pursue a holistic vision.

In several of my chapters, it has been necessary to dip back into earlier decades to support an historical or a critical argument. The segment on Vietnam War novels compared with World War Two fictions, for example, overlaps with some of the material from *American Fictions:1940-1980*; but it also describes the 80s, when the country for the first time began to confront the Vietnam War. "Blacks-Jews-Women," with its references to the 60s and 70s battles, revisits some material from the earlier book, but expands the argument and introduces new writers. The chapter on the short story, however, stands on its own. Although not inclusive, it does contain a broad variety of writers and their sense of America. Their almost unanimously dismal vision of the country must be offset by the fact of the energy of the writers themselves. If America is a fiction, a reflection of reality, a disintegrating giant, a betrayer of its own ideals, its writers, like embattled warriors knocked to the ground, return repeatedly to the fray. In their insistence on *their* America, they have in one respect re-created a personal country as valid as the so-called real one; they have fictionalized a fiction.

Not less pressing in America's fiction, or, alternately, America as a fiction, is the division of the country which we discover in Philip Roth and John Updike. Almost alone of our contemporary novelists, they have returned to the same characters, writing chronicle novels of the kind once popular with Balzac and Zola. Roth's Nathan Zuckerman, the quintessential Jew, and Updike's Rabbit Angstrom, the quintessential Gentile, offer two very different perspectives on America, while themselves proving to be very American. A Jewish perspective set off against a Gentile one-while a simplification, as are all binary divisions-does provide a sense of the last two or three decades: not only who we are but how we think about ourselves.

The Old Guard (alas!) is passing, and a new generation has

already taken over, a commendable one whose only major fault, until *Underworld* and *Infinite Jest*, is a disinclination to go for the big, inclusive, provocative book. The most promising appear to be Don DeLillo, Paul Auster, T. Coraghessan Boyle, Cormac McCarthy, Toni Morrison, whom I catch in "Make it New." There is of course continuing input from Pynchon, Gaddis, E. L. Doctorow, Joyce Carol Oates, Robert Stone, and several others who reach back into earlier decades. These writers connect with those whom I include in the chapter called "The New Realism." To the degree there is continuity with previous decades, the present study will link up with *American Fictions: 1940-1980*; to the degree there is discontinuity, the later book will reveal shifts of direction, even greater uncertainties and ironies than the immediate postwar generation faced

CHAPTER ONE

GROWING UP OR DOWN IN AMERICA

Frank Conroy—*Stop-Time as precursor*
Paul Auster—*The Invention of Solitude*
Richard Rhodes—*A Hole in the World*
John Edgar Wideman—*Brothers and Keepers*
Mikal Gilmore—*Shot in the Heart*
Paul Cowan—*An Orphan in History*
Julius Lester—*Lovesong: Becoming a Jew*
Geoffrey Wolff—*The Duke of Deception: Memories of My Father*
Tobias Wolff—*This Boy's Life*
Edmund White—*A Boy's Own Story*
Susan Cheever—*Home Before Dark: A Biographical Memoir of John Cheever by His Daughter*
Eva Hoffman—*Lost in Translation*
Russell Baker—*Growing Up*
Edward Rivera—*Family Installments*
E. L. Doctorow—*World's Fair*

The key metaphor for the country and for the spate of Growing Up books which were written in the late 1970s and in the 1980s is the hole, the "absence of," or the "lack of." It forms the title of Richard Rhodes's moving memoir, *A Hole in the World* (1990), and is best expressed in Paul Auster's *The Invention of Solitude* (1982). Often, the absence of something or someone is the missing father, not only physically but also emotionally. But it does not have to be the father. It is something understood to be lacking in the country: as if the hole in one's life could be extended into the hole in the life of America. A national emptiness is reflected in these numerous memoirs, themselves a mutant form of fiction/nonfiction. Virtually all are painful experiences, but that is a given of all growing up books: anguish, sense of personal bereavement, mourning and melancholy usually for the lost self; and then overcoming it, at least to the extent that the book about it gets written. The recovery may be slow, threaded with additional problems, saturated with anguish and bad memories-especially that, the bad memories which poison one's sense of history. We observe that in an earlier, classic example, Frank Conroy's *Stop-Time* (1967).[3]

Stop-Time is full of sixties rage, and it serves well as a forerunner of those raging memoirs in which self-destruction limns the protagonist's personality. Conroy's "confession" begins with an adult protagonist driving his Jaguar wildly, seeking the very edge between life and death, daring the outer limits of car, driver, and road. The remainder of the text then explains the wish for self-destruction. The young protagonist, a boy with a brain, has been emptied out of meaning, support, understanding. He is powerless in the adult games played by his mother (his father has left to enter rest homes, then dies) and his stepfather, a Frenchman from Louisiana, who believes the world owes him a living. The boy suffers from such devastating loneliness and sadness that he does not find anything but the void. Close to anomie, he wanders, from New York to Florida, back to New York, runs away, gets less than halfway to Florida, and then returns only because of his half-sister, who has become his sole, although uncertain, anchor.

Injustice and indifference create the void, and young Frank falls in. The void dominates: at twelve, "days were emptiness, a vast spacious emptiness in which the fact of being alive became almost meaningless. The first fragile beginnings of a personality starting to collect in my twelve-year-old soul were immediately sucked up into the silence and the featureless winter sky. The overbearing, undeniable reality of those empty days!"[4] He sees everything around him as nonhuman, and he doubts his relationship to things; he feels that in terms of "snow and sky and rocks and dormant trees I didn't exist, these things rendered me invisible even to myself.... I became invisible. I lost myself."[5]

Discontinuity and disconnection are the battleground on which the war is fought, the book written, the career set. These very different memoirists-male and female, black and white, advantaged and disadvantaged-have come through, although in some instances with worlds so nightmarish they suffer shattered nerves well into their fifties and sixties. The wounds are, we can say, part of the terrain. That terrain, emotional, psychological, physical, is, as suggested, linked to a view of the country: implied in the failure of institutions to help desperately needy children, the lack of concern for family care and values, the economic precariousness of families living without support systems, the absence of adequate health care; and beyond that, the general feeling that anarchy is out there, an absurd sequence of skewed adult lives and random incidents simply waiting to devour victims, usually the young; inevitably, the failure to recognize that families are often no longer families.

Another metaphor is of social anarchy: the predatory adult who becomes the step-parent, the relative, the hanger-on who preys on youth; and in some cases, the predatory beast may be an institution, a non-caring teacher, principal, or entire school. The theme is disharmony, between the child growing up and his immediate society, and then between warring, demonic elements in the child. The most substantial image of all is war: growing up in these memoirs is a large military campaign, with skirmishes, maneuvers, strategies, delaying tactics, losses, gains, advances, retreats.

Possibly the most memorable and characteristic is *The Invention of Solitude*,[6] a brief meditation on absences, with its clear linkage to the late nineteenth-century French symbolist, Stéphane Mallarmé, the poet of voids. Mallarmé wrote of how his work was created: "I've created my work only by *elimination*, and any truth I acquired resulted uniquely from the loss of an impression which, having sparkled, burnt itself out and allowed me, thanks to the shadows thus created, to advance more deeply in the sensation of the absolute shadows."[7]

Auster's "fictional" memoir proceeds on these lines. Absence does not make the heart beat fonder; it defines what the heart might be. Auster's effort is to recreate his earlier years by discovering himself in his father's artifacts after the latter's death. Underlying the quest for clues are the son's insistent questions of where he came from, how he was formed from this invisible man, how he can understand himself when he cannot understand his father, or, conversely, how he can be a father when it is impossible to understand his own, and not least how he can be a son when the father eludes him. The quest for immediate origins is the quest for self, a metaphysical probe into the nature of how people and things arrange themselves; so that the absence of self, the absence of clues, the lack of motives, the loss of linkage become as important as objects. Auster de-objectifies matter in order to make it significant; he deconstructs experience as a means of seeking its elusive center. He recognizes, inevitably, that there is no center; there are only clues.

His search is the fictionalization of his life: growing up with leads, but no finalities. And he finally stumbles on one major clue, his father having witnessed, at nine years old, *his* mother's fatal shooting of her husband. Yet while it is a key clue, it also escapes definition, since Paul learns of it not through his father but through newspaper accounts written by an unreliable reporter–someone interested more in selling newspapers than getting to roots. This is all Paul has–and thus origins come to him as unreliable, decentered, scattered in gossip columns. History is transmitted as possible misinformation; data are important, but not to be trusted. And when all is left, the father remains inexplicable absent, invisible, hidden and disguised amidst the great trauma of his young life.

As Paul searches for traces–his father seemingly left none–he falls outside what was an earlier genre of Growing Up literature. In the chapter "Growing Up in America," in *American Fictions: 1940-1980*, I observed that the forms of this genre tended to be fictions–*Call It Sleep, Studs Lonigan, The Catcher in the Rye, The Adventures of Augie March, Portnoy's Complaint, Go Tell It on the Mountain, The Bluest Eye, them*. Such novels revealed a good deal about American mobility, its pressures, the chances for success or failure; but in nearly every one there is a triumph, if not victory. With several of these works coming in the immediate postwar era, we find the optimism of expansionism, the hope of personal satisfaction, or at least the sense that the self could overcome personal or societal adversity. Many of these books were autobiographical, not in any direct way, but drawing on the intimate experiences of the author–Bellow in Chicago, for example. Paul Auster's version of that genre, now transformed into a kind of mutant fiction/nonfiction, has left behind optimism, hope, triumph. It suggests that searching is itself the metaphor for America. It is a compelling development because it suggests just how strongly the literary mind follows the political-social dimensions of the country. If we pursue a broad range of Growing Up memoirs, we see them as journeys into an America which yields little. The writers have not given up–they have, after all, written their books as both therapy and explanation–but they have limned a country trapped by dysfunctional institutions.

The very Mallarmé resonances of the Auster book suggest exhaustion, enervation, loss and absence, the missing as more significant than the found. It is as though Auster were searching for pieces of a puzzle, and then, after finding them, discovering they do not fit into any pattern. With communication disrupted, there seems little chance Paul, as writer, will be able to make meaningful linkages. The beauty of this memoir is not only its deconstruction of experience and of the form itself, not only its emptying out of an object-filled world, but the quest itself. "You never had the feeling that he [Paul's father] could be located,"[8] an apt symbolic statement for America in 1982, the year when so many of these mutant fictions were published.

When the lack of "location" keeps Paul guessing as to what occurred, he is forced to recreate or reinvent his own life as a fiction. He not only perceives the father but also begins to perceive himself as an indeterminate subject. What is *not* there will help define the son–all this before the major revelation of the family murder. Even his father's role as a married man leads to paradoxes, since he remained a "life-long bachelor who happened to have had an interlude of marriage."[9] Although faithful, he could not endure intimacy; lacking introspection, he did not seem cut out for any role. He took up space without impressing himself on the area around him. As for Paul himself, since he was conceived during his parents' honeymoon at Niagara Falls, he was "a random homunculus, like some dare-devil in a barrel, shooting over the falls."[10]

Unable to be located, the father could not locate anyone else; and so Paul grows up in mists and shadows.

> I was not defined for him by anything I did, but by what I was, and this meant that his perception of me would never change, that we were fixed in an unmovable relationship, cut off from each other on opposite sides of a wall. . . . Like everything else in his life, he saw me only through the mists of his solitude, as if at several removes from himself. The world was a distant place for him, I think, a place he was never truly able to enter, and out there in the distance, among all the shadows that flitted past him, I was born, became his son, and grew up, as if I were just one more shadow, appearing and disappearing in a half-lit realm of his consciousness.[11]

This extraordinary passage suggests a large theme for several of the books in the Growing Up genre: how the parental figure's lack of perception has transformed the child into a shadowy figure, someone without identification: and, further, how that radiates out into the country as itself undefined, shadowy, ominous. We find not the usual individual groping for identity, but a quest for the space one should fill and which is being denied. Not only has the nature of childhood changed, the nature of the larger experience of child, parent, and country has altered.

Kafka's *Letter to His Father* in 1919 seems rather obviously the prototype of this kind of memoir. His plaint was based on his perceptions of Hermann Kafka, the overbearing, boorish, dominating father: not the Hermann Kafka we can ever know but the one his son defined for all eternity. In that perception, the son has lost his space, his own location. The father controls all the territory of parent-child relationships, and has suffocated young Franz until he is airless. He is displaced to a hole.

The "hole in the world" metaphor signals not only family but also the larger arena, as we observe in Richard Rhodes's memoir of that name.[12] Such books–less than novels, more than autobiographies–are, in the Rhodes manner, almost unrelentingly painful to read. Behind the personal pain, however, is not merely the anguish of growing up, but the awareness that as children they have been let down: that despite lip service, the country is uninterested in its children; that they have no safety net until it is almost too late; that the country is infested by sadists, misfits, distorted individuals with infantile emotional responses who gain legal access to children and who can then mold, torture, alter them without interference.

Rhodes's *A Hole in the World* catches the moments when family life becomes warped, twisted, more hole than filler, when monstrous acts can be perpetrated on children. So much adult anger and failure exist out there that it is like a gigantic net waiting to catch helpless individuals in its traps. Instead of growth and development on the part of children, we discover bare survival, jungle tactics, anti-social behavior as responses to emotional deprivation, loss of self-confidence and sureness of purpose in the face of constant onslaughts against dignity. This is no pastoral romance, no sophisticated urban experience. If anything, books like Rhodes's connect to war books, to field encounters in Vietnam; and his young narrator becomes one of those savage Lurps operating alone in enemy territory.

Rhodes's trauma occurs when his widower father marries a woman who attempts systematically to break Richard and his slightly older brother, Stanley. Her plan is to eradicate them, by reducing them into hateful creatures, into bugs she can crush underfoot. She is, in one respect, the Hermann Kafka *perceived* by Franz, only with a more twisted, sadistic personality. Rhodes provides a compelling trope for the process, one based on possession of territory. "In *The Body in Pain*, Elaine Scarry speaks of 'the prisoner's steadily shrinking ground that wins for the torturer his swelling sense of territory.' For two years our stepmother funneled us into smaller and smaller spaces of physical and mental confinement–less food, less room, less nurture, less hope–in order to swell her own. In time, under her vicious regimen, we might have come to occupy no space at all."[13] The image is one of suffocation; and the larger sense of suffocation is the closing off not only of air but also of territory: no more Huck Finn lighting out for big sky country. Life is not expansive, but contracted. One grows "down." The social dimension is not to be ignored. This is, after all, a book of the 1980s, although the experiences come thirty or forty years earlier.

One of the ways Rhodes attempted to counter his stepmother's efforts to squeeze his space was with "flights of megalomaniacal fantasy."[14] We have, here, intimations of Rhodes's great book several decades later, *The Making of the Atomic Bomb*. The spatiality of the bomb and of his book contrasts sharply with the contracting world his stepmother demanded, to the extent she slowly starved the brothers until they scavenged in garbage cans. Like birds of prey, they pounced on any pieces of food lying around. When they were finally removed from her home, the social agency cited their low weight for their height and age. From the home of famine, Richard goes to the land of plenty, the Drumm Institute, where his work revolves around helping to produce the food which will feed him. The Drumm is all spatiality, the openness of the pastoral dream, but not quite a sacred place because death is ever present, in the slaughter of farm animals. Rhodes describes the slaughter with particular élan–it serves as a kind of therapy for his anger, especially the skinning and cutting up of the larger animals, the boiling of the fat, and the rest: the cow as stepmother. But balance, such as it is, is precarious. He will have to pay eventually, and he does with broken relationships and, most of all, alcoholism. The earlier years leave a hole in him the Drumm can only partially fill; and even his scholarship to Yale–as if the gods were looking out for him–is insufficient to fill him. He must endure a painful and difficult adulthood until some peace descends, helped by a particular woman and especially his success as a writer. Only writing, words, language enable the protagonist to regain the territory he was once denied.

Another kind of hole is described by John Edgar Wideman in *Brothers and Keepers* (1984).[15] Here the hole is created by his younger brother, whose life took on radical criminal overtones, leading to a murder charge which put him in prison for life. But there is more–and here the idea of the hole becomes insidious. For after *Brothers and Keepers* was published, Wideman suffered an even greater void in his life when his son stabbed to death his camp friend. No motivation was ever offered, and he is, now, also imprisoned for murder. The stabbing came after Wideman had established the hole in his life caused by his brother, but the son's terrible act somehow fits; as though the Widemans were caught in some cycle of tragic events, like families in Greek drama, where the acts of previous generations are repeated until the Furies are finally, if ever, quieted.

As in so many other books in this subgenera, Wideman uses another's life as a way of entering and re-entering his own: here, the narrator's life becomes, to some degree, a function of the brother's. The "keepers" of the title spreads out to Wideman of course, but to all of society who, he suggests, failed as keepers.

There are extensive arguments here about the shortcomings of the judicial system, about questions of race when the perpetrators are black and persecuted by prison personnel, nearly all of it speculative argument grafted on to questions of growing up. The reach, therefore, becomes far greater than we find in the other books, for Wideman chooses to explore the ambiguities of how one brother turns out the way he does–the narrator, a successful student and athlete in college, a Rhodes scholar, a university professor and writer–the other brother, a petty criminal whose criminality escalates until he is involved in a murder. The "bad brother" is not a bad person, but his career is as inevitably doomed as his older brother's is capped by success. The question is why and how.

While Wideman married a white woman, a Jew, had children, a career, even fame, his brother bonded to the outlaw part of the black world, letting his fortunes ride on the precarious nature of black experience in the inner city. A given in the book is that living in America is a great mystery which some can unravel but which, like a whirlpool, sucks in still others. To change the image, Wideman withstood the Sirens, whereas brother Robby succumbed to them. The narrator's perception is that whites control every dimension of his destiny: whites have surrounded, trapped, created boundaries around blacks, taken away their territory (as in the classic Growing Up memoir), squeezed, and in effect left them for dead. A good part of our response to the book, whether as white or black readers, depends on our acceptance of the overall theme.

As we explore the internal mechanisms of such memoirs, we must ask how questions of survival for Auster, Rhodes, and the Wolffs (for example) differ for Wideman, an Afro-American. Through his observation of his criminal brother, Wideman is attempting, clearly, to move beyond an individual growing up–on his own–to ask what it means to be a black American in the post civil rights era, more specifically in the Reagan years when the President refused to meet with black leaders or acknowledge the existence of a distinct black experience.

Yet this excursion into brother Robby's life creates a curious bifurcation. Wideman's comments are superbly trenchant, creating considerable disturbance not only in himself but in the reader, who must confront painful issues of crime and punishment. But Robby's story, told in *his* voice by the educated narrator, lacks force because it is so stereotypical. It is everyman's street voice, Bigger Thomas's and every other victim's; and it has little or no distinction as Robby's own voice. Furthermore, it suggests strongly that by telling this archetypal story of black youth who gets into trouble from the beginning, Wideman perceives all blacks as victims; and this, too, is stereotypical, inasmuch as the black community is hardly monolithic, but made up of innumerable subcultures, levels, dimensions, varying degrees of experience. The implication, further, is that Wideman as a black American is himself a victim, despite his success; but if so, this is at another level, not at all in the same category of someone like Robby.

The Widemans *are* a family, the mother and father supportive and *there*, their language standard English, not a street language. Given that, how do we explain Robby's voice, his language? Even if Robby consciously tried to speak the English of his peer groups, his language would have reflected a nurturing home, and what he heard there was standard. Wideman's appropriation of a street language for Robby, while understandable in the context of the "two voices" he wished to express, is incomprehensible in its stereotyping of an outlaw black man.

That racism played a part here cannot be questioned, but that racism created Robby is inadequate. As a writer, Wideman needs better motivation, more complicated explanations of how self, race, family, and other factors collide and interact to produce one criminal brother and one socially oriented one. The anger Wideman feels at the hand dealt his brother does need explanation, but it must come from within the writer, not from some stereotypical fallback. Robby had advantages most young boys would envy. His mother has herself maintained a steady course between her own sense of self and the racism which has in part shaped her; his older brother has prospered despite acts of humiliation and contempt which can be attributed to racism. The point is not to deny the virulence of racism, but to suggest there are many factors Wideman has stripped away, those embedded in the fictional or creative side of such a memoir.

The strength of *Brothers and Keepers* is linked to its weakness: from the author's partial recognition that strange forces are at work, that more than racism is involved. What disturbs him is his perception that some of the elements, those unknowns, which went into Robby went into him; that their careers, while superficially at the antipodes from each other, are not that far apart if we take into account circumstances and randomness. In a telling episode, Robby steals the family television set in order to buy two spoons of heroin. The set is replaced by a gift from the author's (Jewish) father-in-law, a generous act which Wideman acknowledges. But when the insurance money pays for the theft, Wideman holds on to the check instead of repaying his father-in-law, even though he has married into this family and fathered half-Jewish children. Unfortunately, this hostility, in which money is the agent, remains unexamined because it diverts from the overt theme of how race plays its role. The particular succumbs to the general.

The Cain and Abel allusions shape *Brothers and Keepers*. Wideman of course develops the book we eventually read; but within that, he is an author writing a briefer book about his brother, using the brother's stories and even words. This leads the author to several considerations, all indicating the fraternal struggle: whether he is visiting Robby in prison solely to gain material; whether the growing closeness between the two brothers exists in itself or develops only because of the needs of the book; possibly, whether the author-narrator is gaining identification and strength at the expense of the brother's loss–he is sucking out his space; whether there is anything left for the two of them when the book is finished, or whether the book has exhausted all they have to say about each other. Once published, the book exists on the outside, beyond prison walls, untouchable by the one whose life fills much of it; and its existence has no real bearing on his fate or condition, which is a life sentence without parole. Even if the book succeeds–and it did command a good deal of attention–the subject, for the most part, remains inert matter, awaiting possibly violent death from inmates or keepers.

While implicating all of us as "keepers," Wideman omits the very element that the reader and the Growing Up genre insist upon: that formative factors have to be dealt with, and the individual must take responsibility for the consequences. The reader must insist that while principles of human behavior are being ignored in prison, the criminal has ignored them in society. From the victims' point of view, it does not matter that the criminal is black, has had a hard background, has mental or emotional problems, was abused as a child, or whatever. Unless in some utopia, the personal background, including race, and societal need simply do not mesh; the one who falls outside whatever the social contract calls for does suffer. And Robby does not even seem to have been dealt a bad hand.

To insist, as Wideman does, that Robby's incarceration is a white plot is to do a terrible disservice to blacks who uphold that social contract as much as some whites do, frequently against far greater odds. Growing up means growing up: Robby failed to, and no one can excuse it. Even for those among us who believe in prisoner rehabilitation and would pay higher taxes tied to that, who believe in increasing literacy among the prison population, who accept the fact that in many instances systemic racism plays a huge role in the criminal justice system, who are adamantly opposed to the death penalty for even the most heinous crimes–for all these people, there is only so much pity or compassion for the Robbys of the world. Whatever the pressures and injustices, they had their chance to grow up; and their victims have no recourse except society's penalties.

Wideman is particularly fine in opening up these areas, in broadening the subgenre into social and political considerations. What are troubling are the stereotypes, surprising coming from a memoirist who is also a novelist. The outlaw black is offered as a given. We as readers must reject much of this; it defames blacks in the larger sense, and it defames all of us by suggesting general behavior based on race or class or ethnic background. Yet Wideman forces us to confront his rages, hatreds, desire for revenge; even while overpleading, overgeneralizing. He makes growing up too much a matter of race when it is personal individual accountability which the open reader must insist upon. The book is torturous, the author tortured, and it does not make anyone happy. And perhaps that is exactly what Wideman wanted to do.

Along somewhat similar lines, Mikal Gilmore's growing up memoir, *Shot in the Heart* (1994)[16] –as much novel as memoir, in fact– gives new meaning to dysfunctional. The Gilmore family, whose most famous product was of course the infamous Gary Gilmore, the murderer who insisted on his own execution in Utah, reaches deep into American life; and the four sons, two criminals, the other two deeply disturbed, are made representative of small-town life. *Wisconsin Death Trip* comes to mind, not small-town utopias, but small-town hells, the nightmarish existence of abusive parents, abusive spouses, alcohol, drugs, wild sexual encounters, with violence and brutality never too distant. The sons, and some daughters, are ushered in and out of reform schools, programs for wayward youths, finally the local and state prison system. Some even make it to the federal penitentiary. This, incidentally, is white America, not the inner city of stereotypes, but white, white America!

Shot in the Heart has echoes of several other books in this subgenera, Wideman's *Brothers and Keepers* most obviously–in which a brother's acts (involvement with a murder) have cast a shadow over the entire family; and even Geoffrey Wolff's *The Duke of Deception*, in which a father creates the contexts which disallow the sons to have normal lives. But of course Mikal Gilmore's story is even more intense, inasmuch as his brother has not only cast a shadow over the family, he has become for a time the most famous murderer in America and has, by his choice, helped to reinstate the death penalty. Utah was the perfect venue for this. The Mormon

Church believes in Blood Absolution, and Gary Gilmore's "blood" when he is executed will provide some redemption for his two murders. Strikingly, Mikal Gilmore's novelistic memoir has the quality of destiny fulfilled: the Blood Absolution of the Mormons coinciding with the deathward plunge of brother Gary, who repeatedly said he had been dying for twenty years.

Mikal Gilmore comes closer to trying to understand his brother than did Norman Mailer in his *The Executioner's Song*. In that nonfictional novel, or novelistic nonfiction–what Mailer called "A True Life Novel"–the author kept butting his head against Gilmore's inaccessibility. Mailer vaunts Gilmore's importance even as his revelations trivialize him. Although Mikal Gilmore cannot fully penetrate his brother's criminality, his slow building of the career as it passes into major crimes, his contextualization of the Gilmore household in which four brothers become dysfunctional, his description of anger and hatred in the mother, whose life was one episode or another of spousal brutality, all, help to explain Gary. Even though nothing can fully open up why a man murders two innocent people in the coldest of blood, some explanations are in order, and here, where Mailer failed, Mikal succeeds.

In all such memoirs, there are really two themes: the subject himself and then the forces in his life which have transformed him and his family into an isolated outpost, here a kind of frontier group surrounded by hostile Mormons. But more than that is the cultural freight such a case brings–I write this as another "double murder" has surfaced in the O. J. Simpson extravaganza. Without his guilt having been established, a good part of the population and the media have treated him as guilty, two innocent people, not shot, but stabbed. The cases, however different in particulars– all unhappy families are unhappy differently–there is the degree of guilt that spills over on brothers, parents, friends. But none can be so intense as with Mikal Gilmore.

The jacket photograph is compelling, Frank and Bessie Gilmore and three of their four sons, Frank Jr., Gary, and Gaylen. When the photo was taken in about 1950, Mikal was not yet born. It is, very much, an American family, posed in a Grant Wood Gothic rigidity, with Frank Sr. looking more kindly than we would expect; but he was already aging, perhaps exhausted. Frank and Bessie: they seem like typical Midwestern farm folks; and the three boys, with their hair carefully slicked down and parted, their eyes squinting into the camera, contain only one discordant feature–the rebellion and scorn in Gary's face. He was already a tough guy. But the photo has other resonances, one of them being the omission of Mikal, who survived the debacle of the Gilmores by breaking away from them. That he had not yet been born indicates how distant he was from Gilmore disaster, how he escaped by an accident of late birth, when Frank Sr. had already done his worst on his family; when his brothers had experienced all the terror and brutality and injustice that only a family can bring, while he was still outside or beyond it. In one real sense, Mikal escaped the family by not being in the photograph, since the camera, whatever else it caught, entraps them in a common fate of misery and criminality.

That is, of course, a family story–the subject and "the others," Gary and the rest of the Gilmores. As a family story, it carries with it symbiotic reverberations: each member demonstrates his or her "love" by way of hurting the others profoundly, physically, emotionally psychologically. Mikal's nightmares, which appear intermittently in the text, reveal terrible acts of violence, destruction and self-destruction–this from the one son who escaped, not dysfunction, but criminality. Yet they all claim love–but it is love in hell; every holiday ruined, every expectation destroyed, every avenue of escape except for Mikal blocked. The archetype for the Gilmores is classical tragedy, rerouted for middle class American life. When the father finally settled down and brought in sufficient money through a newsletter, the Gilmores came to be middle class and there were everywhere possibilities of recovery and stability. But because Frank Gilmore insisted on a patriarchal dictatorship, the family kept exploding into rebellious fragments. Ghosts haunted the family and family residences, for wherever they moved, they sensed shadowy presences both within and without: ghosts that invaded their expectations and destroyed their dreams.

The Gilmores were a small unit of American madness.[17] The book raises large questions about the country, about domestic violence which destroys every semblance of family as community or as societally productive. The waste of it is apparent. Although Gilmore's book is primarily concerned with the waste within his family, including his own inability to maintain relationships in his adult life, like so many other Growing Up memoirs, it reverberates outward. Everywhere the family moves, in its lower to lower middle class status before Frank Sr. begins to make money, the boys' friends are in and out of trouble, on drugs and alcohol, some permanently injured, several dead in crimes against society or each other. The prisons are full of them. Mikal writes repeatedly–and he could be speaking of a large segment of his generation–of how the spirit and flesh of the Gilmores have been traduced.

An entire generation seems to emerge with Gary Gilmore as their most obvious "role model." His notoriety attracted admirers, women, hangers-on. Gary was a star and celebrity, made to order for the proliferating gossip shows and news programs little different from the gossipmongers. He was someone's freak-of-the-day, the sour flavor of the month. He sold newspapers, he created television viewers, he bolstered a market for T-shirts. American entrepreneurism depended on the Gary Gilmores, who blended, in time, into the other monstrous figures with charisma, Ted Bundy, Jeffrey Dahmer, John Gacy; and on into the famous cases of the 1990s. The O. J. Simpson frenzy could not exist without the groundwork laid by Gary. In a sense, what Mikal misses–and he doesn't miss much–is how Gary has become an American legend, like Bonny and Clyde, the James Brothers, the Quantrells, those who killed their way into fame. An entire system requires the Gary Gilmores to create jobs, keep the TV screens busy, sell newspapers.

The only thing lacking in the book is the "selling" of Gary Gilmore. There are several pages on Lawrence Schiller and Norman Mailer: Schiller bought the rights to Gary's story, and Mailer presented it, with Schiller's research, in *The Executioner's Song*. Schiller even produced a film on Gary, and Mikal comes to see the entrepreneur as benign, helpful, even sympathetic. But as Gary becomes a commercial object, lost in the shuffle are the two young Mormon men, victims of Gary's shots, and the Gilmore family as a whole. Utah demanded blood absolution, those firing squad shots into Gary's heart, the outpouring of blood which suggests some redemption; but Gary cashed in, the merchant of death–he sold his story, he made the state bend to his wishes for execution, and he invigorated the death penalty. The system, which claimed justice was done, had not really done justice at all. The quality of Mikal's book indicates there could be no justice, no matter what occurred. Gary's horrendous crimes could not be redeemed; Gary's death was his triumph over the state, and the execution itself only gave greater notoriety to the murderer and left the victims even further in the shadows. When Frank Gilmore married Bessie, everything that was to fall apart was already implicit in the disparities of the union. The hole was being dug. What followed was classical Greek tragedy for middle-class America.

Questions arise. What is so traumatic about "becoming an American"? Does it mean disappearing into the great American landscape as an indefinable blob? Why can't one remain intensely a Jew, or intensely an Afro-American, or intensely WASP, without this frantic search for roots or for rituals to sustain one's life and one's family? Why cannot America nourish what is generally acceptable and yet not threaten what is individualistic about oneself? For Jews, marriage to a Gentile does not necessarily mean assimilation; often, it is quite otherwise. The family retains elements from both parents; a mutant form is created, and that, too, is American. The mutant American, a nation of mongrels, crossbreeds. For example, Paul Cowan's eloquent pleas in *An Orphan in History* (1982)[18] for *aliyah* (that return to Judaism) on the part of otherwise secularized Jews leaves out entirely the psychological forces which drive or energize a person, forces apart from religion, ritual, tradition. They omit the elements which make him, or her, depressed, or suicidal, or unable to function well. Is discovering one's origins the form of "growing up" which will resolve all or part of these problems? In this regard, Cowan's solution to an unfulfilled, divided life is understanding oneself through linkage with one's heritage. The dilemmas, however, could be located elsewhere: in sexual difficulties, blocked emotional needs, a skewed emotional relationship to one's family background, in forms of psychological and even physical abuse, gender problems, disappointments which lie far deeper than religious identity can reach. The root of the problem is not necessarily one's roots. Discovering oneself is a longer haul.

Cowan calls himself an "orphan in history," which means that without the rituals of his heritage, he lived with or in a "hole." His particular hole is filled when his daughter is bat mitzvahed, and the ceremony includes his wife's mother, she of Protestant Yankee stock, but an atheist. Cowan's wife, Rachel, had converted already to Judaism. In this neat way, the circle is completed, with the Protestant Yankee now becoming part of Judaism–instead of the other way around. While Cowan has reversed the American process of assimilation, he has not taken into account that by rejoicing in his wife's conversion, he has rejoiced in something that denies *her* roots, *her* origins, *her* family heritage, which is Protestant, atheistic, and the rest. That, too, is a point of view; conversion turns it into denial. What is further revealing is how small a role God plays, if any, in this equation. It is not God who is wanted, but ritual, history, memory, ceremony, the joys of the holidays; as though the author were seeking more than one day to celebrate his birthday. With the discovery of his heritage, however blunted it is from the original, he is reborn, transformed, resurrected–all those clichés of the American experience which our better fiction mocks.

There are further dimensions to this, aspects which lie at the heart of the Growing Up subgenre and its relationship to the 1980s and 90s. There is implicitly the belief that the quest for religious or spiritual linkage can resolve problems, can even create the context for happiness. Yet this should not be the end, but the beginning; for once the celebration ends, America remains. Cowan does not recognize that the resolution of the historical struggles, this search for community and common history, this quest for shared traditions are all holding actions, a form of illusory control which is transitory. Out there lies *process*, as nearly all of these growing up memoirs acknowledge, and process means there is no finality. The illusion of control is just that, a hopeful fantasy, a temporary act, while the inevitability of America looms. If we don't know this from life, we know it from America's novelists, Fitzgerald's Gatsby, Faulkner's Quentin Compson and Thomas Sutpen, Wharton's Lily Bart, Dreiser's Clyde Griffiths, Hemingway's suicide as the final act in a drama of conversion.

Julius Lester's rather astonishing memoir *Lovesong: Becoming a Jew*[19] is archetypically American, concerned as it is with transformation. If anyone tried to alter the process, it is Lester. His book is in the form of a journey or passage, from someone who countenanced vicious anti-Semitic remarks to his emergence as part of that "hated" community: someone bound to be unacceptable in either group, black or Jewish. Certainly his hostile reception by the Black Studies Department at the University of Massachusetts indicated that anti-Semitism is alive and well in ethnic studies enclaves. In a kind of *Bildungsroman* or apprenticeship-to-life novel, Lester's passage toward Judaism comes when he recognizes he could in himself provide linkage between the two warring communities; all this coming at an historical time when the original close relationship had been destroyed by black perception of Jewish patronization and by Jewish perception of black ingratitude. One hand could not hear the other clapping, and Lester wanted to become a bridge. But the earlier Lester undermines some of this quest for reconciliation and resolution. Some understanding is missing in the following key, perhaps central, statement.

> Many people were very distressed by the remark of Tyrone Woods [a student in an interview involving Lester on New York's radio station WBAI] that Hitler should've made more Jews into lampshades. And people were doubly distressed when I did not disassociate myself from that remark. And I've been asked many times this week [during the winter of 1969, when blacks and Jews fought for control of the New York City public schools] whether or not I am anti-Semitic. . . . I won't answer, because it's not a relevant question to me. The relevant question is changing the structure of this country because that's the only way black people will achieve the necessary power. The question of anti-Semitism is not a relevant one for the black community. The remark that Tyrone Woods made is not one I would have made. It's not my style. I didn't say anything against the remark because I think I understand what he was trying to say. I was aware he was speaking symbolically, not literally.[20]

In his desperation to fill the "hole," Lester misses that Woods's remark *ended all dialogue*. It was a final statement, whatever the intent, and it meant, in effect, the end of idealistic Jewish-black relationships. Lester's failure to understand that language in this context is not symbolic, but literal, makes his subsequent remarks suspect. For Jews, praise of Hitler ends the dialogue, just as for blacks a defense of slavery or apartheid ends that dialogue. Tyrone Woods's comment on Hitler, Jews, and lampshades does not involve whether one is pro-or anti-Semitic, but whether one is pro-or anti-civilization. Language itself has been traduced, and the game is over.

In his quest for a religious identification to fill the hole he apparently felt, Lester sidesteps the queasy question of Jewish race. In his formulation, religion makes a Jew, but for many secular Jews, history and race–whatever those are–matter. Yet by avoiding that area, Lester misses that it is race, not religion, which brought forth virulent anti-Semitism in the twentieth century; and when a black like Tyrone Woods advocates that more Jews should have been made into lampshades, he is getting it on against a race, not a religion. If Woods gains his manhood by aligning himself with those who exterminated Jews, then Lester misses something profoundly psychological and cultural.

Still further, Lester's attempt to bridge Jewish-black differences, however valiant–and one must not underestimate his courage here–nevertheless misses other key points. For example: "That Jews have not supported affirmative action. . . ." Yet affirmative action has had more support among Jewish lawyers, judges, and public officials than among any other white group. To single out Jews as opposing affirmation action because of stands by *Commentary* magazine and similar neo-conservative or reactionary journals is to stereotype a group. Jews in fact have least to worry about affirmative action when it applies to blacks, far less to fear than Latinos, Asians, or Native Americans. Or else, Lester says that the position of the Jews in the world has not changed significantly since World War II. His comment is within a context of his horror at the way some black leaders display anti-Semitism as a badge of manhood or as a way of rallying their troops, and how several have even called into question the legitimacy of Israel's existence. Yet Israel has, obviously, for emotional, political, and even symbolic reasons, altered the position of Jews in the world, and black attacks, while painful, do not really matter.

None of this should be construed as an attack on Lester's own sense of transformation; rather, we must extend the argument beyond religion and celebration and ritual. An understanding of Jewish-clack relationships, if that is at all even possible, must take into consideration these and related matters. Lester has "grown up" into a new experience after discovering that his great-grandfather, Altschul, was a German Jew (married to a former slave), and the book is clearly about the transformational quality of the experience. But as so often occurs with these subgenera of fictionalized-autobiographical memoir, the book raises related questions, and frequently these shaded questions pre-empt or block the personal note.

Another whole category of this Growing Up medium has developed around a different kind of absence, that created by an inadequate relationship between father and son, or in some instances father and daughter; as though in some uncanny reflection of Ronald and Nancy Reagan's implosive family. In these examples from the 1980s, paternal figures loom very large, to the degree one must seek some social linkage. We know that the decade ended with one of the most fatherly books of all, not a personal memoir so much as call to arms for sons to find their fathers, Robert Bly's *Iron John*. Clearly, part of the role Bly's book filled came from the woman's movement, and its perceived threat for men. But male "fear" goes beyond that, into areas of sexual inadequacy (both perceived and real), loss of faith in oneself, loss of sense of mission and direction, inability to cope with enormous cultural change, overall a fear of being swallowed up. Yet despite Bly's high intelligence and ability with language, his prescription is simply another form of voodoo, even when one assesses it for what it is and not for its excesses. It is easy to parody the drums and the nocturnal chants and the scene of men holding hands in common linkage, and their yearning to find the masculine in themselves. Bly's broad group of people, professionals as well as blue-collar workers, all feel a hole in themselves, and very possibly this summer camp get-together makes them feel more in control. But it is coercion of a sort, it evades deeper psychological problems, it fits into the gimcrackery of American religions; it is the Jimmy Swaggart of male bonding, a counterpart to the television preachers who sell their own forms of salvation. It polarizes male-female relationships, and whatever Bly's dissent from this, it is deeply misogynist at the very time when healing, not polarization, is needed for the sake of children.

Iron John is the epitome of these "search for father" memoirs which have appeared so abundantly: Geoffrey Wolff's *The Duke of Deception* (1979), Tobias Wolff's *This Boy's Life* (1989), Susan

Cheever's *Home Before Dark* (1984), Edward Rivera's *Family Installments* (1982), Carl Bernstein's *Loyalties* (1989), Edmund White's *A Boy's Own Story* (1982), the afore-mentioned *The Invention of Solitude* by Paul Auster, Adam Hochschild's *Half the Way Home: A Memoir of Father and Son* (1986), and Philip Roth's *Patrimony*, in 1991. The sickness of the father is frequently the path in for the son or daughter: Geoffrey Wolff's Duke, Susan Cheever's John Cheever, Roth's 86-year-old and now dying father. That "sickness" may take several shapes, whether the mental aberrations of Wolff's Duke, the alcoholism of Susan Cheever's John, the aging collapse of Roth's father, the remoteness of Hochschild's sensationally successful father, the damaging political loyalties of Bernstein's father and mother, the destructive passivity of Rhodes's father. In one regard, the children must learn how to navigate around the illness, or else succumb to it and to life itself.

The main thrust of *The Duke of Deception: Memories of My Father*[21] is the child's loss of empowerment, and this carries over into the companion volume, *This Boy's Life*. Geoffrey Wolff remained with his father when the family broke up, while Tobias Wolff, his younger brother, went with his mother. The two parents were diametrically opposite, and in no rational world should they have ever come together. But they did, and the result was not only a broken marriage and considerable pain all around, but two very distinguished fictional memoirs. When the marriage collapses, the issue is both personal and social. To what extent does the child have any rights? To what degree is he or she involved in the parents' bankruptcy, emotional as well as financial? In what respects does the child become parent to the adult, while the latter reveals his and her infantilism? Does the child or teen have any rights, caught as he or she is in a destiny which is all empowering, rigid, unyielding?

As suggested above, the earlier forms of the Growing Up subgenre were concerned with the working out of one's destiny, however impeded by the individual's own character faults. The newer form is concerned with entrapment of the child in a parental embrace which can be a form of doom. Life with father (or mother) involves a sacrifice of the child's self, or else a distortion of self which lasts into childhood. These memoirs mirror in several respects that breakup of family cited in 1980s statistics: the lack of parental responsibility, or their loss of control; the alienation of a younger generation not out of willfulness but from a desire to survive; the rebellion against authority, since its misuse seems to be palpable, starting in the family and extending beyond to the state and its institutions. But even more, there is an awareness that the center has given way, that the country is anarchic. The children set out as if Adam is in a poisoned Eden.

Common to both Wolffs' books is the fact they developed survival techniques of lying, deceiving, quarreling, of surrounding themselves with trouble: bad for them personally, but good for their potential art. This gave them the stage on which to act, some sense of presence; by acting out anti-socially, they demanded and received attention. Moving around a good deal, attending a succession of schools, unable to settle in, forced to make friends on the run, incapable of putting down roots either in a neighborhood or school, the child insists on his self by displaying one that nearly everyone can find repulsive or threatening.

Geoffrey Wolff describes one such situation, a kind of kaleidoscope of what his life has become. "I entered seventh grade in a Quonset hut set behind Sarasota High School [in Florida]. There were no black kids in my class of thirty, but plenty of kids of a kind I had never before seen, boys with torn clothes and sores on their skin, classmates with breasts as big as my mother's. Ringling Brothers wintered in Sarasota, and midget-sized children of midgets came to my school with regular-sized children of the Tall Man, olive-skinned children of acrobats and animal trainers and the boastful, tetchy get of wire-walkers. I couldn't quite catch the drift of the teacher's Georgia accent."[22] But that doesn't prevent him from being turned on by her–she was pretty, and he stared until she felt uncomfortable.

All this doubles back on the dislocated boy. He suffers stomach cramps every morning, a form of resistance which worries his mother sufficiently to have him examined; there is, of course, no physical etiology. They send for his dog. But the boy plays hooky, and he makes friends with the grungiest kid in the class, Ernie, who lives in a trailer park. He is now twelve, thoroughly confused, unable to cope, unwilling to adjust because he has no norms to adjust to.

His father, the Duke of Deception, is a man of voracious appetites, always trying to be someone he is not; and when he does achieve anything, it is insufficient to nourish his needs. Infantile in his expectations, he is unable to postpone gratification; he requires constant feeding, instant attention. He acts irresponsibly at work–where he has invented his credentials as an airplane designer–and he acts irresponsibly in every other activity. He lies about his ethnic background–he is a Jew, with a Jewish name; he lies about his educational achievements; he lies about his skills. He cons people for services and goods he has no intention of paying back. He willfully deceives and sweet-talks: the perfect medium for the 80s. Gordon Gekko at the end of the decade is the Duke's bookend.

He is, potentially, a great parodic figure, a kind of Falstaff reincarnated as a Jewish con man. But, unfortunately, we never discover the "why" of his needs, although his family is held hostage to his infantilism. Well before the end of this superbly written memoir, we wonder what has made the duke into the Duke. If we–and the author–could only get a handle on him, he would be not only amusing but a figure of enormous interest, perhaps even a symbol for the final decades of the century: the ultimate junk bond man. Running parallel to this biographical sketch of the Duke is the story of the children, Geoffrey and Tobias, the mother, Rosemary, all caught in the wake of the father's chaos and destruction. Like Pan, he creates confusion. The story Geoffrey Wolff tells is of the family's entrance into the valley of death; an almost allegorical journey, Christian's pilgrim's progress, in which it must confront obstacle after obstacle, or else succumb. Once split up, the family lives on a frontier, the frontier not of the American West but of disintegration. When Wolff dies, the grown Geoffrey offers up love, love he can express now that he is free of the Duke's destructive behavior. He says he misses him. Yet what we expect is more anger and hostility; memory should retrieve not love but the feeling something was stolen from him as a child. The reader does not seek a revengeful son, an Orestes, but he does ask for some deeper interpretation of how survival came about, and parallel to that some more profound interpretation of what went into creating the Duke. We recognize that, after all, this is part biography; and biography demands a certain degree of imaginative projection into the subject, a probe into causes and motives. That the Duke was a man who could generate love is clear; but he was also a man who sundered whatever he touched. If Geoffrey Wolff's portrait of his father is accurate—and we assume his reliability—he was poison as a husband, as a worker in every position he held, as a friend, and, ultimately, as a parent. His condition was pathological, and while the son captures a good deal of that, we wonder if by forgiving him he is refusing to admit certain things as simply too painful. What we get to see are the pieces of wreckage of everything the Duke has touched; that is some of it, but perhaps not all.

A decade after his brother exposed the Wolff family, Tobias Wolff in 1989 wrote a very different kind of memoir. *This Boy's Life*[23] is just that: not a biography, although there are trenchant biographical sketches of the mother and the horrendous men in her life, but a fictionalized memoir about the self and its passage from self-destruction into salvation, once again because the boy had brains. Tobias Wolff's memoir is a perfect summing up a certain aspects of the 1980s as mirrored in the fictions of growing up. It is, in effect, a book about children's rights, or, more obviously, how such rights are flouted when parents are caught up in their own self-destructive behavior. The first act occurs almost out of sight, the ill-fated marriage of Rosemary and the Duke. Once the initial misstep is taken, all else, as in a Greek tragedy, unfolds inexorably. Yet there is a certain rightness to the marriage, since Wolff looks for a certain type of woman, and Rosemary chooses dominant men who will first undermine her sense of self and then almost destroy her. She apparently thrives on men who play upon her weak image of herself, although when the chips are down—which is frequently—she reveals considerable strength of character. Yet she does surrender one son, Geoffrey, while she goes off into the nothingness of the blue horizon with the other, Tobias.

The strategy of the book is to present a basically decent young man (we assume) who feels his fate is misfortune; and who, as a result, seeks out what will bring on the misfortune sooner rather than later. Almost at the center of the memoir is a telling passage, when Rosemary has met Dwight, and Tobias—renamed Jack, to seem more masculine—decides to go live with Dwight, see what he is like, and then advise his mother whether she should marry this distant man. Dwight, we know, is a supreme loser: a heavy drinker, possessive, unable to sustain a relationship with a woman or anyone else, deeply jealous and suspicious, with an underlying rage, a man who drives country curves dangerously, in a kind of death wish, a person of no sensitivity or cultural aspiration. He is not even a first-rate stud. Tobias-Jack recognizes how dreadful Dwight is, and yet he reports to Rosemary that all is well, even when she is afraid of making another disastrous marriage. Jack's words are fateful, not only for his family but in the larger sense of the Growing Up subgenre.

> I had come to feel that all of this was fated, that I was bound to accept as my home a place I did not feel at home in, and to take as my father a man who was offended by my existence and would never stop questioning my right to it. I did not believe my mother when she told me it wasn't too late. I knew she meant what she said, but it seemed to me that she was deceiving herself. Things had gone too far. And somehow it was her telling me it wasn't too late that made me

believe, past all doubt, that it was. Those words still sound to me less like a hope than an epitaph, the last lie we tell before hurling ourselves over the brink.[24]

The passage is not only remarkable in its insistence on the boy's powerlessness in the grip of forces squeezing life and space from him, it also creates a crisis in the literary mode represented by the memoir. Whether fully accurate or not, our assumption about Growing Up was that it reflected a forward-looking America; that whatever the difficulties of growing up or carrying on–Holden in *The Catcher in theRye*, for example–there was the sense of at least potential emergence; that however much one is bloodied in the conflict with parents or parental figures (teachers, authorities, police, whomever) there was some degree of conquest for the protagonist. He or she might escape, or even emigrate. Rebellion was the form of salvation; and even if it was inward rebellion, it meant one was acting in good faith, was saving the self, was waiting for the right time to emerge.* Such were our assumptions.[25]

The passage just quoted suggests something else: that the line between personal disaster and emergence is so finely drawn one may opt for the disaster simply as an act of will-lessness. The pressures of the 1980s, on one level, were for one to take advantage of an open system and go for it, become a conqueror; but equal pressures came with the sense that none of it mattered, that it all led nowhere, or that the struggle was not worth the outcome. By

---

* A good example of that type comes in Lorene Cary's *Black Ice* (1991). For her, it is confronting a seemingly monolithic world of wealth and privilege at Saint Paul's School in New Hampshire, where she, a black woman, is a scholarship student. She must make it there as a successful student, and she must attempt to retain her identity. Each confrontation is for her a revelation of what life will bring, not only at Saint Paul's but throughout her life; and each conflict brings home to her that triumph is not permanent. And yet she does come through with it. Scarred, wounded, temporarily weakened, she makes it in order to gain strength later on. Such are her *and our* expectations of the memoir.

succumbing to a preordained destiny, Tobias-Jack will foreclose his life in passive terms; he will not have to fight against the forces which have squeezed him. In letting this unpleasant and violent man put his foot on his neck, Jack has chosen the other side of success, the other side of rebellion. We should not neglect the terrible otiosity of the decade when most of these memoirs were written: the temptation to succumb taking on as much significance as the temptation to cheat, lie, deceive, win out. Uncertainty and ambiguity prevail. The Sirens beckon.

Jack is trapped and he knows it. When he does call on his own few resources, it is to fake his school transcript, fake his recommendations, fake virtually every part of his application. From a friend, he obtains official forms from the high school office, and then he sets forth his plan to escape, to transfer to prestigious private schools like Choate, Andover, and Deerfield (from which his father had been expelled). In the process, he does recreate himself, from a slider and loser into a champ, from someone with no future into a young man who glimpses a future, however imperfectly, through an elite school. In this process of transformation, he gives himself all the qualities he assumes the schools are looking for, an 80s winner. He turns himself–through his own words–into an A student, an Eagle Scout, a powerful swimmer (his school has no swimming team). "I felt full of things that had to be said, full of stifled truth. That was what I thought I was writing–the truth. It was truth known only to me, but I believed in it more than I believed in the facts arrayed against it."[26]

Of course, all the prestigious schools see right through him. But the significant element is that in the forgeries and deceptions, Tobias-Jack has found the means to recreate himself; he has found the bedrock of his best self, and in the American mode he is prepared now to make his way. He is like those outsiders in American fiction who shift from town to town, changing their name and jobs, fathering children here and there, making promises they cannot keep, in some cases criminal types who have assumed entirely new identities. Finally, a lesser institution, the Hill School of

Pennsylvania, idyllically located, is interested. Jack is interviewed by an alumnus in the Northwest, is given a scholarship based on his fantastic credentials, and is outfitted with all the right clothes by this same alumnus and his wife. The boy has won the lottery through lies, deception, forgery, dissembling; he has become that most archetypal American of them all, the imposter or confidence man. Scams work, clearly a morality tale for the decade.

What makes it all the more striking is that Tobias-Jack can't hack it. He flubs his chance. The school proves too much; he knows nothing, possesses no intellectual frame of reference, has no discipline. Socially he rages. With his grades poor, with uncertainty all around him, he drops out and goes into the army. He is unprepared for American success. The traditional story does not work. Tobias-Jack will, later, have another story to tell us, not one of school, but of other ways in which he can transform failure into *his* kind of success, as a writer of short stories and as the author of this memoir.*

Another kind of narrative of rebellion comes in Edmund White's *A Boy's Own Story* (1982).* White's memoir[27] is a kind of gay

---

*   The real successor volume to *This Boy's Life* is Wolff's memoir of his military service in Vietnam, *In Pharoah's Army: Memories of the Lost War* (1994). The child and adolescent has now become a young man, but, strikingly, the terms of survival are similar: chance is at least as significant as will, circumstance as important as determination.

*   In Paul Monette's *Becoming a Man* (1992), growing up gay made him invisible. Closeted, he must efface himself–language itself loses significance, and his development is stunted not only by family but by everything "out there." His "wound" is both external and internal; and he "becomes a man" only when he acts upon his preference. In such experiences, he joins up with nearly all the other narrators of such memoirs, heterosexual or homosexual, male or female, white or black: in their awareness they are alone and destined for some unforeseen doom. They are riding the country to a terrible destiny. Even in a very different kind of growing-up gay book, Samuel R. Delaney's *The Motion of Light*

Catcher in the Rye: an appealing young man confronting his sexual difference. Just as Holden in the Salinger novel fell apart, so White's narrator in his book must confront marginality. It is, also, a tale of terrible loneliness, another linkage with Salinger's Holden. White's memoir is, in addition, a story of father and son, although the father is neither close nor likable. When the narrator's parents divorce, the boy is left with his mother, a self-centered, self-indulgent, unhappy, unsuccessful woman who jerks him and his (hated and hateful) sister around. One-parent families are as miserable in their way as the nuclear kind. The memoir is not concerned with achievement in any public sense, but with the very private way one holds on, seeks oneself, tries to come to terms with difference.

White attempts to explain how he came to accept feelings for men: his fantasies, dreams, mythical visions all filled with a man carrying him off. His fantasy is not too distant, in fact, from Robert Bly's powerful male figure, that father who must be summoned up in the boy or young man as a source of empowerment. White, however, goes further, trying to understand how sexuality occurs, where it derives from, how it develops. His is a quest for origins and sources, not of family but of a tendency or predilection, an ongoing condition which remains mysterious and yet seductive. His feelings create a quandary, and although in one enlightened moment he is able to transcend himself–in a kind of Buddha-like lotus position–he nevertheless makes moves his reason tells him are further isolating him. White's is a parable of self and country.

Loneliness takes several shapes, as any metaphor does: chiefly, distance from parents, who are superfluous: and inability to find a niche, which is why he may have become a writer. As the author of a memoir, he can experience in himself a dualism: by carrying on a dialogue with his past as he attempts to recover it for his present

---

in Water (1988), in which Delaney accepts his homosexuality readily, he finally cracks up in his early twenties. His fuse dims, his energies diminish, he burns out, and he cannot go on. Trying to cover up loneliness with frenetic activity, he failed.

task. The act of historical memory is, of course, self-defeating, since whatever he recovers is colored by what he is looking for, what he chooses to include, and what he, unconsciously, represses. He has fictionalized his own life and sees only the reflection. Withal, it is still a dialogue, in which the writer has gained a companion, someone from the old days, a history filled with people and events, however unpleasant. The memories do provide a sense of self, even if that sense is subverted by how impoverished the self once was.

The first-person memoir, itself an implicit fiction, carries the narrator into a form of empowerment. For White or the narrator, empowerment means conquering a man, having sex with him, and then "disowning him" so that he would not consider himself a homosexual. "Sometimes," he writes, "I think I liked bringing pleasure to a heterosexual man (for after all I'd dreamed of being my father's lover) at the same time I was able to punish him for not loving me."[28] To be his "father's lover" is of course a desire for the father's power, taking on the older man's potency, especially since the father was straight. It is akin to those ritualistic tales in which an opponent eats the enemy's flesh to gain the adversary's strength. The final page of the memoir is a plea for power, which the narrator gains to some degree by entrapping a hippie music teacher.

In this variation on the Oedipal story—White would like to dispose of the mother and "marry" the father—the world of the narrator seems suffused with homosexuals. At his school, he discovers that while homosexuality among the student body is not the thing, the masters are another matter. They are not really "masters," but men in the thrall of deep, terrible secrets which could destroy them. Masters, but vulnerable! The power struggle is confusing, since the sexuality of the men involved is caught between furtive, secretive selves and public, conventional lives. As for the White boy, he must somehow deal with his father as an idea: trounce his father in bed by "loving" him or by trespassing on the older man's hostility to gays by seeking out men. The process is complicated, far more convoluted than we find in any of the other memoirs in this group. Fearful of being considered a mama's boy, White must empower himself with men, while also seeking his father's love and, at the same time, creating the way by which his father can reject him. His needs are triangulated, so that while his narrator proceeds as though by choice, he is actually caught in a cycle of extreme complexity.

More than anything else, the boy must take choice from the father and give it to himself. White has subdivided into three people: ". . . the boy who smelled bad when I was with my sister [her hatred of him is unrelenting]; the boy who was wise and kind beyond his years when I was with my mother; but when I was alone not a boy at all but a principle of power, of absolute power."[29] He discovers *that*, at the end, when he seduces the music teacher.

White is especially good in dream sequences, which become metaphors of the boy's dilemma. His young narrator consistently locates himself outside the self, in the world, or else locates the world as well beyond him, unbridgeable. The process is filmic: an organic part of the autobiographical/fictional memoir in which playback is so critical; and we come to see the boy as part of a film he observes and whose reels he would like to stop. We recall Delmore Schwartz's "In Dreams Begin Responsibilities."

The would-be gay person identifies with all those who lead lives of alienation and feel exiled. And under it all is *The Secret*—when growing up in the 1940s and 50s made it a great secret. White does reveal it to his parents and to his therapist. But he knows that those who listen do not hear. He is thrust back upon himself; and thus his final act, to seduce the music teacher, is his sole way of gaining power, by destroying another.

This is not Huck Finn, finally not Holden Caulfield. The desire to tell this story in the 1980s is linked to the decade, not only to the new confidence gays acquired, but as a protest against withholding secrets when the country was so wide open. Telling is in itself an act of rebellion: a confession to the world which serves as a warning that no one can be throttled by social or political conventions. It is part of that 80s "opening up" which we see reflected in the personal voice even as the system itself runs wild, with restraints removed on stock markets, banks, other financial institutions. The junk bond phenomenon, for one, has its counterpart in the expressiveness of this subgenre; a wild analogy, possibly, but once junk bonds were unimaginable, and so too the confessional note of these memoirs, taking us as readers into previously unimaginable worlds of growing up. Mommy dearest turned inward!

We have neglected until now another very different kind of Growing Up book. For the first part of this chapter, we have dealt with the torturous, pained, anguished memoirs of those who, therapeutically, let most of it hang out: their books, mainly, have been acts of revenge, or else expressions of anger and hostility which otherwise would have remained corrosively bottled up. They have attacked family values, family behavior, the atrocities of stepparents, the injustices of their young lives, the infantilism of their elders, their loss of space, power, even air. The books are weapons against their having been held hostage.

The Reagan years were a perfect backdrop for these emotional outbursts, since politics aside, the Reagan family was a good indication of dysfunction and counterfeit papered over by public displays of traditional values. The Reagans, it turns out, were so private and self-serving the children felt ignored, neglected, outcasts within their own family; and they wrote about it, spoke about it, acted out their rage in various public forums. The meeting here of the institutionalized family–the President's–and the malfunctioning families of our writers is not happenstance. In just this one area, the 1980s, so essential to the Growing Up memoir, were an appropriate time to let it all out. It was a period of expressing the hitherto unmentionable, not least because of the explosion of magazines, newspapers, and talk shows ready to spray the public with gossip, family hypocrisy, alcoholism, molestation, incest, drug addiction, sexual malfunction or multiple relationships, and any kind of bizarre behavior.

There is, however, another kind of Growing Up memoir that

derives from the decade, and it is not necessarily angry, hostile, anguished, or whatever. *It is about growing up*, and it can be witty (Russell Baker and Annie Dillard), or rather solemn (Jonathan Yardley) or part of the immigrant experience (Edward Rivera and Eva Hoffman), or the Afro-American experience (Lorene Cary), or the Jewish (E. L. Doctorow). Serving as linkage between the two kinds is Susan Cheever's very moving *Home Before Dark : a Biographical Memoir of John Cheever by His Daughter* (1984).[28] It fits the Reagan era's divulgations splendidly. Stately, but not overly hostile, it nevertheless reveals anger not at what God hath wrought but at what parents have. Linked to this is Adam Hochschild's *Half the Way Home: A Memoir of Father and Son* (1986).[29] Fathers dominate, no question of that. They represent the power, even in the 80s, when women had long since asserted themselves. Both sons and daughters felt themselves in thrall, especially when the father is indeed powerful and/or famous, as with John Cheever, the writer, and Harold Hochschild, the financial tycoon.*

This is one of the most precarious forms of the subgenre, since it depends on the perceptions of a narrator who has lived with this subject and who has devised strategies, usually, to survive the rigors of that relationship. But what adds difficulty is the fact that the relationship is not that overtly painful or disfiguring to one's personality; the parent is not out of control (even with Cheever's alcoholism), nor is home life unbearable. For Hochschild, in fact, it could be supportive and luxurious, to an extreme. Yet the child growing up knows something is very wrong, for the relationships do have degrees of awfulness, exclusion, and disempowerment. These are powerful fathers who do not countenance too much opposition, and they have trouble expressing their emotions or else express them in secretive, labyrinthine ways.

---

*   Even when, as in Philip Roth's *Patrimony* (1991), the father is not extraordinary, rich or powerful. The problem with such a father is that he holds no interest for the reader; Philip Roth is interesting, Mr. Roth, not at all.

The "hole" in the child's life is his or her desire–of course unfulfilled–to enter into the world of the parent, feel accepted (not necessarily loved), and sense that the father has not taken away the child's space. Yet this is precisely what has occurred. As Susan Cheever describes growing up, she increasingly comes to understand that John Cheever expects all the space in the house, all the space in the family's world, simply all the space. The memoir works on two almost contrary levels: the one which reveals that nothing was so dreadful as to become suffocating; the other which makes anger and hostility inevitable because the parent insists on so much. The drama intensifies when we recognize that the child is so intertwined with the workings of the family that his/her perceptions are both unreliable and reliable. Susan Cheever has a tendency to transform the home situation into theatre, with curtain calls in the front, but with forbidden soliloquies behind the curtain. There are deceptions, intrigues, masks, and disguises–and these are gradually revealed, until the child recognizes she has been living in a drama full of Ibsenian secrets. This theatrical dimension fits well into what we discussed above, the definition of self within the context of another or of others; that blending of autobiography with biography, and all fictionalized.

As a child of high royalty, the famed father, Susan Cheever must find ground between what she observes–all the weaknesses and deceits, the vanities–and what the world expects, a kind of heroic greatness because of a given talent. The battleground is not completely Oedipal, but involves a whole sequence of events and feelings, only some of which aim at eliminating the paternal figure. Part of the conflict bleeds over into class and social issues; into matters of competing literary skills–some of course Oedipal. Often, the conflict takes the shape of the child seeking definition in situations so fluid only the powerful can triumph. While much of this has a psychological etiology, much, also, is part of a pattern of American life: that obsessive need to define oneself in a culture which seems so elastic as to be nonexistent.

Compelling, also, is Susan Cheever's status as a female in a family in which, according to Cheever's Journals, his main family love was for his son, Frederico. What do we make, then, of the daughter's comment near the end of the book? "We had wonderful times. A simpler way to put this is that my father loved his children. . . . As individuals we often displeased him, but as a unit we were cherished and indispensable."[30] Yet just earlier she has said, when she knew he was dying, that "I had come out from the city to love him; but I couldn't do it."[31]

What appears contradictory here may not be that but the consequence of an unreliable witness, despite the seeming authenticity of what the author writes. There are several areas which question her witness, although, paradoxically, these do not weaken the memoir, but, rather, strengthen it by revealing the terrible crosscurrents operating in the family. That Susan Cheever described her father's alcoholism was not new, but that she revealed his homosexual practices was–even though those who had read his novel *Falconer* were not surprised. Clearly, Cheever's struggles with his sexuality created additional tensions. "My father's sexual appetites were one of his major preoccupations, and his lust for men was as distressing to him as his desire for women was self-affirming and ecstatic."[32] Yet although "he loved men," he did not identify with homosexuality and "despised what he defined as the homosexual community: the limpwristed, lisping men who are sometimes the self-appointed representatives of homosexual love in our culture."[33]

To this, we say yes and no. The daughter sensitively addresses the ambiguity of her father's situation: that he had been brought up to "reject homosexuality absolutely," but at the same time he found in it a satisfaction that heterosexual love could not alone fulfill. Yet even as the daughter alertly limns this, we must not lose sight of the hostility underlying her revelation. To speak of her father's alcoholism is one thing, but to write of his homosexuality–when his wife and other children are alive and well–comes from a source of anger and anguish the memoir does not appear to admit. Part of the revelation comes from Susan Cheever's desire to probe the "sham" (her word) of her father's pose as a patrician, when in fact he was not from a "fox-hunting gentleman's world" but from a genteel shabbiness, the shop keeping class he so despised and associated with his mother.

The daughter pierces this scrim Cheever had drawn over his past, and shows that her father, so sensitive in his stories, avoided self-examination. His defense was that his "vices" derived from his loneliness and isolation; and that this was another way–the daughter reveals–of his rejecting family love and the emotional life of wife and children, including Susan.

John Cheever, we also learn, was master of the cutting remark that, as it were, drew a line between him and others, not allowing anyone to cross. Such cutting remarks often focused on "looks." From the daughter's point of view, her father "had expected his daughter to be a beauty." He imagined his child as a dazzling society figure, someone who would catch the eyes of a particular crowd, and whose reflected loveliness would fall on him. The actual daughter, as she describes herself–and perhaps as she sees herself through his eyes–is dumpy, acne-ridden, with a slumped-over walk (from depression?), overweight, with lank hair that fell over her eyes. She is not adorable, nor is she the type who draws the right kind of attractive men. In a devastating paragraph, she writes of how when boys did ask her out, her father "urged them to keep me out as late as they liked." She adds, "They always brought me home early, and they never came back."[3 4]

The home was also the scene of regular marital displeasure and discord, to the degree father and mother repeatedly spoke to the children of getting a divorce. Then, as if they had chosen this as a way of frightening their children, they pulled back and claimed their strong feeling for each other, with Cheever stating that he adored his wife. What gives the book its force and strength, finally, is its presentation of crosscurrents, a Tolstoyan family unhappy in its way. The model seems a "typical" nuclear American family held up as the ideal for the Reagan years; but the actuality reveals how atypical that typical family is, with its secrets, deceits, disguises, lies deceptions, hatreds, desires for revenge and retribution. This is not just a famous family, but also one whose wounds are exacerbated by the father's fame. The key element for the narrator is how her growth has been impeded or impelled, as the case may be; how she agrees to present Cheever in public terms even as we sense the subsurface terms where she seethes; how she feels her happiness has depended on a man who, given the chance, would have suffocated everyone;* how she sided with this man at the expense of her mother, or how she was blinded to the mother by her sympathies for the father. The family is depicted as another one in that long march of 1980s memoirs in which the father is self-serving, when leadership has succumbed to selfish postures, where the social and political dimensions of the country are reflected, however, indirectly, in parental failure.

While not all of these memoirs are battles to the death between father and son, or some other parent-child relationship, all are concerned with how the child or young adult can gain control of his or her life, how he or she can be empowered; and the implications of this are often as much national, institutional, political and social as personal. That sense of empowerment the child gains goes well beyond success, ambition, getting on. It has to do with how one chooses to survive in an America perceived as so emptied out

---

* A complement to the Susan Cheever book about her writer father is Shirley Abbott's about her "bookmaker" father, *The Bookmaker's Daughter* (1991). Abbott's father is not a craftsman of fine books, but in gambling parlance a maker of books. He is, perhaps curiously, supportive of his daughter, saying he never wanted a boy, and this, Shirley Abbott says, carried her through many a trial. He also emphasized reading and downplayed the parties and prettiness factor which doomed so many of the daughter's friends and schoolmates to aborted lives. He wanted a winner, and yet when the daughter began to assert her independence, this once supportive father became frightened and attempted to discourage her normal development. The latter portions of this memoir are concerned with her efforts to emerge as an individual, and in this way she writes the typical Growing Up memoir.

as to allow no space for the individual's inner life as it develops. This is Eva Hoffman's plaint in *Lost in Translation* (1989),[35] as she views the country from the point of view of a Polish emigrant, thrust into American life at thirteen.

The "hole" Hoffman describes probably goes deeper than the emptiness expressed by the other memoirists, for her hole involves nothing less than a restructuring and filling of her existence. As an immigrant, she has had to adjust to a very different cultural perspective, and that in turn has made her into an extremely shrewd observer of the country. She sees the emperor without his clothes. Caught up by the 1960s, she grapples with the entire postwar age, and not least the 80s. The country is a maze, a tunnel, a jigsaw puzzle, a trap waiting for the unwary. What is remarkable about her insight, which follows, is that she sees how uncertain American life has become; so that even those memoirists who present stable backgrounds and family lives–Annie Dillard or Jonathan Yardley, for example–seem like isolated spots in time, a chunk of a bygone era; merely a point of nostalgia.

> Once I step off that airplane in Houston [Hoffman writes], I step into a culture that splinters, fragments, and re-forms itself as if it were a jigsaw puzzle dancing in a quantum space. If I want to assimilate into my generation, my time, I have to assimilate the multiple perspectives and their constant shifting. Who, among my peers, is sure of what is success and what failure? Who would want to be sure? Who is sure of purposes, meanings, national goals? We slip between definitions with such acrobatic ease that straight narrative becomes impossible. I cannot conceive of my story as one of simple progress, or simple woe. Any confidently thrusting story line would be a sentimentality, an excess, an exaggeration, an untruth. Perhaps it is my intolerance of those, my cherishing of uncertainty as the only truth that is, after all, the best measure of my assimilation; perhaps it is in my misfittings that I fit. Perhaps a successful immigrant is an

exaggerated version of the native. From now on, I'll be made, like a mosaic, of fragments–and my consciousness of them. It is only in that observing consciousness that I remain, after all, an immigrant.[36]

Hoffman touches on the paradox that the native American like the immigrant must now seek levels of adaptation. For even as small American villages struggle to carry on traditional values, they, too, are becoming subject to inevitable changes: unemployment, which sends the young people away; death of the railroad and even bus lines, which means the death of the village; abandonment of country roads in favor of interstate highways; penetration of the media and their menu of alternate cultures; the introduction of "summer people" or retirees, turning the village into a vacation mecca; centralized malls, what Joel Garreau calls "edge cities," with their multiple urban cores, which turn the village main street into a ghost town. With even the most isolated places being penetrated or abandoned, everyone has been thrown into the cultural hopper where uncertainty, doubt, anxiety, and, finally, anger insist upon themselves. As an immigrant, Hoffman must assimilate to this even as she develops her "observing consciousness."

She must respond in several areas, but most of all linguistically, which involves more than words and language, but feelings, perspectives, cultural decisions about her life. Through language, she must learn how to respond not only to disruption and discontinuity, but to the uncertainties of America, to expectations she cannot quite fathom, to the abyss which she senses as lying outside the safety nets of her upbringing. In still another paradox, America insists on her rejecting the past, even though that past–screened through a fading Polish language–contains the warmth of a coherent family life, close friends, and a dependable, however fragile, cultural life.

Having lost language, she has lost connections; and that trope serves as a metaphor for the 80s and 90s. One of the enormous difficulties for the writer in these decades is the discovery of a suitable language. So over-heated and artificial has become public language (media, political statements, public claims, and rest) that it is difficult to locate oneself in the private language creative work depends upon. Information is itself at stake. What does the "new" language mean, when so much of that language does not mean, when so much of it subverts language? We may say this was always true, in the yellow journalism of the past, in the deceptiveness of political discourse, in the lies and myths that become part of powerful strategies; but we must recognize that never before has that barrage of artificial, deceptive language been an avalanche.

Hoffman suggests *it is impossible* to discern what language means, unless one enters into the conspiracy to make language mean nothing. Such is her dilemma, and it becomes something considerably more than the immigrant flailing around for support. "Lost in translation" suggests a pivotal or critical time, when loss is nothing less than the loss of Eden, the expulsion from the hearth, the forced recognition of a new order, or at least of some strange beast converging on America.

As a European conditioned by European disaster, Hoffman evokes American disaster, even while, at the same time, she knows that Cracow shaped her cultural aspirations. Her extraordinary piano playing is linked to Poland, whereas in America, it gradually diminishes. When she enters her parents' American home, she feels, within hours, that she's no longer "a hybrid but an oxymoron. My professional self, self-confident, American identity recedes like an insubstantial mirage."[37] She discovers the generational fault line in America, not only for European-born Jews, but also for all. She speaks of her Texas boy friend: "There is a great emptiness, a vacuum within him and there's nothing with which to fill it up. . . . But then he realized that he has never experienced anything. . . . "[38] Hoffman connects this to what she calls "angelism," the Americans desire, she believes, "to become more immaculate beings, avatars of pure ideas." Americans need to be emotionally cleansed, "politically correct angels—and so they ricochet from one vision of

Utopia to another, from a hope for transcendence to disillusionment to the next hope for a more ultimate transcendence."[39]

This reach for transcendental values, paradoxically, instead of creating a spiritual state results in the utter emptiness she finds in her Texas boy friend. It is all reach, not substance. The consequences, further, are that individuals, including her, can perceive not the parts of things, but only the cracks between. Even when things are going well–she has her Harvard doctorate, she is married and has friends and enterprises–she realizes how unstable it all might prove, how flimsy and illusory; and she wonders, like a Kafka protagonist, if she will fall into the seams even while she is pursuing the prize. As a metonymy or trope for the 1980s, this is apt commentary. As we have learned, beneath the glitter of the decade and the promises, there lay a trickily-constructed labyrinth, a potential chamber of horrors for many individuals and for the nation as a whole.

The American disease is anomie, loneliness, emotional repression, and excessive self-consciousness–such is her assessment, and all the above are encouraged by psychiatry, which she herself needs and uses. The American becomes obsessed with his or her own biography; so that the memoir itself becomes part of the "talking cure." For Hoffman, as for so many like her, the 1980s became a cauldron in which possibility is intermixed with catastrophe.

Although Russell Baker's *Growing Up* (in 1982, that popular year of the memoir)[40] does not involve a foreign birth, it does involve a young man coming from a blue-collar background into a sophisticated world of journalism and writing. The experience is based on re-creation: Hoffman with *her* need to resonate from Polish to American, Baker to go from working class Virginia to the urbane halls of the New York *Times*. He, too, must almost learn a foreign language, adopt another culture, and reorient himself in a secular world which offered tremendous emotional and psychological dangers.

Baker's life was not forced to the extremes, even though his natural intelligence warred with the assumptions of his class and time. He does have a mother who urges her son to succeed, and almost alone she recognized he had the goods to emerge. But the route to recreation of self was not easy, although autobiography makes it seem inevitable. After all, by the time we read Baker's memoir, we know he is a nationally acclaimed columnist and humorist, winner of prizes, a man of considerable achievement. Yet when he writes this book, he has to try to recapture the difficulty of upward mobility for a boy from a blue-collar background, and he has to convince the reader it was not simply unimpeded upward movement. Withal, Baker's tale is one of emergence in the American manner. Despite his various hang-ups–shame at his extremely thin frame, embarrassment at undressing before other boys his age– internal demons or external monsters do not push him to the wall. He knows strong women and a supportive stepfather. But the main danger is that he has gone untested, that his brain has remained inactive, and that all the potentiality could be lost. He could have remained marginal. But after attendance at City College, a Baltimore High School, he passes the scholarship test for Johns Hopkins, enlists in the Navy Air Corps and learns, to fly, and from that point on he is engaged.

One difficulty Baker encounters after this Huck Finn-like beginning comes in his relationship with women his age, or the failure thereof. After several half-hearted attempts, he meets up with Mimi, who is drawn superbly. At first sight, she is everything his demanding mother dislikes for her son: she comes from a broken home, with an alcoholic father, possesses little education, holds low-level, dead-end jobs, has no social standing and no real future except to marry a trucker, a woman waiting to be abused in a disastrous marriage. Yet Baker wants to marry Mimi, even while insisting that wartime is not right for marriage. We learn later that the marriage works. Both grow into it, especially Baker, who had originally thought she was not a "good woman," not someone a man married.

While none of this has the heavy freight of pain and anguish we find in the other memoirs, Baker has suffered, and one of the lessons we draw from even this benign growing-up exercise is how close to the edge of failure such an eventual success can be. The life of the American who is upwardly mobile moves inexorably toward the edge of the precipice, and however strong the determination and the intellectual potential, the chances might break the wrong way. The precariousness of it all brings us back to the basic premise, that these memoirs are all forms of allegory, in which while celebrating their own emergence, the writers are really describing how they feel about the country. They are not necessarily antagonistic, but they recognize they are the successful ones, however much they carry forward the scars of their background. There is a cautionary tale here, although one must not simplify. The scale of the achievement should not disguise the possibility that the dragons of failure were all there, ready to gobble up into the infernal regions even these intelligent figures.

Nothing illustrates this more than Edward Rivera's very moving story of growing up Puerto Rican, *Family Installments* (1982).[41] Subtitled "Memories of Growing Up Hispanic," this is a skillfully blended mutational form, of family origins, autobiography, and fiction. The fictional dimension is apparent in the origins, as Rivera creates backgrounds he has learned about through stories and others' memories. The suicidal maternal grandfather and then the other grandfather, the tyrant Gigante, are both shaped as fictional characters whose lives become real as their children appear and give birth to the narrator. The latter is both inside the past and present, and outside and commentator, a witness to people he has not seen. He nevertheless seems reliable, an important point inasmuch as we can accept the precariousness of his emergence only if we find his commentary authentic. This is, in fact, the basis of the mutant form: that even while fictional means are utilized, we believe in the "truth" of the narrator. In so doing, we transform the fictional form into documentary proof, which is another way of saying that *all autobiography*, particularly that focused on origins, is fictional even when we accept it as valid, as true.

Family Installments is an apprenticeship-to-life or education "novel," in which a young man, or woman, is brought from childhood to maturity. Rivera's version differs only in his emphasis on a broader context for his birth, in rural Puerto Rico, among the disenfranchised agricultural workers who own virtually nothing and have no dreams except emigration. But even while they dream of escaping, they fear the huge urban sprawl of New York City, its crime, its vermin, its hatred of them. Despite Puerto Rico's ties to the USA, they become strangers in the city and recognize that New York, tired of immigrants, is less than accommodating. Since their lives on the island are blighted, they have little choice but to come. If daughters, they are beholden to tyrannical fathers; if sons, they are slaves to land which yields poorly. So they pile onto planes, sacrificing themselves so that the next generation, the one Rivera himself represents, can emerge.

The younger generation will have only a slim chance, a single opportunity which, if missed, will probably mean total loss. Yet even as Rivera sees his surrogate narrator, Santos Malánquez, as something of an exile, he also perceives he will fit, however narrowly, into mainland American life. The way in is by way of language, education, working double and triple jobs. Those who can handle this are few, and obviously the first line of immigrants rarely makes it. Slowly, Santos becomes a mainland American, learning not only the language but also the cultural ideology–without forsaking his Hispanic and Puerto Rican heritage. Much of the charm and energy of this memoir comes in the language. Rivera takes the reader inside Santos's mind as he hears English, confuses the sounds and meanings with words similar in Spanish. Gradually, as he sorts it out, we come to recognize how language defines the culture, and until the outlines of words become clear, Americas itself remains indistinct. Central is Santos's experience in parochial school with *Julius Caesar*. When the teaching priest "swears an oath," one student thinks that an oath is always a curse and adds "*maricün*" [faggot] to

'Brother.'. . ."[42] When Caesar tells Caliphurnia to block off Antony when he has "run his course," what course does he mean, a "full-course meal, a race course, an English course?"[43] "Collides" is confused with "colitis." Brother Leary highlights what dunces the boys are and warns them they will never make it to a prestigious Catholic high school, like Cardinal Hayes, which the boys hear as "Carnal Hays," where they hit you with "Latin and logger rhythms."[44]

Yet even while these enormous personal changes are ongoing, Santos does not forsake his "family installments"; he hangs on to memories, stories, origins, traditions, even as they fade in significance for him. He revisits old locales on the island, sees his former schoolmistress, reacquaints himself with the family installments he has just related. But while they contain markers in his history, they have no firm hold; they are definitely the past, not actuality. The past is soap opera of a sort, the trials and tribulations of a desperately poor family struggling on the land; while the present, full of dangers, abysses, possible fatal steps, is existence itself. Life in the old country was not bright. Santos's forebears were not handsome or particularly intelligent. They were uneducated, with a very narrow slit of experience, often illiterate; and yet they did not surrender. He must honor their grit. They struggled against each other, especially the tyrannical Gigante, and they tried to escape with fantasies of rescue, with dreams and plans which inevitably were frustrated. This is no conventional success story. It is hard and grim, full of dreams even as individuals go under.

For Rivera, once he has settled in New York, America's spatiality is confined to the barrio. But that is only physical, for America's psychological spatiality is of another kind, an opening up to almost infinite possibility. No matter how compelling family installments are, they must be escaped; for family, relatives, memories, the island, history, traditions, because of their attractiveness, are traps.

Language is itself one of the traps, since it is the key to moving along, to emerging. Santos walks that edge precariously, making the right moves, but barely holding on. He threads his way into the American mainstream, but immigrants have little opportunity to question what the mainstream might be; it is the Garden at the end of a long pull, and that is all they know. All the familiar obstacles are there: besides the seductions of family ties, there are the turf wars with local blacks; the physical and intellectual intimidation of parochial schools or the violence of public institutions; there are the facts that the writer or "narrator" will be the sole member of the family to emerge or escape the streets or factories and short order cooking jobs. The immigrant does not question values, capitalistic or otherwise, but heads for the prize. Publishing this in 1982, Rivera can still see the prize as worth having, even while he considers the perils of reaching toward it. He typifies the decade– the desirability of American mainstream life measured against the precariousness of every aspect of that life.

E. L. Doctorow's *World's Fair* (1985)[45] is about an organic society, held together by a Bronx, New York, Jewish sensibility. Doctorow, however, is more concerned with the actual growing-up dimension than with biography, although he does not stint on his parents' failed marriage. The title is critical, since it suggests an organic society for a bright, determined child who grows into maturity as a result of the "Worlds Fair." The latter is of course the Fair in 1939-40 at Flushing Meadows, in Queens, New York, the last bastion of civilization before the barbarism of World War Two.

But in small letters, the *world is fair*, despite domestic disharmony, marital problems, the father's inability to keep his record business, his gambling, and, possibly, philandering. It is a just place for a child growing up even in the Great Depression. The child's world offers "fairness" because it is fixed, defined, located, the last time it was; so that "World's Fair" becomes the Garden, sacred (although some very profane things occur there), a paradisiacal place. The world's a fair, and the fairness of the world can be counted upon, until maturity sets in and perceptions change. We can contrast this with another famous fair in literature, James

Joyce's "Araby," a fair, a bazaar, but also a place of disappointment; for Joyce's young boy, expectations turn sour. For Doctorow, however, the "Fair" is a magical place that helps lead him from childhood into maturity.

Although celebratory, this memoir–described as a novel, but really a nonfiction fiction–contains a strong subtext of a child's powerlessness. In a magnificently realized scene, young Edgar is taken by his determined mother to S. Klein's, the long-gone cut-rate clothing emporium on Union Square in Manhattan. The idea is to outfit the boy as cheaply as possible. S. Klein was itself a kind of circus of mothers and children raging through the racks just short of a riot. As the parent manipulates the child, the latter becomes a mechanical figure, a store dummy or clothes horse in this almost endless parade of clothes. He feels humiliated when forced to change in a poorly curtained dressing room, and he senses how exposed, in all senses, he has become. "Little by little as we made our way on this endless pilgrimage I slowly peeled off my clothing, like a foreign legionnaire stumbling under the merciless heat of the sun over dune after dune. . . . "[46] He is coerced into several roles, one more aggressively hostile than the other. "My role in this rite was to lift my arms on command or lower them, to endure having my head swaddled for terrifying moments in a sweater until she [Mother] found the neck hole and brought me back into light. . . . "[47] He is encased, prodded, exposed, invaded, his privacy penetrated, his wishes and desires overridden by this obsessive need to clothe him cheaply.

This is a quintessential childhood scene, repeated in all its variations in this type of memoir/fiction/biography. The insistence on powerlessness–and, by implication, injustice and inequality–is not a matter of chance, coming as these books do in the 80s. Repeatedly, their emphasis is not on coming through, but on the injustices of being manipulated, the unfairness of having no rights, of being uprooted and handled like baggage. There is more to this than modern children and antique parents. There is an awareness that the ship of state has no captain, or that the so-called captain is unaware of direction; that the crew–or child–is helpless in the face of rocks, whirlpools, and other threats; that the ship itself is canting this way or that, unable to determine its destination or goal.

The implications go further. Discovery of self must occur in a kind of vacuum, away from the prying questions or knowledge of the parent. The individual child is isolated, even when childhood is itself a kind of protected cocoon. Despite the domestic hostility between his parents, Edgar obviously does not have a hard time. Yet even so, his revelation of what life is all about comes in a secretive way, when he discovers at the World's Fair that his young friend's mother, Norma, is involved in an elaborate sex scheme in her Fair act. In her water performance, he now glimpses that behind the façade of dancing and innocent play with an "octopus" in a tank, there is another agenda, which is not lost on the adult spectators. Edgar catches certain movements, and he suddenly realizes "I know everything now, the crucial secret, so carelessly vouchsafed."[48]

It comes to him fleetingly, a mere caress, and yet that transitory event encapsulates an entire world. He must keep this information secret, not only about Norma–whom his mother thinks is a guide– but his own discovery of self in this soft porn scenario. This is about growing up, but it is also about the isolation of self, the edge the child traverses, the secret ways in which one is informed and molded. One of the least subversive books in this subgenre– although one of the fullest fashioned and most coherent–*World's Fair* reflects profound 80s concerns. For behind the rather nonchalant and normal growing up sequences are intimations of a fearful world which young Edgar learns to negotiate. Doctorow also has several chapters devoted to other narrators, the voices of Edgar's mother, Rose, and his older brother, Donald. But while these voices do provide some alternate information, it is Edgar's voice which overwhelmingly dominates. He heads toward his destiny, in its way a destiny for his entire world, a world's fair which ends a period of peace in America. After that, all will be new, edgy, uncertain, treacherous. Loss of innocence was a form of doom.

The news is that while the novel struggles to recoup or find its way, this mode of Growing Up literature is alive and well; it has, in fact, engaged some of the best writers of both the younger and older generations. It has helped define a decade in ways we normally expect from our fiction. As perceived from the vantage point of the 80s, growing up is a precarious process, since dark shadows of the 80s themselves dominate memories and experiences. The pain and anguish here are of a different kind from what we saw earlier in Henry Roth or Salinger or Maxine Hong Kingston, or others of that type. The social and political fallout, either directly or by implication, is far greater.

Through reflected images and metaphors of his or her own life, the writer has caught the spirit of the country. The anarchy that lies at the heart of a law-and-order society pokes through at nearly every turn; and the threat of breakup–often more than merely potential–moves from defining family dysfunction and strife to questions of who and what we are, or where we are heading. When these memoirists reflect happier times, they do so as paeans to a mythical past, as part of a nostalgia for memories of Eden no longer recoverable. But most Growing Up memoirs are reflections of lost childhood: part autobiography, part biography, part fiction, a mutational form which indicates a postmodern sensibility, a New Age confessional mode.

Let us hope our writers will build on this; it is, for several reasons, a heartening development in American writing. It of course indicates a reality check on what America is, for good or for ill. It suggests that the anarchy, which has always lain at the heart of a democratic process, is systemic; that defining it will become a major cottage industry in the future. It underscores that we have divided so profoundly in subcultures that novels, which could once capture the sense of the country holistically will no longer be possible or else prove very rare, like DeLillo's *Underworld*. It places the burden of performance on the novel, if it is to retain its place as our chief explorer of identity and self-definition; or else the novel will move into a mutational form. But, most of all, it reveals the lack of coherence and continuity in our social processes: that out perceptions, such as they are, do not so much define America as make it possible to see no definition is possible. The subcultures have taken over, and they are not heartening–however much they are essential to the inevitable development of democratic institutions.

The literary process through the vehicle of Growing Up memoirs has entered into every aspect of the larger society, and it has returned with bad news. One may argue that our writers' perceptions are not the norms, or are insufficient to generalize upon; but, then, we have always used literature, whatever its norms, to read back what kind of society we are or are becoming. Hawthorne, Melville, Poe, Emerson, Thoreau and others in the nineteenth century, Wharton, Hemingway, Cather, Faulkner, Dreiser, Lewis, Mencken, Pound, Richard Wright, T. S. Eliot in the twentieth: these have all provided definition. There is no reason to expect less of this generation. Nay-saying in Growing Up literature is not necessarily subversive of American institutions, so much as it is part of a cautionary tale. The one real negative, however, may be that subdivisions have passed well beyond the point of resolution; that dysfunction and anarchy have already defined us. Very possibly, it may not be too much to claim that in these Growing Up mutant forms our fate is written.

CHAPTER TWO

THE RESURGENT NEW

DON DELILLO, PAUL AUSTER, T. CORAGHESSAN BOYLE, CORMAC MCCARTHY, AND TONI MORRISON

Long before Don DeLillo's ten novels (as of 1992) and those of Paul Auster and T. Coraghessan Boyle, there was a history of what we might call fictions of conspiracy. John Hawkes's *The Cannibal*, various works by William Burroughs, Joseph McElroy's *Smuggler's Bible* and *Hind's Kidnap*, William Gaddis's *The Recognitions*, several novels by Norman Mailer, Thomas Pynchon's *The Crying of Lot 49*, *V.*, and, of course, *Gravity's Rainbow* have all as their main thrust conspiracy, the counterfeit, the artificial, interrelated themes with agendas within agendas. Many of them are concerned with films or filmic processes, mirror images, reflections, the blurring of distinction between artifice and real. DeLillo is a master of this. In *Libra* (1988), for example, Lee Harvey Oswald watches two movies that foreshadow his own action as an assassin. The use of film and filmic techniques feeds the conspiratorial air, since film creates a second track of experience, a record of acting out, and in that process, films shadows an underworld of coherent, organized behavior which we associate with conspiracy, even with terrorism. DeLillo's equations here, linking film and act, amount to a language, a voice, a form of response. If we use film or photographs (as in

Mao II), we take the shadows on the wall as either the real thing or as an approximation of the real thing. This blurring, this inability to distinguish, this disjunction which coincides with all efforts at linkage comprise DeLillo's emblematic America.

In previous decades, Gaddis's and Pynchon's America is full of quirks, eccentrics, the Luftmensch as normal: their conspiratorial, counterfeit, filmic country has no felt sense of security, no linkage to stable forms, no standard of normality. Similarly, Jack Gladney, in DeLillo's *White Noise* (1985),[49] once caught in a conspiracy to kill him and his wife through strange events is not permitted stability or ordinariness. His field of academic study, as chairman of Hitler Studies at the "College-on-the-Hill," is made notoriously unstable by the fact he does not know German; by the toxic cloud which envelops his home; by the presence of some poison in his own body, which will kill him; by his wife's entrance into an experiment which will alleviate her fear of death; by his need to kill her seducer. What may seem to be a stable faculty post, a dependable wife, loving children, all, prove to be menaces. Every personal move is countered by some force or element in American life which is conniving to undermine or destroy Gladney; and yet, withal, he continues with his life as though he can make all the necessary connections. He defies the irrational with reason. He could lose everything, including his position as builder of the Hitler Studies program when a conference reveals his failure to learn German

The reasons for the proliferation of conspiratorial themes in recent fiction are both obvious and not so evident. One obvious reason is the influence of the Kennedy assassination, where conspiracy theories have raged not only in literary pages but also in the political and filmic area. DeLillo's own novel *Libra* suggests that behind Oswald was an entire network of conspirators, some connected to CIA, some disaffected, others linked to Cuban exile groups, the Mafia, and the rest–but omitting Lyndon Johnson and the military-industrial complex. Another reason for the presence of such considerable conspiracy theory is a basic distrust of government, ours and others'. Here we find a curious turn: a still-held belief in the democratic institutions underlying the country and alongside that a disbelief that such institutions any longer protect the individual. The incessant presence of politicians and their epigone selling and reselling themselves has turned the government into an agent of the media; and discourse itself is now viewed as disinformation, not information.

Language is simply another source of manipulation, and here as we have seen we have a major theme; but intensified now until language is perceived as an agent for conspiracy, not as support for the individual or our institutions. A novel such as Walter Abish's *How German Is It* (in 1980) was ostensibly about the German attempt to use language to efface the Nazi past; but it was also about how language everywhere either buries or distorts the past and pollutes the present. Language becomes part of the conspiracy, not so much as the deconstructionists have it–as unreliable and uncertain–but as something which can remake history; in the process, reinvent the present.

Other reasons for conspiracy themes are equally compelling. The conspiracy suggests a kind of patterning of life which otherwise is missing. DeLillo makes a good deal of how bored people become attached to conspiracy and its first cousin, terrorism, because such activities give meaning, order, even organization. A terrorist group is highly stratified, fanning out from cell to cell, each with its own bit of information and its own role in any action; and it has purpose, focus, direction, a point of view. The lonely and empty gain substance. Tired lives are the stuff out of which recruits are made. Conspiracy and terrorism even gain solidity to their language, for while the conspirators may work indirectly, their language has the quality of final meaning: an assassination, a bomb explosion, hostage-taking, or some other act of terror. A related reason for conspiracy theories is that the proliferation of information, much of it trivialized in the process of being disseminated, has within it the potential of making all things seem possible. Conspiracy grows, as it were, in the seams of deceptive language, in the interstices of frivolous feedback.

The emphasis on conspiracy, it appears, is also intimately linked to the proliferation of photographic or filmic images, certainly to the dominant images of television. The ever presence of such pictures of "reality" blur distinctions between image and real. Photography is not life intensified, but lessened. Ambiguity is lost because context is screened out. Photography, film, even paintings create apparent order and patterns where messiness and chaos might otherwise exist. Conspiracy theory feeds on that apparent order, and for DeLillo and others, it becomes the American way. In *Players* (1977), he writes of "terror as purification." In another passage, he tells of how we have underestimated our government, thinking it innocent and ingenuous, when in fact it is entangled in "assassination, blackmail, torture, enormous improbable intrigues. All these convolutions and relationships.... Terribly, terribly interesting, all of it. Cameras, microphones, so forth. Behind every stark fact we encounter layers of ambiguity.... This haze of conspiracies and multiple interpretations. So much for the great instructing vision of the federal government."*[50]

Although this is an incomplete view—it ignores, among other things, how government *nearly everywhere* fails to serve its people—it is a perception which cannot be dismissed. It dominates our postwar literature, and it has had little or nothing to do with the communist threat from abroad or from within. Conspiracy—whether real or perceived—has been home-grown and home-practiced, an American cottage industry based on marginalization, economic triage, racism, the uncertainties of a system which can either reward hugely or punish severely. With the popular media intent on reordering experience on artificial grounds, language fails and conspiracy flourishes.

If there is a long tradition in postwar American fiction of

---

* This was long before we knew for certain that government agencies were experimenting with radioactive materials on unknowing Americans, especially pregnant women and minorities, those least able to protect themselves and least liable to protest.

conspiracy and its parallel phenomena, terrorism and counterfeiting of information, *what, then, is new?* Is DeLillo, among others, merely carrying through on what has been amply done before? The answer is that he, like Auster and Boyle, has found new areas in what seems a well-settled tradition. And what he suggests is immensely important, in cultural as well as literary terms. DeLillo has managed to create a relationship between the larger culture and the way the novel can function in reflecting it. He has not done this in any ordinary or simplistic way, but through metaphors or tropes that catch the incongruities of our existence, even while he compiles evidence that we have no other choice but, paradoxically, to live this way.

One of the most extraordinary of tropes comes at the beginning of *Mao II* (1991).[51] A huge stadium in New York (Yankee) is the venue, and the event is the marriage of 6500 couples, mixed, American and Korean, or other, presided over by the Reverend Sun Myung Moon. He is, in effect, the "new Mao," the controller of groups, mobs, and people's destinies. Marriage here is one form of destiny; and like Mao earlier, Moon arranges lives and alters futures. But what creates this scene so brilliantly is not the ceremony itself, but the way it is angled through the eyes of parents with binoculars attempting to locate their own children. Marriage has become so impersonal, so much a part of control, that the spectators, the parents, are unable to identify their sons and daughters in the mass of thirteen thousand people; and the children themselves are frequently marrying someone they have barely met until that moment. It is all staged, a crowd in the worst sense, an impersonal event of what should be a deeply private one. The venue has echoes not of baseball but of the Roman Coliseum, in which bloody events were staged and presided over by an emperor or Caesar. DeLillo calls up the bloody part of such events, the menace, the threat, the lostness–and yet he applies it to marriage rites, which should be tender, solicitous, reciprocal. The energy of the scene comes in the contrast between expectation and performance, in the desecration of the sacred.

Other factors enter in. Not only is the personal nature of the marriage depersonalized for the greater glory of the Unification Church, its very terms are altered. For among prohibitions, sexual intercourse between the married couple is forbidden until the partners have devoted at least six months or more to raising money for the church. For the parents of these couples, their children have been divorced from previous family ties and organically mated not to a spouse but to a belief, an organization. In reality, we know that several have tried to "rekidnap" their daughters and sons back to their original homes. In the DeLillo version, the parents are bewildered, bereaved; they bemoan their daughter's loss of singleness, and they see her, now, as possessing no distinct needs, hopes, expectations. The entire episode ends with "The Future belongs to Crowds."[52]

The trope is characteristic. DeLillo's brilliance consists of creating scenes which highlight the anomalies, paradoxes, ironies, and absurdities which have infiltrated our society so thoroughly they are thematic. At the end of *White Noise*, perhaps his pre-eminent novel, DeLillo works through disarrangement and disorder, in this instance in a supermarket where the shelves have been altered without warning. The rearrangement creates chaos among the customers, who discern no underlying logic for the changes and who cannot find their favorite brands. "They turn into a wrong aisle, peer along the shelves, sometimes stop abruptly, causing other carts to run into them."[53] Only the generic foods, those white packages lacking brand names, have remained in place. The customers suspect betrayal, conspiracy, some weapons aimed at them.

> ... The men scan for stamped dates, the women for ingredients. Many have trouble making out the words. Smeared print, ghost images. In the altered shelves, the ambient roar, in the plain and heartless fact of their decline, they try to work their way through confusion. But in the end it doesn't matter what they see or think they see. The terminals are

equipped with holographic scanners, which decide the binary secret of every item, infallibly. This is the language of waves and radiation, or how the dead speak to the living. And this is where we wait together, regardless of age, our carts stocked with brightly colored goods. A slowly moving line, satisfying, giving us time to glance at the tabloids in the racks. Everything we need that is not food or love is here in the tabloid racks. The tales of the supernatural and the extraterrestrial. The miracle vitamins, the cures for cancer, the remedies for obesity. The cults of the famous and the dead.[54]

The novel ends. Anarchy lurks just below the surface of what appears to be order, and the extremes which can create riot and panic are never distant from the ordinary. The unexpected can strike from any direction, at any time. Further, DeLillo is eager to demonstrate how the ever-changing quality of life is always somewhat beyond what the players in the drama can comprehend or sustain. His actors as a consequence must play catch-up; thus, the sense of conspiracy, mystery, counterfeit. These are, he recognizes, where a national literature might be located. His *Libra*, on the Kennedy assassination, fits perfectly here, the ultimate mystery and conspiracy in postwar America, *even if* there were actually no mystery or conspiracy. Killing the President, or trying, is an American event. We are so good at it we might offer courses. We speak, usually, of a national literature in other respects, as sustaining the aspirations of a people, as revealing their innermost needs, as presenting them to the rest of the world. But a national literature in postwar America is somewhat different: it is not aspirations, or revelry, but an exploration of forms of lunacy, a revelation of all the fissures, a reflection of differences; so that counterfeit and "truth" are so interchangeable we cannot disentangle one from the other. Secularity has bred a witty kind of cynicism and contempt. No longer a friendly people, we drop out, not in.

Back in *Mao II*, DeLillo takes on still another dimension of conspiracy and the counterfeit: the ways in which celebrity is achieved, how the American calculates his role; and beyond the celebrity is the question of presentation. The assumption DeLillo makes is that the country has become a gigantic stage where people assume roles, act them out, and then confuse whether they are acting or living in a real world. The subject here is Bill Gray, a reclusive novelist who insists on anonymity; as a writer, he recalls Henry Roth, Thomas Pynchon, or J. D. Salinger, or, more recently, Salman Rushdie, whose reclusivity has been imposed on him. Gray nevertheless allows his photograph to be taken, not because he wants to come out into the open, but because he wants to hide more deeply. He conspires to revise the terms of his seclusion, the way Rushdie stresses hiding by appearing.

He assumes that by challenging "the crisis of exposure" he can give himself "a powerful reason to intensify his concealment."[55] In doing this, Bill depersonalizes himself and links his figure to those bodies in the stadium at the beginning, concealing themselves, becoming anonymous in precisely in the very ceremony expected to be public and jubilant. By redefining the level of his concealment, Bill has turned himself into even more of an object: not a person people want to know, but *some they want to know about*. Like Gaddis's Wyatt Gwyon in *The Recognitions*, the more he loathes himself for falsification, the more insistent he becomes about withholding his identity. Everyone else in the novel follows, is part of appearance, as if some filmic process had transformed real lives into reel lives.

Mao is the ultimate cryptic figure, hidden in mists, the model for Bill who "was devising his own cycle of death and resurgence. It made Scott [Bill Gray's assistant] think of great leaders who regenerate their powers by dropping out of sight and then staging messianic returns. . . . Mao was pronounced dead many times in the press–dead or senile or too sick to run a revolution."[56] Similarly, by "staging" his photo, Bill can deepen the mystery of his disappearance. "We travel into or away from our photographs,"[57] DeLillo writes. And pictures with our likeness force us to make choices–whether to look like the picture or to select another look.

Clearly, DeLillo is utilizing comments on self and others that Roland Barthes made in *Image-Music-Text*, or in *Mythologies*. The image replaces the "thing" or subject, and then the subject must live up to the image. In this reciprocal arrangement, the filmic process assimilates the individual, even as the latter struggles to assert himself as real, there, present.

Later in the novel, Bill offers himself up for a French hostage, acting out what he has been all along, a hostage to his desire for seclusion. By gaining celebrity through hiding, Bill has become hostage to the very thing which gives him stature. He also gains his strength from this, since, apparently, he could not exist apart from being a hostage, that is, from being secluded and turned into a photo. Once again, fiction turned things on their end, as it were, so that once fictionalized, the sound byte or photo became credible. In DeLillo's *White Noise*, Murray Jay Siskind, who plans a university department centering on Elvis Presley, catches the presence of the tube as language:

> You have to learn how to look. You have to open yourself to the data. TV offers incredible amounts of psychic data. It opens ancient memories of world birth, it welcomes us into the grid, the network of little buzzing dots that make up the picture pattern. There is light, there is sound. I ask my students, what more do you want? Look at the wealth concealed in the grid, in the bright packaging, the jingles, the slice-of-life commercials, the products hurtling out of darkness, the coded messages and endless repetitions, like chants, like mantras. "*Coke is it, Coke is it, Coke is it.*" The medium practically overflows with sacred formulas if we can remember how to respond innocently and get past our irritation, weariness and disgust.[58]

Yet even as minimalism echoes this, it recognizes the shallowness and falsity of it. In its time, minimalism insisted on a kind of honesty, even as it destabilized language, in fact endangered it.

Because so much has been destabilized, writers from the 1970s, 80s, and early 90s–with markedly uneven results–are attempting to work out whether they live in a real or mirrored world; whether there is substance–whether, in fact, *anything* is worthwhile–or whether they are merely going through the motions from birth through death. A heavy overlay of Kafka and the Kafkaesque is upon this literature, but lacking the Czech writer's witty, bemused belief that through pain and suffering (his!) one gains a point of view akin to survival. Kafka fought against the beast of the apocalypse, the real as well as the imagined ones; whereas American writers are waiting out the uncertainties. Their depression or despondency is such that even sexual energy is depleted or pro forma.

Very possibly more than any other working novelist of his generation, DeLillo is attempting to grapple with our New Age philosophies, or versions of them. He catches the bizarre relationships and associations, the ways in which institutions and institutional beliefs have broken down. He understands that the replacement for the old will not itself endure, whether through mass marriage or terrorism. While there are mysteries out there– *White Noise* is testimony to that–the mysteries cannot be unraveled, or even rationally probed. DeLillo is a master of great images, metaphors, tropes, of uncovering the filmic process as it transforms how we look at ourselves. The wedding that closes *Mao II* in Beirut–perhaps the city of the future, or present–takes place amidst terrorism: a tank with its weapons pointed, a movable turret gun, all the contradictions between the private and public self. Yet the near-dead city refuses to die, since a wedding indicates continuity; tanks, explosions, a turret gun are part of the landscape, but then so is marriage. DeLillo has so deconstructed our life styles that simply to seek meaning becomes the ultimate meaning.

White Noise, the prototypical DeLillo novel prior to *Underworld*, continues his abiding fascination with crowds, here the milling townspeople being evacuated after a poisonous gas cloud appears in their area. But the overwhelming image is one of malaise, the malaise overcoming middle America in the 1980s–*White Noise* was published in 1985, and given DeLillo's rapid way of working, the result of writing in 1983-4. Malaise is typified by the toxic cloud which penetrates into the very soul of the Jack Gladney family. The "airborne Toxic Event," as it is called, is another one of the author's metaphors for our personal lives and our public existence in a post-industrial age, that part taken out of our hands, a kind of national nemesis. The toxic cloud overwhelming the town where Gladney is chair of Hitler Studies is the adventitious event which enters our lives unannounced and creates its own form or havoc. It is disruption, panic, hysteria, a throwback to classical times when a god out of whim could upset the individual life. It is also part of our unconscious, where our fears suddenly become real through some chemical accident or interaction–Three Mile Island as a state of mind. It is the disorder which lies just outside the order we try to make for ourselves; the disorder that lies just beyond Hitler Studies, where the anarchic shadow of the dictator himself lurks.

In DeLillo's view, the environment has become more perilous than the state. We have dared it to collapse, and now it exacts its revenge. It may also kill Jack, who allows himself to be exposed to fumes for a brief time; it introduces mortality into his life, when Hitler Studies seemed to convey on him a kind of immortality. Since he depended for his energy on history, which appears falsely as a seamless presence, the toxic event is the finite in what he believed was an infinite existence. History struggles against the vicissitudes of circumstance; it is the prototypical DeLillo equation.

That black toxic cloud should not be restricted to merely the public event. Its destructive power creates a sense of awe, as though some avenging god. It is as if the Gladneys and their neighbors were suddenly become Job, forced to endure illness, loss of goods, threat to children, personal and public disaster, for some crime they committed, or some wager being made on their responses. The black cloud forces on a godless society the awareness of powerful elements which disallow secular enjoyment; the Emersonian College-on-the-Hill is engulfed by evil. Hitler Studies goes private.

The closest Jack had ever come to God arises when he watches his children sleep, especially girls. "Watching children sleep makes me feel devout, part of a spiritual system."[59] Yet this religious-like experience must be matched by the atavism of a natural disaster, only here industrial and man-made. Every advance in science, like every private feeling of awe, Jack recognizes, is balanced "by a new kind of death, a new strain. Death adapts, like a viral agent."[60] At the very time DeLillo was planning and writing *White Noise*, AIDS hove into medical consciousness; it, too, resembles that toxic black cloud, that nemesis-like intrusion into countless lives.

Jack's wife, Babette, is fearful of dying, and takes a drug, Dylar, to relieve her depression. The couple is in a morbid competition about who is going to die first; although Babette is convinced it is she, when Jack is exposed to the toxic fumes, he becomes the more likely candidate. Preoccupation with death is everywhere, not as a trope for middle class life, but for all life. Gladney, besides chairing the department, teaches a course in "Advanced Nazism," restricted to qualified seniors, with special emphasis on "parades, rallies and uniforms," carrying three credits and requiring written reports. He arranges for screenings of propaganda films, featuring all of the above as well as "physical exercises." "There was no narrative voice. Only chants, songs, arias, speeches, cries, cheers, accusations, shrieks."[61] He introduces students to a culture of death, these students with their jeans and T-shirts, or their walking shorts and rugby-striped shirts. When discussion turns to the plot to kill Hitler, Gladney points out that all plots "move deathward." Babette is herself caught in a plot, forced to commit adultery to gain access to the magic drug Dylar, hoping to allay her depression and postpone thoughts of death, or even suicide. In that dialectic between morbidity and the routine, DeLillo finds his ground, and his work becomes a reflection of the latter decades of the century.

Even more significant in its probe into the complexities of the American character is *Libra*, a novel reaching into our fascination with conspiracies, real or perceived. In some respects, it picks up from DeLillo's 1977 novel, *Players*, in which people cavort as within a film: as actors who screen themselves and then play the reel back to see who they are. They observe, view, scrutinize. *Libra* is the more mature book in the way it carries over the idea of the filmed act: Lee Harvey Oswald becomes a character acting out the role of the man who is supposed to assassinate the President, but who misses and becomes the fall guy. Everyone in the novel has a role: Kennedy himself plays the figure who must be assassinated, part of an event staged for the sake of its dramatic complexities. Similarly, the conspiratorial forces, the CIA, the John Birch society, the Minutemen—all of them terrorist organizations—are also players. The arena is huge, nothing less than the Presidency, but there is no immediate reality to it; it is all a plot in a novel or long-playing stage piece. Its climax is the assassination, the end of Act IV, with the final act yet to be worked out.

In this scenario, Oswald is a small-bit actor who, like a minor Shakespearean character, vanishes from the stage when others take over. According to DeLillo's theory, and it is not to be confused with Oliver Stone's, which implicated everyone in sight, the CIA was active in manipulating Oswald. Present CIA and former ones who had defected to right wing organizations made him their puppet. Kennedy had failed them in their assessment of Cuba, and he was letting Castro win, or at least survive. Kennedy had taken on qualities of Shakespeare's Julius Caesar, and for the greater good of the country, he had to be eliminated. The novel limns the unraveling of conspiracy within conspiracy. What drives the conspiracies is the hatred of Kennedy, but what drives *Libra* is DeLillo's ability to make credible the various forces setting up Oswald. Rather than pointing fingers, the novel is deeply political in a broader sense: that the breakdown of order is a reflection of the disorder and anarchy implicit in the highest levels of the American ruling class.[*]

---

[*] In a remarkable admission of error (April 1995)–leading to 58,000 American and 3 million Vietnamese deaths–Robert McNamara, former Secretary of Defense under Lyndon Johnson, stated that he knew the Vietnam war was wrong, that he possessed no special information beyond what he read in the New York

All America is held hostage to secret, underground plans—as we have learned in Watergate, Irangate, Iraqgate, and, probably, will learn further at the holy gates. It doesn't matter if DeLillo is correct about the Kennedy conspiracy; it may not have gone the way he says. What does count is that he sees American life as having conspiratorial undercurrents which *might have led* to Kennedy's assassination. The details are exaggerated, the claims hyperbolic; but the point is distrust of all official explanations. The validity of DeLillo's point is the way in which America shapes itself through a drifting loner like Oswald and the disaffected elements which are part of America's underground. The mythicized loner or drifter who was once the gunslinger (Clint Eastwood), the ex-marshal (Glenn Ford), the unattached cowboy or westerner (Randolph Scott, Gary Cooper, Alan Ladd) is now a very different kind of animal: a man ready to go underground, to do whatever arises, but on *someone else's* terms.

Oswald has his counterpart everywhere; so that even if he was a lone assassin, he carried out an act innumerable others applauded or would have done had they the means or the courage of their convictions. That drifting, anarchic loner floating free of all safeguards and support systems—in another phase, the serial killer— is the element conspiratorial groups can count on. He is a reflection of themselves: the person or group so disaffected, so confused about his own identity he(rarely she) becomes the tool of ideological forces. Oswald desires to emerge, to be somebody or something; and yet every move he makes for self-improvement moves him ever deeper into the plans others have for him. He is the fly, they the spider, their plans the web; and he is entrapped, does their work, and is rubbed out. Hoping for success, he becomes American failure. He lacks the touch for true deception.

"Libra" is an ambiguous word and title. Foremost, it refers to

---

Times about events, and that he simply supported the Vietnamese slaughter out of loyalty to an elected President. Allied judges rejected that kind of argument at Nuremberg. Is McNamara real, or did DeLillo invent him.

the sign of the zodiac under which Oswald was born, October 18, making him a Libran. Libra in the zodiac, the seventh sign, stands for balance. But it also suggests the word freedom, the root of liberation, and, by extension, emergence. Even as plotters Ferrie and Shaw are planning to entrap him, Oswald hopes to turn his zodiac sign into a kind of freedom for himself. He thinks he will help Castro by killing Kennedy, whose government has been plotting to assassinate or remove the Cuban leader. Oswald, however, becomes the weapon whereby the anti-Castroites can eliminate Kennedy, who might, they fear, break bread with Castro and betray the opposition. Also involved is the Mafia, which looks back nostalgically to the days when Havana was wide open for gambling, prostitution, and other gang sports. Intermixed with this, as noted, are disgruntled ex-CIA and present CIA–for whom Oswald makes the perfect sacrifice. Among other things, he has been filmed or observed at each stage of his journey toward November 22. He is on his way into a culture of death, the "deeper plane" the insider Ferrie speaks of.

Oswald is driven by films, two in particular, *Suddenly*, with Frank Sinatra, and *We Were Strangers*, with John Garfield. Both involve assassination. In the first, the Sinatra character seizes a typical American home in order to set up a base to assassinate the visiting President; and only the family, that part of traditional America, can thwart Sinatra and save the chief executive. In the second, the Garfield character plots to assassinate the Cuban dictator (then Machado) and blow up his entire cabinet. "Lee felt in the middle of his own movie. They were running this thing for him. He didn't have to make the picture come and go. It happened on its own in the shaky light, with a strand of hair trembling in the corner of the frame. John Garfield dies a hero. He has to die. This is what feeds a revolution."[62] When Oswald is caught, he is himself in a movie house, following a plan in which he is to meet Wayne Elko, at a movie called *Cry of Battle* with Van Heflin. Elko, another insider, is planning to kill Oswald, not to help him escape.

The conspiracy itself, a kind of film, features Oswald's

manipulators as set directors attempting to create order out of disparate and disorderly events. As DeLillo states, "A conspiracy is everything that ordinary life is not. It's the inside game, cold, sure, undistracted, forever closed to us. We are the flawed ones, the innocents trying to make some rough sense of the daily jostle. Conspirators have a logic and daring beyond our reach. All conspiracies are the same taut story of men who find coherence in some criminal act."[63] Conspiracies are the sole way we can connect to things; the sole linkage left to us as we subdivide.

The external voice in all this is a researcher named Nicholas Branch, who, after the Warren Commission has done its job, is trying to make sense of the evidence. Branch's work has been contracted for the CIA's "closed collection." Yet he senses the CIA is withholding key information. He recognizes that, while he is being used by the CIA to provide an inside, secret report on the assassination, he is in fact being excluded from what he needs. Branch suspects he is being caught up in a deep conspiracy *against him*, against his efforts. By the late 1970s, the time of Branch's research, the plot has deepened into further conspiratorial recesses, with the CIA attempting to create more distortions. We should not dismiss this as paranoia, for in the 1980s, as DeLillo was unraveling events in and around 1963, America was undergoing something almost comparable: the cover-up of actions in Irangate at the highest levels, of diaries and notes withheld, documents trashed, perjuries committed, indictments filed and dismissed, reaching into the Presidencies of Reagan and Bush, touching on their cabinets, the head of the CIA and his hired guns, the national security staff, and its minions. Conspiracies seemed to have taken over the postwar government, perhaps going back to Lyndon Johnson's deceptive use of the gulf of Tonkin incident as a way of misleading Congress and the American people into entering the conflict with North Vietnam; or further back, to the right wing belief that Roosevelt engineered the Pearl Harbor attack, or at least permitted it, to get America into the war.

In this, Oswald stands no chance, caught as he is between

desire for self-definition and the extremes of ideology and behavior. He thinks he is constructing the kind of rope by which he can raise himself, and meanwhile the rope is waiting to hang him. DeLillo has cast his novel like the great classical tragedies, in which events provide a vise which traps the person who hopes to use them to his own advantage.

But there is a further point, only touched upon above. In some curious way, Oswald, at the lowest end of the scale, a loser, loner, drifter, a failure at everything he tries, is brought up against a man who has succeeded in everything, the President. DeLillo is aware of the parallelism, even of the doubling: both loser and winner have children at about the same time, both have brothers named Robert, both are gunned down. In this vision of America, where lowest and highest touch in conspiracy and acts of terrorism, differences only point up similarities. For Oswald, the assassination is his way of touching greatness, the low and the high and mighty finally encountering each other. By dying young, Kennedy helped create the Camelot myth; by living longer, all the sham would have destroyed him as it destroyed successive Presidents. Oswald's destiny, in this strange equation, is the same as Kennedy's, despite great differences of birth and family; a shooting provides the great democratic equalizer.

As for the shooting–that shooting!–Oswald maintains his first shot hit Kennedy in the back, not killing him; his second hit Governor Connolly; and his third missed. The shot that blew out Kennedy's brains came from someone else in the crossfire of shooters set up by conspiratorial forces. One need not accept this interpretation–although Oswald's marksmanship was suspect, especially given the time frame–in order to see where DeLillo is going. He has set out to do nothing less than to carve out what America is, where conspiracy and terrorism and shooting are the elements which bring us all together. Nothing like an assassination to create community. People grieve, bewail the fates, reach for transcendence through prayer. They feel good. And Kennedy lives more brightly because of the manner of his death. To that extent, Oswald succeeded.

Paul Auster

As a novelist of conspiracy, Paul Auster has created a world as much defined by language as by his theoretical and philosophical themes. Language captures his materials by shaping and reshaping them into certain molds which seem more scenario than actuality. Language is almost always "as if." His "world" is identifiable, clearly his. Through language, he has made it new: the way in which chance plays against individual will; the way, further, in which circumstance turns lives around, the accident around the corner; the disconnectedness of all activities, until they are linked or wrecked by chance; the sense of dwindling resources—whether food, money, worldly goods, dwellings; the marginality of all experience, that movement "outside" which so closely connects his protagonists to Kafka's; the creation of a labyrinthine space which, seemingly orderly, turns out to be random, discrete, circumstantial; the idea of the survivor not as a person who comes through but as someone who can only calibrate the changes in himself (infrequently herself).

In another aspect, Auster has moved fiction into a mutant form—"mutant" in its secondary sense of a new type of organism produced by mutation; *and* a hybrid form, in which fiction and biography cross-fertilize to produce a new variety or species. In Auster's mutant/hybrid reshaping, fiction, biography, and autobiography combine to produce a fresh species, as we observe as early as 1982 in *The Invention of Solitude*. The examination of his father's past is bonded to the fictional reality of Auster's own; history, the past, memory, and fictional recreation produce a new species. Similarly, in his New York Trilogy—perhaps less "trilogy" than just three novels—the product is the result of the bonding of several forms: detective fiction, Auster's own personal details, the use of biographical data for several main characters, and other types of fiction derived from Kafka, Melville, Hawthorne, Poe.

We must return to language. In Auster, realistic, reasonable language defines hallucinatory scenes; whereas in someone like Richard Ford, realistic language identifies the way things seem, not some apocalyptic vision. As we read these and other fictions, we note that American languages, all kinds, glory in their diversity; and yet there is a down side to this. That proliferation of voices and words, although seemingly a boom to fiction, also suggests that language itself has become a temporary refuge and that, in a country which wastes its resources, it can become quickly exhausted or enervated. A constant caveat in speaking of American trendiness is that whatever exists at the present will be dissipated tomorrow, long before the trend or development has the opportunity to develop into substance. Thus, the fear that several of these languages will vanish before they can be thoroughly explored. A corollary of this is that many of them will spit off into streams which are little more than minor variations–the way, for example, that Donald Barthelme's work has become a quarry for a succession of minimalists and neutralists, students following guru.

These are the negatives. The positive element is that American fictional languages can keep us informed of who and what we are. This is no easy business when political language seems more and more surrealistic, when it and popular visual culture demean language at every opportunity. With its multiplicity of voices, serious fiction helps us maintain some balance, keeps us within an actualized world, where language has meaning and is not merely self-serving. What we have witnessed, whether in Washington, on television, or in the daily press, is the destruction of language as a source of meaning. Russell Baker has written wittily of what he calls "Adland," where language has no linkage to the world it purportedly describes; its words defraud language. The free media have thrown us curves, sliders, split finger fastballs. That metaphor of Adland can be extended into every area of our life, except literature. Only in poetry, fiction, drama do we have language which takes responsibility for itself.

The situation is critical. In certain arts of the world, language is perverted to distort reality through a controlled press, to corrupt an entire people. In our society, where we have the perception of a free press, language is distorted casually, usually without any grand ideological plan, although with a mindset. The languages we receive from politicians, news-makers, publicity and advertising people–whether as words, body language, on innuendo–derive from areas distinct from communication. *Fiction* is communication.

Yet when American writers speak of language being their all-in-all–e.g., Barry Hannah's "For me language is always the basic thing. . . . that linguistic reverb"–we perceive they are walking the edge. For implicit in their emphasis upon language(s) is *their fear that everything else in the culture will fail them*; that given the uncertainties of the society and its intellectual base, only language is sustaining. This is a linguistics of danger, problematics, imbalance; and this is precisely what we discover when we begin to see America emerge from the languages of its various writers, whether innovative, retrogressive, or neutral.

The science-fiction writer Samuel Delaney provides a musical metaphor for dependence on a language which is inevitably lost when transmitted. He tells that at a concert of new music one piece "was written for twelve instruments, all of which had to play a different note of the scale–except one, which was left out. The melody was really an absence of that note, which moved up and down, working its way through the composition, a traveling silence through a constant acoustic field of eleven other notes."[64] He then relates that when the piece was "played in rehearsal in an empty auditorium, the missing note was absolutely audible, hovering and drifting through the cloud of cacophony. But when you heard it in an auditorium full of people, the resonance of the auditorium changed, due to the general noise of people breathing, or shifting in their seats, or the new deployment of mass, or whatever. You could no longer hear the silent note."[65]

Paul Auster insistently searches for that missing note, especially in his New York Trilogy (*City of Glass*, 1985; *Ghosts*, 1986; *The Locked Room*, 1986),[66] which deserves wide recognition.[*] Besides Kafka and some obvious American influences, Auster has been deeply moved by contemporary French writing and literary ideologies–he has edited *The Random House Book of Twentieth Century French Poetry* and translated several books from the French, including Mallarmé's *A Tomb for Anatole*. Mallarmé and Robbe-Grillet lie heavily over the Trilogy and perhaps explain the very narrow range of prose, almost obsessively neutralized. Yet Auster demonstrates that such lean prose can have broad potential; and, in fact, if we cite him now and Richard Ford later, we can see that neutrality is of several kinds, several voices.

Auster has created a typical American hybrid, the detective story from Poe and Wilkie Collins overlaid with aspects of French existentialism and German metaphysics; but not in any reductive, prosaic way. His is a landscape of surreal images, not because they melt or bond in some obvious way, but because they are so real and insistent they achieve an actuality of their own. Auster's landscape of the inner city is reminiscent of de Chirico's or Edward Hopper's landscapes of the mind–highly realized structures which seem to lose solidity the longer one peers at them. Auster's labyrinths are not simply

---

[*] The question is whether these three books are indeed a trilogy, even though Auster and the publisher have so labeled it. Names are repeated, some themes do overlap–the pursuit of characters, the detective story aspect, the dwindling of the individual's resources. But the books are not really connected as we expect in a trilogy, which works on continuity, inner coherence, repeated image clusters. This does not reduce the power of the novels or their overall effect, but it makes the trilogy more of a packaging idea than it does a literary one. What does hold them together for the moment is Paul Auster, whose life and experiences lie heavily in all the books; but the individual volumes, despite those overlapping themes and even characters, often work against each other, not together. The novels are really different experiences, each one centered distinctly, except for Auster's own hovering presence.

ways into, where entrances and exits are in doubt, but areas of infinite decisions–the labyrinth not only of place but also of mental connections which may or may not be validated by experience.

Everything in the Trilogy, ultimately, is linked to languages: words themselves, of course, but also the languages of movement, of gesture, of implication. Never straightforward, they have something symbolic, metaphorical, even Talmudic in them. As Quinn in *City of Glass* follows Stillman, the pattern is cabalistic: movement as quest, as means of expression, apart from what the movement individually may come to mean. Auster's fascination with *Don Quixote*–also a source for writers as disparate as John Barth and Kathy Acker–derives from his need to find a novelistic language which goes well beyond "words." Like Cervantes, Auster recognizes that all stories have been told, and what remains for the writer is the means of expression, the mode of communication, discovering the right vehicle.

In Auster, stasis pulls mightily against action. His concern is with the tension created by opposing forces, interiors holding on against exteriors; a metaphor, very possibly, for our times. By taking on the form of search, his novels validate themselves as deconstructed or destabilized elements. The search is not only for oneself, or the "other," the quarry, but a way of entering the labyrinth. His use of Poe-inspired doubling has the usual connotations of victim and victimized, of shadow and shadowed; but also becomes a form of expression, ourselves as amoebic, separating into ever newly formed selves. There is, always, the existential card, the matter of choices, none of them clear. The novels are circuitous, leading back not to people, acts, resolutions, but to themselves; demonstrating that we play roles which cannot be disentangled from the models or patterns we imitate. Circuitry suggests we can never emerge. The fictive world is a labyrinth, as befits the detective story mode Auster assumes; but unlike Chandler or Hammett, he is not seeking solutions to crimes. Rather, he is indicating, through a neutral language, a world of curves, illusions, unrecognized dimensions, split realities and personalities, a braid theory of fiction; the afore-mentioned DiChirico pattern.

Language–here, words–is an instrument of a world which must curve back upon itself because it has no recognizable or definable content.[67] Surrealistic dimensions seem present at every turn, with depths of dream, fantasy, the unconscious, altered states of being. Auster's detectives lose all sense of how long they have staked out a place, or of the place itself; and implicit in this distortion of time and place is an obsessive voyeurism. Although voyeurism is implicit in the detective genre, Auster ratchets it up so that it becomes not only an interest in others, but a way of penetrating into self. His protagonists–Quinn pursuing Stillman in *City of Glass*, Blue watching Black in *Ghosts*, Paul Auster pursuing and being pursued by Fanshawe in *The Locked Room*–ultimately are interested only in themselves. The problem they must solve is an internal one, never defined, never resolved.

Preoccupation with self is obsessive–not only from the protagonist's point of view, but also from the author's. Paul Auster uses Paul Auster, his present life, his wife, even his wife's family. The character Auster fits the real Auster in so many patterns that the reader wonders whether he is in the company of an egomaniac or whether some other phenomenon is present. For not only is Paul Auster recycled as both a real and a fictional character, other characters reappear who are in their way emanations of Auster: Quinn, Stillman, Dark, Fogg, etc. Alternations blur borders between who we are and who we might be, or can be conjectured to be if someone were to manipulate us. This agreed upon, we can see the seemingly obsessive, egomaniacal use of Auster by Auster serving a broader, more metaphysical scheme: that, like Cervantes with his invention of the chronicler who invents Don Quixote, Auster invents a persona indistinguishable from his characters.

As it becomes clear in *The Locked Room*, the act of writing only intensifies the use of a mirror image, Lacan's "gaze." Here, Paul Auster by name takes over the life of Fanshawe,* a man who has deserted his wife and child, left behind a body of work (novels,

---

* As part of Auster's linkage to Hawthorne's fiction, he borrows the name of his

poems, plays), and set it up for his friend, Paul, to assume his life. The taking over of Fanshawe's life at first seems exciting, especially as his wife is attractive and his work gains considerable critical and popular success. Yet the assumption of another's life–maintained by Auster, the character, even when Fanshawe turns up–"locks" Auster in. The titles of the Trilogy, in fact, reinforce the idea of role-playing, moving in and out of others' lives, voyeurism in the broadest sense. A "City of Glass" is a place of endless reflections; "Ghosts" is keyed in to color patterns, where distinctions between reality and ghosts are blurred. "The Locked Room" is the most intense, in that the character (Auster) has locked himself into Fanshawe's life, and by throwing away the key has squeezed out his own shadow, his ghost. He is nothing but Fanshawe, as he discovers when he sets out to write the former's biography.[68]

Auster has discovered metaphors for the ways in which we perceive ourselves. Clues to the enterprise come early in *City of Glass*, when Quinn (impersonating a detective named Auster pursues Stillman, the author of a book called *The Garden and the Tower: Early Visions of the New World*. The book focuses on languages. Once, in the Garden, objects and their names were interchangeable, but after the Fall, names were severed from things, "devolved into a collection of arbitrary signs"; so that language itself was severed from God. From this, Auster extrapolates that the story of the Fall is also the fall of Language. We must infer, all becomes contingent, open to chance; human will or choice has ceased to function according to any pattern. Still further, Stillman writes of a man

---

first novelistic effort, in 1831. *Fanshawe* presents a soul divided between desire for fame as an artist and equal desire for a withdrawn, ordinary life, without guilt, high expectations, self-denial, and the rest. His inability to resolve these drives wills his imminent death; in the meanwhile, he cannot go on. As his conflicted self deepens, even his physical appearance changes; he manifests manic-depression. Auster's Fanshawe shares many of these qualities–and for Auster the divisiveness becomes characteristic of our times, as it apparently did for Hawthorne in his day.

named Henry Dark, himself the author, in 1690, of a pamphlet call *The New Babel*. Only one copy exists, and we learn, eventually, that Stillman has himself created it. It concerns the structuring of a paradise in America, and once this was achieved, Babel could be built. One language and one speech would then be realized–paradise regained–all of this to come to pass in 1960.

The virus of dislocated language here is more than the result of contemporary misinformation and disinformation. We are in a world analogous to mail fraud in Pynchon's *The Crying of Lot 49*, or any of the other paranoiac schemes which crop up in contemporary American fiction and which turn out to be valid. We are, still further back, in Kafka's witty gloss on the Tower of Babel, which he called "The Pit of Babel," suggesting that heaven and hell are interchangeable when language is unreliable. But Auster is going after other game as well. Language is intermixed with voyeurism, and that, in turn, as already suggested, with role-playing. He is attempting to discover where the individual begins, blends, merges with, dies out, becomes extinct, is capable of resurrection. There is beneath all the outcroppings of name changes and role switches a secular spiritual quest; something we associate with Kafka, in *The Castle*, for example, or his "A Hunger Artist." In attempting to probe how the writer becomes part of the process of the novel, Quinn, mistaken for Paul Auster, visits the real Auster, even has a check made out to Paul Auster. The author of the Trilogy is trying to detect how we become indistinguishable from our surroundings, from social expectations, from scenarios which disallow us any say in our own roles. Even as we create roles in order to authenticate ourselves, they are taken from us, our lives borrowed. Even as we seek a language in which we can express ourselves, it proves counterfeit, a Babel. And even as we seek some certainty in our endeavors, we find the arbitrariness of separation, the isolation of individual will from final act. Language is the metaphor of such difference.

Questions of language in Auster demand further inquiry. So much of his work fits into an allegorical process that one is tempted to see his fiction–but especially the New York Trilogy–as a reflection of the 80s, an urban view from someone who considers himself marginalized by both poverty and talent. Auster's world is so destabilized that it often passes into the vision of America we associate with minority or peripheral groups; looking in from the outside, he perceives a world that holds few certainties, few linkages, few sustaining comforts. Everything changes rapidly, as chance works to alter one's welfare, whether money, dwelling, marriage and family, or social position. There are few if any professional careers, except writing and doing detective work. Jobs, such as they are, usually appear in the past or in the distance, not as goals. Marriages, too, like most relationships, are chancy–wives exist in order to be finessed, or deceived, or circumscribed. Affairs do not endure. But most of all, personal resources do not endure. Whatever money or goods one has will not last for more than a small part of the novel, and then the protagonist is faced with husbanding dwindling resources.

Auster replays Crusoe in an urban setting. Parks and streets are places to which one must adapt; and Auster is unique among urban writers for the amount or time his protagonists spend outside apartments or rooms. The loss of dwelling is part of the decline of resources; or else the dwelling is itself cut off, so that a maid's room or corridor serves as bedroom, dining room, kitchen, and bathroom. Dwellings may, also, be caves, as we see in *Moon Palace*, where the cave Thomas Effing inhabits becomes the artist's studio as well as his refuge. Crusoe peeks out from half a dozen scenarios.

Auster plays on enclosures, on contained, dark, narrow places; or else, he can reverse that, and in parks find life closed down even as nature opens up. The streets themselves, as in *City of Glass*, form patterns of deception and disguise. They are counterfeit experiences, in that instead of leading somewhere they become labyrinths which entrap both pursued and pursuer. Streets are the means by which hunted and hunter become indistinguishable; their routes belie the street as a place where one goes, or by which one gets there. The deceptiveness of streets is, of course, linked to Auster's preoccupation with observing, cataloguing, scrutinizing, all acts of voyeurism dependent on unyielding venues. His detectives are on a metaphysical quest, without hard evidence.

Unique qualities emerge. Language is one point of definition, that deliberately flattened out American English, colloquial, but firmly uncolored, so as to convey neutrality, even withdrawal. The language implies a fear of commitment, or at least a hesitation. It retreats before feeling into questions of whether language is itself definitive, what it can identify, whether it connects to objects or is nothing more than subjective rhetoric, the way it fails to cohere to things, which remain beyond its reach. Alongside this problematical language is the paradoxical desire to force communication, to make you see, feel, hear what it is like to push language to its limits only to find it inadequate. Here, Auster resurrects the French poet Mallarmé's hesitation to name things, his quest to get at objects indirectly through their opposite, a form of litotes (in which something is expressed by the negative of its contrary, "not a little" = a lot). One calculates what one has *not by what is there* but by what will be inadequate to fulfill the needs of the future. Whether in the Trilogy or in *Moon Palace, The Country of Last things*, or *The Music of Chance*, the individual is defined by his or her ability to make something last. Or else one is thrust to the edge of the abyss; and what was once wealth, or goods, gradually dwindles to nothing. Nothing now is the mark of former riches. The presence of such fears in the 1980s is surely a response to the inflated sense the country had of itself, its failure to look beyond the edge, and its disastrous inability to have contingency plans when the balloon burst.

In *Leviathan*, published in 1992,[69] Auster has tried a reprise of all his themes. As its name implies, *Leviathan* is a whale of a book in its implications, although not in length or density. And as its name implies further, it has implications leading back to Thomas Hobbes's treatise on individual rights vis-à-vis the state, in his *Leviathan*, in 1651. Hobbes argued the dangers of individualism–he supported fiercely the divine right of kings–and he warned that since all life was a matter of self-seeking, played out in a state of nature, only the monarchy through fear could control it. Men can survive by submitting their rights to the state and accepting its authority. His was a view of life as nasty, brutish, cruel, self-serving, based on a fear of individualism and anarchy, and relying on totalitarian means as forms of enforcement. While Auster is not a Hobbesian, much of his work plays in and out of the antipodes in this kind of world, and *Leviathan* leads directly into it.

The mechanism is, once again, a search, in this instance of Peter Aaron, the narrator, for Benjamin Sachs. Sachs has inadvertently (or not) blown himself up at the beginning of the novel, after several efforts to make a statement about liberty. As a bomber, he has traveled the country blowing up replicas of the Statue of Liberty; and his anarchic activity, falling far outside any government or state sanctions, leads to his demise. Since the social contract has not worked for him, in his perception of it, he has tried to alter it through bombing. Yet even as Aaron seeks to discover the nature of his long-time friend's explosive end, he begins to take on the now dead man's qualities. A good deal depends, obviously, on Auster's strategy of making the internal figure, here Sachs, sufficiently compelling so as to explain Aaron's attraction to him. Yet even when this is not fully accomplished—Sachs comes through as disaffected, disgruntled, not original—there remains the residue of the idea: that if one's life is empty, then following and taking on the persona of another can be fulfilling. Emptiness has rarely been more forcefully argued.

The overall tactic is to narrate successive stories, each linked by chance elements to the others—all of which begins to proliferate into a world that embraces circumstance. From this comes the book. And from that, we can extrapolate that stories are the sole thing to break the silence; that accidents and accidental meetings make stories possible, and without them there is neither life nor experience. Yet the structure of stories can create an almost opposite sensibility: that even while stories "connect," they suggest how discontinuous life is, how destabilized it can become. Dependent on connecting stories, experience may fail to link up and may fall through the cracks, become discrete, disconnected; in effect, experience fails in searching out the story by which it can be expressed.

Here Auster once again mimics his master, Mallarmé, recalling the latter's use of words pursuing some linkage so as to make a poem; or else, in another medium, lines and shapes on a nonrepresentative canvas pursuing some form which justifies their placement there. Sachs has the vision that "everything in the world was connected to everything else," and that is supposed to be the function of stories; and yet, as we know, stories which result from random linkages may illuminate the opposite. At his best, Auster tries to have it both ways. By *Leviathan*, his seventh novel in seven or eight years, Auster has created his world; he has made something new. Through allegory, metaphor, image, trope, symbol, he has mirrored the 1980s; but that world has not yet fully revealed its meanings. Its paradoxes, ironies, contradictions remain. Auster is still playing with us as readers, holding back, as though in some 7-card stud. It will be interesting to see where he will go when and if he writes a more fully fleshed novel. The possibilities (one hesitates to use this word!) seem unlimited.

T. Coraghessan Boyle

The linguistic potential for T. Coraghessan Boyle *is* unlimited, and his is indeed a fresh, bright voice. Nearly all of his early novels and stories are tours de force; verbally sophisticated, witty, knowledgeable, indicative of a well-read person and well-stocked literary mind; a personality who questions everything and sees America in broad satirical terms. Boyle is clearly one of the "new," and yet something bothers: does he settle too readily for the brilliant effect while forgoing the longer, more exhaustive means of handling a subject? Heir to the innovative writers of the earlier generation– Gaddis, Hawkes, Pynchon, Barthelme–along with a strong indebtedness to Kafka, he seems to be searching for some overarching point of view, some syncretic vision of America. Yet at the briefer level of scene, chapter, story line, he is incomparable. No one except Salman Rushdie has his grace, vitality, and energy, a Nijinsky in words. Note the beginning of *Water Music* (1982), arguably his most fully wrought novel to date:

> At an age when most young Scotsmen were lifting skirts, plowing furrows and spreading seed, Mungo Park [the African explorer] was displaying his bare buttocks to al-haj' Ali Ibn Fatoudi, Emir of Ludamar. The year was 1795, George III was dabbling the walls of Windsor Castle with his own spittle, the *Notables* were botching things in France, Goya was deaf, De Quincey a depraved preadolescent, George Bryan "Beau" Brummell was smoothing down his first starched collar, young Ludwig van Beethoven, beetle-browed and twenty-four, was wowing them in Vienna with his Piano Concerto No. 2, and Ned Rise [a London street person] was drinking Strip-Me-Naked with Nan Punt and Sally Sebum at the Pig & Fox in Maiden Lane.[70]

As a satirist, Boyle is interested of course in contraries, the bizarre episodes of the human condition as they confront the ordinary, the encounter of dissimilar elements in unlikely places, the yoking of such elements in a common quest, the unexpected found in the familiar and the familiar found in the unexpected. That is, a hem-stitched America, despite his exotic locales. He is a master at bringing together cultures–as in *Water Music*, with the Scotsman Mungo Park meeting up with Africa in his search for the source of the Niger; or in *East is East* (1990), with a Japanese runaway confronting American life at a writing colony; or in *World's End* (1987), with a triangulated joining of present-day Peekskill, New York, with its Indian and Dutch past. But Boyle's interest in dissimilars goes further. As a devotee of Kafka and *his* yoking of man and animals, he uses the ape in particular as a crossover with man, with wildly amusing results. "Descent of Man" (1979, book publication) begins:

> I was living with a woman who suddenly began to stink. It was very difficult. The first time I confronted her she merely smiled, "occupational hazard," she said. The next time she curled her lip. There were other problems too. Hairs, for instance. Hairs that began to appear on her clothing, sharp and black and brutal. Invariably I would awake to find these hairs in my mouth, or I would glance into the mirror to see them slashing like razor edges across the collars of my white shirts. Then too there was the fruit. I began to discover moldering bits of it about the house—apple and banana most characteristically—but plum and tangelo or even passion fruit and yim-yim were not at all anomalous.[71]

His woman friend is having an affair with her ape, Konrad. The references are to Kafka's "A Report to the Academy" (an excerpt of which becomes an epigraph for the volume of stories); Conrad's *Heart of Darkness*, with its descent into what the westerner sees as a primitive life; and not least Tarzan (also used as an epigraph); with further references of course to Darwin's *The Descent of Man*, which linked man's biological history to his ancestors, the great apes.

Still, despite the satire on relationships in America, on expectations, on sexuality and food, despite the adroit prose and sharply angled scenic conceptions and arrangements, we ask what the reverberations are. We wonder if this is a command performance, dazzling in its working out, but ultimately a pro forma flattening of experience. Boyle, however, can be a deceptive writer, and he does not tip his hand as he works his comic riffs. He seems to be seeking out our cultural icons. "Descent of Man" has all kinds of resonances, including our contemporary enchantment with what is primitive, atavistic, simple, and contrary to urban distractions. Boyle uses cultures and civilizations confronting each other on strange, often bizarre, grounds in order to direct us to our own forms of the bizarre.

The story following in *Descent of Man* is "The Champ," which is Kafka's "A Hunger Artist" reversed: instead of starving, the main character, Angelo D., is an eating champion. Boyle is wonderful on food–offering a kind of "in" joke, since all photographs of him show a man who looks almost anorexic. Yet food dominates his vision, whether the enormous, revolting, monstrous piles of food Angelo D. eats in order to remain an "eating Champion," or else the revolting "delicacies" Mungo Park eats in *Water Music*, or the Japanese foods Hiro dreams of in *East Is East*. A full belly–whether for the starving man or for the competitor who must eat his way into a championship, in "The Trenching Event of the Century"– places food, not sex, not enterprise, not ambition, at the center of Boyle's world. When Angelo D. takes on Kid Gullet, in attendance are Colonel Sanders, Arthur Treacher, Julia Child, James Beard, Ronald McDonald, Mamma Leone.

As if that were not enough, in *World's End*, mad bouts of eating, akin to bulimic binges that are self-destructive, are a recurring presence. Early on, Harmanus Van Brunt, a seventeenth-century tenant farmer in the Peterskill-Peekskill area, is possessed by food insanity. It has nothing to do with nourishment, everything to do with orality, with consumerism. Food consumes him as much as he consumes food. "Harmanus ate till early afternoon, ate till he's ravaged the garden, emptied the cellar, threatened the livestock. . . . The kitchen was devastated, the pots blackened, spatters of food maculated the floorboards, the table, the fieldstone of the hearth."[72]

If food is the central metaphor, far more than sustenance or nourishment, then it reflects, in Boyle's fiction, an American obsession. It is part of a culture not of life but of death, not of satisfaction but of pathology, the sickness of abundance. Food is the emblem of several opposing elements: it can be a sacred commodity when one is starving (Hiro, Mungo Park, the rest home residents in *The Road to Wellville*); or profane, when its abundance overwhelms (as in the stories or in *World's End*). More than that, however, food helps to define us. Even in a story where food is marginal, as in "A Woman's Restaurant," it remains a subtext. A man disguises himself as a woman in order to gain entrance to a women's only restaurant: not for the food, but for the experience of a world where only women are present. Yet it is a restaurant, and therefore, food is associated with women, with a male disguised, with his decision to undergo cross-dressing. Food subsumes sex.

If we associate this near obsession with food, we find linkage with another literary figure who needs constant nourishment and sustenance, Saul Bellow's Herzog. The latter needs more than food, but he revels in forms of nourishment: gourmet meals, emotional support, succoring. Nourished by others, he produces only words. Boyle's characters, while not Herzogs, nevertheless constantly find themselves in situations in which they must be helped, literally saved—and, usually, salvation comes with food. In *East Is East*, Hiro is fed surreptitious lunches by Ruth Dershowitz, one of the writers at the colony off the Carolina coast, Ruth is a kind of Jewish mother, trying to nourish Hiro, as he avoids capture by the American authorities for having jumped ship and then acquired a host of other charges. Hiro (hero? hero sandwich?) Tanaka is half-Japanese, half-American, his father a hippie having passed through Japan. Unwanted at home, Hiro is chased during his entire stay in America. And what sustains him is food, whether insects in the swamp, stolen lunches, or other illicit forms of nourishment. Food is part of Boyle's vision of America, a commodity that can be defined by its "lack" as much as by its overabundance.

In both parts of *Water Music*, the Scottish explorer Mungo Park and the London imposter Ned Rise are put into situations whereby food, or lack of it, fills their imagination and immediate needs. Ned starves in London, and Park starves in Africa as he searches for the Niger River source. But in this considerable novel, Boyle transforms and finally transcends the goods obsession; all his skills, including the culinary, come together in this novel, which can be read as a kind of parable for America as well as an engrossing adventure story in its own right. There are really several stories in *Water Music*. There is, of course, the historical Mungo Park, the

Scottish explorer who traced the course of the Niger and died, drowned, at thirty-five in Africa. Boyle follows the rough outlines of Park's career. But a second story comes when Boyle re-imagines his real character and reshapes him into a fictive one. There is at work here an act of biographical imagination.* Connected to this story is Park's own biography, whereby Boyle fills out the details from Park's life and from his book, *Travels in the Interior Districts of Africa* (1799). A third story, linked to Park's, both fictive and real parts, associates him with a Londoner born into worse than Dickensian and Hogarthian squalor, but survivor of it all, Ned Rise. Here, Boyle creates a tale which parallels Ned in London–as primitive and barbaric a place as "atavistic Africa"–with Mungo Park and his ordeals. The fourth story is the association between Ned and Mungo when they link up on the latter's second journey to Africa. Of these four stories, so far, two are biographical, two are fictive; and we might say that the intertwining creates a fifth story: the way in which Park thinks he directs Rise, whereas in actuality Ned is driving Mungo.

With its reference not only to the Niger but also to Handel's musical piece, *Water Music* is a mutant form. Embedded in its fictional side are numerous biographical portraits of some depth: Dassoud, the Moslem chieftain who works his way to the top through cruelty, murder, intrigue; Allie Anderson, the woman Mungo leaves behind for years at a time, and who finally rebels at being the little lady waiting for her man to return; Boyles, Ned's drunken friend in London; and, not least, Georgie Gleg, a great triumph as a figure whose miserable life is turned magical by his association with Allie, whom he worships at a distance. Through an act of will, Gleg is transformed from oaf and victim to a successful medical man and professor.

---

* In *The Road to Wellville* (1993), Boyle re-imagines Dr. John Harvey Kellogg and his Battle Creek Sanitarium for health nuts, a novel dependent, once again, on food; but here Boyle exhausts his material well before its 476 pages.

The novel is triangular in its geography, extending from Selkirk, Scotland, to London, to West Africa. The geographical triangle suits the geometric proliferation of stories within stories. The literary antecedents are clear, especially for Ned himself, a rogue's tale deriving from the late eighteenth century. Ned lives in filth, thinks in filth, acts out one scam after another to survive. His counterpart–with Conrad's *Heart of Darkness* looming in the background–is another scam-artist of sorts, Mungo. To discover the Niger's boundaries, he must perpetuate one deception after another: among them, offering his African guide, Johnson, a quarto of Shakespeare, then in getting Johnson to return on a second trip with an offer of Milton, Dryden, and Pope, "Leatherbound, gilt titles," the Pope signed. He offers worthless money and goods to the Africans in exchange for foodstuffs and other necessities; he promises freedom to men in a prison colony if they will accompany him, although their chances of survival are slim. To carry out his will, a British-European determination to conquer, he must negotiate his kind of jungle, as much as Ned must negotiate his.

The winning of the American West is background for the exploration, and exploitation, of Africa. Ned Rise's will to survive is the ultimate pioneer's desire to come through; Park's will to discover and chart the Niger is another sort of pioneer effort, where the need to explore pre-empts even the need to survive. Like the American frontiersman or cowboy, Park surrenders all personal comfort–sexual satisfaction, intellectual stimulation, even food–in order to achieve his inner mission. Ned is the opposite. As we see, he rises for material reasons, whereas Park plunges on for the greater good of British scientific circles, as well as his own needs for martyrdom. The allegory is the paralleling of African natives and native Americans: both a group of warring factions, savage in their treatment of each other, allied in their suspicion and hatred of the foreigner, the white man in America, the Moors in Africa, who in the name of Islam have their own agenda of slaughtering and exploiting.

The triangular arrangement works at several levels: English

explorers, native Africans, and Moorish killers as represented by Dassoud and the murderous group he assembles to gain power for himself. The opening up of Africa via the Niger–filling in the innumerable blank spaces on the map–has its counterpart in an America opened up by men and women who filled in the empty places on the map and then exploited the resources. The allegory reveals how societies function, how civilized forces impinge on the "savage races," how racism and condescension operate, how noble aims (and Park is in the main noble) are pre-empted by greed, self-serving, and exploitative needs. Similarly, in *World's End*, Boyle replicates this world of plunder and power in the triangulation of seventeenth-century Dutch exploitation of New York State, Indian victimization, and the 1949 Peekskill race riots. He connects the elements historically as well as fictionally and biographically; but the allegories are clear: the Christian white man plunders, the pagan natives suffer, and the residue remains as racial hatred, violence, and, for many, economic success.

But Boyle is not boorish; he sees both conquest and victimization as part of an inevitable process and, therefore, as comedic. As a satirist, he has a suitable structure and a grand theme, American to his core. The cowboy and Indian set of mind is not far behind. The Africans do not ride horses into battle, but they use canoes, mass for attack, suffer near annihilation by the settlers' guns, until, finally, the Africans prove too ubiquitous and numerous. Employing malevolent schemes, the ennobled explorer himself fills out his crew with murderers, pimps, drunkards, the scum of English society (recalling in America gunfighters, gin-slingers, army riff-raff, sewer rats); and in turn, each has his own need, including Ned Rise, who has risen from the dead so often he joins exploration as his means of escaping another death. For him, survival, not exploration, is all. The novel leaches out much of the late 1970s and early 80s. In its spaciousness, its need for discovery (self and otherwise), its conflict between so-called civilized elements and so-called savages, in its need for a man like Mungo to prove himself, in the violence Boyle turns into entertainment–in all of these, he is writing prototypical American fiction full of social resonances: that hybrid of fiction and biography which has become a curious new subgenre.

Perhaps more than anything else, the spirit of our times is caught in Park's will to make his way regardless of the carnage in his wake. An unknown figure rises, virtually from nowhere, to assume an imperial role. At the end of *Water Music*, the explorer is treated as a god by a colony of pygmies. Although he will drown on his second journey to West Africa, in the meanwhile he has pulled together all the forces of his society to do his bidding and to create a pattern for his life. As a Scotsman, Park possesses all the Protestant ethics we associate with American success, and he is stoical in the face of terrible personal defeat and physical suffering. He is naïve about consequences, and only the wise old Johnson, his guide, saves him from successive disasters; until Johnson recognizes the inevitability of final defeat and vanishes. Boyle here plays on stereotypes: the naïve but driven Scotsman, the all-knowing African; the innocent westerner, with his will to knowledge and power, and the regional native, who knows that all such quests end in disaster. Like the wise Indian in the American western, Sitting Bull expounding philosophies of nature and spirit, Johnson applies local knowledge; and that is superior to anything Park knows, despite his will to power.

Water Music is parable, allegory, biography, fiction, a cautionary tale; but also a narrative of how personal emergence works. Boyle recovers the survival instincts of Dickensian characters; he views the jungle as a far more perilous place than Faulkner's big woods; he perceives the murderous clash of cultures, such as we find in Conrad; he encapsulates the experience of the explorer, the quintessential danger and the suffering for some ideal. In so doing, he brings together the matter of the picaresque, the story of a rogue, as well as the ingredients of the apprenticeship novel, with its emphasis on re-forming and reshaping. *Water Music* is a catch basin of a novel, one of the few contemporary American attempts to be inclusive rather than particular. Boyle runs roughshod over minimalist ideas, not only in the conception of the book but also in its language. He creates an individual rhetoric to match the boldness, nastiness, and bizarreness of his characters' experience. The Niger River itself becomes some magical, totemic force—recalling Faulkner's "old man"—more than river, close to God; and Park's quest for the source and direction of the river's flow has within it a Faustian pact, a sellout to the devil. Although the Niger has great geographical and scientific potential, Park's obsession with it derives from a kind of personal delirium, as though once he had experienced Africa, he had to go on until he drowned in it. He is driven on further than is needed, not for the scientific discovery but for the inner emptiness which only Africa and the Niger can possibly fill.

In historical terms, Park becomes the ultimate capitalist, so energized by personal compulsions, he feels stifled, strangulated, almost dead when he cannot move ahead with his quest. In London, he vegetates:

> And so it goes, week after week, month after month, invitations refused, lectures denied, friends and relatives snubbed. Mungo has become a prisoner to pen and ink, his fingers blotched like a leper's, face pale, spine curved until it looks like an odd piece of punctuation. Day after day he stares at the page before him, eyes watering, progress testudineous, thinking he should never have left Selkirk, never challenged his place in life, never set foot in Africa. The man of action reduced to the man of recollection like some chatty doddering old veteran of foreign wars. It's disgusting. Not at all what he thought it would be. A book. It's a thing on a shelf, complete, ordered, rational—not an ongoing ache and deprivation.[73]

As against this enervation in London, Africa offers a full plate of horrors: cannibalism among tribes for whom white people are the devil incarnate; unspeakable tortures and butcheries; insects, mites, snakes; warring factions, in which Islamic Moors descend on native villages to pillage, disembowel, pirate, or collect slaves; an oppressive, unrelenting climate, the threat of crocodiles lying in wait near river banks, bacteria floating in air and water–all of which make life not too good a bet. With death so ever-present in multiple forms, Park is energized by an inner will: to triumph over death, one needs more than good health. One needs desire, determination, the ability to transcend pain, suffering, discomfort, everything that is anathema to the so-called civilized man. Boyle perceives in all this a kind of balance, in which Africa absorbs the white man, while the latter struggles back to emerge through perseverance, desire, strength of will. It is a tale, apparently, not of the previous centuries, but of our time.

East Is East, eight years later, in 1990,[74] is consistent with the earlier book. It is, in fact, a replication of *Water Music*, with a change of venue. The change offers Boyle an extended, parodic view of America as it has come through the 80s. Here the "explorer" is Hiro Tanaka, who after an altercation jumps ship only to find himself in the "jungles" of southeast America, off the Carolina coast. Whereas Hiro is the civilized being, America fits the Africa of *Water Music*, insect-ridden, jungle-terrained, full of blacks seeking to cut a Japanese throat, whites who carry guns and who are eager to shoot a foreigner, especially an illegal. American food is an abomination compared with the vegetables, rice, and meats of the Japanese diet. Since America's ideas of society have no coherence, the country lacks a center; and its godlessness is evident in the fact that not even the individual body is holy. Americans lack sufficient language for social inter-changes, and Hiro, when pressed, tries to find the words suitable for an American greeting (as contrasted to a Japanese bow and show of deference.)

>Say something, Hiro told himself, say something, and all at once he had an inspiration. Burt Reynolds, Clint Eastwood–what would they say? Americans began any exchange of

pleasantries with a string of curses, anyone knew that—and even if he hadn't known it, even if he were an innocent, he'd seen Eastwood in action. "Motherfucka," he said, bowing to the girl as he shuffled forward to dump his booty on the counter. And to the bewildered boy, in the most amenable tone he could summon, he observed: "Cocksucka, huh?. . . "Shitcan," Hiro said, grinning now and bowing again, as produced the four bills and laid them out on the counter. "Toilet. Make my day, huh?"[75]

As language fails—not merely because Hiro knows only movie English—so, too, does every other aspect of American life, as he perceives it. He becomes, in this respect, not simply an outsider viewing America, not simply a spokesman for a disillusioned author; he becomes an unreliable narrator whose unreliability must be measured against even more unreliable figures, Americans themselves. What Boyle does is to suggest that Hiro's subjective perceptions may be more objective sounding than the voices of those who are distinctly American types. Hiro observes America rotting from within—it is, of course, a *perception*, not a documented reality; and yet, as Boyle assumes the role of Hiro observing, we come to accept that voice, that language, that observation as valid.

By using Hiro as both a reliable and an unreliable narrator, the author plays a duplicitous game. Hiro's perceptions seemingly highlight every American failing: the cheapening of the eating experience as an emblem of the cheapening of all experience, the violence implicit and explicit in the society, the persistent ethnic and racial antagonisms despite lip service to democratic ideals; and yet at the same time, Hiro misses American generosity, the openness of the society, the spatiality which creates its own terms of response, the singularity rather than the commonality of experience. Further, Hiro has his own racial and ethnic hatreds, derived from his Japanese assumptions about this feral land. He sees blacks only as predators and all southern whites as sharing the small town's sheriff mentality. He fails to recognize that the two cultures are so different they cannot be compared; and Boyle's triumph is his use of stereotypes to point up distinctions. As if destined, Hiro commits hari kari when he is finally trapped by the system and his options for escape have run out.

Not to be ignored in Boyle's scheme is the writer's colony with which Hiro becomes entangled. He sees the colony, somewhat stereotypically, as part of that parvenu-ridden, sybaritic dimension to America which contrasts with the simple survival needs of Hiro. The deck is stacked, as they say; and the colony is not only a workplace for losers, it is also the center of terrible jealousies, hostilities, and near murderous anger. What counts, apparently, is not achievement, but reputation; the writers vie for celebrity status without having done the work to underlie it. Here Boyle, even within the clichés of a writing colony, catches the 80s literary scene: where celebrity has pre-empted achievement.

Yet when all the cross plays and ethnic contrasts are worked through, resulting in Hiro's ritual suicide, there is emptiness at the center of *East Is East*. The hollowness is surprising, since *Water Music* had seemed to put Boyle on a literary roll, with his *World's End*, in 1988, winning the Pen/Faulkner award for fiction, then followed by *East Is East*. Much of the posturing in the short stories, where a slick line often negated a brilliant idea, was in the past. Boyle had become a true professional, a writer with all the equipment for a significant breakthrough from novels into literature. With that in mind, we wonder why *East Is East* falls short, disappoints, even when we can cite the brilliance, the insistent voice, the unique Boyle language, knowledgeable, witty, solidly based on close observation, reptilian quick.

One possible reason for disappointment is that the novel *in its conception* does trade on stereotyped; and no matter how witty, the stereotypes remain not particularized but generalized points of reference. Something similar had occurred earlier in *World's End*, despite its fullness: the fatuous, avaricious Dutch landowners, the victimized Indians, the decadent twentieth-century descendants. Further, in the later novel, there is insufficient development of the idea: once Hiro has become our reliable and unreliable narrator, his perceptions are predictably ethnic and racial. Incapable of growth, he must remain the Japanese seaman who has jumped ship into an alien, even primitive society. And that society, seen by him as atavistic, almost cannibalistic in its monstrous violence, does not change, since it is presented in monolithic terms. Hiro's Japanese mentality is centered on one kind of life; America's on another. And so they remain, unlike the permutations and combinations Boyle presented in *Water Music*.

As a maker of literary parables and allegories, as a reflector of American social and political life, Boyle has to avoid the pitfalls of patterning, even when the latter is the source of considerable fun. In his planning, opposites often negate or cancel each other out. If we compare him to those he resembles in an earlier generation, Gaddis, Heller, Pynchon, Vonnegut, Hawkes, Barth, we see that while they, too, are moralists, wits, fabulists, they drive toward some larger dimension, out beyond the self-reflexive nature of their work. In broader terms, Boyle harks back to another "American" writer, the hybrid Nabokov: in his circular way of working, his brilliant and high-toned use of language, his wit and verbal self-indulgence. But he is not so "complete" as Nabokov, and, therefore, his self-reflexiveness seems somewhat vacuous; he empties out his subject—perhaps more adroitly than any of his contemporaries—but when we await some filling in, we are disappointed. There is the danger Boyle will write "entertainments," which even at the highest level is to serious fiction what operetta is to opera. There is, of course, a middle ground, whereby he becomes the Donizetti of American fiction. Yet the skills are so enormous, we wait for more, a vision, a prophetic book, a sense of human destiny that goes well beyond witty stereotypes.

In the meanwhile, Boyle has brought to the English language a freshness and originality, the mark of a major writer striving for the "new." The distinctiveness of his voice goes well beyond whatever shortcomings we find with conceptualization. A few writers in this younger generation have shaped a voice–Boyle, Barry Hannah, Paul

Auster, Ishmael Reed, the somewhat older Toni Morrison; but what some have failed to communicate, withal their skills, has been a larger vision of the country–even when we take into account that often their work is elliptical, metaphorical, filmic, emblematic. They have turned away from a more holistic view–not necessarily a pre-requisite for writing fiction, but a requirement for authors who wish to extend the boundaries of literature and novel making.

Cormac McCarthy

Although an author should not have to bear the burden of his blurbs, Cormac McCarthy's have been particularly difficult to sustain. The problem is not his culpability, but the reputation he is expected to live up to. Attached to his first novel, *The Orchard Keeper* (1965), is praise that probably relates to several later novels as well. The non-literary *Village Voice* calls him a "master stylist, perhaps without equal in American letters"–this for a fairly pedestrian novel. The New York Times *Book Review* says he "puts most other American novelists to shame"–I suppose the reviewer has in mind Bellow, Pynchon, Oates, Gaddis, Mailer, Roth, among others. The Dallas *Morning News* brings in the Faulkner connection, saying that McCarthy "seems to have looked the work of Faulkner in the eye without blinking." By *Child of God* (1973), his third novel, the blurbs now come in from his contemporaries: Ralph Ellison says he is to be envied; Peter Matthiessen states he is "one of our best" writers; Barry Lopez calls him a "contemporary writer almost without equal."

By *Suttree*, in 1979, the publicity blurbs are stumbling over themselves, so to speak. The Washington *Post* calls him perhaps "the closest we have to a genuine heir to the Faulkner tradition." The Cleveland *Plain Dealer* goes a step further, saying that *Suttree* "invited comparison with Faulkner's best"–we assume the reviewer means *The Sound and the Fury*, *Absalom!, Absalom!*, *Light in August*, and *As I Lay Dying*, for starters. Anatole Broyard, in the New York *Times*, having this time possibly read the book he was reviewing, seemed fixated on the dead in McCarthy. After declaring that people do die, Broyard assures us that we won't escape the author's death, who will haunt us, "which is what they are supposed to be." The St. Petersburg *Times* reaches all the way, deeming *Suttree* to be "unsurpassed in American literature." Sorry, *Moby-Dick*.

For *Blood Meridian*, in 1985, the Faulkner comparison looms: the *New Republic* calls him "a literary child of Faulkner, and now Robert Penn Warren weighs in, that McCarthy "has, line by line, the stab of actuality." Warren assures us he "is here to stay." The *Times Literary Supplement* of London, hesitant to praise Americans, novelists or otherwise, says his "sense of the tragic is almost unerring." Alan Cheuse describes *Blood Meridian* as a Western "that evokes the styles of both Sam Peckinpah and Hieronymus Bosch; also that McCarthy "employs a neo-Biblical rhetoric," a "stirring diction unparalleled in American writing today." It all paid off, these blurbs, these pats on the back, these Faulknerian comparisons: *All the Pretty Horses*, in 1992, won the National Book Award. All the stops were pulled out for this one. *USA Today*, known for its literary acumen, calls it "Surely one of the great American novels"; The New York *Times*, a "major achievement." The Chicago *Tribune* assesses it a "genuine miracle in prose"–the comparison is now, not with Faulkner, but with Melville for their common descriptions of landscapes. Many of the earlier blurbs are repeated. The Boston *Globe*, renowned for its dazzling literary reviewers, speaks of the novel's "elegiac rhythms" and of McCarthy's "passion"–one hopes the comparison is not with Jesus Christ; and *Newsweek*, another bastion of high literacy, says he is "a true American original."

Anyone trying to write seriously about McCarthy is, clearly put in a bind. If one wants to locate him in literary terms, there are the comparisons to the greatest figures in American Fiction, Faulkner, Melville, and others. If one wants to see what is original and what is imitative and hollow, one is confronted by something that seems settled: McCarthy is a master, even a legend, and tamper with that at your own peril. Yet McCarthy, in part, can be defended even against his outlandish and outrageous supporters, those in the blurb and hype business. But first we must drop the Faulkner comparison, the reference to Melville, the kudos which make him incomparable, or the finest of American contemporaries. If we return from hyperbole to reality, to the novels and what they tell us, what they reach for, what their limitations are, what they do achieve, we can see them not as a red-skinned answer to pale-faced Henry James, but for some sense of newness in American fiction.

A good place to begin is by asking if McCarthy is an original. He forces several adjustments on the reader, especially on the urban reader–who is, I suspect, his major supporter. McCarthy is not simply recreating something of a West which defies the history books; nor is it that his protagonists commit atrocities of a kind usually met in the Crusades or in Hitler's Germany. These are elements we have become accustomed to. It is that McCarthy can transcend, somehow, the bloodlust of his pages. As the serial killer of novelists, what he brings to fiction is not easy to digest because it seems so uncivilized.

McCarthy rarely asks us how we live, but, instead, how we would live if we found ourselves on the edge. He is our Jack London of the Southwest, but with an even more implacable ideology. The "edge" may be anywhere, but it is usually in the natural world where one is totally exposed, while the individual himself (all men!) may be self-destructive, indifferent to his fate, even suicidal. Fate *is* there, a deadening sense of what lies in store, an inexorable, relentless fate. Individual will is exerted as if one were Sisyphus, but the outcome, while not determined, is fixed within the act. McCarthy's protagonists are, more often than not, entangled as soon as they start on a mission. The American West is not opportunity or escape, certainly nor transformational, but the valley into death. In *Blood Meridian*,[76] for example, the Kid–no further name–joins a band of murderous outlaws whose goal is to kill Indians and collect the bounty on their scalps. The mission is made to order for McCarthy's brand of mayhem and implacability, as well as for the strikingly sharpness of his prose. What the book lacks, however, are the very Faulknerian qualities so many reviewers found in him: Faulkner's depth of humanity, not as some sentimental or nostalgic bit, but as a witty recognition of how life divides, compromises, forces uncertainties, even while the individual struggles on according to a plan of his own. Endurance means very different things to the two authors.

Yet the angulation of McCarthy's prose, its seeming contradiction between obliqueness and visual accuracy, its unflinching clutch of natural events and human weakness, all, create a crisis in any analysis of his work. One must admit that the verbal, linguistic dimensions of his fiction–a good part of his novelty–outrun the conceptual base he starts from. His is indeed a new, jagged voice, a serious revisionist, but mainly in a language divorced from any overall pattern. Running against the contemporary grain, McCarthy wants nothing less than Greek tragedy, the fall of men who pride themselves on their unassailability. Yet when they decline, fade, or, more often, die, they have outlived our accommodation of whoever they are or whatever they are seeking. They seem physical embodiments, not quite human beings: figures who exist so that McCarthy's "fate" can drive them toward some personal doom.

Most critics have commented on the violence and mayhem committed in McCarthy's novels as part of his charm. In *Blood Meridian*, for example, the physical agony is indeed impressive. "They followed the trampled ground left by the war party and in the afternoon they came upon a mule that had failed and been lanced and left dead and then they came upon another. The way narrowed through rocks and by and by they came to a bush that was hung with dead babies."[77] The language is tricky, with the "by and by" indicating a leisurely stroll, then the dead babies hitting us suddenly after we have relaxed. The judge and Glanton in *Blood Meridian* are psychopathic killers who go about their work as other men might make shoes: killing is their business, or else maiming, gouging, slicing.

McCarthy likes to mix blood and gore with piss and shit, as if in some intensified Jacobean revenge drama or an updated *Titus Andronicus*. His books are deliquescent; bodies seem destined to return to their liquid origins. Or else, he gloats over remains, whether human, animal, bird, or unidentifiable. Carrion is a major participant. He distributes blame for the mayhem equally, to whites, Indians, Mexicans. Women and children are almost always victims because in the pecking order they are defenseless; the moral standard we perhaps foolishly associate with civilization is absent, quickly abandoned when his men head out into the wilderness. Men, however, are not only hunters, they are hunted; and anyone in their way, women, children, farm and domestic animals, is sliced up. Whatever the Vietnam War unleashed in America finds its reflection in McCarthy's socio-political view of the 70s and 80s–his killers are free enterprise freebooters, and anyone caught in their path is victimized. His society is, in this respect, a reading of the Reagan years, based on triage.

The mayhem becomes so common in McCarthy's books–*Blood Meridian*, of course, but also *Suttree*, *All the Pretty Horses*, (the first volume of the border Trilogy, *Child of God*, and *Outer Dark*–that we come to take it for granted. Violence comes and goes the way the sun rises and sets. Since we cannot understand why McCarthy needs such violence–next to him, Joyce Carol Oates, who has been called a writer of violence, is suburban–we must isolate the phenomenon on philosophical, ideological, even moral grounds. McCarthy starts from certain premises which make him unique among serious American novelists, most of whom are more heedful of human life, even when personal survival is at stake. McCarthy sees every situation as Donner Pass material, eat or be eaten. He has tasted the things of the world and come away convinced that they are relentless, inexorable, unstoppable; man is merely a temporary dam stopping the flow of pain and anguish. The moral lesson is to look for none.

Suffering comes on in waves. In *All the Pretty Horses*, "He imagined the pain of the world to like some formless parasitic being seeking out the warmth of human souls wherein to incubate and he thought he knew what made one liable to its visitations. What he had not known was that it was mindless and so had no way to know the limits of those souls and what he feared was that there might be no limits."[78]

These meditations, which amount to a philosophical-ideological position, are located at intervals throughout the novels and cannot be disconnected from McCarthy's presentation of nature. It is implacable, far more than anything in Faulkner, where flood, fire, and the rest seem to control men's fates. In the struggle between men and nature, bet on nature–a paraphrase of Kafka's warning that in the battle between the world and the individual, choose the world. Even the horses, the subject of *All the Pretty Horses*, are part of that ungiving nature. Withal their beauty, their flow, their high energy, their independence, they are part of that natural world which only lets in man sideways, or through tiny slits. ". . . and they ran he and the horses out along the high mesas where the ground resounded under their running hooves and they flowed and changed and ran and their manes and tails blew off of them like spume and there was nothing else at all in that high world and they moved all of them in a resonance that was like a music among them and they were none of them afraid horse nor colt nor mare and they ran in that resonance which is the world itself and which cannot be spoken but only praised."[79] If man vanished, the horses would still be running.

McCarthy's world holds no give for men. They hack and cut and shoot and stab, but almost all in the end end. His ideological positioning is that of an amoral god who looks on, and while observing refuses to touch. Needless to say, neither good nor evil exists in this post-Darwinian, post-Nietzschean world. There is more here than the struggle to survive, since most enterprises McCarthy defines are not for survival but for the working out of one's destiny. It is as though one had seen what the end is and then pursued it until it comes to pass. The "middle" is not meaning but process.

Is this a radical postmodern nihilism, one more devastating in its implications than anything in other deniers and mockers? McCarthy does deconstruct our expectations of civility and a civil society, a kind of muscular version of Joan Didion's domestic wars. His meditations are visceral, and they seem to have the full impact of a large-scale nihilism. There are few ideas. The barbarism lies not in patterns or conceptions but in the language itself and in the blind, survivalist activities of marginal men. Horses and men, apparently, belong to the same breed, have the same genealogy. Indistinguishable in their atavism, they blend into each other–men riding, horses running, the two wedded in a common destiny. Everything in McCarthy is in movement–thus the significance of the horse, both a form of transportation and the throwback to a premodern era. While in jail, the young John Grady Cole, in *All the Pretty Horses*, dreams of "horses in a field on a high plain where the spring rains had brought up the grass.... and in the dream he was among the horses running and in the dream he himself could run with the horses and they coursed the young mares and fillies over the plain where their rich bay and their rich chestnut colors shone in the sun and the young colts ran with their dams...."[80] Like the horses, the men never back down.

Because he is so unrelenting, McCarthy presents a conundrum for the reader. As Cornelius Suttree in that novel[81] demonstrates, the survival of the species may take place at many levels. Suttree is a river rat, a refugee from a well-born family, a man alienated from nearly everything connected to civility. Yet McCarthy's sharpness of observation, his incredible eye for detail and accuracy of description, his sense of physical exuberance, his awareness of tastes and flavors most writers pass over or remark perfunctorily, all, do not lead to any psychological probing. Suttree, like the Kind, the judge, various killers, remains unknowable. McCarthy makes almost a fetish of not penetrating, or refusing to infiltrate the inner person. This is, apparently, a conscious decision not to probe motives because that would, in turn, make behavior a matter of choice. He insists on response, reaction, pre-emptive strikes: all the moves of someone backed into a corner and forced to defend himself. His nearly exclusive male world is under siege. But the siege comes not from within but from without; the protagonist creates the pressures by his own actions, and then he must confront what he has educed.

In *Blood Meridian*, McCarthy speaks of war, not as cathartic, but as part of a needful arrangement of historical counters; not even as a pure test of character, but as a juggernaut one goes out to confront because it is there.

> In such games as have for their stake the annihilation of the defeated the decisions are quite clear. This man holding this particular arrangement of cards in his hand is thereby removed from existence. This is the nature of war, whose stake is at once the game and the authority and the justification. Seen so, war is the truest for of divination. It is the testing of one's will and the will of another within that larger will which because it binds them is therefore forced to select. War is the ultimate game because war is at last a forcing of the unity of existence. War is god.[82]

This becomes the most clear-cut statement of McCarthy's sense of process. The individual life is really in service to something stronger; and one could see in this a kind of residual Christianity, of the type Graham Greene often posited in his fiction. According to this line of reasoning, there is an Unknowable–call it what one will– and this Unknowable beckons to all, with war, struggle, bloodletting part of the ongoing process. Man's adversarial relationship to nature is also complementary, since survival paradoxically means, simply, prolonging one's return to nature. There is no surmounting it–only holding it, as it were, at bay. Out there, waiting, looming, whatever the circumstances, is that final move, where the Unknowable will spring. McCarthy calls it war, whereas other may call it some form of deity.

Are we granting him too much of a metaphysical quest? Perhaps not. In *All the Pretty Horses*, when Cole "passed and paled into the darkening land," that "world to come"–the final words–will bring some examination of man's relationship to himself. For that is the subject McCarthy has made his own, carving out even his own vocabulary of arcane, archaic words. That refusal to take on psychological or even moral consequences creates a feral world which is McCarthy's tribute to America near the end of the century.

We recognize that the writer has struck something quite significant in the middle 1990s, a kind of frontier *American Psycho*. Amorality, anomie, lack of community, loss of rational self–all of these are ways of perceiving who we are and where we are going. They are perceptions, not truths written in stone; but for McCarthy's big city readers, the perception is the actuality. McCarthy's revisionist wild West is a perfect model for big city amorality and pervasive corruption. For him, survival means a return to the atavistic self: to the joys of irrational acts which lie deep within myth and legend and far from civilized repression. This is one reading of our culture.

Yet there are cautions. In *The Crossing* (1994),[83] the second volume of the Border Trilogy, several of the cracks in McCarthy's armor show. The first part of the novel is concerned with Billy Parham's effort to save a wolf which has been ravaging cows and calves in southwestern United States. He captures the wolf and takes it to Mexico, where he intends to liberate it–so that it can express its essential wolf-ness. The goal of the entire enterprise is to align man and wolf and to demonstrate that the wolf's wildness should be the measure of all things. McCarthy's extended description–based clearly on the hunt scene in Faulkner's "The Bear," but lacking Faulkner's sense of legend and myth–creates two major problems. What the episode finally reveals does not warrant such length, and the quest to key the sixteen-year-old Billy into the life and world of the wolf during their long trip south falls into stereotypes, even sentimentality. There are other problems as well, revealing one of McCarthy's most stalwart points, which is to avoid all introspection, to make everything resonate with how things get done. We learn an immense amount about the preparation of wolf traps, about the vocabulary of horsemanship and ropes, but nothing about motivation, intent, or inner life. McCarthy, as we know, has consciously eschewed innerness, but after one hundred pages of the trek south of boy and wolf, there is a palpable sense of absence. History, society, a context—all are missing. As things proliferate, absences call attention to themselves.

But this crossing is only the first of three, and while they have structural significance as narrative spines, they repeat without variety. Each crossing contains endless riding from place to place, a succession of meals—mainly tortillas and beans—a sequence of characters appearing regularly with their own philosophies of life, which ultimately blend into McCarthy's doom and interminable encounters of savagery and brutality.

The structure is formulaic. McCarthy has clearly discovered what he can do and does it repeatedly. By intermixing acts of brutality and sequences of movement with long sections of palaver, as gypsies, drovers, cow herders, and old Mexican men become sages, he drowns us in bathos. "He [an old sage] said that far from making men reflective or wise it was his experience that death often leads them to attribute great consequences to trivial things."[84] But the insight here is lost as the old man goes on with the trite sentiment that brothers should care for one another; an example of how McCarthy goes too far even when he has a winner. Later in the novel, still another sage speaks of death: "He said that men believe death's elections to be thing inscrutable yet every act invites the act which follows and to the extent that men put one foot before the other they are accomplices in their own deaths as in all such facts of destiny."[85]

Such sentiments, cast within a Don Quixote-like picaresque, episodic narrative, are vintage McCarthy; but by occurring so frequently, they deaden us. If we cut through the swathes of rhetoric, which veer between Hemingway and Faulkner, with broad touches of London's and Steinbeck's naturalistic determinism, we find what makes McCarthy new, as well as what limits him. The new batch of praise and blurbs should be put on hold: this is not the advent of a fictional messiah, no less the second coming. Rather, McCarthy has carved out something distinct while already revealing all the flaws and fault lines in his fictional armor. He is not growing, or expanding. All that talk of death and destiny and naturalistic consequences is a defensive gesture; no one will get close, and he will eschew psychology as much as he embraces verbal gymnastics. He is unique in his avoidance of love, except for male bonding; and even when there is rare heterosexual play, it is on the run, lacking joy, part of the fugitive aspect of the novels.

We return, inevitably, to McCarthy's penchant for stories–in this regard, like John Barth and their common indebtedness to Cervantes and his Don, and to the picaresque narratives of the eighteenth century. McCarthy's novelty here, however, comes in his use of stories which reveal a harder West than we are accustomed to; to his avoidance of all the cosmopolitanism and sophistication which has consumed the contemporary novel, whether Bellow and Oates or the minimalists; to his ability to find a vocabulary–often a language of particularized words unfamiliar to most intelligent readers–which sharply angles his line of vision; and to the mapping out of a vision which is unyielding, unforgiving, relentless. While including much, McCarthy is perhaps the most exclusionary of our significant contemporary writers. He tells it best when he relates tales, but we must keep in mind he means tales of men (women need not apply).

> ... For this world also which seems to us a thing of stone and flower and blood is not a thing at all but is a tale. And all in it is a tale and each tale the sum of all lesser tales and yet these also are the selfsame tale and contain as well all else within them. So everything is necessary. Every least thing. This is the hard lesson. Nothing can be dispensed with. Nothing despised. Because the seams are hid from us, you see. The joinery. The way in which the world is made. . . . And those seams that are hid from us are of course in the tale itself and the tale has no abode or place of being except in the telling only and there it lives and makes its home and therefore we can never be done with the telling. Of the telling there is no end.[86]

Ultimately, as he publishes more, McCarthy may lose the very elements which reinforce his novelty: his ability to limn the atavistic quality of the 80s and early 90s; his development of a sharply-angled language to communicate his distaste for government, the state, modern life itself; his use of various frontier myths, only to negate them; and, finally, his talent in maintaining enough new stories, instead of recycling all the former ones which worked so well for him.

With *Cities of the Plain* (in 1998),[87] and its aura of Sodom and Gomorrah, McCarthy completes his Border Trilogy. Despite the bravura writing, it is not a notable conclusion. The writing almost carries it, but once we get beyond the rigorous choice of words, the sharply angled scenes, and the spectral appearance of characters, the canvas empties out or is at best reduced. More than ever, McCarthy is indebted to Faulkner, especially to a novel like *As I Lay Dying*, but without the resonance and wit. What is particularly Faulknerian is in introduction of unnamed characters, so that we learn who talks only by way of the talk. We must unravel pronouns to get to the speaker. We sense, also, a Gaddis novel in McCarthy's use of freely floating unidentified dialogue and sharp cutting from scene to scene. Yet withal the hallmarks of a writer's writer here, the novel falters on McCarthy's lack of reach, his inability to get beyond a sentimentalized narrative.

He does make a mighty effort to communicate depth and breadth by way of his philosophical focus. Repeatedly, McCarthy elucidates the point that man is a sum total of his (not her, apparently) history and is linked to that history as a form of destiny. Whatever appears to be free will is, of course, tethered to the historical past; it is just that, only appearance, not substance, not individual life force. Man dances to the puppet master, even when he feels freest. "Men imagine," he writes, that the choices before them are theirs to make. But we are free to act only upon what is given. Choice is lost in the maze of generations and each act in that maze is itself an enslavement for it voids every alternative and binds one ever more tightly into the constraints that make a life."[88] History, not character, is destiny, a thesis McCarthy rides hard.

John Grady Cole, McCarthy's young man, who is very knowledgeable about horses and cowboy ways, is less knowledgeable about women and the ways of the world. Undefined as a character, Grady at the beginning is lost amidst vapid dialogue between cowboys; the novel only picks up momentum when the central quest becomes apparent. What at first seems a fault becomes a method. McCarthy's technique has within it some aspects of impressionistic art: in the way a scene begins to gain definition as one reads through what appears to be skewed coloring, shaped as disorganized dialogue. The quest is Grady's for a prostitute he once saw and who now is in a Mexican brothel, more or less as an indentured slave. The second half of the novel is devoted to Grady's effort to liberate her–but she is murdered and he dies in a matador-like knife fight with the man who "owns" her, Eduardo. In this second half, we find a replay of the *Carmen* theme, with a whore replacing a cigarette girl, and a pimp, Eduardo, as the matador; different roles, but similar ingredients, the somewhat innocent and straightforward Grady embroiling himself in a swirl of corruption and decadence. Like an American Adam, he hopes to transform the corrupted scenario back into one of innocence–to transfer the whore into a virgin, as his lover and wife, and the brothel experience into a Garden. Of course, in McCarthy's formulation, such effort is doomed.

Once doomed, it is also foredoomed, written into history as a wasted effort long before it even entered into Grady's life. The overall theme is grand, part of Greek tragedy intermixed with modern fated romance, all wrapped in the oldest of philosophical questions. But the performance is stereotypical and overdrawn–even the highpoint, the matador-like knife fight between Eduardo and Grady, the worldly, philosophical pimp, and the insistent, compulsively-driven innocent young man who sees only love and redemption. All such values are of course ironic in the light of Eduardo's insistence that Grady's historical destiny is to die, as he does, although Eduardo goes with him. That, too, is part of McCarthy's plan: that even the man who feels he can move outside destiny cannot, that the script is written for him as well as for his opponent. It is, all in all, too symmetrical.

What remains is McCarthy's angular language, pitched at a level just beyond ordinary range. What also remains is how much his novel catches not the early part of this century when it takes place as much as the end. Like so many of his contemporary writers, McCarthy senses a winding down, a loss, the futility of desire, the failure of positive action. Even the violence, his trademark, is muted to a few episodes. In an epilogue, with both Cole and Eduardo dead, in their ballet of desperate knife thrusts, McCarthy plays the philosophical hand. A poor move fictionally, it comes across as pretentious and porous, lacking even the intense language of the narrative. But here he evidently felt a summation of the Border Trilogy was needed, and it fits his "end of" philosophy, a defining moment not only for McCarthy's fictions but also for the decade.

> Its shape [the traveller's life] was forced in the void at the onset and all talk of what might otherwise have been is senseless for there is no otherwise. Of what could it be made? Where be hid? Or how make its appearance? The probability of the actual is absolute. That we have no power to guess it out beforehand makes it no less certain. That we may imagine alternate histories means nothing at all.[89]

The nature of McCarthy's statement here, and a repetition of many similar statements throughout the trilogy, help explain his use of precise and often unfamiliar vocabulary. He names things which are not common parts of the language–*latigo*, for example, as part of the cowboy's gear or *alcahuete* (pimp) and other untranslated Spanish words, none part of general usage. The aim is to substantiate the cowboy's world, to secularize it, as it were; and to reinforce the theme that all else is abstraction, unprovable and unknowable.

McCarthy insists on a world of things. But he does enjoy silences. His cowboys are noted for their clipped, spare speech, so that silence dominates more intensely than even the specialized words themselves. In the cowboy world, silence commands life and death, hard work, hard living, something "pure." Cowboys are the first man, Adam(s) of the open space that once defined America. In their refusal to be anything but cowboys–and they insist there are no alternatives–they are rulers of space, even while they earn pittances and live under hardship. Yet within this tight world of silence and machismo, the men are romantics, and McCarthy, under the eclipsed manner, provides a sentimental center to the novel, and to the Trilogy generally. Grady's quest for his Carmen-like doom is part of a sweetened sense of "saving" the woman, of perceiving a good woman beneath the whore, of carrying her off from her evil pimp, Eduardo; and, not least, his willingness to sacrifice himself if he can destroy Eduardo and revenge the now-dead girl. Within a world of death–and in the novel the brothel is death space as much as the cowboy's world is life space–lives another world not nearly so sophisticated as the language itself, language that speaks, often, beyond the reach of a lay audience.

Toni Morrison

It may seem strange to include as "new" someone who published her first novel a quarter of a century ago. But since I wrote about her work at some length in *American Fictions: 1940-1980*, Toni Morrison has published several novels, *Tar Baby* in 1981, *Beloved* in 1987, *Jazz* in 1992, *Paradise* in 1998, along with some literary criticism. But most of all, her selection as the Nobel Prize winner in literature, in 1993, raised an entirely new dimension. Morrison is now not only an American writer deeply involved with matters of community, race, ethnic dimensions, and language, but also an international writer, in the company of those novelists who have moved outside national boundaries. Also, as a Nobel Prize winner, she is thrown together with other major American winners,

Hemingway, Faulkner, O'Neill, Lewis, Bellow, a group with certain common features. All of this suggests that while she is not quite "new," she requires a fresh look.

A funny thing does happen to a writer on the way to the Nobel Prize: that although achievement (along with politicking, ethnic correctness, geographical divisions, neglected genders and races) leads to the award, the actual awarding of the Prize is often succeeded by a downgrading of the writer in question. Unjust as this may seem, the writer is perceived to have completed his or her career. In several instances, such as Faulkner, Hemingway, and Bellow, their best work was well behind them when they received the Prize; and thus the perception of them in decline or even "finished" was not inappropriate.

The writer leaning toward the final accolade of a Nobel is different from the writer who has crossed the finish line. It would seem to him or her that the career has peaked, since the Nobel is statedly for a "lifetime of achievement." How, then, does the writer go on, especially since age is creeping up? In very few instances does the Nobel go to someone in the peak of his career: Eugene O'Neill, a winner in 1936, is an exception, having been called to the stand at only forty-eight. Yet even for O'Neill, his career seemed over, since no production of his work came to the stage for another ten years.*

All of this is by way of reintroducing Morrison, the post-Prize

---

* Sinclair Lewis was also young, forty-five, when the Prize came in 1930; but he was clearly beyond his best work. Pearl Buck's Prize was so anomalous as to defy credibility, since in 1938, when she was awarded it, James Joyce and Virginia Woolf were still alive and eligible, as were E. M. Forster, Aldous Huxley, and a host of other more clearly canonical novelists. Similarly, the award to John Steinbeck in 1982, when he was sixty, is inexplicable, except that most of the great modernists had died–many unrewarded. Steinbeck had of course by this time long since declined into bathos. In poetry, a different affair, T. S. Eliot's Prize, in 1948, when he was sixty, came well after he had written the work which made the award possible.

author. But there are other considerations besides the Nobel for including her as "new." In the last ten or fifteen years, we have observed intense applications of feminist studies, ethnic studies, gay and lesbian studies, various racial and multicultural studies, as well as more strategic critical techniques for reading. Morrison's work lends itself quite well to much of this: naming, questions of origins and genealogies, narrative devices, story telling strategies, as well as her intense concentration on gender and racial matters. The danger here is to pigeonhole her as a "woman writer" or a "racial writer," however these designations might be interpreted. Equally dangerous would be to apply too heavily to her work deconstructive ideas–although they work well with her, or even semiotics, even though so much of her work depends on tonal and gestural varieties.

Withal, approaches to Morrison as "new"–whatever the angle of perception–are fraught with peril; perhaps none more than to treat her as the critics have, as teflon-coated. More than nearly any other emerging and significant writer of the last quarter of a century, Morrison has bathed in a glowing reception. *Time* and *Newsweek*, noted for their newspeak, respectively called her a "terrific storyteller" and deemed *Song of Solomon* "both a private and national heritage"–comparing it to *Roots*. The Times *Book Review*, the bellwether of how a novelist is to be treated, said *Song* "impresses itself upon us like a love affair," a comment more suitable for a Harlequin romance than for a novel in which many of the characters are called "Dead." The Washington *Post*, in a burst of idiocy unusual even for reviewers, called the novel the "most substantial fiction since *Invisible Man*," which means that in the twenty-five years between the novels, we can ignore *The Recognitions* and *J R*, all of Pynchon, all of Bellow, all of Barth and Roth. The *New Yorker*, which in those days disliked adventurous novels but liked "a good read," called *Song* "a domestic epic–a rhapsodic work. . . it billows." For the first time, a novel is compared to a sail. The Book-of-the-Month Club News qualifies *Song* as "the best novel of the black experience in America" since the Ellison. That sidesteps the fact that Ellison, while focusing on the black experience, was writing about all America, regardless of color, and it was that reach which gave his novel such force and intensity. The critic in the daily *Times* found it a "privilege to review," and the Cleveland *Plain Dealer* found it the most moving novel "I have read in ten years of reviewing," which begs the question of what the reviewer had been reviewing.

How do we get past this hype, much of it doing a terrible disservice to Morrison, since it moves her into realms where she is not "read," but adored. She must be read. And she must be read freshly, anew, without all that terrible baggage of blurbs, hype, adoration. She has, indeed, carved out her own territory, part of it embedded in a personalized, lyrical language and part in her use of an overriding metaphor: that the black experience holds a community together, even while individual lives within it do not cohere. She has, in effect, created a tension between community among blacks and an opposing force, individual blacks who cannot be contained. She has opened up the very paradoxes of a culture.

This differs from white subcultures in several respects, not least because whites increasingly do not possess community values, or need them in the same degree, and their individuals have no rootedness, no place of their own. Blacks, on the contrary, extend help to each other, throw out lifelines in the wake of white intransigence or sheer meanness. When Morrison departs from this scheme, which has considerable resonance, she wavers.

If we revisit *Song of Solomon*, we observe her adventuring into radical political activities for Guitar, Macon "Milkman" Dead's friend. By the time Guitar becomes significant, Milkman has taken over the center of the novel, part of the saga of the Dead family: Morrison's apt metaphor for the black condition and also for its revival. The Dead are frequently resurrected. Guitar's activities, however, seem to be leftovers from another novel–not because they are in themselves unreasonable, but because they do not mesh with anything else. Guitar belongs to a group of blacks called "Seven Days," whose plan is to murder whites whenever a white murders a black. There are seven members to "Days," and whenever a killing of a black occurs on a particular day, that designated day member must commit a comparable crime against a white.[90]

One of the tests for the "Days" comes when the four little black girls are killed in a Birmingham, Alabama, church bombing, and four little white girls will be made to pay, according to Guitar. Yet such enterprises need money, and when Milkman tells him of his Aunt Pilate's gold bags, Guitar is very interested. But in time he forgets his mission and relishes all the good things he can buy with the gold, a fantasy Milkman also enters into. Morrison has positioned herself strangely. On one hand, she has introduced a radical political group, and then, on the other, subverted it by turning Guitar into a bumbling, money-hungry young man. Some of this is connected to her overall plan, which is to show black men as fools and bumblers, even while they remain sexually attractive and available. But the larger question is that her venture into extreme politics exists only so she can undermine it; or else it exists only so that she can demonstrate the desperation of young black men looking for some social/political foothold in a white society. Whatever the specific point, the venture takes the novel astray; and it marginalizes what is Morrison's strength, her grounding of black life in community and, by implication, her assault on white society as disorderly and anarchic.

Further, in *Song of Solomon*, Morrison tries to blend the radical politics of Guitar with a Jason-like search for the golden fleece, bags of gold which Macon Dead Senior and his sister Pilate think they have stumbled upon in a cove. There is, here, an effort to create some of the complexities we associate with *Invisible Man*; but Ellison followed one individual, who came to be a larger-than-life metaphor: not only of the black man turned anonymous and invisible, but of the dehumanizing of all life, black and white alike. Not enough readers have noted Ellison's attack on what has destroyed the potential of America's Eden: racism, discrimination, and injustice, of course, but also the connivance of *all* parties to desecrate what was once a paradise. Morrrison moves on the edges of this, and while it is praiseworthy that she attempts so much, it must be admitted that not everything coheres. Her repeated insistence on community is, apparently, her view of an Eden which is in danger of disappearing. She attempts to catch the loss, and at the same time to capture some of the changes taking place.

The Seven Days assassination squad is one such change: blacks fighting against whites using the tactics of the latter–something Milkman refuses to accept. There is little question that standing behind Morrison's work is a deeply American theme, of the wilderness versus urbanization, in which wilderness bespoke both independence and community, and urbanization in which the individual loses his or her primary identity. The themes derive from both Whitman and Faulkner. Yet Morrison wants to take matters further. Hers is, in effect, a highwire act, and it has become a defining element in her work, from *The Bluest Eye* through *Jazz*, in 1992.

She must make several levels of private and public cohere. Yet Milkman Dead, a third generation Dead, is insufficiently defined to handle the burden laid upon him. The subject is no less than his transformation from a young black man who takes his family privileges for granted, to a slightly older black man who recognizes his responsibilities, duties, and need for contrition in the face of female sacrifices. All of this, further, must fall into line with Morrison's ambiguous presentation of black males; refusing any politically correct or literary stereotyping, she pinpoints their insufficiencies when they are compared with their female contemporaries. While this perception gives her resonance and texture, it creates problematics in presentation not only in *Song* but also in several of her other novels. This is perhaps the pivotal area in her intellectual resources as a novelist.

To move backwards in time, to *Sula* (1973), for example, the titular character decides to take on the entire establishment, but especially the world of insufficient males. She breaks from community and destroys herself, if we read her death from cancer as a metaphor for her struggle against male privilege. But Morrison is hardly through. She is inventive, imaginative, fabulous in unforeseen ways. She mixes her metaphors and gains new ground.[91]

Shaddrack comes out of active duty in World War I a blasted individual, full of hallucinations, wretched, incapable of cohering in any of his functions, wreckage, and, as he suspects, garbage to be disposed of. He must be straitjacketed, but despite his violence, he was discharged from the hospital, which needed space. He is, of course, a human time bomb. Hardly able even to walk, no less function, he is now a free man, with a going-away gift from the government of two hundred and seventeen dollars and a suit of clothes. In some respects, Shaddrack is a black version of Virginia Woolf's Septimus Smith, in *Mrs. Dalloway*, another castaway from the war, incapable of functioning and yet thrust into a society he can never enter. Shaddrack's mental instability focuses on his hands, which seem to him a monstrosity, especially since he had expected to lose them in battle. But he also harbors feeling of unreality, of lacking existence; and his vision, when he has one, is of blackness. Yet, in some way, blackness fits his mood–it allows him to let go of all social restraints, to bathe himself in nothingness. He has fear which is uncontrollable, and while he is not deemed dangerous to others, he lives at a different level. How can he control himself? How can he allay some of the fear? As a solution, he founds National Suicide Day, an annual event on January 3rd, a celebration of death when he can play out all he fears, those actual as well as those unexpected. For the rest of the year, he is able to hang on, because he knows that on one day he can let it all go and contemplate the worst.

In 1920, the Day starts. The townspeople are obviously fearful. They fear Shaddrack, whose appearance is wild, primitive, even barbaric; and they fear the day as a celebration of death. But as the years pass, the townspeople see that Shaddrack is contained within his own mad boundaries, and in time the Day is accepted, as a holiday like Christmas or Easter, or a birthday. In one respect, Shaddrack is reborn on National Suicide Day, and the town of Medallion, Ohio, is reconciled.

With this, Morrison has a great symbolic or metaphorical presence. In this, her second novel, she has caught her vision: a local event with national implications; a personal aberration which becomes acceptable as a community ritual; the presence of a madman who in some way proves a visionary; a celebratory or ritualistic event which serves to create coherence, to underscore a community; the creation of a person who lives "outside" and yet a figure who observes, who becomes the repository of the community's deepest secrets–in this case Sula's and Nel's responsibility for Chicken Little's drowning death; and, not least, the presentation of an individual who while bringing together terrible matters transforms them into something sacred, and instead of dividing the community somehow manages to unify it. In *Song of Solomon*, Pilate Dead serves that function: hiding her madness under a socially accommodating style, but mad she is, in Morrison's best sense.

Panorama has given way to trope. In *Playing in the Dark: Whiteness and the Literary Imagination*, Morrison speaks of race as such a metaphor. Through race, the writer can limn the national character. Race both disguises and reveals, it can be ideological or biological; but it encompasses. National Suicide Day has resonance for race and racial matters, which Morrison increasingly takes up in her 1980s and 90s fiction. *Beloved*, with *its* metaphor of "the secret," is the culmination of that concern.

The Day resonates obviously in racial matters, in matters of national madness (in which all of Meridian acquiesces in the needs of a war-doomed man), but also as part of the gender war, in which women bend to men who try to destroy them and yet resist sufficiently to destroy their men. Implicit in National Suicide Day is Morrison's theme of the sacrifice of a child to the needs of a parent or of a pre-condition: Eva and her son in *Sula*; the situation in *Beloved*, whereby a mother kills her baby rather than let her become a slave; and in several other places where a child's life is aborted.

National Suicide Day clearly acts as a kind of filter for Morrison's vision, her sense of what avails, in the way that the white whale reverberated for Melville or the letter A for Hawthorne or psychopathological secrets for Poe. It is both her anvil on which she can periodically bang and her fallback when she must retreat from untenable or irresolvable situations. National suicide Day is one of those strategies she has cited as the stuff of a "writer's kit." The novels that contain the equivalent of the Day fulfill the complexities which support Morrrison's prose; while those, like *Tar Baby*, which do not, seem to lose their way. Since she writes so compellingly, Morrison can easily be categorized as an author whose work depends almost solely on language. But this would be a misreading: she has become deeply engaged in the configurations of society and the individual, and for this she needs a central metaphor or structuring.

As she has matured in *Beloved*, this need for structure has become more pronounced, whereas *Tar Baby*, with its black and white stereotypes, does not in any way prepare us for the complexities either of *Beloved*, *Jazz*, or *Paradise*. *Tar Baby* is, in fact, programmatic, more diagnostic than fully-fashioned. In its stretch for significance, perhaps more than any other Morrison novel it reaches back toward *Invisible Man*. The central figure, Jadine, is caught between black and white; herself black, she has been educated by Valerian Street, an eccentric white man who owns the "island plantation" where Jadine lives. The question raised by Son, the island intruder and ostensible "bad guy," is whether Jadine has retained or lost her blackness. Her education, her ease in integrating herself in France, her correct grammar and rhetoric wiped out her blackness, as Son perceives it, so that she is caught, anomalously, as neither white nor black, but as some grotesque mutant. Son is himself fixed in his blackness, although unfortunately Morrison presents it stereotypically. His blackness involves everything Jadine despises: he has no vocation, he has neither work nor ambition, he lacks style, he flows with events, gets into trouble, flees, and attaches himself, apparently, only to his small town, Eloe, a cultural backwater. He is the categorical loser. Yet Son strikes something in Jadine, although the attraction of his blackness is linked mainly to his sexuality–once again, Morrison presents the black male as appealing to women not through accomplishment or purpose but through sex.

If Son is a black male stereotype, Valerian Street, despite his eccentricities, is a white stereotype. As a kind of enlightened slave master, he bestows his largesse on all the island blacks who work for him. With his greenhouse as his Garden and the island as his domain, Valerian has created an antebellum Eden. He is tended by black servants who owe everything to him, and whose lives have been corrupted by his largesse. Without him, they have nowhere to go, nothing to do. Valerian is married to Margaret, whom he sighted at a beauty contest, when she was seventeen and he twenty years her senior. He offers her everything an island kingdom holds, but she slowly grows crazy in her isolation as a beautiful object surrounded by other flawless objects. As a pathological consequence of her combined boredom, cabin fever, and feelings of resentment, she sticks pins into her small child, Michael, as a means, somehow, of validating her own existence. In this respect, Margaret becomes the stereotypical mistress: with endless time on her hands, she empowers herself by torturing (not seriously) an infant and small child. This is in many ways a typical Morrison ploy: the way in which a woman seeks control, by abusing or killing her child. Morrison rotates the act into a racial agenda in *Beloved*, and there makes it not only personal but social and political. Here in *Tar Baby*, the sticking of Michael merely seems an oddity in a woman who is more categorized than created.

All this, of course, changes with *Beloved*, six years after *Tar Baby*. Morrison has discovered her world, and it is new and virtually complete. It seems that all of her work in fiction has been leading up to this novel, and it is surely *Beloved* which helped her win the Nobel Prize. It is, in many respects, her most Faulknerian novel, not as a derivative but as her way of having learned from Faulkner's best work how to proceed to maximize her particular kind of sur-reality. *Beloved* is as much a meditation as it is a novel, what we recall from Faulkner's *As I Lay Dying* in particular, but also *The Sound and the Fury*. It is this quality of meditation which gives Morrison's novel its density, its subtexture, and which makes it possible for her to unfold "the secret" which lies at the center of her fictional idea. Such strategies continue in *Jazz*, her novel five years after *Beloved*. Without writing Mega-Novels, Morrison has surrounded her theme, the black as a displaced person. Given this, she has brought together social, political, ideological materials, and for that she needed narrative strategies, ways of unfolding, and a central, overriding metaphor.

Child or infant murder–the Medea dimension–becomes the central trope, and the narrative strategy is to keep the trope hidden within layers of oblique, indirect language until the secret is uncovered by stages. Within the ideological frame of reference is the need to recreate slavery for the contemporary reader, and by so doing imply a commentary on contemporary black life. By framing everything in terms of the black as displaced person, Morrison has in this respect grafted Ellison's invisible man onto Faulknerian techniques for disguising, distorting, hiding. All of this is quite ambitious for a novel that is barely 100,000 words; but because Morrison has so surely captured her material in a narrative strategy, she is able to enclose it, like the Christo wrapping of a great monument.

The black as displaced person has always been implicit in Morrison's work, but here (and in *Jazz*), she exploits it with her entire kit of devices. The displaced black fits nowhere, whether in his or her own community, whether in the north or the south, whether on a tropical island or the mainland; and this sense of displacement leads to self-defeating behavior, even when there is a community. Morrison, in fact, pits the displaced black against her idea of community, and while the latter still has resonance, the individual–Sula, Son, others–heads into aberrant, or self-destructive behavior. The displacement, like Ellison's use of invisibility, is the central drama in black life, whether in post-slavery days as in *Beloved* or in more contemporary terms.

The strategies for presenting displacement hold the key to the success of Morrison's vision. In *Beloved*, she makes extensive use of prolepsis, or anticipation of events, another technique which recalls Faulkner. At the beginning of a chapter break midway through the novel, she writes: "That ain't her mouth." That mouth holds the key to a great mystery. The "her" is unidentified until a friend, Paul D, says it is not Sethe's. But another friend, Stamp Paid, has showed this newspaper photo to Paul D in order to reveal what Sethe has done: that if it is her mouth, then she is the one who attempted to kill her children and did kill her baby. If it is not her mouth, then she is exonerated. Before Morrison reaches this point of disclosure, however, she tells us that a black's face appears in a newspaper only because of some unusual crime, not because of achievement. It is always negative news. Thus in the space of four and a half pages, there is considerable information. There is the anticipation of "the secret"; there is the denial that it could be Sethe, the central female figure of the novel; there is the racial/ethnic point about blacks in the news; and then there is the slow revelation–still denied by Paul D–about the nature of the crime.

In this or similar ways, the entire matter of the novel is divulged. Prolepsis works, moreover, in several ways, not only as anticipation of events. It establishes a detective story atmosphere to the novel– what has happened, who did it, and, finally, what were the motives? Further, it allows Morrison her way with language, which is indirect, oblique, somewhat off-center; so that a sur-real quality is achieved. This sur-real quality cannot be solely the result of language, but must gain its momentum from narrative; and that in turn derives from the proleptic nature of the material which intimates a terrible secret but then divulges it only in small increments. We mentioned above Faulkner's early novels as possible quarries, but his midcareer novel, *Absalom, Absalom!*, is of course the most compelling. Here the unraveling takes the form of ever-receding Chinese boxes, until one is drawn in through narratives and voices into a vortex where the configurations are blurred. The most telling "secret" about black-and-white mixes is based on assumptions and speculations, on the "what if," and this works together with the language to create the sur-real or what some have called magical realism. Similarly, Morrison, working on a smaller scale, has enclosed the inner content in a constantly reshaping shell; so that the reality of the event, horrific as it is, becomes both more and less than real, both more and less than itself.

Prolepsis also works in matters of expansion and contraction, another one of Morrison's devices. Expansion is part of the revelation of the secret: the fact that something momentous lies at the center of the experience of Sethe and Paul D, as well as that of Sethe's now-grown daughter, Denver, and the spectral figure of Beloved herself. The very name Beloved anticipates something expansive, large, as of an angelic presence, a goddess in human form, or some other kind of deity appearing on earth as a sign of divine intervention. For Sethe, Beloved is the daughter whom she yearns to have; and for Paul D and his friend Stamp Paid, Beloved is a demonic figure, the doom that is seeking to bring down Sethe after all these years. The dimension of contraction comes in the very revelation itself; once revealed, the matter, while still horrific,* is distanced and done away with–Sethe has served time in prison, the event past. The contraction keeps it "beyond"; the expansion brings it to the fore, as Beloved in person and as Sethe's stricken conscience.

In her use of decentered language to accompany proleptic events and narrative voices, Morrison starts nearly every brief chapter with a sentence that runs askew to the material. "When the four horsemen came–schoolteacher, one nephew, one slave catcher and a sheriff–the house on Bluestone Road was so quiet they thought they were too late."[92] The relevance of this line–with its recall of the horsemen of the Apocalypse–to what has gone before is not clear. Clarity comes

---

* The death of the baby has echoes of Sophie's choice in the Styron novel, although the contexts are quite different. In retrospect, Sophie's choice to sacrifice her daughter in order to save her son, while powerfully drawn, now seems like a handy gimmick; whereas Morrison's context flows smoothly from history to individual.

only when the scene turns back to the primal act, Sethe's killing of her baby, with the further intent to kill all her children to prevent their becoming slaves. Once again, the obliqueness of the language reinforces the slow revelation of the secret. Beloved herself is part of the anticipatory element in the novel, since she turns up almost dead, and then slowly gets fat (and pregnant) later, a ghost or phantom who slowly takes over the essential household. She does not seem part of anything, until she begins to take on shape (physically and fictionally) as the replacement child who will bedevil Sethe even as she assuages her conscience. Under Beloved's subtle pressure, Sethe slowly deteriorates–she runs out of food, and her slide into hunger is an apt metaphor of the hunger she has felt after the murder of her baby. As part of her angelic mission, Beloved seems to fill, but she also empties, as part of her demonization of the household.

The elements finally cohere: child murder, the emergence of the secret, the presence of Beloved, the needs of Denver, the shifting past and present of Sethe; all caught in a sequence of tensions, metaphors, embodiments. Prolepsis enables Morrison to blend past and present more effectively than in any of her other novels, and this blending is essential to the narrative thrust. For if it is to mean anything, the novel must demonstrate the seamless nature of black life, from slavery through immediate post-slavery days, and, by implication, to the present. Prolepsis allows Morrison to imply, include, surround, and encompass.

Jazz (in 1992)[93] in several ways is an extension of *Beloved*, although less complete and less compelling technically. The theme of the displaced person continues, here transposed to the north, where dysfunction is the order of the day, despite lip service to racial and social equality. The story is the dispossessed, twisted quality of black lives, the result of a situation in which blacks must settle and resettle, a kind of nomadic, gypsy existence which has defined their lives in post-civil war days and torpedoed their efforts at community. Only the moment gives them some sense of respite, and often the moment is just that, without continuity, self-definition, or any of the ordering devices we associate with a measured life. Morrison here continues the Faulknerian verbal stream, with long convoluted sentences, disregard for conventional syntax, the omission of essential punctuation, the use of misdirected or deliberately confusing pronouns, all of it contributing to waves of consciousness rather than a clearly delineated narrative. Such deliberate tactics work toward maximizing the patterns Morrison wishes to impress on black life in the north.

The narrator, while *there*, is gender neutral and hidden; with the main focus on the shooting of a black woman, Dorcas, and her disfigurement at the funeral by Violet, the wife of the man who killed her. But while this is the ostensible story, the seeming text, the subtext becomes more significant: the twisted web of black lives, the dispossessed quality of their existence. And here the convoluted nature of much of the language works well to define the mosaic of dysfunction and of pathological urges which create "the moment" while subverting any continuity or measure in individual lives.

The one area Morrison neglects–which could be a source of enrichment–is that pertaining to blacks who succeed, those who go on to college, make their way as professionals, and establish themselves in some version of the mainstream. By the 1980s, a large black middleclass was visible, with blacks having entered executive and professional posts–more than token, fewer than acceptable–but Morrison bypasses this for the losers, or those who merely hang on to the edges. As a novelist of "black life," she is highly selective; she seems to fly in the face of considerable black stability in the home, as well as in careers and professions. It is true that her losers are sometimes winners, in that they fight on in lives which are perforce stunted, aborted, meaningless except to themselves. Often, they must, like Joe Trace here, remake themselves repeatedly–Joe does it seven times. But remaking oneself, while it means taking on a second skin, also forgoes continuity and, ultimately, self-definition. The black male in Morrison, but also the female, wanders an American landscape, a refugee in his own country. Yet one looks in vain for balance; the wanderer is never juxtaposed to the one with roots, the one who makes a life for himself or herself, whatever the tremendous odds and psychological dislocations.

In one sense, even as Morrison has defined new ground for the novel of the uprooted and the unsettled, even as she has fought to find common interests and community for these very people, she has caught a quite different aspect of the last decades–the need to redefine oneself, to remake the self, to move on. This the black has in common with many whites, since literature by nonblacks also focuses on this: counterfeiting, disguising, faking, all, serve as a continuum with this need to remake oneself. Using the black who struggles to stay afloat, she underscores the instability of the culture from the point of view of those who have most to lose. With the self in a constant process of adapting and readapting, the individual is caught in forces he and she cannot foretell; and while this is, as she shows, more precarious for the black, it is–if we listen to our writers– an all-purpose situation. The instability of American life even while the economy prospered for some reflects how the 80s destroyed the very things it promised.

Paradise in 1998[94] reveals Morrison at the top of the game in her post-Nobel years. While she still does not tackle successful blacks–those with rewarding careers, upward mobility, professional lives–she does combine here her three major preoccupations: community and how it evolves, gender issues, and narrative strategies. The concern with structuring, which was so apparent in *Beloved,* recurs in *Paradise*, and it solidly locates Morrison as a writer attempting something new. For in her method of structuring, however much she is indebted to Faulkner, she has made narrative her own. Telling stories, personal histories, all, are molded into an historical perspective. She has transformed narrative indirection and indeterminism into an effective strategy for suggesting social and personal randomness–that is, history.

In this instance, her community is Ruby, in Oklahoma–

almost in a nonplace which is identified as space in the middle of somewhere–an all-black community. It has been established by male authority as a place which displays black enterprise and autonomy; whites are kept out, as is any personal behavior which might subvert the moral values of the community. Because of this, the Convent–once a place for nuns and now a refuge for the marginalized of society–cannot be permitted to continue; its values, however humanistic and spiritualized in some matters, are condemned as inconsistent with what the male-directed Ruby wants as its "utopia" or paradise.

As against the Convent is the Oven, a large assembly of bricks and mortar, which is permitted for displays of affection, dancing, partying. The point of the contrast is, apparently, that while activity in the Convent is hidden outside of time, behavior at the Oven is openly displayed. Both the Convent and the Oven, as elements of Morrison's community, are sacred places of sorts: the Oven as part of the history of Ruby, and the Convent also as part of history and memory. As sacralized places, both reveal elements of morality: the Convent, despite its name, as evil, and the Oven, despite *its* name, as embodying acceptable Ruby values.

Inside this male-oriented and authority-driven community, the spokespersons are the Reverend Misner along with the leading elements of the community who are those with bloodlines extending backwards into black history. Morrison is really interested in revealing how the women, who live in the shadows, are the major forces in Ruby, whereas the men are energized only by resentment, male chauvinism, and blood feuds. What has happened is that the all-black community has taken on the same negative features of white communities; only the color has changed. As Morrison near the end comments: "A backward noplace–ruled by men whose power to control was out of control and who had the nerve to say who could live and who not and where, who had seen in lively, free, unarmed females the mutiny of the mares and so got rid of them."[95] On this note, the community aspect encounters the gender issue for completion.

The novel's narrative strategies create the aura of a mystery novel, for *Paradise* begins with: "They shoot the white girl first," the white girl being Consolata, now something of a saving force intermixed with witch-like qualities. The posse of townspeople intends to kill everyone at the Convent, but the women rout the men with broomsticks, pots and pans, and a knife; and apparently flee to another life outside of Ruby. The explication of that first line becomes the grounding for the entire novel. Morrison has her way with first lines, using the shock value of a transgressive idea as a way of introducing a mystery or at least a conundrum.

The mechanism of *Paradise* proceeds around gradual divulgation of information. Morrison by now has become a master of withholding and spooning out just enough information to keep her narrative going. But in *Paradise* we observe that her pacing has become glacial, more glacial than in either *Beloved* or *Song of Solomon*, her most representative fiction. The glacial quality of the narrative offers us several options: one, obviously, to experience tedium in the way material is doled out; a second is to see that by revealing detail as a precious commodity Morrison is helping to create a community as it were brick by brick; and, finally the slow pacing allows the mystery to intensify until she can unravel it in the final pages, when Ruby, townspeople, Convent, and gender conflicts all come together in the climactic struggle that defines who and what everything is.

Along the way, Morrison lets her individual stories develop slowly, and even the relationships between characters is not clear until they begin to congregate at the Convent. As readers, we know they are doomed, or at least the one who is white is doomed, and that the Convent has been condemned as the witches of a previous era were condemned. Witchcraft, whether actual or perceived, is viewed through Morrison's eyes as a male-oriented crusade to wipe out uppity females. By identifying the doings at the Convent as satanic, the leading men of Ruby can maintain their power. Identifying women as creatures of the devil is more satisfying to the men than their looking into themselves for their own motives. The one exception may be the Reverend Misner, but he is not sufficient to halt the other nine men from trying to wipe out the blot on their town and return it to what they conceived of as paradise.

In pursuit of her ironic vision of paradise, Morrison has forged an Alexandrine prose, one perhaps, we can say, more Miltonic than any in her previous fiction. It is stately and strangely imperial for someone trying for equality and justice in community life. But whatever immediate tedium the method creates, there is little question that in the 90s Morrison has shaped her voice, distinguishing it from any other novelist. A Morrison novel has its unique sound, and this is a great achievement given the multitude of voices emanating from America's fictions. Withholding, halting, swerving, interpolating, decentering, Morrison has recreated narrative. As she focuses so intensely on black life in America it will be interesting to see if she can broaden her vision to include more successful blacks–not as American black triumphalism, but as a recognition that communities change, that young people migrate to the cities, and that American newness has rubbed off on America's minority populations.

CHAPTER THREE

THE MEGA-NOVEL: DO WE DESERVE IT?

McELROY, MAILER, BRODKEY, GADDIS

Mega-Novels are a phenomenon of our times, a postwar emergence of immensely long novels with a particular pedigree. The so-called Mega-Novel is loaded with paradoxes: it *is* long, but lacks any sense of completion; while it has no boundaries for an ending, of course it does end; it seems to defy clear organization—it seems decentered, unbalanced—yet has intense order; it is located outside traditional forms of narrative, but still employs some conventional modes. Its aim posits disorder, messiness, the chaos of our existence and by extension of our times; nevertheless, its length, complexity, and on-goingness make it a model of order.[96]

As we see with Harold Brodkey and Joseph McElroy,[97] even with Mark Helprin, Norman Mailer, David Bradley,* and Alexander Theroux—as we saw earlier with Pynchon, Barth, and Gaddis—the Mega-Novel is a commentary on the novel form itself. It became

---

* Although *The Chaneysville Incident* (1981) has distinct Mega-Novel potentialities—incompletion and possible unlimited extension- it does not quite fit with the sprawl of other novels in this genre. I have chosen to put it in Chapter Seven: "Black Writers–Women Writers–Jewish Writers– Racial, Ethnic and Gender Segregation."

part of the expansiveness of the 50s and 60s, but in several examples extends well into the 90s. It is an aspect of fiction running parallel to two other expansive postwar developments: Abstract Expressionism in painting and aleatory or randomness in music. While seemingly an offshoot of more conventional fiction, in actuality the Mega-Novel–as apart from simply long novels–is a dominant element in our fiction, neither a subgenre nor a sideshow. At its best, its daring challenges the entire novelistic genre and sets up a conflict at the core of more conventional fiction.

Like its linguistic cousin Mega-Bucks, Mega-Novels has a solid vulgarity to it. Yet that very vulgarity of word gives it an authentic American presence, defines it as an American artifact. Nothing Old World here. Mega-Bucks are limitless, almost infinite–if a person has them, not only is he/she rich, he has unrestricted independence of movement and behavior. The Mega-Novel shares that kind of wealth. William Gaddis's *J R*–perhaps even now still the great unread novel of the postwar era–is a perfect blend of such Americanism: a Mega-Novel about making Mega-Bucks, the protagonist not Huck Finn seeking to escape civilization but a sixth-grader learning how to become an insider, how to make big money in America without producing anything.

The American Mega-Novel is different from the long novels of the past, those associated with Fielding, Richardson, Dickens, Thackeray, Eliot, Tolstoy, among others. Length alone is not the criterion. Those earlier novels, while long, had traditional beginnings, middles, and ends. Our contemporary Mega-Novel muddles conventional elements; in several instances, it seems as though the reader has interrupted an ongoing conversation and must struggle to gain entrance. The Mega-Novel is oceanic, and its vibrations are waves of indeterminate force. It is a battleground of traditional elements pushing themselves against their contraries, an agon of conflicting forces. The Mega-Novel has an uncertain mass, and thus the comparison to Abstract Expressionism and aleatory music. The clear line of Mega-Novel as a literary genre runs from Gaddis's *The Recognitions* and his *J R* through John Barth's

Giles Goat-Boy and, of course, his *Letters*, Pynchon's *Gravity's Rainbow*, Joseph McElroy's *Lookout Cartridge* and his more recent *Women and Men*, to the near current Brodkey's *The Runaway Soul*, Wallace's *Infinite Jest*, DeLillo's *Underworld*, Pynchon's *Mason & Dixon*,* and to a lesser degree, Helprin's *A Soldier of the Great War* and Mailer's *Harlot's Ghost*, perhaps even Alexander Theroux's *Darconville's Cat* and David Bradley's *The Chaneyville Incident*. The latter four, more conventional than Mega, nevertheless move toward the form.

In these novels, we have a literary mode disconnected not only by dimensionality but by fictional ideology from shorter and more popular works by Roth, Bellow, Mailer, Oates, Updike, Malamud, Morrison and others writing in more contained terms. We are here speaking of differences, not preferences. American fictions have been divided into at least two very different camps, and when they speak to each other, unfortunately their tones and the tones of their supporters are mainly disdainful. Fiction has been Balkanized, with most reviewers and critics taking up the cudgels for the conventional and the easily comprehended; while in the universities and among academic readers there is greater acceptance of the more intractable fiction of the Mega-Novelists.

Unlike its lengthy more traditional predecessors, the Mega-Novel has forsaken inclusivity for indeterminancy. Its aims are the decentering or deconstruction of elements rather than gathering in. It is *more mass than content*. It gives up melody for the sake of (often) unheard harmonies. Previous long novels not only gathered in, but set out a given story and limned the general outlines of a discernible society and culture, whether London city in *Bleak House*, Paris society in Proust, the rarified world of illness, death, and recovery in Thomas Mann, even an invented culture in Marquez's *One Hundred Years of Solitude*.

---

*   The Wallace, DeLillo and Pynchon appear in Chapter Nine: The Fictional Nineties.

In an interview preparing the ground for his own near Mega-Novel, titled *The Tunnel*,* in 1995, William Gass spoke of its lack of narrative structure: "It has no continuous style. There are continuous shifts of style. It refuses to place its people even, and some of the characters are caricatures...."[98] Gass stresses the importance of the page "as a person, a place, a particular"; the increase of pages provides a "field of words," and that is more important than the mere putting together of a novel. Gass says that the numbering and consecutive nature of the pages is itself in doubt, something we may recall from Joseph McElroy's first novel, *A Smuggler's Bible*, and his first foray into Mega-Novel territory. Voice itself in this kind of novel is not an identifiable or fixed element, but a contrary, antagonistic force. The voice often has to struggle to emerge.

Our contemporary Mega-Novels have floated free of social/cultural concerns into another area which they have defined for themselves; as if, for them, America's fictional life has drifted free of community and evolved into a unique, self-defining, self-conscious entity. Content is atomic, not coherent. We find it moving toward a distinct consciousness, a behavioral pattern, a restructuring of fictional activity which reflects, not coincidentally, an America which resists definition except as it is reflected in these verbal monuments. These are the stories of America, but the America of such stories lies outside character, scene, and conventional narrative, somewhere in the seams; and all of those words–the waves and avalanches of words–attempt to expose the seams to visibility. Order is redefined as arrangement and composition.

Largeness in our contemporary examples parallels the minimalist vision of silence writ large, or strung out. Such fictions–Mega and minimalist–surrender less and less as we relentlessly pursue them: the light at the end of the tunnel proves illusory, or else recedes the closer we approach. Their seeming randomness of scenes not only subverts inevitability; it threatens order itself. Since

---

* More appropriately placed in Chapter Nine.

the Mega-Novel is a field or mass, it is almost always self-defining, despite its vastness and reach. Its sense of order lies in some subjective area caught between the conscious and the unconscious.

The contemporary Mega-Novel has associations with allegory and fable. Despite its linkage to many aspects of the real world–military, or business, or professions–it nevertheless presents them so wrapped in a self-oriented language that such dimensions of the real world become closer to fable than to realistic novel. The Mega-Novel seriously stretches our ideas of realism. The mention of a "fable" carries us back to William Faulkner's single effort at a Mega-Novel, his much-belabored *A Fable*, in 1954. Having slipped away from conventional elements of plot, character, even motivation, Faulkner intruded into the indeterminate world of associations, compositions, relativities. Granted that *A Fable* does not possess the extreme length we associate with Mega-Novels, it reveals the problematics of sentence and paragraph we associate with the form. Words, sentences, paragraphs are not utilized chiefly for informational or narrative purposes, but for the qualities of massed language, or the illumination of seemingly disconnected areas. Nearly all becomes a forefront; perspective is shifted away from the field of vision. Words are massed for an attack which may never come. In the same interview cited above, Gass speaks of seeking some notational form for fiction, comparable perhaps to Arnold Schoenberg's twelve-tone system. In that, Schoenberg was able to deploy his twelve tones like pieces on a chessboard, either in rows, or inverted, reversed or repeated. The layout of the Mega-Novel has something of that in it. In *Gravity's Rainbow*, for instance, we find not quite a notational fiction, but a series of borrowings from biochemistry, in the cellular structure of the novel. Pynchon focuses on Du Pont's discovery that he could rearrange nature, by creating new plastic effects, through the introduction of aromatic rings into the polyamide (the chain made up of polymers). Through a series of further steps, scientists developed Imipolex G. that insulatory material for rockets. But what Pynchon is really getting at is not weaponry, but the way in which his novel, with plastics as model, can be structured. In the cellular makeup, we find the architecture of the novel's own shaping.

Cellular structure or the like is very significant for the Mega-Novel in general. Mega-Novelists must bind together their material and, despite great length, breadth, and seeming randomness, suggest tight form. Pynchon's cellular structure–which we find also in Gaddis's *The Recognitions* and *J R*–allows for change within constants; he utilizes spatiality with almost abandon, but the cell holds the nucleus or clue. Tyrone Slothrop becomes, at one stage, Ian Scuffing, and yet the new name and new role as correspondent are not a nuclear change, only a cellular one. The center or nucleus, the identifying element, remains, while the actual molecular structure is altered to allow for narrative progression.

The Mega-Novel contains sweeping space, which seems to reflect disorder, but all within a controlling line, which conveys orderliness. Yet despite all the care which goes into binding elements, the Mega-Novel is incomplete and must remain so. The form uses its great extension, paradoxically, to suggest incompleteness; and as noted it accomplishes this by stressing association and composition. Society or culture is internalized into form, and form is part of the modernist stress on arrangement. The Mega-Novel approximates in verbal patterns what line and color provided earlier in abstract painting. Surfaces in this mode are so crowded and complicated because these surfaces carry the weight; what is beneath is submerged in much the way a tall building has a good part of its construction underground. What emerges, then, is not "content" as we traditionally describe or discuss it, but architecture, form, associational matter, mass and cluster. If we attempt to paraphrase what a Mega-Novel "means," we are surprised by how few words we need; by how little it takes to recapitulate half a million words of fiction.

Since there is little in the Mega-Novel to indicate an ending, it evades closure. It is all middles, often with little or no beginning, and, as already indicated, no resolution. Such novels are like elastic bands in their stretchability. As Gaddis puts it in J R, ". . .how could I be inside, there isn't any inside!" Without any inside, there is no ending, only process, a continuum.

Similarly, in *Gravity's Rainbow* and Barth's *Letters*, and especially in McElroy's *Lookout Cartridge*, "insides" are dispensed with. The opening of the latter is emblematic of the type. A helicopter, its computer malfunctioning, hovers over a gridlike area–its uncertainty in space contrasted with the clearly demarcated area below. Since the line of the narrative, its voice, lies somewhere beyond consciousness, the novel commands a sense of dimensionality or spatiality. Our recall of the novel is of an oceanic experience. McElroy strives to discover a realm of narrative which lies both within and without, one that while describing external events is always in the whisper and hesitation of an observer who is uncertain of what is being perceived. Confusion and uncertainty accrue; they do not resolve.

It is clear by now that merely to write a lot of words, as Norman Mailer did in *Ancient Evenings*, whatever else one may say for or against it, is not necessarily to write a Mega-Novel. *Ancient Evenings* is all length; but it warrants being closed off well before Mailer decided to end it. In the Mega-Novel, the material yearns for more; and even after such great length, we recognize we have barely begun. What the genre offers is the opening up of so much fresh territory that waves and torrents of words do not exhaust the author's inventiveness. While there may be no inside, there is an unlimited outside.

Still another dimension to the Mega-Novel is the demand made upon the reader by its language, elliptical, sometimes opaque, slanting in. We know that problems of language have made tremendous demands on the author because such novels usually have long periods of incubation: Gaddis took twenty years between *The Recognitions* and *J R*; Pynchon produces a novel every decade or so; McElroy struggled with *Women and Men* since at least 1976; Barth's *Letters* was the product of an entire career. Our best example, perhaps, from an earlier period when incubation and writing approximated our present condition, comes with Joyce, whose

Ulysses was eight years in the making and whose *Finnegans Wake* consumed seventeen years, almost the rest of his life.

Whatever the problematics, for some readers the Mega-Novel phenomenon is the main literary stream in postwar American fiction; not a subsidiary element superseded by the more popular, and accessible, Bellow, Mailer, et al. Very possibly, when our contemporary period becomes an historical one, the Mega-Novel will be perceived as our unique contribution to postwar literature. What remains to be answered is why America at this time produced this phenomenon. While reviewers and critics have hooked on to categories of Jewish novelists, gays, black writers, female authors, another kind of novel has emerged: written mainly (not solely) by white Protestant males. Yet the question insists: what in the culture permitted or forced something like the Mega-Novel to emerge, and at this time? Does, let us say, a work such as *USA* by John Dos Passos qualify as a pre-war example and upset our view of the Mega-Novel as a postwar event? While innovative, the Dos Passos–although quite lengthy when the three parts are joined–is conceived of in fragments, brilliant segments at times, and that denies the Mega-Novel conception of more subtle arrangement, composition, subversive linkages, conspiratorial, veiled reflections.

One less than literary point: only in America has there been sufficient newsprint and paper for such long novels. The material means must be there, and it has been lacking for most British and continental writers. The real question, however, is why the Mega-Novel has appeared *when* it has–and one answer is that the idea of a fiction without closure represents the spirit of the country. Except for *The Recognitions*, the Mega-Novel is a 60s and after development, and we should not lose sight of the 60s spirit as a hovering presence: the overwhelming sense we were on a frontier of knowledge; that we had glimpsed, however imperfectly, another kind of experience; and that this experience was open-ended, spatial, expansive, resolute but without resolution. Critical of the country and even negative as most of these novels are, they are profoundly American, intensely representative of the American spirit. Pynchon is our contemporary

Hawthorne, Gaddis our Emerson or Thoreau, Barth our Melville—these white Protestants write very close to what America is, and they recognize that the country can be understood only when it is abstracted. That is, as metaphor, symbol, reflection, role-playing, as a process of diverse realities—an America which can be caught (but not trapped) in the labyrinths of the Mega-Novel.

Joseph McElroy's *Hind's Kidnap* appropriately offers us just such a way of perceiving ourselves. In attempting to solve a kidnapping which may not have even taken place, Hind, in this 1969 novel, turns his life into a maze. He is separated from his wife, for whom his obsession with the kidnapping is no small cause; he visits friends, but less to see them than to pursue leads, to voice suspicions; and he revisits old haunts to seek out new information. Each time he visits or revisits someone, the tale of kidnapping is retold, kept fresh through repetition. Everyone is suspected—each character functions as a potential perpetrator. The labyrinth is circular, and Hind is trapped (energized?) in what his own ingenuity and concern have created: he has been kidnapped by his obsession. Application to an artwork is apparent. Hind creates, discovers, shapes, seeks motives, pursues, and is wound in his own bobbin of imagination, narcissistic to his fingertips. The Proustian play of memory is rejuvenated in American backgrounds—a pier, a rural setting, a golf course, a university. Memory works in circular fashion, molding conscious and sub-or unconscious elements, creating a continuous narrative from disparate materials. Kidnapping functions here somewhat like counterfeiting in *The Recognitions*, the stock market in *J R*, rocketry in *Gravity's Rainbow*, the War of 1812 in *Letters*.

We can say, further, that the postwar American novel *as a whole* has been a distinct phenomenon, made up of deeply American elements intermixed with European modernism—and nowhere more than in the Mega-Novel do we find that mix. Yet whereas several American novelists for the sake of accessibility or as the result of temperament ignored more severe technical aspects of modernism, Mega-Novelists took their reading to heart and assimilated

European strategies to American material: the result being the Mega-Novel as a distinctly postwar American phenomenon. Although issues are complicated, we can say that this mode is following the matter of America as a large, sweeping, generalized discoverer of itself.

In the main, the Mega-Novelists have avoided the individualization of ethnic, gay, or female experience and sensed the country as a whole; that in itself insures length, volume, vastitude, oceanic experience. Now that most postwar energies are veing exhausted, it is clear that the Mega-Novel almost alone remains as a reflection of the final decades of the century. When we assert that modernism has passed into history, or become diffused into "postmodernism," how do we account for the Mega-Novel? We cannot leave books like *Women and Men* and *The Runaway Soul*, even *A Soldier of the Great War* and *Harlot's Ghost*, to the reviewers. We should have moved on from there a long time ago.

Women and Men: More Than a Novel

In *Women and Men* (1987) Joseph McElroy is attempting nothing less than asking us to redefine the novel, in ways which Joyce in *Ulysses* and then in *Finnegans Wake* forced us to do. If we start with that assumption, we can comprehend McElroy's effort: he is not writing "a novel" so much as he is working through "a prose fiction" which moves us beyond what novels have usually signified. Some of the resistance to McElroy, as in several of the book's reviews, comes from readers who reject the demands he makes on us; demands connected to his struggle to move beyond the boundaries of what we expect when we open the pages of a novel. McElroy takes us outside, into areas of intelligence, information, linkages which move beyond story, narrative, and other traditional expectations. He is doing here what John Barth has suggested, but not quite accomplished, neither in *Letters* nor in his more recent *The Tidewater Tales*: that testing out of what is fictionally possible; the recognition that the novel genre limits what prose fiction can do and where it can go. For McElroy, sentences and paragraphs are not themselves experimental, the very conception is.

"Wide Load" becomes an unlikely North Star for the McElroy imagination; two words which he repeats and which, along with other key tag words (Leakage, Skylab, Ship Rock) reverberate throughout the 1,200 pages and 850,000 words of the novel. "Wide Load" is itself a commentary on the book McElroy is writing. The description of what it may mean indicates where we are going when we read *Women and Men*.

> A Wide Load being shipped interstate and at this dark hour without benefit of advance patrol–wide and immobile as a home, this unit, and hanging out over the edge of its great, low carrier trailer and out over the edge of the road as if the road's been narrowed or a mountain had arisen widely from a moving molehill, so if a section of us other than the camera being flown beside this night cargo came the other way now, we'd have to swerve off this speeding road. . . . [99]

The conception of the novel, deriving from "Wide Load," is that the relationships between men and women, their linkages, their separateness, their sexual crisscrossing (pre-AIDS) is full of danger we experience when we come upon a Wide Load situation on the highway. We may have to swerve, we may be shoved off; at best we must maneuver carefully to avoid being crushed or squeezed. With the presence of a Wide Load, we must move defensively, our rhythms as drivers thrown off. In our relationships, Wide Load becomes a metonymy of what will follow, just as the opening segment of *Women and Men*, of a woman giving birth, is an early foreshadowing of Wide Load-ing. Wide Load is a danger sign on what may otherwise seem a safe highway.

Since McElroy uses other, similar words which are both cautionary and directive, the novel is all facets, dimensions, expansions, eventually concentric circles of knowledge. Words clearly take on a different significance for him than they do for a more conventional novelist. They come to have a totemic, emblematic meaning. Ceasing to possess their primary function of social or cultural significance, they move beyond into another dimension which has no precise definition or even discernible presence. "Leakage" is another such word–full of potential danger, a source of loss, also part of the second law of thermodynamics. McElroy picks up from his own earlier *Plus* and from Pynchon, especially from the technological dimensions of *Gravity's Rainbow*. This is not to posit analogies or imitations, but to note that two Mega-Novelists recognize science has so changed our perceptions its terminology has pervaded our imagination. "Leakage" has to do with where money goes when it escapes the multiplier, but also with the energy that expires when a motor runs down; it combines with another repeated word, "heat shield," which we know from Skylab re-entry vehicles. Success in the re-entry depends on a heat shield–all that complicated technology coming down to that lifesaver; and so "heat shield" has become totemic for us as we become comfortable with space travel.

The overwhelming concern McElroy demonstrates about spatiality through one of his main characters, the journalist Jim Mayn, picks up from *Lookout Cartridge* and, of course, *Plus*. It indicates him continuing involvement with the extra-terrestrial, the mysteries of life beyond the actual and present–thus, also, the long segments devoted to Indian worship, to spiritual exercises, to the rituals associated with what he calls "Ship Rock." A long novel such as this attempts to recombine everything that has been lost: what has resulted in leakage in our imagination and our cultural history. McElroy describes two very modern characters–Jim and Grace Kimball, operator of a Body-Self Workshop–whose concerns, past and present, strangely blend with each other. As a journalist, Jim is involved in a diversity of worldly activities, but also in those which transcend the ordinary. As a Body-Self Workshop director, Grace works to heal the schism between mind and body, between personal inhibitions and social morality. Although the two never meet, they do encounter each other through the people they know in common and through combinations which make up the body of McElroy's novel. They are, to use a Joycean analogy, like Stephen and Bloom, who crisscross Dublin before finally meeting, an eventuality denied Jim and Grace.

Language forms an envelope or umbrella for events, in which time past, present, and future become indistinguishable. The writer is not concerned primarily with chronology; rather with lateral or horizontal movement. The so-called "Breather" interludes illustrate perfectly McElroy's conception of time; for these segments, which appear at intervals, are attempts to break away from historical narrative into simultaneity. What Joyce attempted with streams and free associational material, McElroy achieves with lateral movement, as well as historical positioning through the "Breather" episodes. Language, then, is for the purpose of illumination, a seer's tool. Areas which are developed in seeming isolation–like Mayn and Kimball themselves–are linked through commonalities, as molecules are combined in model compositions. Words are part of a field of force, not of sequences; language is massed, as well as massive, and it never informs us precisely where we are because we are, at once, everywhere.

Despite the plethora of scientific, historical, and mythical detail, *Women and Men* becomes quite abstract. While there is no lack of information, including a good deal of sexual history, kinky and otherwise, all of it is buried in memory traces, dreams, hallucinations, Proustian "taste trips," moments of transcendence. Little of it grows from a defined narrative, or from formed character. McElroy is attempting to capture the piecemeal sense of everything, the fragmentation of elements as they pass through us, as they become part of an informational structure and then achieve evanescence as we approach them through reverie or memory. Everything is part of a retrieval system, and the perfect form for this is the Mega-Novel, with its magnitude rather than final shape.

Women and Men opens with a delivery, a pregnancy which has come from nowhere, with unidentifiable people, their backgrounds superseded by the birth. There is labor, stretching, straining, all process, no beginning. Movement seems arbitrary. Although the novel is tightly structured and organized, for the first-time reader its proceedings appear circumstantial–the hundreds of episodes indicated in the text would appear to have no clear positioning or sequencing. McElroy could have begun with Grace as easily as with Jim; or he could have re-adjusted their backgrounds, intertwined them differently from the way they appear. The novel is an expanding universe, including the trap of black holes for the unwary or the inattentive reader. In *Lookout Cartridge*, which seems the closest relative of *Women and Men*, McElroy prepared us for this process. In that novel, as in this one, we recall an oceanic experience; rhythms of waves, avalanches, torrents of language, scenes, events, where the line between science and humanism is blurred.

All is dimensionality. Yet it is not achieved by inclusion of courtship, marriage, death, such as we find in older long novels, *War and Peace*, *Middlemarch*, *Clarissa*, or others like them. It is gained through metaphors of existence, through suspension not only of information but also of our means of receiving it. Memory is constantly manipulating reader response. We become part of the aura, the atmosphere, rather than caught up in the events of the novel. A very different process is at work from what exists in conventional fiction.

Very little can be validated or has objective existence. In one respect, McElroy's gigantic novel is a blown-up version of what we see in Paul Auster's minimalist New York Trilogy. If we link the two–one overarching and massive, the other reaching under and lean–we find two bookends of "languages" for the last decade or two; both based on a litotes, that affirmation achieved through denial. Auster denies the validity of our empirical experience, denies the very metaphysical basis of our perceptions; whereas McElroy inundates us with experience and then denies that it can be "located." Both are coming at our sense of the last two decades as intermixing an indistinguishable reality and unreality. We have moved beyond naturalism, realism, existentialism, romanticism, even modernism; all ideological "isms" have succumbed to a form of life based on the affirmation of denials. Both agree that clear affirmation is impossible, although McElroy insists he remains optimistic. Yet the very structuring of his novel leaves little room for a stated optimism, since its premise is that distinctions can no longer be made: one is moved in and out of memory, where reality and unreality are interchangeable.

In common with some other Mega-Novels, *Women and Men* has little "matter," but is all phenomenology. The use of litotes creates areas of doubt and uncertainty, so that all that remains is sensibility. The huge spaces which exist "out there" can as readily be huge spaces which exist "in here": external and internal inseparable. Women and men become women-and-men.

The Mega-Novel has developed its own languages of difficulty: not only because the writer is willfully challenging the reader, but also because it demands its own kind of cosmic prose. Part of the language of the Mega-Novel–and this is basic to *Women and Men*– is repositioning of the voice of speakers or commentators.[100] Often we do not know the derivation of the voices; and while this is temporarily disturbing, it serves a longer-range function of developing a novel whose languages seek their own definition. Words take on an unworldly aspect. McElroy is the master of this dimension of novel-writing: that ability to come at the reader from all sides simultaneously, to subvert linear narrative without recourse to streams of consciousness, to provide a freely-associated context without going completely inside. All is disguise, veils, mists, even deceptions. The aim is not only to disorient, but, ultimately, to reorient the reader in a different context of reality; to break the thread of the realistic novel even while including realistic scenes and events.

Yet despite great length and even longueurs, *Women and Men* seems fragmentary. With words and voice so suggestive, we become aware of their lack of inclusiveness; the more we are offered, the more we resonate with and expect. The Mega-Novel, it seems, is the ultimate deconstruction of fiction: not leveling it, but disemboweling it of its traditional realistic functions. Language moves *around*, not *through*, subject and events, deconstructing our verbal expectations, even our structural ones. Chiefly, we come upon a form which makes the American experience as open-ended as fiction can envelope, which negates any possibility of closure and makes words and structure as well as experience spatial. The expansiveness of the mode, and of the McElroy novel, suggests that the spirit of the 1960s still lies heavily over one dimension of fiction: that even while minimalists have burrowed into neat holes, other writers are seeking an opening out that has little to do with miniatures.

Women and Men works on discontinuity, on shifting of styles—the so-called "Breather" segments are themselves interruptions, even while providing background and historical depth. Because we are confronted at every turn by a bend or curve in the labyrinth, we can never settle in. This unsettling process is really a turn away from previous innovative fiction, different from Joyce's work; for lying beneath *Ulysses*, in fact, is a fully traditional, mythical story. Underneath *Women and Men*, however, is a different conception of how fiction should function—it does not return us to ancient myth, nor to modern adaptations. It is a penetration of sensibility, memory, recall, the individual historical past; it is a personalization—one might suggest a "narcissusization"—of all matters, so that objectivity melts into the subjective.

In still another way, *Woman and Men* distances itself from the more common run of fiction, even from other Mega-Novels. It presents itself as a form of meditation, a private affair which we, as readers, happen to overhear. Fueled by some unrevealed energy, it does not appear to derive from an author, but from an inner world filled with words, stories, linkages.* McElroy has taken us in a

---

* A kindred spirit in this regard is not only John Barth but Salman Rushdie, especially in *Midnight's Children* and *Shame*. This is still, near the end of the century, one of the frontiers of contemporary fiction.

strange way to the center of another earth, where the language may be ours, but the modes of expression–the languages of contemporary communication–have shifted their ground. The words are like silent prayer suddenly allowed to emerge.

Conscious and unconscious, as well as all states in between, blend. Even our expectations of states of consciousness are deconstructed. When we speak of meditation in a novel, we usually mean a flow of words and energies set off from narrative or from "story," interiors interrupted by external shifts. McElroy does provide chapter breaks, even spacing within chapters, as well as the "Breather" segments–but all of these are seamless, continuous. The spaces rest the eye momentarily, but do not affect the flow, which comes on as if driven by avalanche force. The import of this is to create not only seamlessness and continuity, but something close to Henri Bergson's ideal in which ordinary memory is suspended while pastness breaks through unimpeded.

While not quite Bergsonian, McElroy attempts to find that inner world–truly a language–which borders intuition, reverie, pure memory (not pastness). Since so much of *Women and Men* is "backgrounding"–Jim Mayn's, Grace Kimball's, others'–a reliance on reverie or pure memory is essential; especially since McElroy blurs pastness and presentness. Mayn's journalistic activities bring him into touch with a broad range of interests, from rocket launchings to South American politics (particularly Chile and Allende); strip mining, with its linkages to the Indian past; multinational elements, with their interrelated military conspiracies. Using Mayn, McElroy can tap the entire country–not least an abiding interest in Indian lore, brought to Mayn by his grandmother, who relates the tale of a princess of Choor who is connected to a Navajo prince. It is a tale of magic, spirit, unworldly presence, since both the princess from Choor and the Navajo vanish: he into the as yet uncombined parts which will make up the Statue of Liberty. Such flights of fancy are not unusual in a novel embracing Indian belief in spiritual presences even while anchoring itself in contemporary realities (the military, politics, conspiracies, international strategies).

Much of *Women and Men*, therefore, has something of the magical science-fiction we associate with the earlier *Plus*. Even our uncertainty about the narrator–who is he? where is he? is he a Chilean under torture? is he isolated somewhere, in a reverie?–is part of McElroy's dissociation from traditional fiction-making. Jim Mayn's voice appears to dominate the novel, but we should not assume he is the narrator; he is really the narratee, the subject of a narration which is about him in ever-widening concentric circles. Similarly, Grace Kimball, while a lesser narratee, is also the subject of ever-widening circles. Her group is less sensationally involved, since her Body-Self workshop includes more routine activities than those attributed to the journalistic Mayn. Yet in some special way, Mayn and Kimball connect. His mother a suicide, his marriage a shambles, his son isolated and alienated from him, Mayn pursues that inwardness also found in Kimball's Body-Self workshop therapy–nudity, masturbation, coupling, acting out of one's feelings. The arena is different, the internalization similar.

One way of reading *Woman and Men* is as a kind of Joycean detective story. Will Jim Mayn be able to piece together the fragments of his life, or will he fail? These are stories from the past, miseries of the present, his vision of a future when two people, launched into space, become intertwined–a vision in which sexuality and individualism are eventually subsumed into a single consciousness. All of this is underlain by entanglements which prevent the reader from pursuing any particular thread; since the strategy is to make all threads indistinguishably one. The strategy is also to fold Grace Kimball into Mayn's life without their actually meeting, although both live in the same apartment complex. For several reasons they do not encounter each other, the most obvious being that they represent different halves of the human experience. But a more subtle reason is that by overlapping, intertwining through personal acquaintances, interweaving through paralleled experiences, they are acting out what women and men are.

Connection *is* impossible. The approximation of their meeting is a metonymy of gender differences.

Although the novel opens with a birth–the consequence, not of a test tube, but of a sexual encounter–the entire novel which follows posits the ultimate impossibility of a complete interfacing between male and female. The novel is constructed on paradoxes. Grace Kimball's Body-Self Workshop suggests that connections can be made, within the individual himself; but the larger sense of the novel denies that ultimate meeting. The solitariness of each sex, of each individual within that sex, dominates. The shadow of D. H. Lawrence hovers over the personal tensions.

A basic structural concept conveys McElroy's sense of women and men who interact even when they fail to meet: his use of homologies. The homology works curiously, both deconstructing the novel, disemboweling it of its traditional realistic functions, and yet giving it volume and breadth. A labyrinth, *Women and Men* seeks spatiality: endless, it yearns for closure; a seamless narrative, it is in actuality a meditation. Through the homologous process, each segment of system refracts other segments and systems. The term has a biological origin, signifying the evolution of an organ or other part from the same or corresponding source: i.e., the relationship of a leg and an arm of a person to the leg of a horse, the wing of a bird, the pectoral fin of a fish. With such techniques, McElroy gains the desired effect of overlap, endless variation, evolution within a social-cultural context. In another respect, Mayn and Kimball, among others, can be viewed as refractions of each other; not unique, but linked ultimately as homologous.

Homologies inevitably lead to an epic sense, since man is homologized to angels and mythical figures, as well as to dimensions of history and technology. McElroy perceives linkages everywhere, as though carrying through a theory of correspondences in which what is man-made connects to what is heaven-sent. This is his sense of epic, and if a poet, he would be Rilke. In one respect, he decentralizes the epic (recent history, the Indian past, the cosmos in transition); in another, he recreates it from small elements (man's yearning for breadth and size). Like *Gravity's Rainbow*, the archetype of this kind of fiction, *Women and Men* moves in rhythms that alternate large and small. In an interview, McElroy indicated his interest in remarks Rilke made in the eighth of the *Letters to a Young Poet*, written on August 12, 1904. Rilke writes that if it were possible for us "to see further than our knowledge reaches, and yet a little way beyond the outworks of our divining, perhaps we would endure our sadnesses with greater confidence than our joys."[101] Our purpose is to open ourselves to the new, to comprehend when it appears and not to "grow mute in shy perplexity." The key aspect is our ability to see beyond our knowledge, and it entails opening ourselves up to what may at first seem alien. Our "sadnesses" in this respect are constructive, inasmuch as they enable us to reach toward the unknowable.

If, in fact, we asked what *Women a1nd Men* is about, we find little "about"; only a process, a method or sequence of strategies. Its "aboutness" is itself an endlessly curving fictional epic of overlappings and repetitions. It seems akin to the new physical explanation of the universe as part of "string-theory," where nothing is linear or geometric. All of this, in turn, is linked to McElroy's effort to peel away layers of understanding, conceptions, the past, in order to reach into some mythical core. That repetition of words and phrases cited above is part of the pattern: to turn language into incantation, to force us to re-perceive common expressions so as to replace familiarity with surprise, even awe. Simplicity heightens difficulty; difficulty heightens simplicity. Skylab whirling around the earth every ninety minutes reminds us that a "flying house," as McElroy calls it, has become part not of our extraordinary but our ordinary experience. The mythical and spiritual enter into our routines. In such ways, we absorb the great.

McElroy's basic architecture of this huge novel rests on three shapings: the waves of consciousness already cited, in which spatial and temporal concepts form rhythms tied to myth and spirit. Then there are the long segments devoted to city life, life in the fast lane.

The urban episodes offer a different pacing, obviously a different spatial-temporal dimension. They depend on rapidity, speedy changes of pace, and require less of the reader's attention span; whereas the episodes devoted to consciousness are much slower, more considered in their rhythms. The third shaping takes place through the "Breathers," meditations by people (souls) awaiting reincarnation. The Breathers sections, as noted, are continuous with the first scene of the novel, a birth episode; and we can see these segments as having something of the unborn foetus responding to a world which he or she will shortly enter. But the Breathers are not simply a tour de force of gossipy prose; they permit McElroy to comment on matters religious, social, political, even historical. The detail here is awesome, the author demonstrating a keen attention to the disposable detail we all absorb in our daily reading.

McElroy is deeply committed to a liberal-left reading of America's history: critical of our treatment of native Americans, and himself inspired by the Indian past. He is concerned with our recent policies toward Chile, with the overthrow of Allende and the imposition of a brutal, repressive regime. He finds entire dramas in the episode of the U-2 pilot Powers, and in how in the 60s that episode sundered American-Soviet relationships. He brings back Coxey's army of the unemployed and its futile march, in 1893-94, on Washington, where it was dispersed and many of its leaders arrested for trespassing. But there are several other, almost as important, leitmotifs, all of them signifying to McElroy some way in which America is held together or, conversely, fragmented. Often these motifs are fanciful, or take place within an area of dream and reverie. Like Barth and Pynchon, he is fascinated by technologies, here the way in which information can be analyzed and exchanged in micro-electronic systems; counterbalanced, however, by an opposition to technology, the way in which an Ojibway medicine man devises a tapeworm process for losing weight. McElroy fiddles with a secret submarine which hides off the New Jersey coast and has as its goal the smuggling of a revolutionary opera into South

America–part of the pervasive Chilean theme. There is, as ever, that Skylab or house orbiting the earth. But these are only beginnings. We have the various enterprises into which Mayn enters as a journalist: strip mining in the West, in once-held Indian territory; Ship Rock itself–one of those word groups, like Wide Load, which enter our imagination during the entire length of *Women and Men*. Moon launches, which fail, are juxtaposed to other moon metaphors which grow from Indian myths.

Little of this is clarified. These moments, leitmotifs, references to history, spiritual elaborations, flights of fancy and reverie are all buried deeply in a nonstop, tidal wave narrative. McElroy evidently embraces the earth as an energizing system, so that even in those processes which subvert life or undermine the earth itself, he finds vitality, a spirit he can communicate in this novel. He has, as though a Ralph Nader of the fictional world, found in our rape and degradation of the land everything which has gone wrong; but he has also found counterbalancing elements in spirit and soul which live. He sees random destruction, but also patterns of recovery; doomsters and calamity-prophets are not given their way. The Indians are always there, with their life-saving myths, their spiritual guides, their tall tales of spiritual encounters which contrast with our modern technologies. Through the haze of this material, McElroy is insistent that such stories are not simply fanciful, but living memories, part of a recall which can save us. If we struggle against this flow, then we find ourselves inside a fictional nightmare; but if we cease resisting and give McElroy his head, we experience America. For this is a novel deeply about America and what it means to be an American. What begins as a birth is really the birth of a country, a national attitude, a "race" distinct from any other.

The association of Mayn and Kimball illustrates the multi-level quest: *he*, moving outward, or into history; *she*, exploring body-mind, blending, trying to achieve individual balance. In this equation, it does seem Mayn has more of the author's ear than does Kimball; for his world appears more significant, with its worldly events and historical detailing. Kimball's world is important, but it is also kinky, a source of some titillation, a little off the wall. Since it is therapeutic, it seems more of a female world and, therefore, less momentous than the male world of cosmic events. In the equation of men and women, women appear less concerned with the larger issues; whereas men are less involved in matters of health or balance. Yet despite what appears to be a certain inequality of concern, both sexes are deeply involved with earth, with the kind of America which will emerge from their endeavors. McElroy has some of that nostalgia for an America which was, once, thought to be Edenic; the new Zion, the new Earthly Paradise shining through.

Yet not all is a nostalgia trip; rather, an effort to find realignments between fragmentation and the possibility for wholeness. McElroy is interested in finding some holistic approach to American life; but not in any cheap or easy way. The result is an extremely difficult quest for retrieval, one that places the author in the line of an unlikely group such as Cooper, Hawthorne, Melville, and Faulkner. For all of these, the country pre-empts individual stories, even while individual stories remain significant, the source of narrative energy.

McElroy is particularly careful to make certain that language does not become the totality; that is, not solely circuitry leading back to itself. That is a real danger in a novel where words pour forth seemingly uncontrolled by any definitive speaker. McElroy has devised several strategies to alleviate or block this eventuality. He has decentralized his epical sense, always bringing the larger, cosmic dimension back to individuals and to historical events–an example of his theory of small as beautiful. Then he has found information clusters by which we live, so that just when we expect to be wafted off into verbosity, we experience déja vu, or at least some linkage to recognizable experiences. Further, he keeps digging away at history, at those things which did occur and which he can repeat often enough so that they shape words or undermine language with events. Finally, he insists on tensions between large and small, history and individual, body and self–an insistence whereby emotions can be touched and expressed.

Despite the brilliant successes of this method, however, we should not be blinded to some shortcomings. There *is* a coldness and impersonality to relationships that, it seems, should prove otherwise. Mayn's failed marriage, his alienated son, his feelings about his suicidal mother are all handled to preclude reader empathy. Mayn himself denies certain feelings by insisting on facts; he also denies history as a way of remaining sane, but in that act, he turns deep emotional attachments into forms of reason. McElroy here is walking the edge: he does not want to fall into sentimentality, obviously; but also wants to avoid the cynicism and irony writers like Barth, Gaddis, and Pynchon are prey to when their feelings might be touched. He wants to demonstrate disintegration, the ways in which feelings are fragmented; but in so doing, he cannot overdo feeling. Therefore, for all the soul-searching which does occur, the novel is curiously impersonal. We find Mayn's denial of personal history little more than a rationalization, a means of avoiding his emotions. Even Grace Kimball's more emotionally developed life, as leader of a therapy workshop, trails off into sexual openness rather than a broader-based range of expression. Given the nature of the enterprise, there appear few ways McElroy can tap the emotional life.

Yet there is more. One point, throughout, is that all stories are incomplete, all narratives fragmented, all personal intimacies impenetrable. This is a given of the novel, what we accept as part of the vision. Since incompletion and impenetrability leave little leverage for deeper feeling, this helps us accept the emotional impersonality. In this respect, the very ground rules of the novel preclude any significant emotional attachments.

McElroy decenters or destabilizes the novel even as he builds its volume. The subtext of the book combats the main idea, which is to establish the ways in which women and men relate to each other. The subtext shows the impossibility of this; how in their inability to meet, the sexes implicitly reveal their inaccessibility to each other. Which novel do we credit? There are, in fact, two, and we must read both, accept both. There *are* relationships, but in the final run of things, they do not work—only inwardness, selfness, self-absorption flicker. Each effort at closeness is frustrated by events, by character. Love and separation play an unending game of one-upmanship. Two people joined into one—that is posited as a good; but it is also a loss, because it means the sacrifice of individual traits. The good is the conflict, which can be overcome; the disadvantage is that in concession and compromise, the singleness of the person leaks away. We yearn, the book informs us, for both union into one and separation. The books keeps opening up and closing down on that movement of self and other: dissolution of union and yet asymptotic movement toward oneness.

The novel ultimately subverts everything it goes after. If beautiful is small, McElroy can posit it only by creating hugeness. If tensions between individual and society/cosmos are to be accommodated, the individual must concede his place. If singleness is to shape itself into union—as, near the end, we discover—then singleness is sacrificed. Given the human condition, each movement or idea is a paradox, and that, too, is a language for the last decade or two. Without wallowing in bathos, McElroy has found a means of expressing human need and desperation.

Absences play a large role. About one-fifth through the novel we find a long episode on the "Departed Tenant," where absence, not living in, is the key factor. The "Departed Tenant" is one of several such metonymies which help suspend *Women and Men* between all-inclusiveness and absence or lack. At one point, the tenants had been perhaps four, then only one, then departed and missing. But the departure may have been only temporary, for the new tenant fears the former one has returned and been admitted by the superintendent. As it turns out, the departed tenant had his own key, and without the locks being changed, it was simple for him to return. Yet while the former tenant is not dangerous, he creates a threat by his very shadowy presence, by his potential. He is in this respect like history or Mayn's personal background, the suicide of his mother, and all those other pressures which hover just beyond words. The departed tenant also has power, for it is possible he may retake the apartment, sublet it to someone else; that is, displace the new rightful tenant. Questions of ownership arise, and questions of propriety–all part of the potential threat posed by someone moving around New York with a key. McElroy does not sustain this episode, but it does become a metaphor of the hovering sense he is such a master of; those shadows, threats, presences, pressures which exist all around and beyond us. *Lookout Cartridge* was based on such a metaphor, as was *Hind's Kidnap*.

Linked to the departed tenant motif or metaphor is the abiding one of emergence. Mayn must emerge from the background of mists, a parental suicide as well as the Indian lore of his grandmother; and Kimball must attempt to get past blockage into release through mind-body therapy. As process, emergence is deeply related to memory, recall, history, hovering. Early on, McElroy gives intimations of his procedure, by speaking of reliving one's life as if one has the choice, "from start to finish, every fuck-up, with every pain, every downer you've endured already...."[102] Given this option, what would one do? There is, of course, no response, simply the pondering of the question; but it is interrelated with emergence, pressures, forces working on us. Even if we choose another life, we cannot escape what remains beyond, pressuring us; and if we choose to remain what we are, we have accepted the motif of the departed tenant–the shadow, the potential, the threat.

The Breathers function here, also. Although we may think these episodes are connected only to the "breathing" during natural childbirth, an early motif, Breathers are also momentary escapes from what is pressing upon us. If, as McElroy insists, our present must take into account the future, just as it must somehow deal with the past, then Breathers are linkages between temporal modes: escape on one hand, reminders of what binds us on the other. The Breather is used, then, to reinforce the paradoxes implicit in our methods of dealing with our lives. While it provides a temporary escape or relief, it is by definition only momentary; like breath itself, it allows a pause, not a resting place.

In still another respect, we need Breathers to escape the torrent of prose which threatens to entrap us. Part of McElroy's function is to capture us, the way Proust creates waves of words and recall to prevent any discernible exit points. *Woman and Men* is all entrances–into present lives, past events, historical dimensions–but offers few if any exits. One of the very few comes in Kimball's Body-Self Workshop, but that does not necessarily carry over. It, too, is a Breather of sorts, merely a pause. In this scheme, the Breather segments, as well as other interruptors, destabilize the very structure McElroy is building. They are more than tensions or counterbalances–they permit us to breath instead of smother under the word waves; and they help to atomize, however briefly, what is unwieldy largeness. Breathers, accordingly, take on a literal role–giving us breath when we might go under, as in the following:

> Like the universe–which, while not We, approaches (always a mile or two too late) the receding idea which proves that We ourselves are neither that universe, nor it us, nor are, very much of the time, that articulating commonality heretofore capable of accommodating a multiplicity of small-scale units, which, it has occurred to us as we have curved through the bodies of our history a work without a gear, locate us as (no joke, no future joke) what is within Mayn and within the elsewhere-busied Grace Kimball and others as what they don't know about each other and a world which "there" is outside-growing, too.[103]

The convolutions are about relationships of sizes, large to small, and about our relationship to our past and to each other, within that expanding largeness and contracting smallness; and neither can know much about the other. The confusion in the statement is perhaps broader here than elsewhere, but it suggests how McElroy refuses to relent, even when he asks us to come up for breath.

Another kind of Breather occurs in a segment called "Alias Missing Conversation," a Joycean reverie highlighting Mayn in New York. He is a tourist not only in the city and its sights but in history and memory; the freely associated material moving back and forth, up and down, laterally, a reverie creating its own dimensions. Called "known bits I," this segment is a sequence of New York City scenes which incorporates one of the book's key ideas: the way in which people who do not know each other nevertheless touch. It is a McElroy preoccupation that large numbers of people who do remain strangers come so close, on the street, in a conveyance, or in some other way. Almost touching: that is a constant. In another kaleidoscopic city scene well on in the novel–called OPENING THE VOID (Smile)–McElroy crowds the pages with people from Grace's and Jim's circle. Seen through the eyes of a New York State prison inmate, the movement is swirl, a street cocktail party, full of real and potential violence, eccentrics, and historical references. Running almost one hundred pages in itself, the "swirl" is one-twelfth of *Women and Men* and works together with the Breathers and the three "known bits" episodes to give lateral dimension to the more historical segments.

The reader's engagement with the novel must be as relentless as the writer's obsessive energy in getting it all down. *Women and Men* establishes its own terms, since it is futile to compare (or contrast) it with other contemporary or even past fictions. It borrows its directives from itself, which is not to say it is altogether self-conscious in the manner of Barth's *Letters* or some of Gaddis and Pynchon. No, the problems lie elsewhere, in the reader's willingness (or not) to allow McElroy's attenuated and at times fatiguing book to overwhelm him; reader-response here is essential in ways different from what it means in other novels. McElroy has a vision he insists upon, and he must bend fiction to his uses in order to unroll that vision. The vision comes first, the novel as its subtext; and he has remade the long novel into something quite distinctly his own. If we grant him his premises, his is a unique language in our march toward the third millennium and its unknown beasts.

HARLOT'S GHOST: the CIA as Movie

We are in the post blowjob era, and Norman Mailer doesn't seem to know it. Or at least in *Harlot's Ghost*, he tries to give us a thrill with fellatio, as well as other sexual positions that we now take for granted in print or on film. Yet he is after big game–this is a whale of a novel, Mailer's effort to reach for grand themes on the order of Melville's having reached for whales. The contemporary whale is the CIA, no less; and its activities, starting in postwar Berlin and extending through the 1960s and 70s will be Mailer's anchor. Hang on, he warns us, as he takes us through a roller coaster of conspiracies that lie behind the country's covert political process. And hang on, while a typical Mailer character, here Herrick (Harry) Hubbard, insinuates himself into every major decision of the CIA in those decades. While fatally flawed, the novel attempts big things.

The publication, in 1991, of *Harlot's Ghost*[104] ("Harlot" is Hugh Montague, modeled to some extent on the legendary CIA operator James Jesus Angleton) was notable in several respects. Besides being the "big book" Mailer has been promising us for over a decade, its very ambition as a Mega-Novel type provides an opportunity for a broad review of Mailer's fictional career. We walk a precipice of his own making–since he has proven to be several kinds of novelist, from the neo-realism of *The Naked and the Dead* to the experimental, be-bop, rock-and-roll, Burroughs-like *Why Are We in Vietnam?*, to the documentary style of *The Executioner's Song*, which Mailer insisted on calling a novel, to the overloaded, stillborn, clogged *Ancient Evenings*, to the massive, sprawling *Harlot's Ghost*, with its allegorical title and content, in which Mailer hoped to take the country by storm. Further, *Harlot's Ghost* is only the first installment, 1282 large pages of text; with the assumption that the "completed" novel–if we can use the word "completed" with such a Mega-Novel—will come to 2500 pages, the longest single novel ever published.

Harlot's Ghost opens up all the old questions, themselves ghosts of sorts in the Mailer canon. The real question is why Mailer with his considerable intelligence, his ability to squeeze language, his courage in confronting what once were sacred objects, his underlying wit (more of line and phrase than of scene or passage), his effort to broaden fiction onto a world stage, his willingness to walk the edge and dare the public, his refusal to be dull and comfortable—why with all these weapons at his command he has not proven more of a master, or even a force. *Harlot's Ghost*, if we spin off from the title, opens the Pandora's Box, and from it Mailer's phantoms rise and circle the reader. His shadow is everywhere in the novel, and from these glimmers and intimations we must conclude that *his ideas* have held him back, ideas which have occluded into traps. In what is arguably his most effective fiction, *Why Are We in Vietnam?*, a quarter of a century before *Harlot's Ghost*, Mailer was able to call up his entire bag of tricks; and the result was impressive, an essential piece of Americana, a combination of *Huckleberry Finn*, *The Bear*, and *The Great Gatsby*, along with a whiff of Mailer's real hero, Hemingway. Language, technical control, the wide screen (Texas itself, the background of the Vietnam War), the sexual play all held together, perhaps because there was a real center.

But the ideas so solidly rooted in the 60s, when Mailer also wrote his best nonfiction, have little significance in the 1990s. He is caught in a time warp. These ideas are now like bunkers and water traps on a golf course, and each time Mailer takes a hard swing to get out of the rough, he lands not on the green but in the sand or in the trees. He tries again and again to chip out, with sexual liberation, acts of derring-do, heroics, self-testing, masculine flexing; but he suffers from longueurs, the fate of a man—if we change the sports analogy—who feels he must hit a home run each time he comes to bat; or to keep the golf metaphor, who must hit a hole in one. All those passages in which he hopes to be bright often only succeed in dimming the lights, tamping down the meaning, and suggesting that Mailer has lost his way.

Part (not all) of the difficulty is that Mailer never attuned himself to some of the strategies in modernism. He need not have been Gaddis, Pynchon, Hawkes, Coover, or others like them–he could have remained Mailer. But his effort to broaden the screen, an insistence we find in *Harlot's Ghost*, results only in a plethora of words, the language of blah. He needed strategies, techniques, angles of perception and perspective, voices to get around the talkiness. Since he remains a neo-realist–in a straight line from *The Naked and the Dead*–he has no place to hide when the piled up words become impossible to listen to.

We are caught up again in the interminable discussion between Cummings and Hearn in *The Naked and the Dead*, efforts not to delineate a point of view *but to write one's way into a point of view.* In *Harlot's Ghost*, the prose wobbles until something will, perhaps, hove into view: "Kittredge [married to Hugh Montague, "Harlot," later lover and wife of Harry Hubbard, our narrator] and I were fabulous lovers, by which I do not intend anything so vigorous as banging away till the dogs howl. No, back to the root of the word. We were *fabulous* [mythical, legendary, or just terrific?] lovers. Our marriage was the conclusion to one of those stern myths that instruct us in tragedy. If I sound like the wind of an ass in whistling about myself on such a high note, it is because I feel uneasy at describing our love. Normally, I cannot refer to it. Happiness and absolute sorrow flow from a common wound."[105]

This is not an isolated passage, but exemplary. Besides the quality of the prose, the language suggests a problem with point of view. Harry Hubbard is our controlling narrator, perhaps unreliable, but the one on whom Mailer has chosen to hang 2500 pages of novel. How are we to take this? Is Harry pulling our leg? Is he an emblem of American youth after World War II, caught up by the need for adventure, intrigue, conspiracy, forced to compete with a legendary CIA agent-father? Is the need to be a super-duper lover– one linked to fable–part of this quest for American manhood? But more than that, is the entire book to be taken as ideas and history or as comedy and burlesque? The paragraph above is parodic. More than pretentious, it is overkill. No one cares about Harry's cock, ass, prowess in bed. Either he measures up or he doesn't. Mailer still insists on being the Iron John of the boudoir. That old idea of the masculine principle delineated by sexual prowess dies hard, even when the culture of the 90s had turned.

The problem with the paragraph and all it represents is not only that it cheapens Harry Hubbard, it makes him invisible. Despite all his coming and going, his sucking and being sucked (pre-AIDS), his insinuation of himself into most of the major policy issues of the time–despite all this, he is paper-thin. He is the reflection on the screen, not even the actor in the drama.

What we observe in *Harlot's Ghost* is something of the dilemma Mailer encountered in *The Executioner's Song*, his nonfiction/fiction book of 1979 about Gary Gilmore, the murderer who demanded his own execution. Mailer insisted that *Song* was "A True Life Novel," fudging the lines between fiction and nonfiction. Apparently, he needed a novel after so many years without one. But nomenclature aside, the book showed Mailer falling into the seams, claiming more for Gilmore than the record provides. While the killer stands for something large in Mailer's mind–perhaps as a kind of Raskolnikov–he is little more than a punk in a hyperbolic documentary. We observe no motivating factors in Gilmore, he has little perception of what he has done–he has shot a gas station attendant and a motel manager–and his activities are more hyped than profound. The book lacks consciousness, resonance, the feel of a character who is worth 1000 pages. There is no *there* to Gilmore; there is only Mailer's romanticization of crime.

Some of this is continuous with *Harlot's Ghost*; only now Hubbard can commit crimes protected by the CIA. Missing, however, is any rationale. Harry has no ideology beyond a kind of unquestioning patriotism. Revealing little in the way of self-knowledge, he is willing to commit any crime which the CIA concocts. He does not question the whys of the Bay of Pigs action, or the Cuban missile crisis; he simply goes along. He speaks of his love for Kittredge when she is married to Hugh Montague, but his "love" never appears to go beyond a physical attraction. Ideas, such as he has, are linked to proving himself against his father, trying to protect his rear against Dix Butler, a macho homosexual, devising long letters to Kittredge about CIA business. There is no Harry to Harry, no itness.

Mailer makes much of the Alpha and Omega of human character, by which he means conflicting and differing impulses, Alpha as order, Omega disorder. The consequence is a clash within the person for the supremacy of one or the other, and on that will depend the individual's behavior. But the Alpha and Omega concoction is simplistic, part of that carryover we cited from *The Executioner's Song*. Alpha and Omega in a sense gets Mailer off the hook; he need not attempt a greater depth psychology, since he can attribute behavior to a kind of Nietzschean struggle, a yin and yang, but without the shadings. His resolutions are often in sexual terms—an erection for Hal, Harry's father; a good entrance into Modene Murphy for Harry himself. There is no "as if" or "as though"; no historical memory beyond personal stories or origins, or personal gratifications; no speculation on how the individual fits into the wider world, despite the momentous events conjured up by the CIA.

A corollary: Why would someone with Mailer's liberal politics choose the CIA and present it with some considerable admiration? Have we all been wrong about the Company, and is Mailer instructing us in a differing perception of the organization? What is it about the CIA that should grab his attention sufficiently to generate a potential 2500 pages of fiction? One is driven to respond that the CIA gave Mailer the ultimate in masculine participation, Iron John working for his country. A man could prove himself by the way he walked the edge of conspiracies, threatening situations, arcane operations. Everything could become a test: intelligence, craftiness, courage, ability to demonstrate grace under pressure. Mailer's use of the CIA recalls Hemingway's insistence on seeking out German infiltrators in waters around Cuba during World War II, whereby Hemingway became his own CIA, FBI, and armed forces.

But the involvement with the CIA goes much further, deep into the Mailer psyche, what we also glean from *An American Dream*, a 60s novel. The CIA provided Mailer with masculine fantasies which we observe in the earlier novel, either as projections of what a man wants or as a parodic vision of what men are like. Rojack in *An American Dream* has it all, Ph.D., television show, Congressman, marriage to a wealthy, well-connected woman, but, most of all, sexual prowess so that he gets to screw the Marilyn Monroe character even while she is involved with a big dick black man. It is, Mailer might say, all a dream. But it is a dream or fantasy continued in *Harlot's Ghost*, since Harry Hubbard here is able to intrude in some big-time screwing episodes.

By associating himself with the CIA, Harry also associates himself with Modene Murphy, based loosely on Judith Exner Campbell–involved with Frank Sinatra, John F. Kennedy (one of his several ports of call), and Sam Giancana, the Chicago Mafia don who later ate a load of lead while fixing himself veal and peppers. In this crowded scene, Modene, an airline hostess when she has time to be on her feet, finds Harry satisfactory, second only to Kennedy. But Harry can gain consolation from the fact her attachment is not to Kennedy's cocksmanship, but to his need for her, his vulnerability, not to add to the fact that he is President and she hopes he will divorce Jackie and marry her. This is an American dream spread out far and wide, and the net includes Robert Kennedy with Marilyn Monroe–as close as Harry gets to *her* is to screw the woman who is screwing the brother of the man screwing Monroe. It is attenuated, but there it is!

The situation is made to order for Mailer: sex is danger, bedding down is part of a large scheme of events; prowess is measured against others' performance: Kennedy's fame and power, Sinatra's reputed schlong, Giancana's threat to rub everyone out. All this is played out against the aegis of the CIA–while we thought it was undermining unfriendly governments, we were unaware that its operators were toiling elsewhere.* Harry aspires simply to be James Bond–Ian Fleming and 007, in fact, are never distant.

There is considerable conflict in all of these elements. The ambitious reach Mailer reveals is commendable: to do nothing less than to find a metaphor for America in the postwar years, to identify that metaphor as the CIA. Then to present a young man in an apprenticeship-to-life novel "growing up" through his CIA roles, to intermingle him with the great events of the day: Berlin when Soviet pressure was greatest, Bay of Pigs, the Cuban missile crisis, the Kennedy assassination, the beginnings of the Vietnam intervention. Yet, unfortunately, the parts do not cohere. Once again, it is in good part the fault of Mailer's ideas; the conception might get by, but the ideas, and prose, sink it.

To blend the pageant with the individual required a very different kind of technique. It needed the very kind of modernistic strategies Mailer has avoided, although he does try to mix it up with letters, a journal, and narration. Then he would need a very different narrator, a different personality. His use of a typically patriotic American who grows up with a CIA father and who wants to get into the act leaves him little room for breadth or depth. Harry Hubbard may be brave, but he doesn't seem too bright. Further, the events themselves become self-defeating: their outlines are familiar, whether the invented conspiracies or material picked up from (acknowledged) sources. Freshness is not all, nor is ripeness. This is a young naïf's book, not an elder statesman's.

Still further, the material, which is of historical significance, is diminished by those Mailer stalwarts: male sexual prowess; women with insatiable appetites (not for food); flirtation with anal sex, a carryover from Rojack's reaming the German maid in *An American Dream* and then expounded on ad nauseam in *Ancient Evenings*; the alpha and omega thing, which simplifies and reduces, while

---

* Perhaps this is the real reason why Aldrich Ames, the Soviet mole, could escape detection for so long!

Mailer thinks it complicates; the hero worship when power is at stake. Mailer has a thing for Robert Kennedy, seeing him as "maternal," as a safe harbor for those who suffer, rather than as a man on horseback, the one-time supporter of Joseph McCarthy* and Roy Cohn, later as attorney general a man who moved so slowly into civil rights as to provide little cover for those who were taking huge chances. There is also the admiration for John Kennedy, even though Harry is jealous he must share Modene with the President. Staleness dominates.

The problem is that Harry Hubbard and all his endeavors for the CIA are irrelevant in current cultural terms, which is the sole way we can take him; and the CIA is itself a kind of film playing before us without meaning. We cannot stand back and admire the cool of an Allen Dulles (also his prowess, according to Mailer, as a cocksman on the Washington social circuit), the wisdom of Hugh Montague (a talky, tedious Angleton), the macho nonsense of Hal Hubbard, Harry's father, or any of the rest. The CIA is a movie, and Eddie Murphy should play Allen Dulles as a figure of fun, with Robin Williams as Kennedy.

Mailer has taken us within a dreamland, but not one he figured on. His solemn figures playing with all the toys provided by the CIA–safe houses, secret tunnels, name disguises, role reversals–are parodic: not at all characters in a novel but adults playing boys' games. What do we make of the one Jewish CIA agent, who is gay? Is it a typical insider Mailer joke, since for him Jewish men lack balls and gaydom here is a downer? Or Libertad? She has undergone a sex change operation, and men going to her for her vagina are really jerked off by her oily hands in the dark. Mailer can get in his little joke that her plumbing is off, even while men fall for her. Yet the sex, such as it is, is only part of some bazaar, like the kinky stuff in the Berlin homosexual episode.

Did the novel need an editor? Probably, but editing was not

---

* McCarthy was the godfather (this before Mafia boss Sam Giancana entered the Presidential world) of Kennedy's first child.

the main problem. In a somewhat disingenuous Author's Note at the end of Part One (1282 pages), Mailer says that when he told people over the last seven years he was writing a novel about the CIA, nearly everyone exclaimed, "I can hardly wait." Perhaps his friends felt that through the CIA as a gigantic metaphor for America in the postwar years, Mailer had found his whale of a subject. Or else, people were stupefied by the idea–after all, Mailer moves in liberal, left wing circles. Whatever the expectations, however, he has let it all get away from him. The long novel, and especially the Mega-Novel, requires the kind of discipline he does not appear to have. It–and here we mean the Mega-Novel, not simply any long fiction–also requires *ideas* which have almost infinite expansion. Mailer closes down; his alpha and omega is reductive, not expansive. The neo-realistic assumptions from his earlier work clearly hobble what should be a phantasmagoria of American postwar history. Mailer may use the CIA as his underlying structure–the way Gaddis used a school in *J R* or the art world in *The Recognitions*, or Pynchon, rocketry, or McElroy, a metaphysical quest for reality in *Women and Men*–but he also digresses into marginal matters. He is too much the storyteller for a novel of such length to be shaped according to the controls the mode demands. An unformed or unshaped Mega-Novel leads to sprawl, self-indulgence, probing of unrelated areas, loss of focus, inevitably to a destabilization of the very thing the author is consciously pursuing.

Contradictory impulses in Mailer lead to incoherence. He desires, above all, to shape a vision of America in the last three decades, in somewhat the same way those dialogues between Cummings and Hearn in *The Naked and the Dead* and the political dialectic in *Barbary Shore* earlier shaped his sense of the war and its immediate aftermath. He wanted not only a summing up but also a control, something he could grapple with as big thinker, manipulator of language, perceiver of subversive truths. He hoped to point out the contraries in the American character, manifest by alpha and omega. The CIA trope was perfect: an invisible empire funded lavishly and run by men whose only control derived from themselves, all ringed by danger, secret ploys, powerful sex, possibilities of outwitting other, arcane strategies, disguises–those cryptonyms which enabled real people to take on fantasy names and roles. Furthermore, the CIA allowed Mailer to play devil's advocate: the leftist New York Jew could toy with the ultimate gentile establishment. This is not to be dismissed: Mailer finds in the intrusion of the alien Jew into gentile, right wing territory the kind of daring enterprise which tests a man: and he is willing to take the heat as devil's advocate in order to show that a Jew can not only infiltrate this outpost of Christian political fervor but also be gay. All of this is endearing.

But the problems poke through. If Harry Hubbard does not impress us and we turn to the other major characters, we find minds full of blah, blague, trivia; and yet they are presented as extraordinary. The dialogue is dormitory-level, and yet it, too, is presented as inspirational. The love of Harry's life, Kittredge, is described as a "genius." Here, early on, is an indication of her genius mind at work: "'I've always found Freud congenial,' she said. 'He was a great man with bushels of discoveries [he sounds like a farmer], but he really had no more philosophy than a Stoic. That's not enough. Stoics make good plumbers [in a way that CIA agents would make poor plumbers?]. The drains go bad and you've got to hold your nose and fix them. End of Freud's philosophy. If people and civilization don't fit–which we all know anyway–why, says Freud, make the best of a bad lot'"[106] This would be a fitting speech for Kittredge if Mailer were parodying her; but he takes her quite solemnly, not only as a haunting beauty but as a mental giant.*

Hugh Montague, "Harlot" himself, is a rock-climbing enthusiast, claiming that it builds character and will. It also gives us a glimpse of the transcendental, and before he permits Harry to

---

* Kittredge's first name is Hadley, which links her to Ernest Hemingway's first wife, Hadley Richardson. Mailer can't forgo that Hemingway linkage, even though here his chief sexual opponent is not Hem, but Jack Kennedy.

become eligible for the Company, the latter must pass a rock-climbing test. One wonders if the CIA makes its other decisions on this basis, and whether the country has been secretly manipulated by men who find in rocks some notion of God. Harlot pontificates: "I suspect that God is with us in some fashion on every rock climb. Not to save us–how I detest that tit-nibbling psychology–God saves!–God at the elbow of all misbegotten mediocrities. As if all that God had to do was preserve the middling and the indifferent [the CIA philosophy?]. No, God is not a St. Bernard dog to rescue us at every pass. God is near us when we are rock climbing because that is the only way we get a good glimpse of Him and He gets one of us."[107] Surmount your terror on the rack face and you climb to a higher fear, which "may be our simple purpose on earth."[108] Is Harlot getting off on his rocks!

Such disquisitions fill the early parts of the book and, unfortunately, establish cartoon-like figures whom we are expected to take seriously throughout the 1282 pages; and, we assume, through the next 1200. Eventually, Harlot dies, whether by accident, murder, or suicide, but that is still in the future. In the meanwhile, he emits more and more blah. And when he is not speaking, or when Kittredge is not writing long letters of blah to Harry, we must listen to Harry's father, the legendary Cal. Cal not only enjoys capers, he enjoys philosophizing about them; and he refuses the age gap with his son, attempting to outrun, outwrestle, and outbox him: Abraham and Isaac going at it, or is it Laius and Oedipus? Cal represents that ultimate masculine father, and Harry cherishes him–there is no question of Mailer's point of view. The result is a ludicrous scene about two-thirds through the novel when they do everything but compare dick size. Iron John comes home.

What remains? The vision thing, as one former CIA director called it, is there, as is the ambitious reach of an enormously talented writer. Mailer desperately doesn't want to be out of it–and that, of course, is all to the good. Big, sweeping literary endeavors are always welcome. But he has stretched himself into self-parody. Mailer doing Mailer leads to burlesque, not high seriousness. The language reads like a comic version of all of his worst faults, and the posturing should have ended in the 60s with *An American Dream*. It is a hopeful sign that Mailer will not allow himself to be fossilized as the grand old man of American fiction, but performance is still the thing. *Harlot's Ghost* stretches for Mega-Novel significance, but somewhere in this vast enterprise a possibly tidy novel of 3-400 pages has lost its way.

Every now and then a remarkable literary mutation comes along which is so mauled and misunderstood by reviewers and critics that the book for the time gets lost. This occurred with William Gaddis's *The Recognitions* in 1955, now with Harold Brodkey's *The Runaway Soul*.[109] The latter is of particular interest as a Mega-Novel since it is a fiction in the (auto) biographical mode, in fact a kind of mutant form of biography and autobiography, or else an autobiographical memoir transformed into a fictional mode.

The Runaway Soul is a true Mega-Novel, immensity without inevitable closure, an exploration more than a definition. Its sequence of voices, as in biography, seems to derive from both within and without, from a middle area between conscious-and unconsciousness. A monster of self, this book helps define an enormous range of emotional and private life. It is, in one respect, the ultimate in the life of the individual consciousness, and, apparently, it cannot be everyone's cup of tea. Most clearly, it is not for daily reviewers, nor even for those with weekly deadlines.*

---

* Without getting caught up in diversionary tactics, we can say, also, that some nonfiction books–those of great length and density, those heavily textured and with psychological orientation–are a mismatch for reviewers. Not only are the latter pressed for time, they lack the knowledge, the free play of intellectual inquiry, the critical tools for dealing with such books. When they cannot grapple with a book, often they dismiss it as "academic," as though the academy were the enemy of books and reading. Also, their readership is never far from their minds; they are careful not to offer something their audience might have difficulty with. Expectations must be met, books sold, publishers mollified. In

Those comfortable with Updike, Oates, or Bellow, or other quality writers like them, apparently cannot handle long, convoluted, difficult novels not only by Brodkey, but also by Gaddis, Pynchon, McElroy, to name only four. These books require another dimension of reading, a sympathy with innovative, often opaque narrative strategies, an ability to enter into difficult contexts, an openness to the fictional process in all its mutational abundance, and the tolerance, in several instances, to withstand longueurs, and even missteps.[†]

When we take all considerations into play, the Brodkey novel is a pioneering piece of work, a testing out. Rather than letting down his audience from his previous collections of stories–several of which are incorporated here–Brodkey made *The Runaway Soul* into the apex of the short story writer's craft. The man who wrote the stories has matured into a many-leveled writer. Unfortunately for many critics, the book appears to disregard its audience, becoming an introspective journey of such proportions that the reader becomes lost in byways and labyrinths, so private in places that one follows only with peril; and, overall, so full of private hatred, anger, hostility, and reactive energy that the emotional life within is always near disintegration. Brodkey writes:

> The reality of being empty, of being defiled by grown-up life–by love among other things–the distillation and con-

---

this respect, an entire industry depends on a certain kind of reviewing and a certain kind of reviewer. Nonfiction books, whether trade or university press, that fall outside this pale rarely make it in, or only as exceptions, and very slowly.

[†] An exception is Robert M. Adams in the November 21, 1991, *New York Review of Books*, with a serious, mainly sympathetic review. Adams makes a real effort to understand the book, to see its multiplicities, and to valorize its strategies. However, the review title, "A Good Minestrone," while witty, does subvert the whole enterprise–probably an editor's idea of an amusing way to deal with such a self-oriented novel by making it sound like a cookbook.

centration of love is the heart of long-term fucking, perhaps too of the efforts on one's part to rule one's life. To understand one's choices, even that one has made choices and the connections and parallels, the threads and gimmicks of the foreseen: all that happens in a certain somewhat literary, French tone, in emptiness. She, Ora [his Harvard lover], *fights* to see that we love, that I do. . . I really don't know why: I know it is a human and not an absolute thing. It scares me. . . makes me uneasy. . .makes me ironic and superior. . . .[110]

The emptiness goes well beyond the hole that the narrator, Wiley Silenowicz–adopted at two by the Silenowicz's–feels as an adoptee. It moves well beyond accommodating difficult adoptive parents (while his blood father is still alive and able to send support checks) who fight constantly and try to destroy each other in the boy's presence. It, the hole, goes well beyond the sexual imagery which underlies nearly every aspect of the book, mainly heterosexual, but also homosexual, as Wiley teeters on one edge or another. It goes beyond Wiley's own comprehension of his precarious situation, as he confronts the abyss of his own existence and recognizes how fragile his sanity is. The emptiness goes into the very metaphysical condition of life as Brodkey forms it–in the tradition of Kafka and the French literary elements frequently alluded to.

Emptiness, however, is not merely negative, but a force to be reckoned with, containing an energy of its own. Brodkey turns emptiness, *his* black hole, into a weapon, part of his sensitivity to the nuances of his responses; and part of his sexual makeup. To confront and struggle against emptiness, he must mount a mighty offense; and it is that offense which compels Brodkey to keep coming at his material. Emptiness becomes the great equalizer as well as the great obstacle. It gives Brodkey, and Wiley, a handle on life, as it were. It takes on spiritual significance, although outside any conventional sense; and it does create a kind of sacred condition which allows Wiley to "float," when he might otherwise sink. It shapes the fictional equivalent of the biographer's search for the source or origin of his or her subject's creativity, the imagination or epiphany which makes the subject unique.

Emptiness shapes the meaning for Wiley's life; and Brodkey, as biographer of Wiley Silenowicz, must discover the many ways of this black hole. One way in is through chronology. The narrative is based on interruption, from infancy to adulthood, with numerous side trips, including those as brief as twenty minutes. Time loops shape the labyrinth and valorize the emptiness. Wiley is born in 1930, in a single page, then removed to 1944 (for four brief episodes, when his adoptive father, S. L., died), then moved back to 1932, when he is two years old, forward to 1956, for an episode with his Harvard friend Ora, returned to 1932, at two, then forwarded again to 1956 only twenty minutes later. At other stages in the novel, Wiley returns to the times when he was thirteen, fourteen, fifteen, for extended episodes with Cousin Daniel, Leonie, and Remsen, one heterosexual relationship, two homosexual. There seems no apparent reason for this division, except that Wiley's blood mother dies when he is two (1932); but 1956 seems arbitrary. The twenty-minute break in 1956 is not developed as a temporal idea; and the return to teenage sexual experimentation could have come chronologically as well as through interruption. Meaning must lie elsewhere.

These cuts back and forth, some in long, swooping episodes, themselves full of time loops, make no overwhelming statement in themselves. Little in the novel "adds up" conventionally. Like an adventurous biography or autobiographer, the novelist works more on association, which the accommodating reader comes to accept. The associations describe Wiley's inner workings, both early and later, his sexual adventures, his relationship with parental figures, most of all with his extraordinary creation, his adoptive mother, Lila, not to mention his adoptive sister, Nonie. The grounding must be not the "why" but the "how."

As we know from "A Story in an Almost Classical Mode" (and

the volume containing it), Brodkey is splendid on mothers and sons, his speciality, one might say. That story is more than a shadow piece for the novel. The relationship the son has with his mother is the emblem of a broad journey Brodkey encodes for the reader. The key word is journey. The language serves as a sucking-in force, so that once the reader is engaged it is not narrative that captures him, but the pull of words which create their own kind of labyrinth. The journey takes several turns and operates on several performance stages: the inner journey of the protagonist Wiley which is dominant, extensive, and exhaustive; the journey toward knowledge–sexual, psychological, familial, intimate; the journey we associate with the transcendence of the individual, toward some process of self-recreation and transformation; finally, the journey toward spiritual awareness of our place in the world or universe. The latter is not in any traditional sense a religious quest, but a metaphysical grappling with the nature of our existence, which Brodkey hopes to achieve through language. The young boy is a reader, but reading alone is limited; he must discover the words which approximate *his* thoughts, reaching back past his conscious mind into some region of the unconscious. The blurring of narrative, the confusion of realms, the privatizing of emotions, the convolutions of Wiley's story, all, are part of Brodkey's quest for the way in which that "unconscious realm" can be penetrated.

Yet his aim is not to resolve the forces which may lie in the unconscious. To penetrate to the shadows does not mean he can bring matters to the surface, or claim special archeological powers. Quite the contrary. To penetrate close to the kingdom of the unconscious is to discover the process by which the unconscious functions. If he can bare Wiley's deepest thoughts, going well beyond the traditional therapist's goals, then Brodkey can probe not the matter of the unconscious–which is unknowable–but possible ways in which it works. Process, not results, is all. The neo-Lacanian implications of this for fiction as well as for biography and autobiography are immense, not the least in terms of narrative and psychological probing of the creative mind. Brodkey seeks epiphanies, just as the fiction writer and biographer seek those moments in the subject's life which provide transcendence.

To express his quest for penetration, for his ability to transcend, he describes numerous passages of "reaching," some of them quite convoluted. These are passages which soar from earth to heaven and back again, part of that openness in which the writer yearns for ultimate freedom from traditional restraints. "The Talmudists," Wiley meditates, "Who proposed a contraction of God–called *zimzum* (I think)–to allow in the abandoned space the world to exist with its inhabitants condemned after Eden, to moral choice– separately from the omniscience or Omnipresent God–also proposed never listening to women. Or rarely. What my mother hinted at was her sense that thought was the track of wake of the truth but wasn't the whole truth but was as strange, as ambiguous, as subject to interpretation as Biblical text was for the Jews–and for others."[111] The thought here is both simple and very complicated. It intertwines zones. After the Fall, Jews were allowed a space of their own, without God's omnipresent interference; and this Wiley extends to the exclusion of women, a misogynist idea not out of keeping with the Old Testament. Yet from this, what he extrapolates further is Lila's assumption that truths lie beyond thought as much as the Biblical text allowed for freedom of movement beyond God.

In a related passage which also suggests transcendence, Wiley notes that Lila lets him "peek at reality. . . . She lied about reality– both about the crimes there, the pains, the assertions of will, the blindness and the rest of it, and about the limits that the crimes perhaps do not go past. She lied about the degree to which we [Wiley and Nonie, his older troubled stepsister] were not in Eden and the degree of absolute innocence she, and we, had."[112] But that is not all. "But, you see, then, Nonie and I, S. L., too, we were in Eden part-time, when she allowed it. And, sometime, we were sent out by assassins from a castle to deal with reality."[113] Her commands were always ambiguous, for Wiley could not know if they derived from her desire to permit him into Eden or were part of her expulsion of him from the Garden.

The language of a sacred place of course links several aspects of Brodkey's thought here; where the family, a "holy family," is traduced by the reality lying outside; where the children are offered a sacred resting place, only to be expelled by a remark, a domestic argument, a discontinuity, a reckless bit of behavior. The sacred place should seem, at first, to be the area God has allowed them, safe from evil committed in the Garden; but then that is vanquished with words or with a sleight of hand. Whimsey controls more than rules. Brodkey must struggle to maintain Wiley's persona against Lila's attack; in much the way the biographer must entangle and then disentangle himself or herself from the subject.

As a presence, Lila is both an archangel and the devil incarnate; her alternate roles right up to her death are necessary fixtures in Wiley's mind. Even Nonie, his wild, unfocussed, difficult, half mad stepsister is often an extension of the wild and half mad Lila. The latter is a grey eminence, someone who dogs Wiley into his eighteenth year, even as her words nudge him toward some transcendence.

On her dying bed, Lila sends for Wiley-now a freshman at Harvard-in order to set the record straight, if we assume anything she says is reliable. As a narrator, she may be no more credible than the novelist/biographer. Many of the scenes at which Wiley was not present or was too young to understand are now filled in–she becomes witness, once again with her reliability in question. In a curious reversal of roles, she now becomes Wiley's biographer, and in her way she subverts Wiley's efforts to write her life. The subtext of all of Lila's assertions is that she must rationalize and defend herself; that while we may think of her as candid, she may really be deceptive and incapable of containing her venom. "Wiley refers to her: she meant to be remembered–to have earned her way. She was a fatal, mortal Scheherazade, a Morgan Le what's-it, *fatale* to the end–innocent by virtue of death, virtuous chiefly as a come-on–how startling she was for me."[114] His assessment of her, in this critical segment called "Love Story," reveals sexual machinations Wiley was not privy to earlier. His sister and Casey, an older female relative, were having a covert affair; Wiley's blood mother was in love with her maid; and more. Lila's intent, superficially, is to educate Wiley in the ways of the world, but nothing is quite that simple. We move deeply into both fictional and biographical matters, especially those questions of reliability, of validating information, of choosing points of view.

We have to reckon with several factors which reach deeply into this mutant form. Like a biographer, Wiley is himself the funnel for this information for the reader, via the dying Lila. Her motives are not clear, and, therefore, her narrative of events is clouded by mixed motives and her dying state. Wiley is himself grappling not only with what happened, but with how those events–those true, those perhaps imagined, those in the shadows–have molded him into what he is. As any narrator, he is himself not a reliable witness, even though he is reclaiming his own experiences. The autobiographer is no more grounded in truth than the biographer. He is unreliable not because Brodkey wishes to deceive us, but because Wiley has become so subjective that everything has been transformed by inner need and ego. In his compulsive need to know, and to transmit that knowledge to the reader, he, Wiley, has placed a pattern on experience and events which are themselves open to question. Indeterminancy is key. The result may be numbing, soporific, or exciting as the case may be, but the narrative unfolding has, in fact, almost infinite possibilities; thus the great length which usually characterizes this mutational form. Mutation may be the generic label, but discontinuity and disconnection are the catalysts. In these areas, the Mega-Novel thrives.

Even as Lila narrates her "stories," even while Wiley questions her veracity, he suspects her of deception, and argues she cannot be trusted; nevertheless, she becomes, for him, the link between past and present–as if she were the biographer shaping his life. Part of the adoptive process, he feels, is that pastness has been discontinued from present. His blood mother died when he was two; his blood father continues to send support money, and his adoptive parents are the ones he related to, even when he feels they are more cousins than parents. As for his "sister," Nonie, she is of course not related by blood, but is part of a blood group from which he is excluded. That exclusion in Brodkey's hands is like the expulsion from the Garden; somehow, in the boy's and adult's mind, the linkage by blood to parents is an aspect of the Garden from which he has been excluded by the circumstances of his adoption. He also feels cut off from what he was, since his "stories" are not experienced in a natural setting, but in an unnatural one. As he moves around with various relatives, he is both included and excluded: part of that edginess which makes him want to accommodate the stories of the dying Lila. To carry our analogy to the next stage, it is as though Wiley suddenly found himself in a biographical study and had to grope his way to familiar coordinates against the biographer's own shaping.

The motif of this huge, sprawling text is caught in the evocative title, the story of Wiley/Brodkey as "a runaway soul." The author tries to capture it in a few words, although the title resonates throughout. "The *runaway soul* goes groping–and plunging–flying and lying–and trying–and dying…."[115] The runaway soul evokes the spatiality of adolescence and young adulthood in America, the spatiality which while offering so much is also an entrapment; the sense of escape linked to the where to? of the run. But the phrase also involves other dimensions: to run away from oneself, into unknowns–here chiefly sexual and social; to run away from familial relationships, here two sets of mothers and fathers, a sister who is less than sister but more than cousin; cousins with whom homoerotic games are played. The runaway soul, also, must grapple with stabilities, which turn out quite otherwise, volatile and unpredictable.

Most of all, the runaway soul is a wild, primitive thing, itself so volatile it can hardly be contained. Much of its wildness comes from almost ungovernable sexual urges, but not all; some from the need to find anchors when one's background has proven so mixed, strange, uneven, even destructive. The "soul" must run away from Lila and Nonie, from the influence of half-crazed women, into a world of maleness, which itself does not prove satisfactory. Self-discovery is at the core of the runaway soul, but it is never resolved, never finalized. The "soul" forbids closure.

As we know, the 1980s lent themselves to a whole spate of mutational autobiographical/biographical/fictional memoirs, although pointed more toward memoir than Brodkey's work. We have discussed several: Richard Rhodes's *A Hole in the World* (published 1990), Paul Auster's *The Invention of Solitude* (1982), John Edgar Wideman's *Brothers and Keepers* (1984), Tobias Wolff's *This Boy's Life* (1989), Susan Cheever's *Home Before Dark* (1984), Edward Rivera's F*amily Installments* (1982), Carl Bernstein's *Loyalties* (1989), Edmund White's *A Boy's Own Story* (1982); in 1979, Geoffrey Wolff's *The Duke of Deception*. In these memoirs, it is apparent that the time, the 80s, and place, America, have come together to give birth to a particular kind of book. As with Brodkey's sense of adoption, discontinuity and disconnection are the battleground for 1980s memoirists. Their wounds–some of them severe–are part of the psychological wounding of the country: the failure of institutions to help desperately needy children; the lack of concern for family care and values; the lack of emotional maturity in parents; the economic deprivation of families living without support systems; the absence of adequate health care for those just outside systems; and beyond that–particularly in the Brodkey book–the general feeling that anarchy is out there, an absurd sequence of skewed adult lives and random incidents simply waiting to devour victims, chiefly the young. Families are, quite clearly, no longer families. The basic theme is the disharmony between the child growing up and his or her immediate society, and then, in the next stage, between disparate elements in the child.

Growing up in these memoirs is a large military campaign, with skirmishes, maneuvers, strategies, delaying tactics, losses, gains, advances, retreats. The big news is not that these memoirs constitute a new subgenre but that they are so clustered in one decade: they suggest, among other things, rebellion, revolt, insurrection against the holiest of institutions, the family, and beyond that the state or government. The primary trope is the "hole," characteristic of the memoirs and of the Brodkey novel, the hole outside and within. The question is how to fill it. It devours, engorges, consumes, in some primitive peristaltic way. The "hole" is linked to Wiley's inability to define his own story. "It is genetically *weird* to be adopted. From deep inside yourself, what you are is stuff that is visiting, not entirely, not even all-in-all, but enough that you feel like an intruder even in grief, even when it's your own grief."[116]

What creates the emptiness in the runaway soul is the feeling nothing is real; "he" is not my real father, Wiley says, and he extends that to virtually every aspect of his existence. The dual parents dwindle to none, or else the dualism is balanced out by the nothingness. He speaks of the hole, which creates a doubling action, to fill it or to evade it. "I want to avoid my [adoptive] mother and sister . . . I don't want to be part of their dealing with their father's and their husband's death."[117] Even though he came to the Silenowiczes at two, they represent the hole, not the filling of it. He enters their weirdness, becomes a supplement to it, serves as a crutch for them, but can never be part of the family. Their story and his can never coincide. Two young sons died, both in the care of Nonie, and she is suspected of having done in one, possibly both, although nothing could be proved. Wiley is the replacement, and Nonie treats him with both contempt and flirtatious interest. While she is adamant, half mad, ungiving, a would-be Medea, Wiley develops as fragile, uncertain, sexually confused, undirected for the most part. The desire to run away is of course to achieve self-discovery, but also to validate himself as a person; unfocussed in his identity and direction, the adoptee hopes to seek the Garden outside the home, possibly in himself.

In several respects, then, the Brodkey novel is a Growing Up fiction but a mutation that, as it were, devours all genres. Very late in this novel, about 400,00 words along, a passage encapsulates what the runaway soul must confront both inside and outside itself. The context for the passage is compelling. It comes in a section called "Leonie's Fiancé," in a long chapter-like segment titled "Leonie or The History of a Kiss," a segment that also includes "On Almost Getting Laid." The hundred pages plus of this interlude are among the most Proustian of the Brodkey chapters, with the "kiss" the rough equivalent of Proust's tea and madeleine. The kiss here is supposedly the prelude to "getting laid," but it proves to be something else entirely, since the enormously long episode ends with masturbation. The kiss functions as a means of centering different kinds of information, including speculation on the entire range of one's sexual activity, male as well as female. The following passage allows Wiley/Brodkey to spin out intermediary ranges of experience, areas close to reverie and fantasy, recoverable only through a kind of personal therapy which blindly seeks out words. Brodkey targets nothing less than an innerness impenetrable by language.

> . . . the evening is a pimp. The finality of the sexual terrain is terror-cum-outcry in the scandal of being male, not as a preliminary as in my experience so far, but at being given a huge white world, whitelit, brief, briefly comprehensible, in regard to others' destiny–a gambler's intrusion on further time–and on life . . . romantic distances are not real distances–not like time or like going out into a river. Romantic distances ache with their breakability…. The childish part of me, the leftover blondness of what I am, is a dirtiable, naughty sunlight warmingly touching her. She was–supple– some girls I'd fooled around with had collapsed after a while into woodenness and fluster into being rooted and heaving twigs and leaves in a wind, sexually. The clumsy intimations of how anarchic and ungeneral the power is in love in each person–love in regard to one's own self, which is all one can know from immediate experience–one's own powers and

defenselessness in regard to that interfere with one's perceptions: the sickening and deliciously sticky sense of guilt and innocence fixes one's eyes, inward and outward–not everyone can bear this stuff....[118]

The play of reverie here is carried on chiefly with women, Lila, Nonie, and Leonie, with later interludes with Ora, when Wiley is a Harvard student; although some homoerotic episodes exist as well, with Daniel, his cousin, and then Remsen, plus other minor figures. But the chief line of reverie derives from women, not only as sexual creatures but also as femaleness itself. Brodkey is trying, among many adventures, to discover the very significance of what it is to be female, what it takes to be male. He does not accept received information. Here autobiography merges into biography, the subject as narrator of his own condition, and then fictionalized, so that biography and autobiography become submerged in the creative "I."

Much of Wiley's sexual experimentation–some episodes running on at great length–is concerned not with sexual fulfillment, certainly not with reciprocity, but with the way in which mechanics (kissing, foreplay even forms of penetration) and feeling can possibly become linked, or else fail to connect. By way of sex, he is seeking another dimension in life, and thus the episodes of seemingly endless speculation and, yes kissing. In kissing, he senses the ways of the world. "One of the things you feel in a kiss is the degree of susceptibility and resistance of the other person to being ruled and how nice (and submissive) you are each being now or not. I could feel in her that she was a death-or-freedom girl . . . No one to joke with."[119] This is with Leonie. But Nonie, too–she nuzzles and tempts, half seduces her stepbrother.

Sex is not a completed act–there is little enough of that in the 835 pages of the novel. Like autobiography itself, it remains "open." But sex is prevalent almost to an obsession. The way in which one is aroused, or led along, the way in which one comes together with another, all are far more significant than orgasm or even satisfaction in the act. The point of view is male, but Brodkey goes further than any contemporary American male author in trying to understand the femaleness of the female. The biography of a woman, chiefly Nonie, is as strong as the (auto) biography of Wiley.

Brodkey spends a hundred or more pages trying to penetrate into Nonie as an individual, as a woman, as a daughter responding madly to an almost mad family. Wiley speaks of Nonie–whom he hates through most of the novel–as having "a lasting tact about some of the pragmatic realities of childhood."[120] She has fought off madness, perhaps she's been mad, perhaps, even, has committed the unspeakable act of smothering one or two of her brothers. Although uncharged, Nonie grows up with Lila believing her daughter has killed one or two of the small boys, and that is a factor in the shaping of the relationship–as it also rubs off on Wiley. The latter comments: "But that tact [about the pragmatic realities of childhood] turns outward and is clearly part of a case of Nonie's being the center of decency in her system, the central repository of civilization; she is a young girl of suffering semi-equilibrium now, a consciousness stretched taut over certain inadequacies of consciousness."[121] Wiley is writing this after Nonie has burned to death in her house, married, mother of five sons, all of them "black-mooded, difficult, detestable,"[122] unsuccessful from Wiley's point of view. But now as the writer of Nonie's story, he has to come to understand her terrible fight to win her personal war: "We're all trash but in different ways."[123] By attempting to understand her, Wiley hopes to understand how he is like her, suffering comparable pain.

As the "writer" of all these stories and also as the subject, Wiley is both narrator and participant in a panorama of pain. We know from several of the longer stories in *Stories in a Classical Mode* that agony cannot be evaded. Brodkey is a master of ceremonies at a spectacle in which pain is played out in three rings. He controls the circus, with each act in it as a form of pain–to the extent that it is a defining moment, a test, so to speak, a time when one can assert oneself as a human being. He derives from Kafka in this respect: the moment of pain is not negative, but a testing ground; and without pain, the individual slumps into otiosity.[124] Since pain is the subject, the motif, the spine of the novel, the sensation can be prolonged indefinitely: the more episodes of pain–familial, sexual, growing up–the more the book can be extended. The first segment of *The Runaway Soul* is titled "Life on the Mississippi," indicating the journey Wiley must take.

If pain defines the moment and, in its way, defines the person, then Wiley must struggle to come through. He can never settle for less than the struggle within himself, and he catches this in a Kafkan and Proustian image. "If it is like being locked in a coffin, rather than a cell, then it follows that it is sensible for the senses to bulk up so in one's consciousness that every fragment or color and bit of small registers and not nostalgically but as a blur of clarity of something largely not to be explained here, merely experienced and to be thought about later and known then if it is to be known."[125]

Narcissistic though *The Runaway Soul* is, it goes beyond narcissism and defines how one can look at oneself. With Wiley as analysand, we can perceive the entire novel as a sequence of therapeutic sessions, with time leaps, and chronological convolutions. Without regard for any censoring device, the novel is the process of a consciousness unfolding. The consciousness will be as candid as it can ever be, although we know that the narrative given to the analyst in therapy is not the original or "Ur" narrative, but one molded and shaped, even as the biographer molds and shapes his or her narrative for the reader. We know this, but even so, we see in Brodkey's exploration the possibilities of the "ultimate self": not as a pleasant boastful thing–unlike the Mailer mode– but as a weak, deplorable, often repellent element. Brodkey is not attempting to prove how great he is, but to display how, despite all his weaknesses, he has at least the strength to come through. He is not vaunting himself, as many did in the 1980s, but seeking the roots of consciousness, as a man of the 1960s, when the project began to take shape. While a writer like Mailer seeks power, control, the Napoleonic energy to command and triumph, Brodkey eschews the larger world, seeking the energies which will enable him to burrow in and turn his pain into writing.

In a curious twist, personal, religious, and political intertwine. Despite playing with religious imagery–in his "affair" with Ora, for example, her name suggesting oratory, a religious service, prayer– Brodkey eventually folds the religious into the political in its broadest sense. The religious element recurs in the desire for a transcendence which never occurs; in the desire to turn words and language into forms of transformational or sacred worship; in the pursuit of spiritual imagery, as in the moth image that comes with Ora, a "giant, fluttering moth," which may be a personal image for some godlike or divine experience. Repeatedly, Brodkey searches for ways in which religious imagery and personal, private sacred images can suggest and define human experiences; and repeatedly, he comes away empty-handed.

The consequence is that the religious and spiritual must be given over to the political, by which we mean something territorial. Wiley is constantly seeking the ground on which he can win, although we must emphasize that he rarely "wins," moreso that he avoids losing. In his repeated teenage sexual affairs, he plays with power and control: at thirteen, with his cousin Daniel, whose homosexuality he perceives; a year later with Leonie, who is ten years older and engaged; then at fifteen, with Remsen, also older, by two and half years. These "affairs," such as they are, do not end in sexual satisfaction; rather, they are staging areas or arenas where power games can be played out. But the control and power gained from the sexual games are not expansive or cumulative; they do not make Wiley into a powerful person. Unlike Mailer's CIA operator in *Harlot's Ghost*, they do not give him any prolonged sense of his increased strength. The events with the older men and women are merely stages, without any accumulation of wisdom accruing from them.

The political elements, accordingly, reinforce the acquisition of knowledge which helps Wiley to become a writer. By the time he has the affair with Ora at Harvard–Ora, who cannot come to orgasm–Wiley has published some stories and is on his way to becoming Harold Brodkey. The auto (biographer) has become the fiction writer. He has not become more resolved or settled as a person, but now he accommodates knowledge that may become part of the process he calls writing. As suggested above, Brodkey is searching for some "truth," however invalid that search may be when the subject is one's own consciousness. But he is not to be distracted: he seeks fiction, not biography. "If everything is possible to belief," he writes, "then one might throw oneself from the porch in the conviction that one might fly. We have only small laboratories of time and limited abilities and we have large wonders and great horrors to deal with; and often a vastly unconquerable unhappiness stands in our way–so we had better be limited–limited in terms of knowing anything–limited in terms of fidelity to abstract truth since, then, lying has special importance. Because then the truth is testified to by the lie, by its, the truth's, not being what the lie is. It exists then."[126]

Prototypical Brodkey, the prose takes us to the edge of an idea, that since we have only "small laboratories of time and limited abilities," we must be limited in our aims; that is, in our desire to get at the truth. But the swoop of prose encompasses more, for Brodkey then can move to his real point, as he enters the interstices between fiction and biography: that truth is not some abstract principle, as he has implied, but an element which is tested by a lie; so that truth remains after the lie has been leached out. But even that is not certain, inasmuch as we are dealing with "truth"; and what remains after the lie is gone may not be truth at all. All we count on is possibility, an "immediacy." Brodkey follows this with a typical symbolic passage, about sleep as a journey carrying one into "a merciless transience of light that proposes itself as stillness and absolute meaning and as theater. . . ."[127] The echoes of Baudelaire, Mallarmé, and other French symbolist poets are not by chance. Brodkey wants to note that sleep as a journey is not unlike our movement in our waking life, where reverie and fantasy are themselves a kind of theatre. In the center of that theatre is a stillness, which is a form of life-in-death or death-in-life. This is the ambience the individual moves around in and the soul running is the way in which that somewhat transcendent movement can be captured.

The life Brodkey charts for Wiley is a kind of opera (opera sets are rarely far from the novel's imagery) which can be a fearful experience for a boy growing up. If pain is the center, and the ability to withstand it the process, the fear of isolation from normal events and activities can be intense. Wiley speaks of his fear of "having no mind except a specialized one. . . I didn't think I was smart; I thought I had very limited possibilities. . . . I didn't see how to exert will without doing damage."[128] One salient fear is that his isolation will condemn life, that he will become a prisoner of his own imagination. The perception is revealing, in his recognition that the very internality that gives him the material for his reveries and fantasies may well entrap him; so that he becomes a prisoner, unable "to escape from those postures."[129]

The Brodkey journey, twisting this way and that, forward and backward, all as part of some timeless, unconscious process, leads to an amusingly titled chapter called "David Coppermeadow," caustically modeled on Dickens's Copperfield. As an adopted child, Wiley feels he has been both wanted and rejected, feelings which are intensified when he visits uncle and cousins. They are rich, he is an upper middle class pretend; and he senses how they move to different time schemes from his. He is, once again, the odd fellow out, unwanted, an adoptee; and as in his other ventures, he must be accommodating in order not "to have worse memories about oneself."[130] Words, even expressions of feeling, cannot mitigate being an adoptee. It is a state of being, an unconditional situation. "You are not perhaps a person quite. . . ."[131] He is a pet and an enemy, an intruder in the family of three, "an outsider–a distraction–a possible ally. . . ."[132] He becomes a reclamation project for Lila, an unknowable commodity for S. L. He is not sure who likes him, or if their tie to him is simply a matter of duty. His own father, after all, is alive; so that the death of his mother when he was two does not mean that Wiley had to be put out for adoption. But all drop away: his father then dies, as does S. L., as does Nonie much later, and also Lila, in between, of cancer–that terrible cancer as we know from "A Story in an almost Classical Mode."

Implicit in Wiley's survival is the subtext of violence. Not only is Nonie suspected of having killed one or two of her brothers, she is involved in other instances of both physical and emotional violence. The contradictory nature of her parents during her childhood leads her to a barely subdued public character which disguises a personality based on anger, hostility, and violence. That she dies in a blaze is not happenstance; she is herself part of fire, mephitic in her undertones of distress, deceptions, desire to shape her femaleness, her frustrations and inability to control elements despite a dictatorial nature. That subtext of violence lies everywhere, in Wiley's adoptive father's rages against marriage, family, household; in Lila's overwhelming need to break out of what she has herself created for herself; in the cousins, with their labyrinthine tastes, disguises, anguish; in Nonie, as stated above; and in Wiley, whose gentleness of manner cannot hide a need to get under the skin, to make life difficult or unbearable for others. He refuses any easy commitment to romance, nostalgia, certainly not to love, not even to affection. He bends and melts and reshapes himself in relationships, until all that remains is that unformed self: like an octopus in its many reaches.

The Runaway Soul resists categorization and classification. It is a screed, but then it is also the biography of a family. Ostensibly it is about a search for love, or self, or definition, or all three. But it goes much further than those sentimentalized quests; it aims for the divinity in human life that is not basically religious or spiritual. Brodkey, in other words, is seeking what can never be recovered: the sacredness of self when all the siren calls are secular; the divinity within the individual who fears, most of all, his separateness from the main body; the spirituality of human aspirations when spirit and God and church are themselves commodities. *The Runaway*

Soul is a plea for letting all the un-reason in the individual and in the world around him (or her) have its rope; unleash the forbidden, the inhibited, the unspeakable, and see what is there. Brodkey reaches for an epiphany. But once that is attempted, as this mutant reveals, no matter how much is opened up and spilled out, we sense that at least as much still remains. Brodkey is not finished. Like all biography/autobiography, like all Mega-Novels, it is incomplete; the narrator is not up to the narrative. Or, conversely, the narrator is too much for the narrative. The fictional auto (biographer) has met his/her subject; one must lose.

In his latest Mega-Novel, William Gaddis in *A Frolic of His Own* (1994)[133] has followed his previous efforts: to find in systems all the elements of disorder, and then to present those disorders as the system itself: the art world in *The Recognitions*, the world of finance in *J R*, now the world of law. The legal system, Gaddis recognizes, has nothing to do with justice; and since the two are so separated, it is possible to reveal how law is based on disorders so schismatic it might be the San Andreas Fault of our modern world. "Justice?—You get justice in the next world, in this world you have the law,"[134] so begins the novel; reminiscent of Melville's "Call me Ishmael," which calls attention to the narrator's marginalization, as the Gaddis opening points to an acute division. Both are elements of America, since Gaddis is representative of those most American of writers, Melville, not to add Hawthorne and Emerson.

One of the givens in the Mega-Novel world is to reveal the rifts, divisions, schisms, and holes in what might seem to be an ordered and rational world. Mega-Novels live off the disorders which lie just below the surface of relationships, systems, institutions, organizations, or merely individual lives. Disorder, in time, becomes the major arena, for it is disorder which helps define the American character, especially as we passed from the 1980s into the 90s. Divisions and subdivisions affected nearly all people, most of all those dedicated to finding in the legal system some continuity with the past. A litigious society is obviously based on people who assume their world is rational, ordered, organized on some principle of logic. Gaddis has latched on to that kind of false hope in continuity, in a justice system which flirts with the Supreme Court and with history which returns his major characters to the Civil War. History, social arrangements, class and caste, race, all associated with some kind of continuity, come under scrutiny, only to be parodied for dividing us far more than they might bring us together.

What is parodic about Gaddis's treatment is how people believe in systems even as systems at every turn in their lives fail them, whether in what they write, or in the cars they drive, or in matters of inheritance. People believe as though justice were finally to be theirs, when it is the law they must deal with, a different order of being. The centerpiece of Gaddis's novel is Oscar Crease, a representative of the artist (of sorts), a man muddled in his outlook and in his ideals, but someone also obsessed with money. He is a typical Gaddis "artist" in that he sullies his art even as he insists on its purity. He sees around him the savagery of a society willing to sacrifice him and what he considers his art–his almost interminable play about his grandfather's experience in the Civil War–to the grossest needs of the marketplace; and yet he, too, cannot ignore its rewards.

He also believes in the law, which he confuses with justice– and the novel is in one large respect an unraveling of his ideals, his naïveté, his innocence in the face of the legal system. In several areas, Crease is a grownup version of JR, from Gaddis's 1975 novel about a grade schooler who sets out to make a fortune from trivial items, who becomes caught in forces he cannot possibly control and rides a roller coaster of fortune and decline. Oscar is also a kind of Philoctetes, the wounded artist, the man isolated on an island with his stinking foot and his "bow," which is the instrument of his art. The job for Philoctetes is not only to suffer in himself, but to suffer for all mankind as he languishes on his island. In a distortion of the Sophocles *Philoctetes*, Edmund Wilson, in his famous essay ("The Wound and the Bow") argued for the "wounded" artist and insisted on a society which must take the artist as he is, wounds, warts, stink, and all. Gaddis reworks the myth to emphasize the Philoctetes-like tension in Oscar–between the desire for isolation, where he can indulge despair, and the equal desire to return to a world which he has come to disdain.

Oscar may seem an unlikely vessel with which to create such a large theme, but the would-be playwright is caught in several levels of experience which reinforce his inner decisions. Despite all his muddle and unexamined motives, he holds to his idea, to the force of art in a decadent society, to the power of the artist as the last holdout in a society gone so corrupt it must rely on the law to maintain it. The artist stands at the barricades, holds back the floodgates, puts his finger in the dike; but he is deeply flawed, not at all heroic in any traditional sense. He is, nevertheless, there when everyone else has deserted his (her) post for easier rewards. Inadequate though he is, Oscar stands alone, surrounded by the vultures who jab into his flesh and bones. He presents himself as a god: "To get back to work! couldn't she see? spending all day here trying to capture these voices of men a hundred years ago swept by the tide of events toward the end of innocence? to bring them to life caught up in the toils of history, struggling vainly with the great riddles of human existence, justice and slavery, war, destiny, things are in the saddle and ride mankind in Emerson's voice"[135]– all to be cut short by a marketplace shark, "tin trivial" interruptions.

Yet before we go too far with the "artist figure," we must examine the language with which Gaddis invests him. Oscar speaks in clichés, in verbal stereotypes–"swept by," "toils of history"–which points to the very flaws of his vision. Preferable in some ways to those he sees as persecuting him, he is nevertheless part of the very scheme he thinks he is opposing; for he enters into the verbal trivialization of his own product, by way of Gaddis's endless supply of clichés for him when he expresses himself. The artist may think of himself as the savior of mankind, but is in fact seriously limited. He attacks others, while misperceiving himself: "Sunday mass nailing down their immortality one day a week so they can waste the rest of it on trash, or the ones who squander it piling up money like a barrier against death while the artist is working on his immortality every minute, everything he creates, that's what his work is, his immortality and that's why having it stolen and corrupted and turned into some profane worthless counterfeit is the most, why it's sacrilege. . . ."[136]

But if the law interferes in all segments of the artist's life and intervenes in every aspect of the novel, it is, after all, only words. They dominate, as they have in every Gaddis novel: an avalanche of words which help reinforce his work as a Mega-Novel. Language can expand into everything, and it seems eternal and unending, like the scenic proliferations of Oscar's Civil War play. It rolls on. The words are not only in the flattened-out scenes of Oscar's play, which Gaddis mocks for its pieties and sentimentality; words pour out of an ever-playing television set and flow from the mouths of unidentified speakers–the reader must identify them by their vocabularies and grammar. Words do not permit seams or silences; Gaddis is the least silent of contemporary writers, since he recognizes that words serve as a barrage which eventually batters down everything. Thought is itself confounded by words, unable to form or escape; and words do not permit completion. Interruption, lack of closure, fragmentary phrases and sentences characterize speech. With so many words coming at us, with so much undifferentiation, we search the page for difference–typefaces, punctuation aids, tones, nuances. Mail intermixes with television, radio with speech. "There was always mail, even the trash it was still mail wasn't it? something important that might have slipped into a big sale on camping equipment, washers and dryers, choice pork roast center cut like that invitation to lecture on Shiloh almost thrown out with porch and patio furniture, outdoor barbecues, snow tires and God knows what, the oil bill, trash removal $26.75 he punched out on the pocket calculator x 2 with a month's arrears and the window lit up with 8s end to end. . ."[137]

Co-equal to the words pouring from these sources are those emitted from the telephone, a ringing device as a harbinger of another onslaught of words. Frequently, telephone, television, speakers, mail, and Civil War play words blend together into a simultaneous performance, a synthesis in which syllables come at us so rapidly and at the characters so insistently they run over each other. Gaddis tries to capture the simultaneity of syllables deriving from various sources, an aural experience which should involve orchestration; but lacking that, he rushes them together sometimes using different type faces to gain prominence for one voice over another, yet just as frequently leaving the reader to pick his or her way through the avalanche. The strategy is perilous, for the novel could become formulaic in its very innovation; and yet also is highly susceptible to the best of Mega-Novel practices, its sense of disorder, mess, sheer chaos in our daily lives.

That inner world of Oscar's Civil War play, in which he tries to justify his grandfather's behavior and which becomes the subject of the novel's major legal action, is all words: monologues and dialogues, little or no action, just talk. This talk matches the layerings of the legal briefs, when Oscar sues on grounds that his serious play has been plagiarized and turned into a trashy and very successful film, *The Blood in the Red White and Blue*. But he is also suing over an automobile accident in which he has been significantly injured, and in turn is being sued on several fronts. What he considers as his art and his dignified position (he is actually an unsuccessful academic, untenured, an adjunct hanger-on) have been subsumed to legal arguments. Gaddis has mastered legal language so as to present it parodically; when it speaks for itself, it demonstrates that it generates its own comedy.

One legal case swirling around Oscar is based on a sequence which enthralls the American public: a dog, Spot, has become trapped inside a huge outside sculpture; and the question, in abstruse legal jargon, focuses on the rights of the artist and the humanitarian need to dismantle the sculpture to free the dog. Obviously, the public becomes embroiled, expectedly on the side of the dog and against the claims of the artist: a typical Gaddis strategy in which the integrity of the art object must hold its position against the onslaughts of those bred on sentiments from *Hard Copy, Entertainment Tonight,* or *Readers Digest.* Gaddis himself speaks of the original site for the sculpture as "epitomizing that unique American environment of moral torpor and spiritual vacuity"[138] that is requisite to his [the sculptor's] artistic endeavor.

The book's title has vast resonances in the layering of language, as it applies to law and, more broadly, to American culture. Harry, Oscar's brother-in-law (married to Oscar's stepsister, Christina) says that the hapless Oscar "goes off on a frolic of his own writes a play and expects the world to roll out the carpet for."[139] What is a frolic? Christina asks. Harry, a lawyer, calls it just a phrase which comes up sometimes in "cases of imputed negligence." An employee, for example, does something outside of his job description, such as putting "out an eye shooting paper clips with a rubber band they say he's on a frolic of his own, no intention of advancing his employer's business his employer's not liable"–the employer would possibly be liable if he knew about this horseplay and hadn't tried to stop it. Before Harry finishes, Christina interrupts to say that Oscar's play is different from shooting paper clips. It is hardly a frolic. But Harry tries to put the work in context as a longwinded affair about his grandfather–he wasn't hired to do it, "about somebody seeking justice nobody paid him to did they?"[140] It's not as though Oscar is a playwright–he never writes another–he simply becomes devoured by this singular effort.

The attempt to characterize Oscar's sincere (but over-inflated) work as a frolic is connected to the way legal language can be used to redirect everything into reductive categories. Christina charges Harry with saying everything in terms of "a whole legal brief." But what he is doing with the resonant word "frolic"–with its reverberations of pranks, merrymaking, fun acts–is turning it into something condemnatory so that it can be fitted into a legal system which constricts, displaces, distorts, and deceives with language. Oscar's effort, admittedly a piece of sludge, is not permitted to keep its integrity even in terms of how it is characterized or mocked. From Harry's point of view, the play is not only a frolic, in the eyes of the law on the level of shooting paper clips, but a means by which Oscar can spit at the world for rejecting his work. For Harry, the legal realist, Oscar has created a persona for himself as an artist, and then is behaving as though the persona were the person. His interest in legal action, according to his brother-in-law, is not based on law, nor is his play based on artistic principles–both are founded on resentment; most of all, on Oscar's need to act out his fantasies that he is civilization's last man interacting with cultural thugs.

Gaddis plays his usual double game, which is open-ended, as the Mega-Novel demands. He can condemn the legalese, which he displays parodically; and at the same time he can undermine what seems to be the last stronghold against legalese, the artist and his art. As in *J R*, he can vaunt language as the means by which we deceive and corrupt, at the same time use language as a way of expression which attempts to move beyond deception. The artist is imperfect, art is imperfect, and both are subject to some of the same parodic handling as the legal system. In the case concerning the sculpture in which the dog Spot becomes trapped, Gaddis has his epitome: a reprise in some ways of Wyatt Gwyon's predicament in *The Recognitions*, a counterfeiter and yet purer and more idealistic than those who shape his career or sell his work; and the world of JR, a young boy so formed by the financial culture that he can build an empire founded on sand, deception, and corruption of youth.

Most of all, language corrupts. Art in trying to counter the subversion of words is self-corrupting, often false, frequently its own parody–as Oscar's Civil War play turns out to be. Art does not save, although there is no other salvation: thus the litotes-like conundrum Gaddis poses. While the artist holds himself (or herself) above cultural thuggery, he is himself always tainted by the dissolution he disdains. Oscar argues he is not interested in money, and yet money dominates his thought as much as artistic integrity. As in *J R*, nearly all is breakdown; entropy underlies all systems, not only law. Communication and information have been traduced, language reduced to multiple acts of deception.

A refrain for the novel is that the clock is running, the familiar cry of the legal profession and a blast of fear for the layman. The "clock is running" has within it several paradoxical elements–reminiscent of Joseph McElroy's refrain "Wide Load" in *Women and Men*. The running clock is of course directly associated with billing procedures; so that when Oscar's lawyer snacks, Oscar wonders if he is being billed for soup and sandwich. Time is money: the ultimate statement of a financially oriented, self-consuming culture. But the running clock has other, even more sinister dimensions: that the culture cannot even enjoy its time without measuring it in billing. In another respect, that "the clock is running" suggests an asexual society, since the clock pre-empts feeling; when money counts, when billing is all, all other activity by contrast is trivial. Not only sex, but all relationships are subverted by a running clock, inasmuch as once the profane is established, every act is tarnished. And, of course, time is running on, and out!

What is remarkable about this Mega-Novel is how integrated all elements are, one of the most difficult accomplishments in a form which seems endless and open-ended. *A Frolic of His Own* could have gone on indefinitely: with extensions of what are already long excerpts from Oscar's Civil War play; a further extension of the law cases and the introduction of new cases; the continuation of Oscar's difficulties, more appeals, more legal statements; the presentation of additional people to expand the swirl, to create further maelstroms; and so on into a novel far more than the present almost 600 dense pages.

Yet except for the play itself, Gaddis has managed to put it together; and the way in which he has accomplished this is part of the novelist's craft, often so missing in those, like Mailer, who simply write long books. Gaddis avoids sequencing and seriatim narratives through several strategies. Paradoxically, he does this through his use of narrative itself. He has conceived of narrative in very personal terms, for he has complicated the reader's usual expectations of first and third person. Pronominal blurring[141] is one key to the Gaddis method. When we examine a representative passage, we find that pronomial blurring occurs through interrupted, incomplete speech, through bending of syntax, and, most of all, through the proliferation of voices implied but not identified. Early in the novel, Oscar receives a letter, "Dear Professor Crease, he's got one of those awful typewriter that writes in script. Perhaps my earlier letter did not reach you."[142] The writer goes on about Oscar's grandfather as a member of the Supreme Court and the subject of a book on the Holmes court, when suddenly a voice comes in, "you're not planning to see this person are you?"

In the single paragraph, we have three dissident voices: the writer, with his or her request; Oscar's own interruption on the "awful typewriter"; and the voice of his stepsister, Christina, warning him. Yet the three voices proliferate through implication: the "Dear Professor Crease" opening comes from Oscar, but in a direct statement different in tone and attitude from his comment on the typewriter; and then the voice of Christina which is both cautionary and almost indistinguishable from the very request the letter writer is seeking, an interview with "Professor Crease."

Pronouns no longer dominate as distinguishing features. The narrative sucks in the reader so as to become an active player, since sense derives from what voice the reader ascribes to the words: not just the identity of the voice, but its tones, attitudes, gestural quality. There is body English in the words, an implied semiotic language the reader must discern. While such a method may prove disconcerting to readers in a hurry or disinclined to read carefully–reviewers, some critics, readers fed on lesser stuff–the method proves binding. It gives Gaddis a tool to make his material cohere, since he established early on confidentiality with the reader. In some curious way, he demonstrates that other authors' use of pronouns distances text from reader; whereas elimination of pronominal dominance links text and reader and creates a coherence often lacking long, complicated books. In McElroy's *Women and Men*, a much longer work, the narrative is held together less by traditional means than by the author dipping in and out of conscious/

subconscious tones and attitudes. Pronouns there, too, are blurred. Such ambiguity, paradoxically, binds.

The master for this blurring of voices is Faulkner, especially in his *Absalom, Absalom!* For Faulkner, the problem was the extent to which a narrative–or what passed for it–can be established when all texts are embedded in personal histories which lack objectivity. Each character has his/her story to relate; and this is certainly the case with Gaddis's roster. In addition to telling their stories, the characters are play-acting roles in dramas of their own making–certainly this is true of Oscar, who focuses only on those matters which lead back to himself. So if all is subjective, the problem becomes how one tells and retells. Gaddis recognizes that the probable order of characters' stories has little to do with the way he must present those stories as the novelist's arrangement of his materials. One kind of discourse insists on a chronological sequencing, but the characters, caught in memory, role-playing, and self-expression, cannot always fit themselves into the chronologies which exist in the author's plan. Accordingly, we observe something of a clash, between the conventions we expect in ordinary sequencing of events and the actual way in which the story unfolds: what becomes a kind of sub-textual narrative: there, but not visible.

That subtextual or even invisible narrative is caught in our expectation of pronouns–*he* this, *she* that, *it*, etc. When that is missing, we supply the pronouns, but silently and tentatively because our assignments are not always clear, or identifiable. Thus, as readers, we are engaged intensely, not only to figure out who is speaking and to whom the words are being directed, but in other areas as well: in the very way the novel is to be arranged, concerning past and present; in definition of events themselves; in attempts to get beneath the characters' posturing and, in Gaddis's case, beneath the stringent irony. That engagement, seemingly so necessary in an open-ended subgenre like the Mega-Novel, makes textures, voices, memory, into forms of narrative. It permits Gaddis to project a seemingly unending text without the fear it will drift or float away; and even the barrage of words the reader cannot escape has within it strategies of coherence, identifiability, and purpose. America lies defined in that barrage, nowhere more incisively than in this kind of Mega-Novel.

A NOTE:

Another possible candidate for inclusion as a Mega-Novel is Alexander Theroux's *Darconville's Cat* (1981).[143] The arguments for inclusion are of several kinds: a multiple-layered narrative; an extended and innovative play on language; the presentation of several other forms or genres within the text–poems, a play, essays; the sense of open-endedness in the author's experimentation with postmodern narrative forms and with language; and, most of all, Theroux's ability to move about in texts without restrictions as to voice, tone, point of view. All these suggest Mega-Novel strategies, and they help invigorate the novel.

Yet there is another side to this, and that is a kind of sub-agenda to Theroux's book which moves it into a heuristic, sermonistic, pedagogic venture. The novel is, in reality, not so open-ended as the strategies would seem to indicate, but closed in a moralistic system, and, therefore, not at all what the Mega-Novel suggests. The latter does not settle or resolve; it does not even offer options. It in effect creates a world neither moral nor amoral, not even nonmoral; and it has no message, no play between good and evil, or love and hate, or between God and Satan. *Darconville's Cat* is another kind of fiction altogether, a kind of New Age pot pourri, possibly more message and moral imperative than fiction. For all its inventiveness of forms and languages, it stumbles over itself, more essay than assay.

A further entrant in the Mega-Novel category is Richard Powers's *The Gold Bug Variations* (1991),[144] with its play on Bach's Goldberg Variations, but more evidently on Poe's tale "The Gold Bug." The main movement in the lengthy Powers novel is a search: of a geneticist, Stuart Ressler, who, at the time of Watson and

Crick, is attempting to crack the genetic code. This quest has within it qualities of both science and art, and it immediately calls up an earlier Mega-Novel, Gaddis's *The Recognitions*. The Powers book takes the form of a detective story, as two people much later, after the event, try to discover what Ressler was up to: plot moves which recall the trail Wyatt Gwyon in *The Recognitions* leaves, or the trail he tries to disguise. Just as Gaddis examined how art is "done," so Powers analyzes how science and knowledge are defined. In one respect, the couple seeking the scientist are like those attempting to duplicate a kind of double helix pattern: they will, as it were, intertwine with the scientist, a literary version of the double helix, if they succeed.

The key is the unlocking of the mystery, not only of the genetic code but also of Ressler himself. "I need to know exactly what happened to Stuart Ressler between 1957 and 1983,"[145] the narrator says. As in good Mega-Novel conventions, *The Gold Bug Variations* plays on the indeterminancy of time. The narrator, O'Deigh (a name itself linked to day time), describes what occurs on a given day in history in her assignment as reference librarian; but this specific information is juxtaposed to her uncertainties about the larger picture, the facts about Ressler himself, whose goings-on remain mysterious and obscured. To "know," then, means to go beyond the factual details of what happened to what it suggests, how it resonates, what patterns it fits into. Fiction blends smoothly with biography, and, to some extent, with autobiography. O'Deigh's job, so to speak, deconstructs history; while her more active mind reconstructs it, or attempts to. "The language of life is luck,"[146] and the prototype of human experience itself lies in the mysteries of inheritance. The trick, as Mendel posited it, was to find the hidden recessive gene in biology.

Despite an innovative use of language and a sharp sense of structural strategies, *The Gold Bug Variations* does seem derivative, much Gaddis, some Pynchon, a little Barthelme, a trickle of Auster. The pursuit recalls *The Recognitions* and *V.*; the clipped language is reminiscent not only of Pynchon but of Hawkes; the irony and wryness suggest Barthelme; and the search for the authentic amidst the artificial and the counterfeit recapitulates a large strain in postwar American fiction. While the Powers novel is an ambitious undertaking, and commendable for that alone, its reverberations are considerably minimized by its derivative qualities; as such, it loses thrust as a Mega-Novel, or as something unique.

CHAPTER FOUR

THE NEW REALISM-HOW NEW IS IT?

FORD, BELLOW, CANIN, OZICK, STONE, ACKER, BANKS, OATES, BAKER, MATTHIESSEN, PROULX

Realism is not what it used to be. Startling about the "New Realism" in American fiction is how stretched realism itself has become. Like the country, it is often unrecognizable. If we think of the term historically, in Dreiser, Lewis, Wright, Wharton, Cather, Anderson, even Hemingway, and earlier in Crane and Norris, we recognize that while realism was never narrow in these writers, it is now as broad as fiction itself. It is, in fact, tempting to view the newer forms of realism as the be-all of mainstream North American fiction of the last twenty years. As America changes, the newer realism seems to define the way most of America insists on seeing itself.[147]

A case in point: the work of Richard Ford, especially his *The Sportswriter*, in 1986, and *Independence Day*, nine years later. To move back momentarily, however: ordinarily, realism is linked to American pragmatism and empiricism: we see what we see, we understand what we understand, and we perceive what exists out there. Realism tends to disregard and displace a literature based on fantasy, magic, or spiritualism. It also seems to exclude elaborate techniques, in which the "normal" is deconstructed or reconstructed, reshaped, refocused. In many of its guises, although certainly not in all, it parallels journalism; it least parallels poetry, although some of its prose may be "poetic." Our traditional realists are usually not associated with experimentation or innovation in narrative; no Faulkner or Joyce for them, although they may play around with involved temporal sequences and interpolated or interrupted scenes. They are, all in all, straightforward, their narratives clearly defined so that the reader feels comfortable. Strategies, narrative or otherwise, are rejected as alien to the very realism that such authors purport to present.

Yet our sense of this kind of realism must be expanded. Our "new realists" offer up much more psychological apparatus than did earlier authors in this vein; they have also moved into some experimentation with language. Narrative itself has become entangled, although not to the extent we find, for example, in Faulkner, in his *Absalom, Absalom!*. Even part of the "magical" or fantasy aspect we do not ordinarily associate with realism has been appropriated: internalized, ghost ridden, shadowy materials as subtexts. We might cite a novel like Cynthia Ozick's *The Messiah of Stockholm*, but also novels by a group as disparate as Richard Ford, Russell Banks, Joyce Carol Oates, Robert Stone, Joan Didion, and Alice Walker. This entire book, in one respect, could have been written from a "new realist" perspective, including authors as different as Cormac McCarthy, Gaddis, Pynchon, and most of those I have cited as "new." As in all things, the question becomes one of degree; there are realists and then there are realists.

Richard Ford's work is such a good place to begin because while he appears so neutral, so traditionally realistic, he is, in fact, an internalized, shadowy writer with profound psychological contexts. Like so many "new realists," he is not quite what he seems. *The Ultimate Good Luck*, in 1981,[148] is a working-through of some of the pressing influences on Ford, the presences he had to escape or control in order to define his own kind of realism. He was clearly caught up by the tough guy novelists, Hemingway, Chandler,

Hammett, perhaps the western writers, Max Brand, Zane Grey, Luke Short, even Louis L'Amour. All flow with excesses of masculine juices. *Good Luck* is a book a writer has to expunge from his system; not because it is poor or insufficiently achieved, but because it is not the style the writer is most comfortable with. He, or she, writes his way into what becomes his middle style often through a book that seems to come from a very different corner of his talent. *The Ultimate Good Luck* is Ford's working through: that hard, tough guy pose, full of ungiving, inflexible thoughts and sentiments, so much at odds with the later more flexible, more sensitive tones and verbal dimensions of *The Sportswriter* and *Independence Day*.

Not that Ford was that young when he published *Good Luck*, at thirty-seven, or even his other novel, *A Piece of My Heart*, at thirty-three. Considering that twenty-five is now the age when writers establish their presence, a writer in his early to later thirties is a mature man; and, therefore, it is all the more remarkable that Ford was able, by *The Sportswriter*, in 1986, to redefine his voice and write one of the more compelling novels of the last twenty years. Withal, what makes it compelling is language; and what makes it distinctive is the author's refusal to let traditional realism dictate its terms.

But before we move to that, we should observe that in his protagonist, Harry Quinn, in *Good Luck*-foreshadowing Frank Bascombe in *Sportswriter* and *Independence Day*-Ford limned one of his characteristic peripheral men. A Ford peripheral is a dropout, and he represents a country that the author identifies as having become peripheral-that is, lacking wholeness. Early in *Good Luck*, Quinn is presented:

> He had a sense when he joined the marines that the country he was skying out of was a known locale, with a character that was exact and coordinate and that maintained a certain patterned feel. A thing you could get back with if you had a reason. But that patterned feel had gotten disrupted some-

how, as though everything whole had separated a little inch, and he had dropped back in between things, to being on the periphery without a peripheral perspective.[149]

With that recognition, Quinn becomes a Ford tough guy who is not really tough. He does carry a gun during a tense time in Mexico, and although he does kill people, his level of survival lies not in killing or in shootouts-no Cormac McCarthy, he-but in trying to find some ground he can stand on. He seeks something *his*, even though he has involved himself in a situation that almost sucks the life out of him: an anomic girlfriend (Rae), her druggie brother now in a Mexican jail, dealers who believe the brother has ripped them off, and a trigger-happy Mexican army, shooting guerrillas, terrorists, civilians.

Quinn's desperate maneuvering to save himself and Rae is part of his self-defining. Like other Southern-Western writers, Ford emphasizes space, the individual discovering his own space amidst vastness. He is not community or social-minded; his concerns start at the smallest common denominator, the single person usually standing against a stark exterior, overcome by problems which, seemingly, emanate from some indeterminate world. He must sustain himself through his own reserves; he cannot count on others.

Ford's new realistic stance removes him and us from naturalistic determinism, from the dominance of things, from a cradle to grave struggle against social forces and from the destructive enticements of America itself. Unlike DeLillo and even Auster, Ford uses family as something his protagonists must separate from, or avoid, or maneuver around. Their ability to handle this separation is an indicator of their ability to survive the poisons flowing from institutions, attachments, and other destructive elements. In some final sense, although Ford's men stand alone, they are not unilaterally macho or aggressive-once again, distinguishing themselves from more traditional realistic protagonists. They may be passive, like the sportswriter Bascombe, but their enterprises, nevertheless, will force them to keep part of themselves separate;

in Bascombe's case, on the road, in alien hotel and motel rooms, in casual affairs of the heart, in writing sports stories which, somehow, do not connect. Through it all, these protagonists insist on holding to their own stories, to the possibilities of shaping or reshaping themselves-a key to the new realism of the last twenty years. They do not fall victim to history or to pastness.

They must work through uncertainties, usually by way of some inner resource that is inchoate and incoherent. Ford established this early on in *A Piece of My Heart*. As even the title indicates, the search is on, the quest for one's heart. The theme reaches its peak with Frank Bascombe in *The Sportswriter* and *Independence Day*, passive, laid back, trying to be cool, concerned where his heart is, yearning to understand not the world but his place in it. He must not invent but reinvent himself. As the country has reshaped itself, so must he.

Even Ford's short stories repeatedly carry this point: that self-definition comes only by withdrawing into what one is, after some quest or pursuit which proves fruitless except for the eventual discovery of self. In "Rock Springs," Early tries to define himself by running, stealing cars, keeping one step ahead of whatever is pursuing him even as he pursues himself. Space is all, even as he dissolves into it. Similarly, Sims, in "Empire," caught in the spatiality of the country, "felt alone in a wide empire, removed and afloat, calmed, as if life was far away now, as if blackness was all around, as if stars held the only light."[150] Seemingly lost, he is undergoing the characteristic Ford oceanic feeling as part of his effort to achieve self-definition, *even* as he recognizes it may prove impossible.

In the process, Ford discovered that language need not be bizarre; it can be characterized as "neutral." In *The Sportswriter*,[151] it does not move startlingly in any direction, there are no extremes, and it serves its primary function as a narrating voice. It puts us at ease. Although it moves in and out of the protagonist's voice-the novel begins *Moby-Dick* like, "My name is Frank Bascombe. I am a sportswriter"-there is no effort to achieve interior monologue or streams of association and consciousness. The interior voice of

Bascombe remains one of steady narrative quality. Yet Ford's great achievement is that with this basic tool, a neutral voice, he is able to gain a wide range of emotional and psychological life. The point he makes is that his novel of neutral narrative, without flourishes, dazzling derring-do, metaphysical flights, or deterministic doom, may also be representative of America-and this achieved without his dipping into stereotypical language.

Ford has gotten the neutral voice down so perfectly that his sportswriter is a representative American, spanning in his modest way the entire breadth of the American experience within its middle ranges. This, too, is a new form of realism. No psychopathic behavior, no manic flights, no violent undercurrents, no morbid pressure from environment, heredity, or immediate society. Bascombe is merely a good chronic depressive, characteristic of a type in the 1980s, when the hype of the 60s and the blandness of the late 70s resulted in a laid-back, somewhat cynical, somewhat passive response to whatever lies out there. He already knows, or comes to learn when he visits a paraplegic former football player, that activity, yearning, willing of self end up in the same place; that the mature person, as Emerson counseled, must try to have good days, or even good moments, and forgo sweeping ideas of happiness. Nothing extends, nothing lasts, nothing goes much beyond a momentary high. Then, when it all recedes, one is back to a chronic depression, for which Ford's neutral prose is a perfect vehicle. This is not Hemingway nihilism; it does not end in suicide; the voice is, in fact, the only possible voice of survival.

The quiet, almost bland language of *The Sportswriter* turns out to be a representative medium for the new realism of the 1980s. It perfectly accommodates the novel's assumptions: a sportswriter who must lose himself in the achievements of others in order to express his own opinion. Swallowed by other people and events, Bascombe emerges only in the word, which, as he recognizes, is insufficient for emotional life behind the event or personal motive. A man on the road, rueful, not joyous or seeking thrills, a broken marriage and a child left behind, withal a keen awareness of human frailty in carrying out his duties; a country which never coalesces, a personal life in which nothing is resolvable, relationships momentarily satisfactory but fleeting and not repeatable, days in hotels and motels where life is regurgitated as detritus-all of this is part of the neutrality of the Ford novel.

> I am always hoping [Bascombe expresses about a quarter through the novel] for a great surprise to open in what has always been a possible place for it-comradeship among professionals; friendship among peers; passion and romance. Only when the facts are made clear, I can't bear it, and run away as fast as I can-to Vicki [his new companion], or sitting up all night in the breakfast nook gazing at catalogs or to writing a good sports story or to some woman in a far-off city whom I know I'll never see again. It's exactly like when you were young and dreaming of your family's vacation; only when the trip was over, you were faced with the empty husks of your dreams and the fear that that's what life will mostly be-the husks of your dreams lying around you. I suppose I will always fear that whatever *this* is, is *it*.[152]

If the 1980s and 90s have meant anything to those who see beneath the hype and the degradation of language, it is that America has become part of a finite world. *The Sportswriter* shadows that finite world, without subverting momentary pleasures-occasional good sex, a fine phrase, a meaningful gesture. But anything beyond is the language of the foolhardy, unperceptive, and hypocritical. When Bascombe visits the paralyzed football player, Herb, he is made to understand what the sportswriter does not write about: that a man does not face his decline and uselessness with courage, but with hostility and self-hatred. All heroism is squeezed out. After the benefits, the fund-raisers, the fine words, what is left is a crippled man confronting the rest of his life. There is no relief, only days piled on days. This is the language America evades, of course, but it is the language it must face. Bascombe tries.

Ford found the perfect career for his protagonist. He has matched language, individual, and society to job, then job and its implications to what he wants to say about individual and country. A sportswriter is in a strange position. He is honored for his knowledge of games and for his prose, but he is, after all, writing on the sports page, not as part of the more significant death culture on the news pages. He is someone interested in games and players, which places him somewhere in the category of child-man, boy-man; not fully adult or serious, since it is, all in all, only a game. And athletes, while honored and rewarded extraordinarily, are not really serious people; they get paid for playing, for being part of an entertainment that in nearly all sports carries one back to childhood. The athlete, rightly or wrongly, has not been given credit for much intelligence; and his or her education, such as it is, is nearly always suspect, even when good grades result. Anyone who writes about such players is, accordingly, neither serious nor adult, not a mature person, even a marginal one.

Frank Bascombe has assimilated all those ambiguities of his career. He likes being outside: riding the rails, or taking planes, poking into the private lives of others, being a temporary in-and-out type, living in hotels out of suitcases, experiencing pickup affairs, getting his copy from whatever tidbits the athletes drop into his lap. His job does not require enormous expenditures of mental energy, simply certain deftness, a turn of phrase, a sense of language, since so many sports stories repeat each other or are homogenized. The fan expects courage, determination, will, the desire for victory-and the sportswriter feeds this expectation. Sports are an alternative to the news pages and obituaries, and woe to the sportswriter who fails to provide that alternative. Like film critics or Hollywood observers, sportswriters deal in their own kind of reality. He, or she, signals speciality, without being anyone or anything in particular. The sportswriter is often most read, but, socially, least regarded.

Furthermore, no matter how excellent, the sportswriter does not have to engage himself deeply; the pursuit is, as noted, only sports, a childish reflection of life, not life. In still another area, sports writing means that Bascombe can move in a world of men, other writers, the athletes, their coaches and trainers, and publicists. This is a compelling point, for Bascombe is very much aware of himself as a man, and when he is not on the road, he belongs to a Divorced Men's group. Ford's protagonist is responding to the feminist movement, not with overt hostility, but in his drawing back to the support of other men, a kind of forerunner of Robert Bly's woodsy men beating drums, chests, and perhaps their meat. But Bascombe's world is laid back, uncommunicative, without emotional intensity; he identifies with those who clamp down on their feelings, especially since all his emotional life has been directed to his son's death. Bascombe *can* feel, as evidenced by his superb musings on his young son's end, but he parcels it out, husbands it, does not engage in display.

But there are other emanations of Bascombe. As a kind of double for the sportswriter is the unfortunate figure of Walter Luckett. Luckett seems perfectly ordinary, but he has had what he considers an "accident" in his past, a homosexual encounter that has unsettled him and made him in his eyes incomplete. His encounter is no big deal for Bascombe, but Luckett refuses solace from those who try to pep him up. The crossover comes in Frank's own inability to be pepped up. Although reasonably optimistic about himself as a writer, he feels incomplete emotionally, drained, enervated, playing out the game, an old athlete well past his prime but still in it for the money. Like Walter, with his dread of what he did, Frank experiences an undercurrent of doom, the fear he cannot pull it all together. Walter's suicide is a manifestation of one area of Frank that has rejected commitment. But there is still another side, reflected by the crippled football player, Herb. Frank interviews him, and is full of the usual approaches, to cheer him, tell him he has something left; but Herb refuses all sympathy or support. He stares into his paralyzed condition, and he knows his accident has made him permanently incomplete. This, too, becomes part of Frank's recognition of self.

In this triangulated arrangement, Ford is fictionally reshaping one's perception of the decade, reaching deeply into emotional matters but not taking the self to impotence or destruction. His insistence on the ordinary with an intense outreach is key to his kind of realism. An instance comes with Frank's lady friend, Vicki, a hotdog of a woman who refuses the depression and withdrawal she perceives in Frank. She insists on her own kind of reality, which blinds her to everything outside her immediate vision. Frank is nervous in his visit to her home, a right wing, redneck setup (in his eyes) that he tries to understand. She and her family represent the country, he the outsider, and the two cannot possibly mesh. He speaks too much, he misses the need for silence, and he errs on the side of effort; to the extent she realizes he does not fit. This absurd family suddenly closes ranks, and Frank is on the periphery, shut out because of some perceived deficiency. Yet because of his split self, he knows things Vicki can never know; he knows about the "small empty moments" that cannot be avoided. He knows that his withdrawals alternating with his talkiness are part of self-destructive rhythms every sensitive person experiences: *they* are the norm, the ordinary. He also knows she will lose interest in him the more he attempts to reach her; he knows Vicki wants something-and he is not sure what it is-but he cannot give; and yet he tries to talk his way into it. He reaches out to embrace those "empty moments," and they engulf him; they lock him in as a sportswriter.

What remains strong and true are his memories of Ralph Bascombe, the nine-year-old wasting and dying. That is the one anchor in his life, the singular moment when he can concentrate all the hopes and failures that have gone into him. It is death, not life, which grabs him. "In his last days," Ford writes, "Ralph changed. Even in his features, he looked to me like a bird, a strangely straining gooney bird, and not like a nine-year-old boy sick to death and weary of unfinished life. Once he barked out loud to me like a dog, sharp and distinct, then he flopped up and down in his bed and laughed. Then his eyes shot open and burned at me, as if he knew me better than I knew myself and could see all my faults."[153] Somehow, Frank cannot get past this scene. The novel, in fact, begins with a vigil he and his former wife hold at their son's graveside; it is the determining point.

What Ford has captured is an extremely complicated kind of life, and he has done so in language that by avoiding all extremes becomes a guideline in the new realism since the 1960s. As we have observed, no hyperventilation, no hyperbole, no extreme scenes or emotional outbursts, no hard violence, no brutality of spirit, none of the anomie and nihilism we associate with twentieth-century American fiction. There is a rootedness to the language, just as there is to Frank; and yet beyond or under the rootedness is that awareness of the terrible sorrow of life, that negation and emptiness in the American soul. Frank must seek out his experiences on the fringes, in a fringe career and with fringe women. He has denied himself complacency; and yet even as he drifts toward the suicidal Walter and the paralyzed Herb, he insists on that small space the individual keeps to provide self-definition.

There is a parable for the 80s buried in here: not a simple message, but one loaded with complexities. Below the patina of a basically moral and ethical life lies the despondency of the particular experience, the shakiness of the enterprise, the inability to make connections, the awareness of destabilization everywhere-death of son, breakup of marriage, suicide of friend, crippling of player(s), the uncertainties of who and what one is, the inability to find one's location, and the difficulty of recovering the space whereby one gains definition. Avatar of the new century, the sportswriter says it all.

Sequels often disappoint, but *Independence Day* strengthens Ford's position as the advocate of the "new realism"-extremes brought to the center by way of a mediating prose, the abnormal made to appear normal. With this novel, Ford is perhaps working through what Updike tried with his Rabbit Angstrom sequences, providing a Frank Bascombe for each decade. In several respects, *Independence Day* is a book for the 90s-and it could have been placed in that chapter-as much as *The Sportswriter* was a book for the 80s. One difference with the Rabbit books is that Ford has not lost his tone and become bombastic or overwrought. If anything, the later book is at least as incisive as the earlier and, in its way, reflective of a decade, of 90s confusion, desire for direction, and withdrawal. If nothing else, *Independence Day* is a cautionary tale: not for its warnings, but for its implied moral message, directed at the individual. It is a recognition that American will, determination, even desire have leveled off; that if the individual is to come through, he (less so, she) must settle for different goals from those in the frantic 80s or even the divided 70s.

In the later novel, Bascombe has gone from sports writing to real estate, a shift that cannot be lost on us: from the ephemeral, from gamesmanship, from peripheral writing, to something as substantial as houses, land, furnishings, architecture. As Ford comments:

> ... people never find or buy the house they say they want. A market economy, so I've learned, is not even remotely premised on anybody getting what he wants. The premise is that you're presented with what you might've thought you didn't want, but what's available, whereupon you give in and start finding ways to feel good about it and yourself. And not that there's anything wrong with that scheme. Why should you only get what you think you want, or be limited by what you can simply plan on? Life's never like that, and if you're smart you'll decide it's better the way it is.[154]

This is a culture of "let's settle." Real estate is the emblem of America; the home as part of the "hut dream," in which the individual and family think of themselves as part of an Eden-like setting. It is a perception, not a reality. Although this exists as a long tradition in American fiction, Ford runs it by us with a distinct twist. In more conventional terms, the home is sanctuary, sacred, a holy place where the family works through its years as part of a community *but also* as a separate, independent unit. To be an adult, one must own a home and a piece of property; but whether or not it is actually part of the American dream, it is definitely part of a mythic sense of a return to the Garden, to a life when one was free to achieve or fulfill oneself. It was, obviously, a mythic experience, a fantasy or dream; but it embodied an America that could still think of itself as rural and innocent even as it became urban and criminal, even as its rural life turned increasingly sour with drugs, crime, bigotry. The reality, however, did not negate the fantasy aspect of the ideal. But here Ford breaks with the conventions and reveals how one must settle for far less. Yet without giving up entirely the idea of the dream. This is the perfect emblem of Independence Day, the holiday during which all the novel's activity takes place.

As in *The Sportswriter*, all life is triangulated. Here the points of departure are: the home, the individual life that is both free and restrained, and the outside world of "independence," embodied in the annual holiday. While the Fourth has lost most of its original significance, it does in part recall what the individual owes to himself and to the community: what is emblematic in the home, in real estate, in the individual, and in social space. Working through 1990 millennium ideas of dispersement, displacement, and alienation, Ford is trying to discover where the center holds-his abiding commitment to that neutral world where upheavals are contained in seemingly ordinary prose. A real estate agent, divorced, his dead son still weighing heavily, with a teenage son now a trouble spot, Bascombe needs to put together a life. As he says early on, the sad fact "about adult life is that you see the very things you'll never adapt to coming toward you on the horizon. You see them as the problems they are, you worry like hell about them, you make provisions, take precautions, fashioning adjustments; you tell yourself you'll have to change your way of doing things. Only you don't."[155] What Bascombe experiences, instead, is what he calls the "Existence Period," a practice of his middle years in which he ignores much of what he dislikes or what seems "worrisome and embroiling."[156] The new realism insists on pulling back.

The Existence Period-very close to that Emersonian injunction to experience good days, mentioned above-is the neutral ground where Ford operates so well and where his prose can surround ordinary situations without distorting them. The Period is also a norm, a median area, more than simply "space." It suggests a place of sanity amidst the swirl of disturbing developing events: his rebellious and emotionally sick son, the murder of a black real estate agent with whom Frank was having a casual affair, the remarriage of his wife to a wealthy twerp who takes himself very seriously, the ups and downs of the real estate market itself, all emblems of Frank's own emotional and psychological sliding responses. Deep within that swirl is what calms the maelstrom of events and feelings, the Existence Period.

By allowing sufficient withdrawal of self to insure sanity, the Period, at least in part, symbolizes the melancholy 90s, when withdrawal, retreat, passivity seem the only survival mechanism against folly. Whether such a perception is true or not, Ford does capture the "feel" of the era: the real estate metaphor, which includes tending one's own garden, establishes terms in which temporary sanity becomes possible.

The novel moves inexorably toward a disaster, although the calming effect of Frank helps deceive us on the way to catastrophe. His Existence Period must be put to the test. It comes in the perfect "middle ground" of American experience, Frank's trip with his troubled son, Paul, to Cooperstown, the home of baseball's Hall of Fame. Paul is recalcitrant, emotionally upset-still dismayed by the death of his dog, not to speak of his brother-unable to deal with his parents' split, but highly intelligent and perceptive in his bearish way. Frank sees the trip-a custodial event not fully acceptable to his ex-wife-as a way of creating some relationship with his son, on this Independence Day holiday. But disaster is implicit in the endeavor, for while Frank has reached deep into his Existence Period for survival, Paul has not found any anchor for his hostility and anger. His sole way to create interest in his hostile feelings, when minor disturbances and a bashing language fail, is to find some way to become injured. This he does, once again in that American middle ground, in a batting cage at Cooperstown when he ignores all safety measures and is struck in the eye by a baseball. The eye may be lost, but reconstructive work on it enables Paul to come to some terms with himself; and it enables Frank to reach more deeply into himself, for some meaning, beyond his Existence Period-independence day for both. Lest we think they have found happiness, Ford has the holiday parade in Haddam, New Jersey, Frank's mythical kingdom, skirt close to the cemetery where his first son is buried. That death will never be laid to rest, even as the Existence Period has permitted him to come through bad days into better ones.

There is no happiness, but there is accommodation. Ford leaves open the question of a successor volume to *Independence Day*. He mentions that Paul, upon recovery, may come to live with him during his crucial years; he, Frank, may get married. He has forsaken his Divorced Men's Club, and he appears on the edge of entering what he calls his Permanent Period, what Erik Erikson would call his stage of maturation. That period would be the long-drawn-out time when he would try to comprehend the mysteries of a broader life; but that remains for another book and, quite possibly, for another decade when the folly recedes or else takes on a different perspective. This level of uncertainty, ambiguity, possible directionlessness is, also, part of the New Realism. Few certainties, there!

If we wish to see the failure of the Old Realism, we need look no further than Saul Bellow's work in the last two decades. Since winning the Nobel Prize in literature, in 1976, Bellow has recycled and further narrowed his tones and views, already expressed in *Mr. Sammler's Planet*. His single tone is a detestation of the modern world, of modern women-those totems of breakdown in civility, most of all of what men have become. He is our poet laureate of hatred, of modernism and modernity. He is our plimsoll mark for such feeling, exemplified in *More Die of Heartbreak*, in 1987,[157] or in other work before and after.[158] His men are done in by scheming women, or by women with their own priorities; and while the men may seek some moral center, they are all part of Bellow's detestation of who we are and what we have become. Hatred is fine, but Bellow has not found either in language or strategies the means to make it meaningful.

If any writer has been done in by adherence to a political ideology, left or right, it is Bellow and his deference to neo-conservatism. Once magnanimous and able to stretch, he is now squeezed, tight, provincial. Short on ideas, short on ways to deal with a radically changing world, neo-cons sound liked tired Carlyles, offering only readmission to an earlier age, medieval, Victorian, or others, as alternatives to contemporary rot. Bellow's handling of such matters could, of course, still be significant if he had found a language for his diatribes; but his is a tired realistic language lacking in nuance, unsustained by wit (wit has become jokes!) uncompelling in its nagging insistence on how wrong we have become. Not ripeness but screed is all.

Bellow is good in revealing how joyless life has become, but his perception of that is not cast in wider terms, such as we find in Richard Ford, where lack of joy is associated with uncertainties and ambiguities in life which we must learn to handle. Bellow's assault on modern life is sour, without resonance, and without the grounding in character that might make it, psychologically, part of the New Realism; or else in language which might break from the tired clichés that express hatred of women (all those marriages and alimonies have apparently corrupted Bellow's ability to write objectively about women) and their "liberation." The personality of our time may be diseased, as he suggests in *More Die of Heartbreak*- it is hard to dispute that; but he has no way of connecting it to a larger vision of life, to lives which do go on, despite Bellow's inability to find the language for them. Rarely an innovative writer, he was nevertheless at one time a stretcher, a seeker, an explorer. Now he has pulled in, burrowed into secure ground, set up defenses against attack; and his prose has lost its gloss, its sheen, its brightness. The old realism lacks reverberation.

A more representative example of the older realism is full of the kinds of energy missing in Bellow even while the manner or method provides us with a benchmark of the older form. I have in mind Ethan Canin's *Blue River* (1991).[159] It is, in many ways, admirable, and possibly most admirable of all is how Canin shows us that realism in its traditional sense can still hold us. Two brothers have to come to grips with the fact that while they seem so different from each other they, in several respects, curve around to share numerous traits. One brother, Lawrence (Sellers), seems possessed by demons; he has a shriveled hand, which his mother feels he was born with because she felt such hatred for his father. He pursues a self-destructive course (stealing, drinking, hanging out) until his eighteenth birthday, when he apparently assumes responsibility for his life: holding a job, getting degrees, settling down. But in actuality, he is still demon-struck, an arsonist, a man who gets a young woman pregnant and then abandons her, a divisive force within his family from his lair in the basement of their house.

The other brother, Edward, is six years younger and, therefore, a follower for much of the novel; but he grows up and becomes quite the opposite of Lawrence. Edward turns to medicine, to ophthalmology, acquires a devoted wife, a son, a well-appointed home, and passes for a good citizen, which in the main he is. His appears to be the settled life, the opposite of his brother's drift. At the beginning of *Blue River*, after a long separation Lawrence visits for a brief time, intruding into the tightly organized life of his brother and creating a vague threat to Edward's wife and son.

Edward must rid the household of this driven, demonic brother, and he does so; but he himself has his own form of disturbing realism. He has a penchant for driving a lonely, curving, very dark road at night and closing his eyes for seconds as the car hurtles along. As a doctor, he is fully aware of the potential of this act, he and his dog in the hurtling car, the darkness overwhelming, the curves beckoning to disaster. He believes he may meet up with

Lawrence ahead, but he also senses he is twinning his brother's self-destructive mode. Even as he puts his life on the line, he hopes to find some transcending idea, some transformation, some inner sense of what he is doing, even what he meant when he drove Lawrence away earlier and, now, once again. The novel for the most part concerns brothers in somewhat the same way as John Edgar Wideman's *Brothers and Keepers*. As in the Wideman, while one brother is criminal, the other more respectable one also has criminal tendencies, although of a lesser sort. The brothers, seemingly so different, twin.

But manner is our concern here: the telling as much as what is told, the how more than the what. Much of *Blue River* takes the form of an extended commentary by Edward directed at Lawrence, now lost to the reader's sight. The coordinates of the novel remain solidly placed: objects, things, persons, relationships. There is little or no departure from a factual world, although there is some magical fascination with fire-fires are set, observed, and eventually traced to Lawrence. Yet fire is a device, not a form of magic. In Canin's hands, the older realism goes further than objectification; it goes into expectation. The reader's level of expectation is that matters will be worked through; that the objectification of things will extend to an objectified resolution; that whatever lies "out there" will eventually be clarified; and, finally, that even the mysteries-Lawrence's fires, Edward's blind driving- will have their explanation.

It is not simply that Canin always fulfills these expectations; it is that he is reassuring that he will, so that we assume, even when matters remain occluded, that they will be resolved. We are put at ease with a narrative that has its bizarre moments precisely because we can expect the bizarre to be enfolded into the recognizable, the assumed. Darks become lighter; shadows emerge into recognizable shapes; magical moments dissolve into motivation.

In a key passage full of modulations, Canin suggests how knowing is possible even in areas of great ambiguity: "In a facile way I [Edward] pointed out to him [a psychiatrist] that driving with my eyes closed on a wide nighttime highway pre-empted any foolish risk I might take in an operating suite, and though at this explanation he nodded forcefully and blinked down into his beard, I knew in the quiet way I have always known things in my life, that this was not exactly true."[160] Even the ambiguity here is "explained," and whatever demons exist in Edward are discoverable, identifiable, controllable. That defines traditional realism.[161]

Cynthia Ozick's brief novel, really a novella, *The Messiah of Stockholm*, in 1987,[162] seems to defy the New Realism mode. It is, after all, part of the search for the Messiah, and it raises the question whether the savior-the Jewish one, this time-has really arrived, or whether, as in the past he (not she) deceives us into thinking he has come. Yet in the very quest for the messiah-whom Ozick wittily locates as a potential deception within potential deceptions-she turns the matter of faith into an everyday affair; in fact, into writing. For this messiah is a manuscript, not a person; he is part of writing, and he must be treated as someone who exists only as words. There are no apparitions, sightings, ghosts, shadows-simply the words, the title of a novel reputedly lost, by Bruno Schulz, the Polish writer shot down by the Nazis. The locales for this messiah are not the heavens or the whirlwind, but a newspaper office, a bookstore, book-lined rooms.

In Ozick's version, the "god" has been brought down, or up, to the word. Lars Andemening, a minor book reviewer on a Stockholm newspaper, conceives that he is Bruno Schulz's son. Before he died Schulz had composed his masterpiece, *The Messiah*, and Lars tried to discover it while establishing his role as son to this now legendary father. When his would-be sister turns up with the manuscript, Lars must deal with several layers of deception and possible fact-in this respect, with what the messiah himself represents. Late in the novella, he determines-although without certainty-that she is a fake, that the manuscript she brings to him is a forgery, that he is being taken in by a group of confidence people and so he burns the manuscript in the amphora where it has been stored. Doubt remains-as it remains with the messiah. Lars cannot accept the reality of the manuscript, even though he has himself insisted on its existence and has maintained he is Schulz's son.

Ozick's work, then, is an attempt to recreate or recover a past that does not exist; or which exists only in fakery and flummery. *The Messiah* may well have been destroyed in the camps, as Lars believes; and yet there is the possibility it can surface-he has placed his belief on that. So his faith is tested, and he comes away recoiling and yet uncertain. In the face of the loss of everything in the Holocaust, there is the need to create a simulacrum of the past; but that past forces everyone into a deception in order to recreate a history that has been blanked out. Lars has helped shape a legend and enters into it, but when confronted with it cannot accept its reality. He has insisted on a monster that he must destroy, literally burn away. But the novel is also about "waiting"-for the messiah, for the manuscript, for the correct word. And what makes such an original idea come to life is Ozick's ability to turn the fanciful and the apparitional into something real, tangible, however false it may prove to be.

There is always the question whether Schulz's messiah is the true one, the one for whom the Jews have waited; but for lack of verification, one worships the false one, until he, too, must be destroyed. Lars's burning of the manuscript is his recognition the true messiah has not arrived; but Ozick's point goes beyond Lars's. For she has determined that the sole way the messiah might arrive is through the impulse that he might be real; through the possibility that truth lies not in words but in the desire of the believer. Here realism is stretched to include what is usually given to romance: the idea or ideal makes anything seem credible. Here, the New Realism includes what might not be, and by extending the "possible" it insists on forces older forms of realism often neglected.

As the title suggests, Robert Stone in *Outerbridge Reach* (1992)[163] was attempting to stretch his kind of realism into realms of possibility rather than simply depicting events. Much in this novel will recall his earlier work, *A Hall of Mirrors*, *Dog Soldiers*, and *A Flag for Sunrise*, in which a life on the edge can either go under or else gain substance through the prospect of change. It is a typical American subject, found in both the Old and the New Realism. For Stone, however, unlike most of his realist predecessors, the point in not winning, but becoming engaged. Process is all. One measures oneself through a test that may prove self-defeating; but, nevertheless, to enter into the test is the sole proof one is alive to possibility.[164]

In Stone's 1992 novel, the realistic possibilities of the narrative often give way to the quest, to the inner journey, to matters which have significance only within the individual, here Owen Browne, an Annapolis graduate. Browne has left the navy and when we meet him he is selling boats for a yacht brokerage in Connecticut. Now in his forties, American-style handsome, with muscular build and regular features-a version of the Marlboro man-he is on hold. He has been married for twenty years, with one rebellious daughter, unable to deny his career has reached a dead end. He appears to be a Fitzgerald character, with no second act to look forward to. When the owner of the yacht company-a man who runs a multinational corporate empire, a Robert Maxwell wannabee perhaps-vanishes in what is a typical 1980s scam or kiting scheme, Browne jumps at the opportunity to take over a yacht in a round-the-world race. Unfazed at being alone, he is in fact overjoyed at the prospect of a solitary trip. The race will be his test; it will bring out everything that he perceives as having gone wrong in his life and will either correct it, or make him confront irremediable failure.

In this brief description, we see the archetypal American strategy: the test or ordeal, the need to define and redefine oneself; but also matters which break from conventional realism and probe into the capabilities of the individual, into his very soul, as it were. A parallel plot line, and one more in keeping with the older realistic tradition, is the "shore" equivalent of Browne's test. His wife, Anne, is left behind, of course; she has attempted to stop his participation in the race because she fears the impact on their quiet, safe marriage. She suspects what will occur in feelings, attachments, loyalties, and the rest. But once she sees her husband is resolved, she agrees to help.

Hovering in the background is the filmmaker, Ron Strickland, and he is now prepared to come to the fore. He is an aging 1960s man, a Stone man-we envisage Nick Nolte in the role-maker of documentaries, a leftist (anti-Vietnam War documentary), a man who dabbles also in pornography-he has made a porno film about a prostitute, Pamela, who hangs around him. Strickland is himself facing an empty life and is seeking some fulfillment; cynical about permanent feelings, he hones in on Anne once her husband has gone chasing his chimaera. His insistent point is that her marriage and life have become stagnant, that while she has settled for less, "more" is possible. He recognizes she fears change because it will disrupt her cozy, complacent, deadening existence. He will become her "test." They enter into an affair, and the sex is, apparently, terrific. She becomes his slave of sorts. Husband and wife are now on somewhat parallel journeys-he to nature and she to human nature. A dead marriage means that one or both must break out, however destructive this may prove.

After the first part of the novel ends-a part given over to set-up material-the parallel lines of husband and wife make up the second part. Once this pattern is established, and we have gotten the feel of Browne's frittered-away life, we can accept his need for a challenge. To recognize that need and to act upon it is little less than the aphrodisiac of power. "The trick," Stone writes, "was to take pleasure in knowing what was true and to deprive the rest of the world of that knowledge. That was the power suggested in the Bible stories. The power of command over reality consisted in being party to its nature and possessing the knowledge exclusively. All at once Browne understood that such power would always be denied to him."[165] Yet he must battle against accepting that perception. There are, clearly, tragic potentialities here, in that the individual yearns for godlike powers only to recognize he will never possess them.

Yet Browne will test that very perception. Before sailing, he cuts and punctures himself badly, an accident that gives him the kind of mythical stature enjoyed by Philoctetes, the "wounded artist." Browne's act now becomes chancier, but he perseveres, and the wound heals-further expanding the mythical potential, to Parsifal or Jesus. One of the problems in the novel, in fact, is that Stone must constantly move the realistic material into mythical dimensions as a way of disguising his characters' stereotypical qualities. Browne has little to recommend him, a Fitzgerald retread; so that Stone moves him into higher realms. Similarly, his wife is an exhausted creature, waiting for something to enter her life to give it shape. Neither is engaging in himself or herself.

Once the race begins, Browne keeps two logs, indicating how perception of self and self-deception are intermixed. One log informs the monitoring group he is ahead; the other reveals how far behind he actually is, how he has been spooked by the venture. Like Martin Decoud in Conrad's *Nostromo*, he drowns himself, unable to handle a solitary existence. And on shore, film-maker Strickland, the seeming agent of change, is himself done in, as his logs are stolen, his video taken, his film project aborted. In this by now typical Stone view, the agent of change, the outsider-here an aging hippie, out of touch with feelings-comes to grief when his project collapses, a project based to some extent on self-deception.

Conrad lies heavily over the novel. The protagonist immerses himself in the destructive element only to be dragged down finally. He must efface or sacrifice himself in order to produce a greater show of self and ego. He emerges, if ever, only by submitting himself to the force or element that will, inevitably, prove self-destructive. Conrad, however, conveyed grandeur through prose and expansive contexts, through juxtaposition of character and setting in inventive narratives. Stone attempts to reach beyond mainly through the larger dimensions we call mythical; and in so doing he yearns after a newer form of realism. If elements, finally, do not quite mesh, we must nevertheless praise the effort to break out; for as Stone implicitly recognizes the old realism is no longer viable.

Surely reinforcing the New Realism are forces outside literature itself: mainly, the awareness that violence and anarchy have become part of the landscape, not only in the inner cities but in the higher reaches of government. The broken Presidencies (and the contempt we feel for them before they break), the assassinations of various leaders and spokesmen, the revelations of corruption at all levels of government, industry, and financial markets-all these reveal a kind of anarchy far more systemic and damaging than anything in the inner cities. This is not to underestimate that inner city breakdown is no less a sign of anarchy. All such activities, high and low, help create the deceptive illusions by which most Americans must still cling: that we are different from other countries in our democratic institutions; that we still represent progress; that despite subcultures and breakaway groups, we are still united, with common purpose; that despite all the signs of disintegration, decline, and moral flabbiness, we are rich, productive, unbeatable, and prepared to lead the rest of the world into the twenty-first century. Such illusions help feed New Realists because self-deception can no longer be caught in conventional terms. If we live in a perceived counterfeit culture, our fiction must reflect the larger fictions, and this is where New Realism flourishes.

Who catches this more aptly than Kathy Acker, especially in *My Death My Life By Pier Paolo Pasolini* (1984)![166] Pasolini was, of course, the Italian film director (as well as a writer and painter) who was murdered under particularly sordid conditions by his homosexual lover. Acker uses Pasolini, and his work, to reflect a counterfeit culture, along the way probing how that culture is shaped.

Acker has made a career of carving out from culturally based artifacts an imaginative interpretation of modern culture. She is a (mild) pornographer, synthesizer, a hostile and outraged rebel against complacency, respectability, and every version of bourgeois values. Breaking with conventional realism, she uses montage, verbal streams, self-reflexive devices, a tough guy language, and ever-shifting narrative strategies. We find some or all of these in *Kathy Goes to Haiti*, *Blood and Guts in High School*, *Great Expectations*, *Don Quixote*, and, more recently, in 1990, the three-part *In Memoriam to Identity*, much of it built on a rereading and reshaping of the Arthur Rimbaud legend. The import is to confound realistic expectations with a different kind of literary experience, more innovative than most but still close to what we are calling New Realism.

The Pasolini novel begins with a riff based on *Hamlet*, with a decided view of it from the feminist side. Hamlet's Maid, for example, accuses him of planning to marry Ophelia for her money; and Hamlet himself hopes to be a representational painter. "I will represent the poverty of spirit that the powers behind Reagan endorse. Economic poverty. Social poverty. Political poverty. Emotional poverty. Ideational poverty."[167] Acker then moves to her own version of *Romeo and Juliet*, in which Juliet asks her young lover: "What time tomorrow will we be able to fuck?" But Juliet also revels in her fame: "I'm getting to be so incredibly famous when I walk down the city street, people have to stop and ask me for my autograph."[168] Juliet is a liberated woman, on the attack: "Most men would rather fuck corpses than other women. How do I know this? Because men pay prostitutes but they don't pay other women to fuck,"[169] the implication being that, sexually, a prostitute is little better than a corpse.

Throughout the early pages of *Pasolini*, Acker seeks coordinates for his own violent, seedy, sleazy, and productive life. In *her* world, events occur without logical explanation, a point she carries into every aspect of American political and cultural life. In Pasolini's senseless death-a man he had had sex with drove the director's car over him-she sees the irrational, illogical, inexplicable world; and with this insight she runs wild. Hers is a rambunctious talent; at its worse, out of control and tedious in its yearning after meaning; at its best, witty, incisive, corrosive, inventive, and disturbing. Her tough guy, violence-prone language indicates she will not be typecast as a "woman writer," and her expressive use of narrative forms signals that she won't be constrained by traditional realistic modes.

In investigating Pasolini's life and death, she attempts to get inside his world by paralleling her own life to his death. Typical is her cross-gendering-he male, but gay, she female, but butch. In that crossover and the ensuing confusion of realms, she finds the disarray that exists in the larger culture. Her language, for example, is one traditionally given over to men, to male writers-she will out-tough Mailer. She breaks all rules, all expectations of character, narrative, and scene; she uses sex as a commodity, not as love or romance; and her gender switches provide her with hegemony over male roles-women can act out what men usually clutch to themselves. She goes through feminism, however, into the "beyond" of forbidden desires, loss of repression, thoughts of cross-sexual appetites, murder, mayhem, violence, and cannibalism. Her political references indicate that whatever the individual does, no matter how brutal and violent, it cannot equal what the government and its leaders do. The state is the ultimate obscenity, not the individual who commits unspeakable crimes. Given the wanton nature of government and its leaders, anything or everything is left open for the individual; he or she (usually she) is freed up to pursue her obsessions, desires, needs. This is the Enlightenment Acker, with a strong taste for de Sade.

In her quest for tropes somehow to align Pasolini's life and death with the broader culture, Acker takes great risks. She is willfully not a safe writer. She rejects all fallback measures, all safety nets. Like the wild junk bond traders of the 80s, she throws the dice with abandon, knowing that a throw of the dice will never abolish chance. She forgets odds, bottom lines, literary security. She cracks open genres, narrative strategies, character presentation. She goes for the cliché or stereotype, which she wraps in irony and sarcasm, as in the following:

> Yellow people are taking over the United States of America.

> They own the vegetable groceries, golf courses, fashions, technological designs, and car-manufacturing plants. Unlike us, they believe in wisdom. They are going to make the sage the American Vice President [Bush} and instill desperately needed anti-materialism.
> They wear two-feet-high purple hats trimmed in fur. Their eyes are the eyes of insects. Their men have tongues which move up and down a hundred miles an hour. Their men like whips better than cunt hair.[170]

And earlier, before this ironic stereotyping, she writes:

> An unknown man tries to kill Reagan, but instead drops William Casey. Reagan becomes more paranoid about his power. He and the sage plan to kidnap, bring up in secret, and if necessary murder the remaining Kennedy children. They have to act, as the wise man says, in accordance with the overall historical imperative.[171]

Obviously, the New Realism here has moved to new ground. But Acker's work, withal its subversion of the novel genre itself, is an extended version of realism. Using real people and events as grounding, she builds elaborate metaphors in trying to understand the culture. Pornography (mainly soft), anti-social language and thoughts, mocking statements about government and authority all work together to broaden the realistic mode, however extreme her methods may seem on first look. Perhaps even someone like Dreiser would have understood, although I suspect Wharton would have condemned her to her house of mirth.

The chance Russell Banks takes in *Continental Drift* (1985)[172] is his attempt to blend opposing forces in the two tales he tells. He had a choice: he could have made them complementary or else he could have played them off against each other-in either instance, the position is full of pitfalls. In his effort to bridge both choices,

Banks stretched the grounds of realism; he, in fact, established it with new lines, in his narration of two stories which, seemingly so distinct, can in some way become unified. The two tales are of Bob Dubois, an ordinary man, a New Hampshire oil burner repairer, who migrates to a small town in Florida; and a Haitian woman named Vanise Dorsinville, who migrates from Haiti toward the Miami area. Near the end of the novel, in an unlikely way, the two lives intersect.

Banks's daring occurs not only in bringing the two lives together, but also in his effort to gain a realistic hold on cause and effect. For while there is some sense of inevitability, of doom, destiny, fate-all those realistic/naturalistic dimensions-there is also a contrast in lives which creates another dimension. Even as Bob Dubois (Bob of the Woods) heads toward an inexorable doom once he leaves a fairly secure (but narrow) existence in Catamount, New Hampshire, Vanise's life begins to open up, despite the ordeals she must endure in order to make it to America.

The intersection of the lives, then, is both structural and interpretive. Writing in the 1980s, Banks captures an America that is failing lower middle class white men (perhaps *all* lower middle class families). This America seems to hold out promise if one moves, but it then closes down and the moves prove to be a chimaera. The "dream": comfortable house, new car, boat, and the rest are illusory. Yet even as this kind of America is beyond the reach of the Bobs of this class, so, too, it still seems a beacon of hope for those far worse off, Haitians, for example. But Haitians could be anyone of color from extreme poverty or oppression who views America as salvational. Although there is something stereotypical about this-America failing its own even as the disadvantaged from beyond cling to the country as hope and opportunity-there is also the element of truth; and the truth becomes more compelling when we see it fictionalized. Fictionalization provides reverberations lacking in the reality.

The way Banks avoids stereotypes (most of the time) and stretches realism comes in the "fantasy" subplots molded into the narrative. One of these involves Bob's brief affair with the physically alluring Marguerite Dill, black daughter of his helper in the liquor store bankrolled by Bob's brother, Eddie. The affair has something of master-slave, plantation owner and female worker, but it also carries Bob into a black world and prepares the text itself for the entry of Janise into his life. His drift into Marguerite Dill's routine is something of a fantastic leap-gathering up in its intensity some of the subconscious, his desire to break from a bourgeois life and move into supra-real sex (as portrayed), his need to live on the edge, even while maintaining some middle class surface. In the relationship with Marguerite, Bob can move outside himself, into an undefined "beyond," certainly outside of what his wife and children expect of him. And the affair takes on something of an idyll; besides great sex, there is the excitement of the subterfuge and the exhilaration that he is breaking through social bonds.

Another level of this "fantasy" life comes when he meets Ted Williams in a fishing tackle shop, and he is thrown outside himself, into adulation and confusion. He almost loses speech, and he forces the former baseball player to mumble a few words toward him.

These and similar episodes prepare the reader for the "fantastic" tale of Janise, Banks's combination of Moll Flanders and Brecht's Mother Courage. As she moves from island to island in her journey to the American shore near Miami, Florida, she is abused sexually and physically, she is brought near death, she loses her baby, and she can be saved only through a kind of voodoo. The novel breaks all traditional realistic boundaries in these latter segments, where Janise is caught up in voodoo practices orchestrated by "Brav Ghede," whom she believes has saved her from drowning. This embodiment of Haitian mystery parallels Bob's belief in the "awesome and mysterious" powers of the Haitians he is illegally smuggling on his boat. These mysterious powers are something implicit in Bob from the beginning, however; and while such powers make him test out the limitations of who and what he is, they are also the source of his decline and death, at the hand of Haitians.

Banks has moved us in and out of the undertow of realism and naturalism. He is fully aware that Bob "has no conscious plan, no intent," that he has given himself "over to forces larger than himself-history, the unconscious, the future. And once he has done that, he has lost "track of the sequence of events,"[173] lost track of who and what he is. Having decided to forsake the security of a painfully provincial life in New Hampshire-where he is on 24-hour call to repair oil furnaces-he becomes a modern-day Columbus setting out into unknown territory. Haitians emblemize that unknown: the mysteries of the black, their supposed primitivism, but also Haitians as the geographical location of that unknown within Bob which he feels he must explore. Doubling Bob in some way is his brother, Eddie, who has moved into equally dark territory, dependence on mob money.

Eddie lives with dark secrets of his own, a surface of success, with failure, and worse, in the not too distant background. Each major characters lurks in the shadows, with the possible exception of Bob's wife, Elaine, who yearns for stability even while she accompanies her husband into dark territory; even as he sinks ever deeper into what he had hoped would be "life," but which turns out to be merely another kind of living death. Ineluctably, he is drawn into one morbid enterprise after another, until his path closes in on Janise's, on what is in effect a slave ship. Then she, as slave, must survive what is an enterprise aimed at destroying her and everyone with her. She emerges from the shadows to survive; Bob emerges from the shadows to seek his own death.

Despite the stereotypical moments, Banks has grappled with something that was becoming apparent in the 1980s, when prosperity seemed to be just what Eddie, Bob's brother, thought it was: there for the taking. What was, overall, great for the upper part of the economy proved to be debilitating, even disastrous, for the lower middle class white man. Bob stands in for that entire generation of men in their 30s and 40s who found themselves buried in jobs with little or no future; where they could say they were alive, but not living. What made this so particularized in the 80s was the decade's appeal to those with panache and flash, and its gleeful dismissal of those who could not keep up.[174] Bob's brother tries, but his façade rapidly crumbles; whereas Bob more slowly sinks, from furnace repairer to liquor store operator to driver of a boat smuggling in Haitians. It is impossible to read this novel without the background of the decade in which it was written and published. The main characters, as if to emphasize their divisions from each other, all speak different languages: Janise, literally, cannot speak English; Eddie's English is a street language, punctuated by curses; Bob's is more neutral, but it is, nevertheless, the language of yearning doomed to failure; Marguerite Dill's is borderline, between standard and a so-called black English; Elaine's is the language of forbearance. Each addresses a different self in a different tongue; and part of their inability to connect is the fact they speak past each other. When Marguerite and Bob split, he asks if she has taken up with a black boyfriend, and she says she has, an indication she is trying to focus on a language and story she can identify with, whereas Bob never finds a language which fits because he cannot find an identity which gives him leverage.

Implicit in the novel, then, is Banks's manipulation of realistic factors, language and dimensions of fantasy being the most compelling, in order to reveal how the decade is splitting apart. Further, he reveals how white insistence on its traditional power, now under peril, results not in greater power (which is the prerogative of most realistic fiction), but in the demise of the participants. The one who comes through is Janise, bereft of all goods, caught in a strange land, language-less in that land, and yet a survivor. This break with realism has its message.

With *Black Water* (1992),[175] Joyce Carol Oates has carried to an even further degree her break with the realism of her earlier work, for example in *them*. Here she speaks out as Mary Jo Kopechne, the young woman unfortunate enough to get into a car with Ted Kennedy, in 1969, when he was drunk, out of control, and inattentive. She drowned; he saved himself. The break with traditional realism occurs in several ways: in the freely associative passages where Mary Jo (here Kelly Kelleher) muses on her life and death; in the hallucinatory passage of the Toyota as it hurtles rocket-like toward doom with the drunk, careless Senator at the wheel; in Kelly's slow passage toward death as the air bubble in the submerged car begins to recede and with it her life.

In another respect, the funereal ride is the mirror image of the one in *The Great Gatsby*, with Daisy Buchanan at the wheel and Gatsby the fall guy. Reversed genders, similar results. In Oates's presentation of the "case," Kennedy is the "Senator," described as recognizably Ted: robust to overweight, face filled with veins from years of drinking, the superficial charm of power and famous connections, attitude suffused with the kind of carelessness which recalls, once again, the Buchanans in the Fitzgerald novel, the carelessness of the rich.

What makes Oates's telling so incisive is the way in which she juxtaposes Kelly's awe of the senator and her desire to seem attractive to him with his abandonment of all but his desire to score. As a means to getting laid, he pays attention to her; an attention that she thinks goes deeper. In her eyes, he has singled her out as someone special; whereas in his eyes she is just another conquest in a long line of young women the Kennedys have considered their property. Power is their thing, and while it draws Kelly to the senator, it is also what helps kill her: for the senator is focused on power, whether over her, the Toyota, or simply in general. A young pretty woman is a way to exercise that power, and he drives his case with her as hard as he drives the Toyota. Oates's description of the senator at the wheel of the car approximates a kind of sexual play, as he brakes and gives gas to the engine, in bursts, while the car surges, falters, picks up, drops off; and, finally, when the sexual energy is gone, the car sinks into the muddy waters where Kelly drowns.

The hallucinatory quality of the novel, and the concomitant move into the newer realism, occurs primarily when Kelly flashes back-she has in actuality died, but Oates keeps her mind moving along her routine, her preparations, clothes, makeup, perfume. This touch reinforces Kelly as an innocent in the mating game who has completely misread the senator as someone interested in *her*, when he is of course interested in young women. She is his fling of the moment, someone he can readily charm with his position and male aggressiveness (masked by what seems to be an interest in her). As she drowns-as she in fact has drowned-she awaits his saving arms; she claws at the idea of his returning to pry her from imprisonment in the car seat. Her mind is on life, even as the senator has saved only himself. As he moves toward his damage control team, her air bubble having been exhausted, she fills with muddy, oily, scummy fluid entombing the car. Like a foetus trapped in its own amniotic fluid, she has been discarded by her "parent" figure, the senator old enough to be her father. She is Iphigenia in his Agamemnon quest for power: once the accident occurs, he must get his support team into action so that he can sail back to his old role as a notable statesman.

In several respects, Kelly has bonded with the senator as someone standing in for her father: she has written her undergraduate thesis on him (one is amused at Brown University having sanctioned such a topic), and she sees him as the liberal father of the Democratic welfare system-the father of us all. She seeks, as his daughter-to-be, to learn from him-he will tutor her in the ways of the world and all the while shield her. But of course his interest is less than father and more like lover, an in-and-out lover at that. The young woman who graduated summa cum laude, with a thesis entitled "Jeffersonian Idealism and 'New Deal' Pragmatism: Liberal Strategies in Crisis" (a kind of Groucho Marx title), is attempting now to act grown-up. A good Catholic girl, she protests to her parents that she can take care of herself-and so she does, with a willfulness that kills her. In Oates's hands, the senator is all attitude, above the law, one part turned toward the electorate, the other turned toward "black water" where terrible things recur in his life. Two-faced, he will escape. One-faced, Kelly will suck up the remaining air and then suffocate when he has left her nothing to breathe. The senator has sought a young woman for amusement in a motel, but has instead dispatched her back into a womb, a dead foetus.

Having avoided the traditional realistic route, Oates had found the new perfect vehicle for her rage: rage at Kelly for believing a man, for following him into what she thought would be a pleasure dome, and for believing in him even after he has abandoned her in the deep. She has filtered Kelly's first person voice as hopeful victim, and she has added her own comments, in the third person, but by way of Kelly's mental processes even as they are being snuffed out. Italics create a kind of transitional language between Kelly's own story, which she strives to locate and tell, and Oates's, which of course encompasses Kelly's and the senator's. We see the senator through Kelly's adoring eyes, even as he plans his escapade, that weekend's screw. Black water is the fate of a woman who believes a man, and black water is doubly the fate of any woman who believes in a politician. If the politician is a Kennedy, one can expect to be wasted.

When we look at Nicholson Baker's first two novels, *Mezzanine* (1988)[176] and *Room Temperature* (1990),[177] we can repeat that realism is not what it used to be. In a Baker novel, the realism is so intense it is equivalent, visually, to putting one's nose up against a painting and then trying to describe it. Size, perspective, distancing, shape itself, all, become distorted; so that, ultimately, realism gives way to some supernal experience, not quite surreal, not quite real, not quite abstract. To work in those crevices of artifice is Baker's mission. The paradigm is clearly Proustian, since Baker draws on real moments interrupted by long meditations on "meaning." Early on, for example, in *Mezzanine*, he interrupts his meditation of the need for a shopping bag when making a purchase, and the interruption, which runs almost half a page of small single-spaced type, includes the experience of buying a periodical one is ashamed of being seen with, *Penthouse*, or *Oui*, or *Club*. In that segment, all part of interruption within interruption, Baker writes of the modulations between customer and saleswoman over the purchase of a salacious periodical, where dominance between purchaser and store becomes a dramatic confrontation; how the semiotics of tone and gesture influence the nature of the experience; and then even what it might lead to, as customer and cashier begin to bond at this local 7-Eleven.

Proust suffuses the book, giving it not only its philosophical grounding but its strategies for interior narratives; its privileged moments-those moments which provide a kind of epiphany, like Marcel's tea and madeline; its tightness of argument which wrenches every bit of juice from a situation or event, however slight. But even more than that, Proust allows Baker to turn the seemingly trivial into the significant; to turn molehills into mountains, in much the same way the French writer could intensify an apparently insignificant detail into the stuff of a social arena. Along the way, just as Proust redefined the nature of realism, so does Baker take on traditional realism and trump it on its own grounds. By putting events under a microscope, Baker has so intensified details that they take on immense proportions-and in the best sense of it, we are as readers made to assimilate and comprehend differently. The very best of the new realists force upon us alternate perspectives on objects, events, relationships, situations, circumstances. They wring the unfamiliar out of the familiar. Here Baker excels. Even when the strategies and methods become tiresome, we accept that tiresomeness is often the sole means to upend pre-assumed postures.

What, then, do we gain in perspective? Like Gulliver in the land of the giants, Baker dissects the familiar by probing into its crevices. When Gulliver peers at skin, he sees pores, tiny pimples, pits or crevices, hills and mountains, all part of what once was a familiar and taken-for-granted landscape, the body's skin covering. In like manner, Baker breaks down the large into small, and then reprocesses the small until it takes on gigantic proportions, until it overwhelms, and forces us to look beyond the large into its minute components. By overstressing our sense of ordinary realism, by overwhelming it, as it were, he makes us into voyeurs. All the things we would normally pass over are now stages of perception and meditation. Using long footnoted material, Baker carries on corollary or longitudinal arguments, stretching his case further and further, as though all experience were infinitely elastic and expandable.

One of the wonders of the method is that even while Baker focuses on the almost invisible detail of processes, he is aware of the larger sequence of events. When he buys books, has his shoes reheeled, pays several bills, has an address stamp made-in all of these, he recognizes he has set into motion a gigantic production machine, aimed at fulfilling his needs. "As I walked out of the office-supple store," he writes, "I became aware of the power of all these individual, simultaneously pending transactions: all over the city, and at selected sites in other states, events were being set in motion on my behalf, services were being performed, simply because I had requested them and in some cases paid or agreed to pay later for them."[178] Entire industries are maintained and oiled by virtue of his simple activities-rubber for his address stamp, for example-so that he becomes part of a vast, oceanic process even as he worries about shoelaces, heels, and escalator steps.

This linkage between large and small reinforces the Proustian presence. For Proust uses the privileged moment, the persistence of memory, the need to recall and lay out past sequences as part of a social strategy. Implicated in the recall of the narrator Marcel is the entire social scene of Paris, with the Dreyfus case foremost as a social-ethnic-political conflict. Nothing so grand exists in Baker, but implied in the miniscule observations of his narrator are those workings of the larger world. Near the end of *Mezzanine*, the narrator's musings take into consideration what he calls "mid-frequency ideas," which lie below the usual "level of thought-vocabulary"[179] and which relate the individual to the world. These subjects of thought are graded according to the number of times they occur each year, in descending order with L. (a woman friend) first, followed by family, and continuing on through the large range of matters which takes us into the world, ending with "Kant, Immanuel," scoring only 0.5, whereas L. scored 580.0.

Room Temperature, two years later, seems a similar kind of novel, but it does reveal differences. If anything, Baker has become more self-enclosed, more narcissistic in his concerns with self and self and others, with others' revealing themselves to him, and he to them. Ostensibly about a feeding session with his infant daughter, Bug-that Proustian moment which becomes a privileged moment of revelation-the novel roams deeply into the narrator's relationships with his wife, his sister, with a scooping up of the past and his childhood memories. While there are some excursions into "knowledge"-Robert Boyle, Isaac Casaubon, and other theorists- the main thrust of the brief novel (barely over 100 pages) is the narrator's self. Some of the selfness is particularly strong, especially when he speaks of how he and his wife manage their devotion to each other or how he expresses his feelings toward his newly born daughter. Family homage here is intermixed with that intense detail Baker has made his trademark. If we see *Room Temperature* as a successor to *Mezzanine*, we find him trying to invent new ways of getting at a world made static by observation and memory. Nevertheless, a dead end looms.

From these two books, we would expect Baker's next steps to be interesting in his expansion of the new realism: to see, for instance, whether he can utilize his Proustian sense for something larger, without losing sight of his penchant for something smaller. A more recent book, *Vox* (1992),[180] vastly more popular than *Mezzanine*, is a tour de force of masturbatory fiction, but it's a trivial entertainment, not a fulfillment, and certainly not a development. Similarly, Baker's amusing little book called *U and I* (1991),[181] a "True Story" based on his adulation of John Updike's work, is a sport, a step toward archness, coyness, and, in many of its comments, misjudgment. But along the way Baker shrewdly assesses his own first novel: "I wanted my first novel to be a veritable infarct of narrative cloggers; the trick being to feel your way through each clog by blowing it up until its obstructiveness finally revealed not blank mass but unlooked for seepage-points of passage."[182] If read as a way into his own work, not into Updike's, then *U and I* resonates. The book suggests Baker's intense commitment to writing, to words, to the power of expression, and to originality-even if he dramatically overrates Updike. What one carries away is not only therapy for the writer, but a fierce commitment. Writing, we hope, will follow.

Like *Vox*, however, *The Fermata* (1994),[183] is a misstep, attributable, I believe, to Baker's slavish devotion to Updike's fictional lasciviousness. A piece of voyeurism, it takes obsession with self to another level, more obsession than realization. Baker's narrator, Arnold Strine, has the ability to enter the Fermata or Fold; a "Fold-Stop" occurs when he, Strine, remains active and alive while the rest of the world pauses. He has developed several techniques for triggering the pause, during which time he can observe women's body parts, undress them, have them engage in sexual activity. There is an idea here, but Baker focuses almost solely on sexual matters, chiefly on the narrator's ability to control women who cross his path. His look is a form of rape. As a consequence, the novel fulfills some generalized, degraded male fantasy world, but neither parodic nor ironic, it is not sufficient to sustain a book of 300 pages. There is some stretching of realism here, back into H. G. Wells's *Invisible Man*, but it is of a kind which is self-defeating: it transforms realism into obsession without altering our observation of ourselves or the world.

Far more successful is Peter Matthiessen's *Killing Mister Watson* (1990),[184] the first part of a trilogy, in which he disrupts what could be a routine story with a Rashomon-like effect, presenting conflicting views of Edgar Watson, a successful rogue farmer and businessman in the Everglades part of the Florida Gulf Coast, the so-called ten Thousand Islands. Matthiessen surrounds Watson with points of view, from historical documents, newspaper reports, letters, gossip from neighbors, statements of sworn enemies. In several respects, Watson recalls Faulkner's Thomas Sutpen, in *Absalom, Absalom!* Sutpen is commanding, mysterious, brutal, without moral compunctions, all "thereness"-and he succeeds, for a time, in carving out an empire, his Sutpen's Hundreds. Having created his own space, he survives because of the fear he engenders;

likewise Watson, whose frosty, hard look indicated implacability. When he arrives on the Gulf coast, his reputation accompanies him, as the possible murderer of the famous female outlaw Belle Starr and others. His life is steeped in legend, and his silences-he gazes, but rarely speaks-reinforce the mystique of his presence. By maintaining silence, he comes to mean all things, in much the same way Sutpen challenges all convention by insisting not on language but on looks and then acts.

But we return to Matthiessen's strategies in the novel. By taking a basically realistic situation and context and turning it into points of view, he has underscored realism with uncertainties. This "new realism" suggests several things: the unknowability of human character-obviously that; the difficulty of discovering evidence or establishing documentation; the question of information or disinformation and how each is transmitted; the very question of justice and law in cases where proof is replaced by gossip, rumor, intimation; and, not least, the sense that language has failed, even when the actual words derive from people caught in intensely real settings. We never get to know Watson-such is the externalized method-just as we never get to know Faulkner's Sutpen. But that unknowability is not authorial slippage, but his way of asserting that what drives each man is unfathomable; that behavior in men who create empires, or try to, is an *x* factor; that men who are feared because they can intimidate and brutalize not only do not need language, they need only the mystique of their presence. Besides all else, there is, here, a chilly political message.

Finally, since it is solidly wedded to geographical place but also contains elements of magic, ghostliness, and transformation, Annie Proulx's *The Shipping News* (1993)[185] fits well into the New Realism. Set on the Newfoundland coast, the novel focuses on local types as they interact with Quoyle and his small family, two daughters and an aunt. When he arrives from small-town America, Quoyle is torn by conflict: ungainly and fat, a low-level performer, a man obsessed with a wife who cheated on him and is now dead in a car crash, with two daughters who evidence instability, a man of few prospects since he has been a less than spectacular newspaperman; but also someone solidly rooted in the belief he must do his best for his daughters. Newfoundland coast is an area as much of fish as of people, fishing boats, fishermen, fishy food, fishy smells, balanced by domestic violence, by children violated by fathers and by priests, by terrible acts of self-destruction. Everyone lives on the edge of potential disaster. Yet somehow Quoyle plugs along and finds his spot.

But the line of Quoyle's narrative often takes secondary place to the weather, the change of seasons, the onset of fog and blizzards, the knottiness of harsh life containing its own rules of life and death. Most chapters are introduced with drawings of knots taken from *The Ashley Book of Knots* and elsewhere. These images function in several ways: they keep us rooted in the primitive level of life on the coast; they show us how people survive by tying the correct knot; and, metaphorically, they suggest that nearly all life here is knotted to something, to the past, to tradition, to a history of destruction and disaster. Life is not linear or sequential, but, indeed, knotted.

What gives the novel its edge is the precarious nature of the life these Newfoundlanders experience. In the best of times, they suffer shipwrecks, drownings, other kinds of violent loss of life; but now they are confronting another danger, that their way of life is being phased out by more modern methods, newer technologies, foreign invasions of their fishing areas. Not only are they being invaded, they find all the old ways of making a meager living slipping away; not only marginalized, they are being erased. The paper Quoyle works for, the *Gammy Bird*, exists, increasingly, because of coverage of disasters, domestic violence, rape, child abuse; it needs a car wreck in every weekly issue, and when car wrecks are not forthcoming, the editor digs out old footage and photographs. With the fishing areas swept clean by Japanese and Russian shipping vessels, the local men move further and further out into greater danger as inshore fishing becomes inadequate. The weather is a constant factor, inconsistent, discontinuous, treacherous one day, sunny the next, like the life itself. The younger people, in particular, have nothing. While they do not commit suicide, as they do in the northern reaches of Canada, they are suicidal, in acts of life that often morph into acts of death on the road and on the sea. The population is dwindling-fewer marriages, fewer children, the young leaving for St. John and further south.

However powerful the physical dimensions of life here, an even more powerful element in the novel, however, is the prose. Proulx mixes sentences with partial sentences, fragments, groups without a subject, or lacking a verb; so that word groups come at us like darts or missiles, sudden blows. While she rarely avoids comment, the comments are seemingly tangential, elliptical, and yet incisive. The sharpness of observation is rare even in realistic fiction, along with a sense of place attuned to nature, rocks, hills, grass, animal life, birds, water and its innumerable variations as the seasons change, the dangers of nature as well as its pleasures and comforts, the harshness of snow and ice and lack of heat, the sheer discomfort of the place together with its startling beauty. Its ghosts, moreover, are never far from its actualities.

Beauty derives often from absence: the lack of amenities, the fewness of jobs, the revolting nature of food based on the cod, the potential of danger, the lack of a future, impending disaster on the road and at sea. The prose works so well because it parallels and reinforces portent. Short, pithy phrases-again, the frequent absence of sentences-create the aura of impending catastrophe; and yet Proulx is not precisely Naturalistic-nature or natural forces, or genetics, do not always claim victims. People sink into alcoholism, but some escape; men commit terrible crimes against children and spouses, but many are kind; people dare nature to do them in, but some are spared.

Some, like Quoyle and his aunt, despite meager resources, fight back with reasonable lives, with the will to move along incrementally, without illusions but also without despair, and they make modest gains. In some respects, Proulx in *The Shipping News* recalls Richard Ford's *The Sportswriter*, where pleasures are small and almost incidental, gains are measured in inches, not yards or miles, and staring and absence are signs not only of despair but of measuring, time out, calculating one's interests, allowing matters to percolate and settle down. Beyond tragedy, there is a measured sense to life. Normalizing Realism and some aspects of Naturalism meet, as the genres overlap and squeeze meaning out of each other. The details of daily life in very harsh conditions encounter the irreversibility of natural forces, and neither triumphs. Victories are small, deriving from marginal individuals who rise to the occasion. In her accomplishment here, Proulx mirrors one prevailing sense of the Nineties, at a time when normalcy was balanced by portents of disorder. In both the best and worst of times, neither wins.

A word on Postcards:

Postcards (1992)[186] reveals Proulx's indebtedness to Faulkner, especially his *As I Lay Dying*. The Bloods of *Postcards* and the Bundrens of the Faulkner novel are kin, in their common descent into marginality. The Blood farm is deteriorating as the younger ones leave and the work becomes impossible to handle, while the Bundrens deteriorate because the family is imploding into madness, unwanted pregnancy, and loss of goods. Aside from naming-Jewell as wife of Mink, Loyal as son, Mernelle as daughter, Dub as son, Loyal's girl friend as Billy-the presence of *As I Lay Dying* is evident in the narrative switches, the brief chapters, the concern with natural disasters. In the Faulkner, fire and water rise up against the Bundrens; in *Postcards*, it is rage, arson, the lack of suitable land for growing, too many cows for too few hands, the utter lack of resources.

The great success of *Shipping News*, in addition to the fine angulated prose, is its density, its focus; whereas *Postcards*, withal its use of postcards for purposes of information and irony, becomes too diffuse. Characters rarely seem significant for the weight placed on them: among the younger generation, Loyal, who has murdered Billy, ends up as a mere survivor of his own poor choices, and Dub becomes a stereotypical American success. Even their mother, Jewell-if we compare her with Faulkner's Addie Bundren (who dominates while lying dead in *As I Lay Dying*) lacks focus. Splendid writing and inventive narrative strategies cannot themselves create coherence.

CHAPTER FIVE

THE SHORT STORY-WHERE IS IT TAKING US AND WHOSE LANGUAGE IS IT?

PART ONE: THE SHORT OF IT

If we examine where the short story is taking us, we cannot disengage it from the "languages" of contemporary American fiction. For nowhere more than in the short story has language, in its multiplicity as an American lingo, exploded. Just as the short story has demonstrated our diversity, so, too, has language become the vehicle of such diversity. The languages in our short stories have become as numerous as those in modernism itself, then in postmodernism, and beyond.

Language here is more than the words a writer uses to express a style or point of view. It refers to methods of arrangement, the total mode of expression. Language is linked to ways in which the writer manipulates the reader, the means of expression that becomes the writer's signature. It is also body movement, gesture, silence, tonal varieties, open spaces, interiors, secret selves, manifestations. If language is the expression of multifold voices, then it adumbrates an American scene and American vision.

One evident characteristic of the contemporary short story is its revelation that diversities do not add up to unity, but to isolation, separation, unique, disconnected subcultures. The more languages we create, the more we are cut off, not only as African-Americans, females, gays, Jews, WASPs, Latinos, but as tributaries and streams which seem part of another country altogether. What this proliferation of languages has done is not only to energize our fiction, but also to atomize America. Instead of a country, we perceive countries; instead of a culture, cultures; instead of a defined geography or map, spaces. If we translate what we hear in those short story voices into some historical perspective, they tell us we are experiencing a country which lacks substance or body, surely wholeness. No longer a nation, we are fragmented to the degree that, from the literary point of view, we should not speak of American fiction but of America's fictions.

The short story in its post-Vietnam era manifestations has caught up to modernism and then pushed beyond it. It is, in fact, no longer a short "story," for the noun part of the designation has always presupposed traditional attitudes toward fiction and literature. "Story" assumed continuity, cause and effect, even plot-all subsumed under realism; it stressed the relating of a tale or tales, and it assumed some fixity: teller, audience, someone responding, even a place. "Short story" has given way to "short fiction," which is a neutral designation of any number of words in prose. But this is *not* the *New Yorker* type of story, all middle and little or no beginning or ending. Quite the contrary! The *New Yorker* story, or what falls under that rubric, is really the old-fashioned kind with an "in medias res" trendiness. The writer becomes type cast. That version is like central casting: the writer, like the actor, fits the slot.

Short fiction has no slots, no central casting, nothing so defined. In many of its forms, it moves toward abstraction, imitating in words what painters came to almost three-quarters of a century ago. William Burroughs, a writer of longer rather than shorter fictions, was distinctive here, someone whose influence became pervasive not only because of his loose forms but because his language fitted the newer kind of "stories." He innovated a more fluid, hybrid language and genre, as did William Gaddis, Joseph Heller, Thomas Pynchon-all workers in the longer forms. Although words cannot "abstract" in ways colors and arrangements can, there are means of emptying out the verbal canvas. Such writers we might call "emptiers." Their vision of objects and shapes moves them away from representation. They would, if they could, create Cubist masterpieces, geometrical forms, lines and points and planes; they would do the Kandinsky thing, on the order of his pioneering work in the 1910s and 20s. The emptiers are still fighting the battle of modernism; while nearly everyone thinks modernism is over-that even postmodernism is finished-the larger struggles have by no means been won. Read book reviews, high and low, and see the resistance, even anguish.

Not only is short fiction in the emptiers' hands moving toward abstraction, it has for a good many decades been moving toward minimalism: not spareness so much as incompletion and fragmentariness, *despite* a plenitude of words and even descriptive language. Minimalism, incidentally, has social and political resonances, in addition to literary significance. What we note is the loss of "tale" or "story" and the shaping of a fiction through bursts of language or swatches of color, along with burglary of other genres. None of this is quite new, since these borrowings have been the stock-in-trade of short fiction since the advent of modernism; but we see now a compulsive intensification of these earlier trends. And for several reasons we see it more decisively in the shorter form than in the longer. Serious shorter fiction has taken away our familiar world. The novel cannot quite do that-it runs on too long, it has recognizable characters and scenes, it must have a sense of time and place. But shorter fiction is under few of those obligations, and thus it can subvert our notions of the familiar.

Guy Davenport's stories, *Eclogues*, published in 1981[187]-and ignored in nearly all studies of contemporary American literature-convey how "languages" and the newer short fiction function. "The Death of Picasso," originally in the *Kenyon Review*, is a fiction presented as an assemblage, a verbal collage. With its dated headings derived from the French revolutionary calendar, its setting of two men on a tiny North Sea island, its recreation of a kind of Greek idyll, complete with flute playing, the story would appear to be far from America and American concerns. Yet Davenport is slyly establishing a medium through which America can be approached: through its now mythical Walden Pond experience. The two men in this Greek idyll-the Professor-narrator and a much younger man named Sander-act out their own scenario in the light of Thoreau's isolation in the past and Picasso's death in the present. "We hear on the radio that Picasso is dead. He was ninety-two."[188] The conception is clearly to generate an atmosphere of revolution: the calendar itself, Picasso's artistic breakthroughs, his insistence on renewal, references to Van Gogh, the two men pursuing an "antisocietal" existence on an isolated island, Thoreau's "anarchy" in the background. Paragraphs of meditation, intermixed with Sander offering himself up to the Professor and a description of routine activities, make up the story; with Picasso's death hovering. In this unlikely mix-which may be everything or, for the less engaged reader, virtually nothing-Davenport has discovered a language and also a medium, another kind of fictional statement.

Davenport would seem at the opposite end from the emptiers, the minimalists who understate and "under-language" their prose fictions. He supplies a tidal wave of referential material or planes of existence, brought together in ways that recall Picasso's method of yoking dissimilars. The packed language results in a commentary on America in the re-use of the Walden myth as it blends with the Picasso representations we all carry in our heads. Davenport presupposes we perceive with Picasso's eyes, so that the report of his death is really a rebirth of his images. The writer's method, however, is really not that different from what the minimalists practice; for his energies are directed at forcing new perceptions by creating unusual or eccentric combinations; he empties us out of preconceptions, as a way of making us see ourselves unfamiliarly. Like the emptiers, he removes the ordinary, the expected. History, geography, sexual pairings, artistic creation, acts of imagination, observations (the Professor keeps a journal, a text about the text) are all ways of commenting on our discontinuity, an acknowledgment of how we live in a multitude of subcultures which only connect when someone like Picasso dies and alerts us to both our divisions and our potential for wholeness.

Those whom I label emptiers perceive objects, events, even history as the enemy; and their landscape-when it can be discerned-is saturated more with language than with representation. The sounds of language, the feel of it, its oddity when repeated, the disconnectedness of language from feelings and from things: all of these are characteristic. Such emptiers are often referred to as postmodernists, rather than modernists, because they stress a linguistic, self-conscious circuitry. For emptiers, space is not what is around things, but a medium that can be explored as apart from things. Time serves not to reinforce history, but to subvert it, an ally of discontinuity. Among them: Guy Davenport, Walter Abish, Donald Barthelme; on the margins, Frederick Barthelme, Raymond Carver, John Barth (in his *Lost in the Funhouse*), Gilbert Sorrentino, William Gass (in parts of *In the Heart of the Heart of the Country*).

How did the emptiers come into being? Although it is always difficult to pinpoint what a literary tendency or movement means in the larger cultural context, we can hypothesize that polarities in short fiction-almost a war between methods-reflect deep divisions of perceiving and thinking in the culture itself. Matters of perceiving may be linguistic, racial, sexual, emotional; broadly cultural, they create dualisms: of words and objects which, somehow, link up for the traditionalists (whom I call "fillers") and which fail to connect in the emptiers. In brief, one side sees continuity, the other discontinuity. When we speak of the gulf between the two groups, we are describing a large cultural divide, between those who seek certainties (the fillers), even if they do not always find it, and those who see indeterminancy, which allows no resolution.

For fillers, certain aspects of realism have returned. The fillers, in the main, satisfy those exhausted by modernism and its insistent demands on our attention. Whereas emptiers are frequently nonrepresentational, fillers find that words define things. The battlefield, not restricted only to shorter fiction, raises large questions of how we define reality, then how we represent it. That struggle is no longer between high and low culture, but between different ways of perceiving.

Typical fillers are Saul Bellow in his latest work, also Mark Helprin, Joyce Carol Oates, Tobias Wolff, Alice Walker, Toni Cade Bambara; to a lesser extent, Ann Beattie and Bobbie Ann Mason, and others who edge the emptiers. Whatever their other virtues, they do ride waves of imitation; while voicing trendy assumptions about society and its culture, they explore older modes. Because they have not sought appropriate forms for whatever may be new about their subject matter, there are divergences between what they tell us about disconnectedness or fragmentation and the means they employ to tell us. The fillers are often more accessible than the emptiers because their world is so recognizable; and yet, as if against the grain, their subject is often the unrecognizability of the contemporary world, its distancing of itself from our ability to comprehend it. Inevitably, such writers may appear at odds with themselves.

Emptiers make no pretense to immediate appeal. They have the arrogance of the avant-gardeists: their vision first, the reader secondary. Some writers such as Ann Tyler, Bobbie Ann Mason, and Tobias Wolff may seem like emptiers because their stories are often all middle. But they are not incomplete enough. Emptier fiction has qualities of "stretch," not completeness, which suggests it has entered a world where line, point, plane-Kandinsky's painterly categories-extend into infinity. These fictions have a geometric, plane-like feel to them; and the experiences they limn lie in the interstices of known reality, a kind of phenomenology in which works-however abundantly *there*-must fail. Emptiers are not morally superior; they are more adventurous. Their language finds them straining not after lyricism-the mark of writers such as Helprin and Walker-but after an epiphenomenal language that owes at least part of its existence to the indeterminacy of nineteenth-century

French symbolism. Suggest, never state. Language on the edge of delirium or pathology, appearances rather than thinginess, secondary rather than primary characteristics, all, define such fictions. When emptiers strain for meaning, it is not the meaning of who we are, or how we behave, or what we should do-but meaning linked to states of being, in which we have floated free of routine. The world is spiritualized, although without spirit; it is all "para" or "meta," above and beyond immediate expectation.

A good example of an emptier comes in Coleman Dowell's dozen or so published short fictions, which have appeared in various avant-garde magazines. During his lifetime, Dowell never gained much of an audience, but he deserves a second look as an artist with the highest ideals. Although better known as a novelist, he used short fiction as a way of "floating free," of gaining mysticism and intensity which, he felt, no writer could achieve either from story line or objects. In "My Father Was a River," part of a group of childhood scenes-themselves defiers of standardized growing-up stories-Dowell set himself the talk of demonstrating that his father *was* indeed a river. The trope moves to become actual. And behind that was the even more difficult task, which was to define what a child is. The parents:

> My mother was a light woman, quick and evanescent. When she entered a room she had already left it. Her beauty was contained to the point that little of it showed. When my father entered a room it became too crowded, for there seemed to be too many of him. He extended himself so that he sat in every chair and filled each corner. My father was feral; if he filled a room, he became the forest. My father was a river, a fox, a mountain lion.[189]

"The world is full of abandoned meanings," a character in Don DeLillo's *White Noise* says. The Dowell story fits, as do most of the emptiers'. In the Dowell, the brief passage is, mainly, spatial: not only the child viewing the disproportionately large father as filling all space, but the space of an idea which has superseded physical qualities. This is a message from "beyond" which makes all realistic depiction secondary to the magic or legend of the father; in which, as if in some African or New Guinean legend, he can be transformed into river, fox, lion. Under these conditions, how does a child grow up? How does the child, so spatially distanced, himself become a father? Dowell is working through not only the excruciating difficulty of growing up, but also the even greater difficulty of trying to pinpoint when the transformation of child to adult takes place. The meaning of that lies in abandoned places.

Guy Davenport's other collections, *Tatlin: Six Stories* (1974)[190] and *Da Vinci's Bicycle: Ten Stories* (1979),[191] which, despite their plethora of information and detail, are nevertheless examples of the emptiers' art. In nearly all of these pieces, we find that negative connection between objects and the space around them that is characteristic. Davenport is a miniaturist, a minimalist, a decentering force in the short story. "Tatlin" concerns the Soviet polymath and his idea for the Monument to the Third International, planned as a kinetic structure perhaps one-third of a mile high. It was, generically, a sculpture, structured of scaffolding within which would hang a cylinder, a cube, and a sphere, all of them revolving at different speeds. Its overall effect as a building was of a spiral, a space-age mechanism, in which dynamic and kinetic energy as building-sculpture would be the physical counterpart to the power of the revolution. The idea, based on the redistribution of space, would link spatial concepts with political, social, cultural changes. When Trotsky criticized it as folly, it was never built.

The European equivalent of this is the Italian fantasist Italo Calvino; and Davenport's work reminds us of *Invisible Cities*, cities not of things, but of spaces emptied out, and both of them recalling the master of this, Borges, where everything is an abstract of the real. That kinetic Tatlin architecture which was to serve as a social and political symbol of revolution is an apt metaphor for the emptiers. Such voiding of traditional significance is not nihilistic, not a denial of Western culture, but a witty affirmation of form meeting history.

Perhaps even more than Davenport, Walter Abish is concerned with cleansing words, renewing them so that we re-perceive and re-think. With his Viennese background, his adolescence in Shanghai, Abish is less American than (say) Davenport, Dowell, or the Barthelme brothers (Donald and Frederick). That he brings to short fiction something of Europe's traditions and thus straddles two cultures becomes apparent in his key volume of short fiction, *In the Future Perfect*,[192] as well as in an earlier collection, *Minds Meet*.[193] Characteristic are "The English Garden," "Crossing the Great Void," and "In So Many Words," which should be read along with "Ardor/Awe/Atrocity." In the final two selections, Abish is not writing stories in any traditional sense: he is placing words on a page, as an abstract painter lays paint on a canvas. He uses words in sequences to explore verbal potential, ideas of narratology, information theory, and other determinants in our otherwise casual use of language. He is subverting casualness to destroy the idea of sequence (plot, story, narrative) which deadens language through expectation. In his sense of English as something special, he hears sounds, tones, and linkages which the ear born to the language neglects.

"Crossing the Great Void" is concerned with space, mapping, geographical locations, all as tropes of how we attempt to locate ourselves within our own lives. The map creates several possibilities, not only of space, but of mental concepts superimposed on a territory or even an idea. Our map of this or that is a phenomenological process, an effort to rein in something unbounded, an attempt to conceptualize what seems unrestricted. In the "Great Void," one Zachary is trying to reach the center of the desert, where somehow he will not feel the void; but the center is as much void as what is around it. Through maps, voids, spatial concepts, he attempts to cross over into meaning, to find coordinates for our present state. Once more the painterly analogy is well taken: the painter as someone mapping territory on canvas, seeking the equivalent in paint of a mental disruption, an aberrant circumstance, a distancing between oneself and the rest.

"The English Garden," which foreruns Abish's now classic *How German Is It*, links many of the strategies with a more traditional narrative. The volume title itself, *In the Future Perfect*, is itself part of a linguistic ambiguity, since the future perfect in English is bizarrely dualistic. The future perfect suggests both time and space; while obviously a temporal mode, it does indicate future stretching. And yet it is a future which has been retrieved, since it is part of a perfect tense, a past tense. Dual times pull against each other, as they do, overall, in the volume. This is a typical emptiers' ploy: to establish countering or clashing temporal modes, and then to locate such temporal tensions in a spatial dimension.

The story at hand illuminates the method, while also suggesting something very meaningful about history and culture. Germany is presented as a coloring book, and this coloring book must be filled in before we can understand the Germans and their country. It is the, by now, familiar map strategy. "Nothing is intrinsically German, I suppose, until it receives its color."[194] It is mind which "makes" Germany. Creating, coloring, mapping *are* existence. The idea is satirical: Germany is a chameleon, and implicitly we all are to some degree; history now depends not on "fact," but on maps and colors, acts of mind. "Minds Meet" is another Abish fiction: Minds Meet? Or Minds Meet! Information is *not* conveyed. The message, as in Kafka, Nabokov, Barthelme, Borges, and other emptiers, is that there *may be* a message behind the shadow, and *that* is the message.

No discussion of emptiers would be complete without consideration of Donald Barthelme's short fiction. Barthelme struck what would become his characteristic mode: to show what America is like *after it is voided*. The stories describe not only landscapes of exhaustion-nearly every modern writer, emptier or filler, does that-but staging areas where one waits, in vain, for modes of renewal. Barthelme's creation of a language was a way of circumventing the exhausted, turning it into something meaningful by stressing its platitudes. His language is not neutral, as many critics have described it; it is fierce, hostile, demanding, relentless. Language is a juggernaut that metaphorically crushes everything as it rolls on. What remains is the detritus of a culture of plenty, described in a language that empties plenty out, reduces it to terms and phrases. It is a culture of vital desolation.[195]

Emptiers have turned innovative short fiction into an expression of the culture, as much as, earlier, cubists, abstractionists, surrealists made comparable efforts in another genre. Edging the emptiers, but more traditionalist, are Raymond Carver, Frederick Barthelme, Ann Beattie, and Bobbie Ann Mason-the list is not inclusive. Technically expert though many of their short stories are, the writers are what we might call re-achievers, recreating well what has already been created. They fall into a paradox: that while they seem terribly "real," they have sidestepped the more intense questions of what constitutes reality-how it is presented. They do not trivialize the form, but they are, with some notable exceptions, derivative emptiers. Their most representative technique-and what connects them to emptiers-is their flattening out of their prose, their deadening of experience, a kind of homogenized emotional life-their sense of echo and reflection. They are, to a large extent, inheritors of the *New Yorker* style, not in the obvious way of John Updike, but as imitators of its chic emptiness.

Consider Ann Beattie's "Colorado" and "Dwarf House," her "A Vintage Thunderbird"; Frederick Barthelme's "Shopgirls"; Raymond Carver's "Cathedral" and "A Small, Good Thing"; Bobbie Ann Mason's "Shiloh." The latter embraces a typical emptier proposition, which implies-rightly or wrongly-that America, whatever its financial and political success, is anomic, directionless, shadow not flesh, surely neither spirit nor blood. As symbolic of that dark shadow behind the affluence is Shiloh, the Civil War battle which, while proving a huge Union victory, almost destroyed both armies. Shiloh becomes a metonymy for a disintegrating marriage: American disjunction or emptiness presented as its own civil war. Every aspect of American promise is fragmented. Mason's

America is emptied out because of profound disconnectedness, human as well as material.

We find in these marginal emptiers an ideological commitment to the idea, but a paucity of technical resources to convey their vision. While they appear to be mod, they reject some of the basic premises of modernism: its skewed relationships to objects, its difficulties of language and location, its uncertainties about linkages between people and things. Yet they have apparently been deeply influenced by the "moment" or the epiphany, a phenomenon which, falling outside of realism, subverts a rational or ordered experience. At their best, they communicate that moment as if they were creating a new language, and that, possibly, gives them the feel of innovation.

Many of the would-be emptiers are "echo" writers. Often their echoes derive from those who are contemporaries or only slightly older, in the way writers like Tama Janowitz, Frederick Barthelme, and Jay McInerney are indebted to Joan Didion, Donald Barthelme, or other spare writers like Raymond Carver. No influences here from Chekhov or Faulkner or Joyce or Kafka or Conrad-they are, apparently, history. Our contemporary echoers attempt to link themselves to innovation and to experimentation, but, frequently, they fall short. Frederick Barthelme, for one, achieves something beyond minimalism; yet his formula is unvaried. His achievement is in the world of semiotics, a language in which tones and gestures become of equal expressiveness to words. Barthelme often works by litotes, where the element revealed is the result of negating what he may seem to mean.

He negates middle America even while presenting it, but except for a kind of anomic tone which does fit, he lacks the technical resources for molding message to language-what emptiers attempted to do and what the fillers have avoided. Barthelme's characteristic scene is the indeterminate, intermediate world of fast food, casual affairs, indifferent couplings, a "drive-by" culture. He lacks a base or structure, even a point of view to anchor emptiness. Anomie has its limitations. Bartheleme's people are white middle class, inauthentic in every respect, even when their feelings are engaged. Unfortunately, he has not discovered any valid language for this world, except for empty phrasing, statements lacking resonance, silences which hinder words. If the aim is to capture aimlessness or formlessness-and Barthelme is excellent at suggesting that-his shaping does not communicate the coherence of aimlessness. As we know from Beckett and others who pursue anomic visions, that is what language must be about.

Other "echo" writers are Jay McInerney and Tama Janowitz, who in the later 80s seemed to captivate all the lesser forms of the press when they became celebrated as celebrities. They purported to be emptiers-that is, those concerned with seeking out newer forms-but once the reader got behind the flash, there was little substance. In "You and the Boss"-the Boss being Bruce Springsteen-Janowitz attempted something culturally meaningful: the deconstruction of fake heroes and heroines. She deglamorizes Springsteen into a yenta of sorts. So caught up is he in adulation, he cannot distinguish among his wives; his culture is kitsch, and he's uninterested in sex. We have no idea if any of this is true, these being tropes of the rich, famous, and adulated. He wants a child named Elvis, male or female; a wife with a lobotomy would be just fine. Along with Michael Jackson, Jack the Ripper, Reagan (the then President), Hitler, Stallone (after several Rocky's and Rambo's), and Ali, he belongs in a wax museum. "The Boss" becomes part of American facelessness. Except for Warhol's fifteen minutes of fame, he ceases to exist, having become little more than a dumping ground for our fantasy lives. The other stories in *Slaves of New York*, with their casual sexuality, hyped-up drugs, and sadomasochistic behavior (straight and gay) are all ways in which past heroism has been debased into moments of fame, highs, flash. We burn up rapidly, or melt down, like wax under flame.

Language that edges the emptiers' world is found in Lorrie Moore's "How to Be an Other Woman," from *Self-Help* (1985).[196] Moore has found a kind of Woody Allen-like language to describe what it means to be the "other woman"-not the wife, but the disposable mistress. Her use of language is precarious; tip it another way and it fails to be either ironical or amusing. Or else it could be precious, or platitudinous. But in some of the stories, especially this one, she holds it all in perfect balance. It portends well-although her novel *Anagrams* the following year suggests that her achievement lies in the shorter form.

Moore is concerned with the battlefields of gender struggles: the metaphors are all martial, not marital. The "other" woman defines how the female finds herself outside, although Moore does not examine how the philandering man's wife also becomes the "other" woman. In a slangy, colloquial, hip lingo, Moore zeroes in on the way it looks from the outside of any formal rules; a mistress is a disposable item, the eternal outsider, and the one with no apparent rights. Language meets subject. "After four movies, three concerts, and two-and-a-half museums, you sleep with him. It seems like the right number of cultural events. On the stereo you play your favorite harp and oboe music. He tells you his wife's name. It is Patricia. She is an intellectual property lawyer. He tells you he likes you a lot. You lie on your stomach, naked and still too warm."[197] When he asks how she feels about that, she asks, "What is intellectual property law?" He grins and responds, "Where leisure is a suit."[198] The emptiness here derives from the gaps, the silences, the distances between words and feelings.

Still on the edge of emptiers is David Leavitt. In his collection *Family Dancing: Stories* (1984),[199] language wells up from undertones, secret currents, undertows. Often what is unsaid becomes a language of its own. This undertow derives from depths: whether from one's homosexuality or cancer, the individual is left to deal with what is his or her territory. The determinants are internalized; and, therefore, the stories are for the most part incomplete. In the title story, "Family Dancing," the young man whose graduation from prep school is being celebrated wanders off with his sister's male partner. Meanwhile the young man's mother has problems which make her oblivious to what her son is revealing. Her husband has left her in middle age for a younger woman, and while she has herself remarried she still yearns for the first husband. The family "dances" around each other, hiding his or her secrets and pain. All feelings are undercurrents, swirls of balletic recognition of self. The story works at this interior level and even generates a particular language of the unspoken, although externals are ordinary, even trivialized.

Another writer who falls between-and one who deserves a wider reading public than he has obtained-is Barry Hannah. On the surface, Hannah seems the opposite of an emptier; but his use of language, his sneaky strategies for holding a note, his confusion of realms, all, are aspects of the emptiers' arsenal. Often, he finds air where one expects people or things. Hannah writes of exhilaration: music (especially band music, John Philips Sousa), sex (all rippingly healthy) fetishes (feet are a specialty of the house), and violence (fists, knives, guns). He tries to deny despair by insisting on energy. Unlike Paul Auster, who empties out with a vengeance, Hannah exudes an energy which is, however, a disguise for chronic depression. He reaches out to emptiers.

His America sings; it doesn't waltz but rocks. It is full of eccentric personalities, packed with romantic ideas of love and sex. A manic language, lyrical and flowing, becomes part of that love. The undertow of violence, alongside love, is distinctly American: Hannah's native Mississippi and the South are far more uncontrolled than New York City. In the collection *Airships* (1978),[200] "Testimony of Pilot" is exemplary. Arden Quadberry enters a world through his saxophone, like Roy Hobbs with his bat Wonderboy in Malamud's *The Natural*. Both tools of the trade are phallic, but both are transcendental. The wonder is the wonder of America. Hannah:

> The new boy was Quadberry. He came in, but he was meek, and when he tuned up he put his head almost on the floor, bending over trying to be inconspicuous. The girls in the band had wanted him to be handsome, but Quadberry refused and kept himself in such hiding among the sax section that he was neither handsome, ugly, cute nor any-

thing. What he was was pretty near invisible, except for the bell of his horn, the all-but-closed eyes, the Arabian nose, the brown hair with its halo of white ends; the desperate oralness, the giant reed punched into his face, and hazy Quadberry, loving the wound in a private dignified ecstasy.[201]

This life-paragraph embraces a world in a language that becomes part of America's language; and yet it questions things-the horn, the reed, the very face-even as it celebrates them. While Hannah gives a good deal, he implicitly is taking away; the balance is between filling and emptying. His use makes possible the structuring of an unreal world full of terrible events, revelations, all attuned to something just beyond what we consider mainstream. Two worlds, at least, are operational: the one in which people merely respond and the one in which they step over the line into sex, violence, or music; the first depressive, the second manic. The prose fits the surge of orgasm, rising, a crescendo, the long withdrawal into despair, until relieved by the next riff; the prose of band music and jazz, lifting and releasing, then falling back.

Hannah's *Ray* (1980),[202] cut down from an original 400 pages, is now a long story, a little over 100 loosely printed pages, with brief chapters and rapid shifts, lots of white. One of its triumphs is the use of dual narratives, with Ray in both the third and the first person: "he" and "I" shape an American language because they are concerned not only with breaking out, redefining boundaries, remaking oneself, but with an implicit gap between third person and first person experience. In the middle of "he" and "I" is not "you," but an unknown, that gray area of American silence which cannot be communicated. Thus, amidst his burst of words Hannah has his silences, as well as his abandonment of things or people characteristic of emptying.[203]

What keeps Hannah placed between emptier and filler in *Ray* is that despite the strong intimations of despair and depression (an emptier demand) there remains a culture for his defeated, homeless, or beaten down creatures. In his south, they do not fall through the seams, as they do in the northeast; they contain resonance, history, contexts. Even Jeb Stuart, defeated in the Civil War, reverberates with energy. "Sabers, Gentlemen, sabers!" ends the novel. Withal, his characters are not displaced persons. His eccentrics carve out their own lives; life saves, even when it seems to be swallowing its victims. Hannah's words and scenes, at their best, bounce off the page, the result of a living language that serves the angle of vision.

In assessing the "fillers," we must be cautious. These writers, Updike, Bellow, Roth, for starters, helped form the prose of the more immediate postwar world; along with Malamud, Mailer, Flannery O'Connor, Carson McCullers, Styron, Vonnegut, Heller, Oates a little later, they shaped our contemporary literary language. They joined with other voices, some of them in the 50s, but most in the 60s and 70s-like Gaddis, Pynchon, McElroy, Coover-to make American fiction the most exciting in the Western world. But by the 1980s, their voices, with the exception of Gaddis, Pynchon, and that group, was no longer a representative language, nor was their sensibility sufficiently broad and instructive to mean much for the final two decades of the century.[204]

None of this is to be construed as a negative response to their considerable accomplishments; in fact, the sole criticism would be that the more popular ones-for example, Mailer, Styron, Bellow-ran from those innovative practices which might have given their voices more breadth, without the loss of particularity which was their strength. Few of them can offer us an entry point into the 80s and 90s. America is in the process of the kind of change the country has never before experienced, when the very sense of it as a nation is being challenged; and yet its fictional voices from the past keep repeating themselves. Bellow rants at American life from the vantage point of the affluent, and since winning the Nobel Prize two decades ago has given his name-in blurbs and otherwise-to one self-defeating book or idea after another. What was once growth is now rancor and peevishness. He expected better of old age. The other writers have continued to publish, but they recirculate themselves. Styron has written compellingly about his chemical dependency and his acute depression-a moving book, but about himself. Mailer's work has been, and continues to be, about Mailer.[205] All their fifth acts sound familiar.

Some of the more recent writers, those surfacing in the 70s and 80s, have found it difficult to create languages that capture more than particularized or isolated elements. This becomes clear whether short or longer fiction. With some exceptions, the languages we saw proliferating in short fiction have not carried over into broader fictional ideas. And the shorter forms are, also, showing signs of enervation. It is as though the exhaustion which seems to characterize the country-that indifference to larger issues, the loss of flexibility, the intense self-absorption-has created an opening for filler writers with their more traditional ways of proceeding. Different though they are, Updike, Bellow, Helprin, Walker, Tobias Wolff have one thing in common: they have eschewed the very world they are attempting to delineate. They turn their backs on silences, white spaces, pauses, intervals, seams-those strategical elements which communicate resonance and reverberation beyond the word. Yet as we indicated above, a discontinuous America, one splitting into innumerable subcultures, cannot be captured by literary techniques which suggest continuity, wholeness, rationality.

There must be some medium, some language, which suggests emptiness, the sense of the country as a vacuum or as an abandoned place-*as these writers perceive it*. Bellow, for one, struggles against himself; for even as, in *Herzog* earlier, he sees the country emptying out, he cannot tolerate emptiness. He is a compulsive filler, with people, scenes, witticisms, hot arguments-what he does so well to prevent rest or breathing space. He is always *there*, like a mother shoveling food into her kid, and in this few can equal him. So in his shorter fiction-*Him with His Foot in His Mouth* (1984, but with stories going back to 1974)[206] and the novella *A Theft* (1989)[207]-Bellow cannot avoid putting into traditional language ideas that need different expression. Emptiers can suggest more by sidestepping direct expression; fillers have to say *it*. Messages, statements of faith or lack of it, sound hollow when revealed in traditional ways. Bellow proceeds as if languages of expression have remained static; that words mean now what they have always meant.

We observe in shorter fiction-to a lesser extent in the novel-the struggle of emptiers to maintain the flow of modernism against fillers who oppose it. The term "postmodernism," or even "post-postmodernism," has soaked up a good deal of what we once thought of as modernism. Fillers embrace postmodernism-its eclecticism, its validation of realism, its subversion of style itself-as a means of denying that modernism still has some infiltrating influence on the culture. At stake now is nothing less than cultural hegemony, not too different from those in Paris who tried to boo Stravinsky's "The Rite of Spring" off the stage and those who insisted it be played a second time; or those who mocked early forms of Cubism and abstraction and those who perceived what art was insisting upon.

There is little question that fillers, the neo-or pseudo-realists and anti-modernists, have won the day with reviewers and critics, as well as with the popular press and media. The prizes, with few exceptions, go to those who present their work directly, based on clear-cut narrative, with an evident chronology, a minimum of linguistic ambiguity, and less psychological probing than the subject may call for.[208]

In an America so intensely focused on self-interest, on subdividing into groups, on conserving narrow rather than broad views, emptiers face a bleak present. The entire sense of the 90s is to deny the emptiers their role. They can be difficult, they do upset expectations, their abstraction often leaves us afield and awash, their linguistic experiments and problematic use of language make us yearn for "meaning," and their subversion of traditional ideas through irony, ambiguity, and paradox forces us to rethink our own forms of trivia. The cultural crisis is not political but in the broadest sense ideological, and short fiction has been an excellent battlefield. It indeed does show us where we are-but where it is taking us depends on where we want to go.

PART TWO: THE FICTIONAL LANGUAGE

Although this chapter has been concerned mainly with the short story and its languages, several of the arguments bleed over into longer fiction, especially when the authors have also been short story writers. Joan Didion has flirted with minimalism, but hers is more of the terse phrase, the concise statement, the understated than it is of anything smacking of minimalist, or emptier, strategies. In *Democracy* (1984),[209] however, she made a strategical departure. Through the mechanism of incompletion, she was clearly seeking a distinctive language to accommodate the minimalist prose she had made her signature. The verbal expression is characteristic-cut off, elliptical, sharply angled, the vision paranoiac. But language here-in the broadest sense of means of expression, point of view, gesture-depends on narrative angulation, some twisting of the material out of its expected shape. Didion innovates: a self-reflexiveness in which she introduces in the telling both an "I" and a "Joan Didion," entering the narrative as herself, then as her persona. This is a form of language, since it creates a dialogue between first and third person. "Call me author," she begins, with its whiff of Ishmael. The "I," a reporter, tries to put together her novel even as she becomes aware of Didion looking over her shoulder. Yet the promise of the strategy begins to wilt when we meet another one of Didion's wimpy women, Inez Victor (née Christian). Inez has lost much of her life when she married the prominent Harry Victor; and she further loses whatever is left when she must struggle with a hippie dropout daughter, a flaky son, and, not least, the publicity thrust upon her family when her father flips and murders his own daughter and her Hawaiian lover.

It was impossible for Didion to make sense of this mash, unless she planned a Tolstoyan-length novel; but, nevertheless, she has reached for meaning through linkage: that yoking together of disparate elements into some pattern that struggles against the indifference of matter. She heaves toward significance; as if hoping to reveal a language by which neutrality, indifference, the fateful shrug of life can be withstood.

Another writer who moves back and forth from short to long fiction (for shorter forms, *A Night at the Movies Or, You Must Remember This* (1987)[210] is Robert Coover, whose *Gerald's Party*, in 1985,[211] was seeking a metaphor for America; that is, a suitable language for a particular vision of the country. In passages in *The Public Burning* and in the long story "The Baby Sitter," Coover had used not only frenzied bunches of words but frenzied situations, what we also find in Gaddis, in both *J R* and *Carpenter's Gothic*, and in Philip Roth's 1990s novels. In such a tour de force, frenzy becomes a miniature world, bounded only by its own excesses-a darting, insistent language, shifts of perspective, rapid changes of dialogue, often without immediately clear references; an aesthetic based on chaos, turmoil, and churning as the sole way of capturing an American vision. Coover has been and remains a master of chaos, although it can lead to excesses-perhaps that is its strength. Chaos in *Gerald's Party* becomes a self-oriented entity, a micro-world. After a young woman named Ros, who has slept with most of the men at Gerald's party, has been murdered, even the police who arrive become partygoers. The celebration of sexual degradation, violence, messiness, disruption comes to exist for itself: not simply a get-together of friends, but a prophecy.

Unlike minimalists Didion and Frederick Barthelme, Coover is all oral excess-chewing, licking, sucking, tasting. People are always consuming, but rarely retaining. With the toilet broken, guests relieve themselves anywhere, even while the food intake intensifies. Yet death is all around; not only Ros, but also her husband, Roger, and the painter Tania. If the celebrants permitted, the party would become a funeral. But so intent are they on having fun that the deaths become, for most, merely part of the general mess. Gerald's wife, the perfect hostess, cleans up, serves, puts things away, clears debris-as if all that counted, despite the deadly interruptions, was the momentum of the party. She remains oblivious to Gerald's own pursuit of Allison, a married guest; and she leaves the "rational" arrangement of the house to her mother, who cares for the young Mark.

Coover's "language" here is his effort to capture the chaos inherent in our lives as we pursue familiar ends. Working against the churning party is the attempt to keep ordinary things rolling: unplugging the toilet, hiding sexual activities from the child, keeping the debris under control. Our lives in the small area remain on course, become even tidy, while beyond us surroundings crumble. The house is itself destroyed: curtains used as napkins, outlets stopped up, carpets smeared and stained, furniture smashed, junk food squashed everywhere, drinks poured into every receptacle; blood, semen, saliva, and alcohol indistinguishable liquids. Excess has become the norm. The language here is of contraries: Coover's insistence on the trivial things of the world as they bounce off each other and become a gluey mass of fluids and solids, erasing all distinguishing traits from objects and from the people who own them. It is not the language of despair, so much as of the "second coming," the face of chaos, the anarchy that is part of ordinary lives. It is also the language of a violence that is not only urban but also suburban, not only poor but middle class and beyond, not only minority but distinctly white.

In other areas of language-alien to most short story writers-we observe an advocacy or issue-directed form of expression; and this mainly in the hands of black writers. Even Latino writers-for example, Oscar Hijuelas, in *The Mambo Kings Play Songs of Love*-are less issue-oriented and more concerned with individual lives and Latino-Hispanic-Chicano culture. The partisan surge from male Jewish writers and to some degree from white women has more or less ended. Only Philip Roth plugs along at specifically Jewish situations and paranoias. Blacks still feel outside-their designation as African-Americans an indication of that outsider status-whereas Jews and white women perceive themselves as having moved into the mainstream. Jews do not represent themselves as Polish-Americans or Russian-Americans; white women do not label themselves as Jewish or Catholic or Protestant; Italians are no longer Italian-Americans. Among women, only Mary Gordon is referred to as a "Catholic writer," although much of her work describes her struggle with Catholicism, not her representation of it. In any event, she is half-Jewish. Whether Jews and white women actually are mainstream, they have for personal reasons forsaken the advocacy positions of the 60s and 70s.*

Part of the reason for Saul Bellow's ineffectuality is that he has lost his subject. The Jews of the immediate postwar years, caught in such a triumphant novel as *The Adventures of Augie March*, are now as integrated as Irish and Italians, not only mainstream but establishment, except in the corporate world, where Protestant males still hold the fort. Only blacks remain as advocates, critical of the entire structure of American life, not merely of blacks' position within it. No group is better positioned to find a language suitable to protest marginality or even, in some instances, triage. Their protest has been expressed in both shorter and longer fiction, although it is longer fiction that has made the impact.

I have in mind John Edgar Wideman and Toni Morrison (both discussed at greater length elsewhere), John Williams, Alice Walker, and Ishmael Reed. Advocacy fiction creates particular problems for language, since the reader's expectation is of a standardized, realistically based prose which lays out problems, issues, and ideologies without much elaboration. This is not necessarily the reality, but it is the expectation. Accordingly, the writer who advocates or reveals worms in the body politic and social comity is up against several obstacles. Alice Walker discovered this in *The Color Purple* (1982).[212] Language had to cover a great deal of ground,

---

*   Even when the so-called "Jewish novel" was flourishing, many Jewish writers-Mailer, Heller, Doctorow, as starters-did not identify with Jewish life, religion, themes, or Jews. I take this up in greater detail in the chapter "Blacks–Women–Jewish Writers: Racial, Ethnic, and Gender Separation."

from issue-laden matters to conventional narrative to emotional depths and horrors that on occasion lay beyond words. Among some of the issues: questions of gender difference, feminism, master-slave and husband-wife relationships, but also blacks' connection to Africa, women's relationship to other women, deep questions of race and racism, even to matters of appearance, profound psychological questions of whether physical attractiveness can prevent degradation, or, conversely, whether physical unattractiveness can lead to degradation.

Each issue is of considerable significance, and for language to function here it must reach heroic heights; one kind of language might not prove adequate for such severe modulations of content. The author would need an arsenal-which is why it is less difficult to define language in shorter fiction, where a single element or tone is involved. Walker had, in effect, created for herself an almost impossible task; for language which works for Celie's life with her husband is inadequate when the author comes to the strong advocacy parts, the experience of Celie's sister in Africa. Here, language must range from the tortured aspects of Celie's nightmares to her glimpse of Eden. The equation is clear, Africa as Eden, America as degraded and degrading. Furthermore, besides a shift of language, Walker needed more space if she were to make this point, since it is not self-evident, at least not the part in which Africa seems like a prelapsarian Garden. Which Africa? The countries ripping themselves apart or those on the edge of bankruptcy? Which America? Mississippi or Maine? The matter remains to be proved, fictionally proved-not ideologically-and for that Walker lacks the right words. Ideology has overtaken expression. What works so movingly in the personal area has little weight in the political arena. *The Color Purple* lies in Walker's presentation of life through letters, a mode that creates voices, and through voices interrelationships. For this, she has a suitable language. Yet, ironically, this very workable mode struggles against the language selected for advocacy, for issue-directed areas. The epistolary method pushes inward, where Walker is strong; the issue-directed verbiage pushes outward, where Walker is ideologically correct, perhaps, but literarily flat. The epistolary dimensions are compelling in their critique of Mr. and of Celie's expectations; whereas advocacy bleeds off into matters that cannot possibly be developed in a book of this length.

Although in another section of this book I have commented at length on Toni Morrison's body of work, some further words on her *Tar Baby* (1981) are appropriate here. Morrison is unsurpassed in her ability to root people in their place, in delineating what seem ordinary lives, in using the seemingly trivial as a trope for a large sense of life. In *Tar Baby*, however, the advocacy parts-to examine black-white relationships where each representative of his or her race becomes symbolic-falls precipitously into stereotypes. It is as if the book were several short fictions that had to be blended into a novel, while the strength of what becomes the novel lies in the shorter segments. The first stereotype is Valerian Street, who, as a wealthy man, had settled upon a Caribbean island as a kind of benevolent plantation master-surrounded by an entourage of black workers; a master-slave relationship modern style, where money, whiteness, and caste buy everything.

The setup is literarily untenable, while perhaps ideologically sound as a partial metaphor of contemporary America. The exaggerations that fit the political agenda debilitate the literary one. Although the blacks are the stronger figures, they, too, are stereotypical, along with cliché-ridden scenes. Valerian has helped Jadine, daughter of his cook and houseman, gain an education; and she, in turn, takes up with Son, a prototypical black man from hell. Son is so stereotyped he has no particular features: lazy, uneducated, a great stud, physically magnetic, and insistent on "going home," even while he has lived undetected in the Street household. When Son-the name makes one wince-encounters Jadine, he mocks her education and aspirations; he insists that she must have traded sex for education with Street. All locales-even the Southern town where Son lives, Eloe-are stereotypical, including Manhattan, the Caribbean island on which Street has his estate.

The naming of characters seems allegorical, and yet they are cast in realistic terms: Valerian, a medicinal plant, a sedative; Son, Son of? Sun? Oedipus searching for a father?; Ondine, a water sprite; Jadine, jade, a jewel or treasure. Caught between a realistic, advocacy point of view and allegorical characters, all located on an island with a whiff of the Garden, entire elements are never developed. Morrison's lovely lyrical language has few ways of connecting.

In Ishmael Reed's *The Terrible Twos* (1982),[213] a basic language that is satirically very promising becomes predictable in its manic leaps. Once again, what might have been effective in short fiction, a truly inventive jive language, does not work well in longer forms. The idea is based on language: that he who controls Christmas (and Santa) controls America. Control takes the form of information and communication; words reign. While American business hangs on to Christmas as a cornerstone of its commercial empire, two offbeats named Saint Nicholas and a dwarf-like bellhop named Black Peter plot their own games. As a running commentary, the novel becomes an attack on every segment of the Reagan administration and of every previous one: their racial relations, governmental excesses, treatment of the poor, disregard of ethical values. Nelson Rockefeller, for example, is roasted for his handling of the prison uprising at Attica. Santa Claus himself suggests a boycott at Christmas time-giving up our consumption of toys with the aim of bringing business to its knees.

This is Reed's "language" at its best: the discovery of a plot or strategy that defines an insane situation. But the language only occasionally sings; the strategy wears out. Savage satire of the kind Reed has in mind, an issue-directed, advocacy-oriented fiction, requires more. Language becomes solely words, all talk, little grounding. There is no validating embodiment of the idea, solely the satirical treatment of it. It is politically correct rage, but so hyperactive every moment is flash and throb. Gags keep coming-a kind of Robin Williams riff-the attack unrelenting, leaving the reader with no base, no breathing space. All reality is lost in hype. Shorter fiction might have contained the brilliance of the verbal gymnastics; longer fiction can hardly be sustained in this way. The fiction of advocacy, we must conclude-however praiseworthy many may find its social and political aims-strives too hard for meaning, loses itself in rhetoric, reaches for stereotypes, and pursues issues larger than the novel's particular structure can sustain. One of the few novels able to combine language and advocacy was Ralph Ellison's *Invisible Man*. Language there expands beyond words and phrases to shaping of scene, to the creation of spaces, to the sense of interaction longer fiction demands-not resolvables, but interactions.

Another category, that of "growing-up" books, autobiographical but slipping into fictional modes, has added immeasurably to the American language. Here, as I illustrated in an earlier chapter, various styles appear: narrative intermixed with speech patterns of considerable density, experimentation with the integration of dialogue and narrative, innovative ways of capturing personal experiences and reshaping them into a blend of biography and fiction. We see, in fact, the creation of a fresh genre, a break with realism and yet not a complete negation of this most American of modes. The freshness of the genre lies in its daring to discover narrative strategies which slice through strict categories. We note the fictional quality of these "memoirs," but also the nonfictional, biographical nature of them. Especially in the raw depiction of parent-child relationships, we observe a "new language," an effort to catch the discontinuities of the 1980s, in particular.

Although of novel-length, William Gaddis's *Carpenter's Gothic*,[214] in 1985, is a suitable cap for a discussion of languages; especially when we set it alongside another kind of foray into language, Jay McInerny's *Bright Lights, Big City* (1984). In a curious way, *Gothic* has short story potential. The reader is encapsulated in voices, in constant sound; yet the sound, as if part of a shorter fiction, never completes itself or resolves the ostensible subject. Gaddis perceives American life as part of a television script, the ultimate shadow on the wall. His interrupted speech parallels what occurs during programming: small segments of a story interrupted by news flashes, advertisements, public announcements, coming attractions; another round of the program, followed by another sequence of interruptions until the required time expires. Then: a sequence of between-program bits and pieces, coming attractions later that night or on other nights, followed by advertisements; then another program with its own sequences, on through the evening. Life reveals itself to the viewer as five or ten minute segments, or even briefer, from product advertisements to flashes of sinkings, bombings, tornadoes, fires, war killings, subway murders, mob ruboffs.

While we all accommodate ourselves to this presentation of "information," it does influence our modes of perception. To catch that mode is Gaddis's job, and to transform that perception into words, into a new language of seeing, is his m. o. What we observe on television is not that different in other media: the newspaper breaks off a story, then embeds the remainder in a nest of advertisements-so that an impending or ongoing way is nestled amidst sales of Snapple at the local supermarket or a new line of fashions at a posh department store.

A nation of brief segments characterizes Gaddis's world in *Carpenter's Gothic*.[215] This is a novel of interrupted life, those interruptions and discontinuities which, ultimately, shape a language of who and what we are. Just as J R's machinations on the stock market are forms of adolescent conspiracy in that novel, so Paul Booth here is involved in conspiracy within conspiracy. A major one is the creationist plot to take over American schools by outlawing evolution. While seemingly part of a right-wing ideology, the creationist movement is in actuality a radical, revolutionary force, a form of anarchy in the realm of intellect.

Part of the book's "language" comes in Gaddis working through the paradoxes of what has occurred in American life; whereby the right wing has become radical, extremist, revolutionary, and liberals and left-radicals strive to maintain the status quo. In such realigned political forces lies a new perception, and of course a new way of expressing it: a view of how paradox has created such gaps in our understanding that perception must be expressed in new ways. Paul represents the conspiratorial nature of the right wing as he tries to help the Reverend Ude (based broadly on Jimmy Swaggart), an evangelist who prefigures the holy rollers in the news. Intermixed with this is a further conspiracy to take over gold ore fields in Africa, where bribery, extortion, and other kinds of deception abound. Everything about Paul is, in fact, deceptive. Claiming to be a Vietnam hero wounded in action, he has in reality been fragged by one of his own men. Everyone else enters into forms of deception, whether government people, the Reverend Ude, or the sympathetic McCandless, from whom Paul and his wife Liz rent their "Carpenter's Gothic."

Whatever the paradoxes of American life, Gaddis never lets us forget the fragmentary nature of it. Fragmentation has so entered our lives that verbal expression had become bereft of grammar, syntax, cadence; our mouths emit sounds and words, but not sentences, surely not paragraphs and coherent statements. Impulse has transformed discourse. The multiplicity of events is so enormous that language can no longer capture them. The lives of the central characters are diluted by newspaper headlines and television game shows, making lives and programming indistinguishable, or at least overlapping. All coherent life is deconstructed, making it difficult to separate the reality of the character from the role he or she is playing. Only Liz seems to be playing herself, or trying to; and her reward, after years of psychological abuse by Paul, is to be murdered. For the others, role-playing, wearing of masks, taking on of personae-all the paraphernalia of a modernist and postmodernist scenario-are inseparable from Gaddis's transformational "language of conspiracy." In the Gaddis world, nothing is what it seems, and that "nothing" is his metaphor for an America that has lost touch with itself. His is an alternate globe, where the "role" becomes people's signature; so that they are removed from the ordinary world by the way they conceive of themselves, by the way others perceive them. They hope to be self-created, but to the extent the role takes over their lives they are unable to fit themselves back into their skins. Their efforts in either direction create a distinct "Gaddis language."

One final word, on "language as cool." At the other extreme-and at another level of accomplishment-Jay McInerney in *Bright Lights, Big City* (1984)[216] aims at a language of aimlessness. This is a novel about minimalist death, and it requires its own mode of expression. Deadly coke becomes a metaphor for life, not in itself a bad idea. One lives for the rush, the moment of velvety feeling, the high; all the rest-work, trivial routine, communication with others, bourgeois rewards-is a downer. In this respect, McInerney has found a language for upper middle class desolation, the desert of life that has, in reality, passed from merely urban to suburban and even rural areas. Coke bliss is not only a substitute, it is an alternate experience; as we say, another language.

Yet, withal, a language that must collapse. McInerney's twenty-four-year-old pursues the coke experience in New York's discos, and the downtown scene becomes a metonymy of the country: coke as a way of dropping out of or protesting Reagan's America. This beat, dropout scene has something of the "On the Road" and "Easy Rider" quality of the 1950s and 60s, except that McInerney's young man can drop in as well as out. A fact checker at a magazine patterned closely after the *New Yorker*, he finds everything about his job restrictive, suffocating, inadequate-as it must be in contrast to the Edenic bliss of the coke high.

Yet despite some fine sharp passages, McInerney does not perceive his material fully. Through the mists of blow and the anxiety of work, there lies in his young man a firm linkage to nostalgia, stereotypical experiences, the cliché of the "good guy" woman (Megan) who cooks, cares for men, sleeps with them, shares their miseries, and in time is deserted by them. Other young women fall into familiar types: the fast, drug-ridden young vampires of the discos, contrasted with the steady fall girl like Megan. What seems hip or cool is not that at all. It is old time stuff gussied up. Megan is really not a "girl," but a mother; the others whores, a familiar equation. The role of the former is linked to nostalgia for a

Garden experience-dough and bread making at the novel's end are part of that desire for rural salvation. We can say that in this stereotypical, even platitudinous, response the protagonist needs coke as a way of regaining that lost Eden. Discos, weird young women and their guys, destructive scenes reminiscent of Andy Warhol's factory, sexual as well as social kinkiness are all substitute vehicles for mom's tit. Peruvian or Bolivian flake must make do in lieu of validating one's personal life.

The staging area of death is the *New Yorker*-like magazine, with fact-checking squeezing out life. The protagonist is suitably trapped: between work that suffocates and play that portends an early death. The equation, which comes hopped up in bright language, is, if not infantile, then reductive-although the lights are bright and the city is indeed big. The downtown world of cool and blow is as old hat as Kerouac beat. What McInerney once referred to as his group of writers and editors being "a galaxy of our own" is, in reality, a falling star exploding into unidentifiable fragments. Yet in another novel published right after *Bright Lights, Ransom* (1985), McInerney does not reach out for "new languages" and wrote a very effective book about a young American living in Kyoto, Japan. Ransom tries to purify himself through classes in karate; and McInerney's telling-except for the final shootout at the O. K. corral-indicates how talented he could be if he stayed with more conventional, less cool, forms. In his case, striving for new languages fails; more traditional realism succeeds. Finding a suitable, original language, whether for the short story writer, memoirist, or novelist, remains an American dilemma.

CHAPTER SIX

SECOND WORLD WAR AND VIETNAM WAR FICTION: CONTRAST AS CULTURAL DIFFERENCE

Vietnam War novels and even nonfiction (such as Caputo's *A Rumor of War*, Kovic's *Born on the Fourth of July*, Herr's *Dispatches*, Hackworth's *About Face*, more currently Sheehan's *A Bright Shining Lie*) are, in a sense, removed from history, roving outside time and space.[217] The fiction writers who turned to the war-Tim O'Brien, James Webb, John Sack, John Del Vecchio, Larry Heinemann, Philip Caputo, Rod Kane, Robert Stone indirectly-have converted it into an ahistorical aberration by thrusting it almost entirely into a present disconnected from past or future. By handling it in this way, they make the war more nightmarish: that is, so removed from anything familiar in time or space it hangs there, itself a fantasy life of sorts. What distinguishes Vietnam War fiction from that about World War II is its disembodied quality; it is dissociated from anything occurring back home or even back on the base. It is disconnected even from the men experiencing it. The men enter a surreal area when they fight: jungle, sky, whirling coptors, a phantasmal enemy, loss of distinction between friend and foe. Ground itself loses its context.[218]

One of the key differences comes in what our side considered a victory. Victory in Vietnam was measured in terms of body counts; the number of enemy dead determined whether we had won or lost an engagement, whether we were winning or losing the war. In World War II, the measure of victory was land, ground gained against fierce opposition; often not much ground at all, but nevertheless earth and land were measures of success. One took an island in the Pacific, which was a land area; one did not gain victory by killing 30, 300, or 3000 Japanese. Comparably, in Europe, one advanced and took villages, towns, and cities from the enemy; German dead, even when numbers piled up, did not become a measure of triumph. The distinction is a crucial one, and not merely grisly.

In citing body counts in Vietnam as ways of claiming victory, our side in effect admitted defeat before we got started and helped create the surrealism of the effort. For if we assumed that Asian populations extended to near infinity, any number of human sacrifices were possible, and Asians, we said, did not value life as much as Westerners did. With those assumptions-and they were stated at various times during both the Korean and Vietnam Wars- a body count becomes meaningless; since the other side could afford to lose an indefinite number of men, women, and children and still return with more. When land or ground is the test of victory, the assumption is that a country and a people exist in some finite sense; and if you take away the ground belonging to them, you defeat them. You do not need to kill them all. The premise of the body count, however, is that eventually one must kill the entire population if need be to achieve final victory. Implicit in the body count is the notion that friends as well as enemies will be caught up in the death nets; and, after all, it makes little difference, since friend and enemy in any event cannot be distinguished.

With two such different emblems-ground in one war, death in the other-writers will structure responses to the wars that will be entirely distinct. When you attempt to end the war by killing off the population, the indifference to human life becomes critical, and there is, implicitly, a racial assumption: that the people being killed have no viable culture, make no difference in the world, are so different from us that their deaths lack reality. People are indeed "wasted," as the expression was used; turned to waste matter, defecated, and even our side was wasted, placed in body bags little different from the garbage bags used back home: bagging the garbage or dead leaves. The concept of war gives way to a concept of denying another's culture; denying life itself, so that death, not victory, becomes the prerequisite of all thinking about the war. Michael Herr's *Dispatches* catches this better than the novels do, and his description of the Lurps, the ultimate killers who are atavistic in their response to the war, reinforces the sense that the war is not a struggle for people's allegiances but a way of reducing the population in areas where people do not matter.

If the aim is to win ground, there is the recognition that territory underlies a viable culture; that towns and villages and cities are the foundations of real people's lives. The people, however evil their state, are not ghosts or phantoms. In the Vietnam War, however, so much of the fighting took place in and around undifferentiated jungle that it created disorientation; that, in turn made death, not land, the measure of victory. An enemy lurking in the jungle, refusing to come out to fight, refusing indeed to be distinguished from those loyal to the government makes of everyone with an Asian look something of a spectre.

Furthermore, the Vietnam War was the first one in which America was a client state. We did not come in as the primary conquerors-to-be, but as an invader of a culture in which we were advisors, lookouts, special forces; where we sneaked in the back door as warriors. Only later did we take over the running of the war; but before that huge buildup of American troops after Johnson's Presidential victory in 1964, we were at the mercy of our local allies. This had not happened before-in World War II, whether the Pacific or the European theatre, American forces acted as the army of occupation. Our leaders did not clear political and military matters with local chiefs; they acted in their own best interests. In Vietnam, the wishes of the South Vietnamese had to be taken into consideration, and this nearly always, as Neil Sheehan describes it, through placating and bribing corrupt officials. What this did was to create a distaste for our side as well as for the enemy. This indifference to human life encoded in body counts is implicit in the political arrangements.

The lack of differentiation between friend and foe, the sense that the world had receded, the recognition that individual sacrifice meant little or nothing, the ever-present jungle as phantasmagoria or spectre all made the men hang together in the presentness of Now. War has always thrown a body of men into an intense present, in which past and future, whether personal or the world's, must become secondary to the Now situation, where life and death play themselves out. But even given that all wars accentuate Now, the Vietnam War was almost unique in the Now-ness of its terms. For its soldiers were indeed cut off, since the war became increasingly unpopular at home, and from the beginning it was a vacillating process, with no clear goal of what victory meant. Caught up in that, the men had only the present each day as one fewer they would have to serve. In World War II, men were in for the duration, if they lived; whereas in the Vietnam War, they served for a set time, one year, or two, depending on their enlistment. Thus each day had a different durational quality-soldiers did not look forward to the end of the war, as they did in World War II, but to the end of their tour of duty.

This emphasis on Now-ness meant that Vietnam novels and nonfictional forms-"near novels," we may call them-had little political or social fallout.* There is almost none of that political discussion such as we find in *The Naked and the Dead*, none of the

---

* Or in a collection of individual experiences in Keith Walker's *A Piece of My Mind* (1985). Here, mainly nurses speak of their tours of duty in Vietnam, and we are struck by the absence of context, the lack of a bigger picture, for their intense, painful, and courageous acts.

political symbolism or allegory of *Catch-22*, none of the social potential of *From Here to Eternity* and *The Gallery*, none of the overt ideology of *The Young Lions*. The reasons are of several kinds. The majority of World War II war fiction is European-based; and even in a book like *The Naked and the Dead*, where the main action takes place in the Pacific, the political discussions are more appropriate to the European theatre. Since several writers of World War II novels were themselves of European background, many of them Jews whose parents and grandparents had emigrated to America, it is clear their focus would be on political matters pertaining to Europe, not Asia. Furthermore, many of the writers were from the Northeast, or had settled in the Northeast and the New York area-which made them especially responsive to Europe. The Pacific War, in fact, had little political resonance, because "politics" as such were connected simplistically to the attack on Pearl Harbor. Little was known or thought of Japanese culture, or of historical events leading to that attack. Politics, however, were nearly always present in the European-theatre war novels. More on this later.

In the Vietnam War, there was an absence of political ideas or ideology because Vietnam or that entire region had no historical meaning, no past or present, no contextual significance for Americans. Most would have been hard-pressed to find Vietnam on a world map even during the conflict, no less before it began to become a killing ground. In addition, the racial differences made Vietnam as a political entity seem far beyond anything an American could assimilate, even if geographical and historical understanding were better in this country. In still another respect, the Vietnam War was a covert one. Americans did not know that by 1963 Kennedy had sent in over 11,000 advisors, many of them far more than advisors. For most, if their sons were not fighting in Vietnam there was little knowledge a war was occurring there until well into the 1960s. All of this inevitably affected the way the war was described in the novel: fiction, especially war and combat fiction, cannot exist in a vacuum. The lack of knowledge of what was going on reinforced the Now-ness of the novel, the ahistorical quality of the conflict and the intensity of given events, not the war itself. What we saw in James Jones's *The Thin Red Line*, with its intense attention to one particular World War II battle in the Pacific, becomes the major mode for the Vietnam War novel.

As a consequence of all these factors, the Vietnam novel, unlike its predecessors, does not become gigantic or oceanic. It is not of Mega-Novel size, a term I have used elsewhere to indicate a particular kind of fiction that can, theoretically, go on seemingly endlessly. Although war and combat novels as a genre do not go on indefinitely, since there is usually a climax, victory, or some other resolution, the great length of several World War II novels takes on Mega-Novel dimensions: *The Naked and the Dead*, *The Young Lions*, *From Here to Eternity*, for examples. They were, indeed blockbusters in their complicated presentation of several kinds of materials: varied groups of characters, historical backgrounds as well as personal pasts, political ramifications at least in the Mailer and Shaw novels, as well as long narrative passages either of battles won or forays undertaken. In the Jones novel, social politics of the 1930s is implicit, with the novel ending with the attack on Pearl Harbor; but even before that, the presentation of Prewitt has within it caste and class ideas deeply linked to Depression-era conditions. Further, Jones's use of an insistent Naturalism suggests a strong ideological component: Naturalism as an implicit attack on the way the country has arranged itself, so that the individual is lost amidst large, unforeseen factors created by others or by circumstances. Whatever the precise mix, these three novels suggest a large, inclusive, political, and historical interpretation, for which the war is the ultimate catalyst.

This Mega or blockbuster mode is not to be found in the Vietnam War novel-which is a reflection of the kind of war it was and the kind of quandary which the novelist found himself in. When a Vietnam War novelist did want to extend his range-as in Tim O'Brien's *Going After Cacciato*[219]-he followed, however adeptly, in the footsteps of *Catch 22*. Cacciato's squad pursues him to a spot where they think he is trapped, but he eludes them. This is the last phase of a realistic narrative; after that, we enter a fantasy world. O'Brien's book chronicles the fantastic journey of the squad as it chases Cacciato across Asia and Europe toward the "capital of the world." Cacciato himself remains shadowy, even though he seems to help the squad when the Shah's secret police, the SAVAK, are about to execute them. Along the way, the American soldiers pick up a Chinese girl named Sarkin Aung Wen, who represents something very real, for she hopes to create for herself a life apart from the army.

The main thrust of the novel is that fantasy journey to Paris, a kind of magic carpet flight across Asia. Crossing the journey at several points, ten in all, are holding actions, comprising the "observation post." These brief sections, pages rather than chapters, recall the Promenades in John Horne Burns's *The Gallery*. Facing toward journey aspects, yet themselves static, they hold the action back in the real world of Paul Berlin's first day in combat. Paul is one of the men who take off after Cacciato, and he becomes the registering consciousness of much of the novel. The "observation post" is a four-hour watch Paul stands, and it provides commentary on his dreams and perceptions of events. The segments are spaced in irregular patterns, which allow basic rhythms to emerge, with closeness giving way in the middle pages to distant spacing, then returning to smaller intervals, the end as at the beginning. The idea is ingenious, in that its static element-the post never moves, of course-works with and against the fantasy journey, while giving it grounding and still affording it dimensions and alternate possibilities.

Playing against the "post" and the journey is a third element-the description of Paul's first day in combat. The interplay of these elements gives us a three-part frame: the present of the journey, the present of the observation post, and the present of the combat experience, from which he had run only in his imagination. Little (except Cacciato's pursuit of Paris) is future, or past; all is Now. That Now-ness-intensified by the running together of several elements in some kind of modernistic phantasmagoria-is characteristic, as we have noted, of Vietnam War fiction.

Although it is nonfiction, Michael Herr's *Dispatches*[220] is such a remarkable piece of imaginative prose it reaches toward a fictional statement about the war. Its language owes a great deal to Norman Mailer's breakthrough in *Why Are We in Vietnam?*, possibly *his* finest fictional effort. Herr's achievement is that he found a prose commensurate with the world he was describing: men in shadowy combat, killer coptors, the "Lurps," those special killers, the fantasy world which Vietnam became for anyone who looked beyond the mere killing grounds. What Herr achieved was something none of the novelists of this particular war even reached for-that language itself, apart from the scenes depicted, which would prove to be a verbal equivalent of the war experience. Mailer had reached for that in his Vietnam War novel, in which Nam appears only in the final page. Herr tried for it and was quite successful.

At its best, Herr's language goes into musical phrasing, and the music is the characteristic sound of the war, rock and roll. Frenzied, death-like beats, pounding, noise beyond noise-rock and roll fitted the type of army which formed to fight that war; quite different from the more democratically-based army of World War II. Rock and roll with its raunchy tones, its explicit sounds, its overtones or rough dealing was itself a language; and in it Herr found his own. "Breathing In" is a section that opens the book, and it is itself a paradox, since breathing in indicates one lives. In the section, one dies. "Holy war, long-nose jihad like a face-off between one god who would hold the coonskin to the wall while we nailed it up, and another whose detachment would see the blood run out of ten generations, if that was how long it took for the wheel to go around."[221] That wheel going around seems to be the wheel of chance, to see which casualties would be dusted off, and brave officers are not popular because they get their men killed.

By 1967, when the whole tone of the war had turned, Herr sees only spooks, those who had bought the ideas of the New Frontier and then became its "saddest casualties." ". . . left now with the lonely gift they had of trusting no one, the crust of ice forming over the eye, the jargon stream thinning and trickling out: *Frontier, sealing, census, grievance, black operation* (pretty good, for jargon), *revolutionary development, armed propaganda*. I asked a spook what that one meant and he just smiled. Surveillance, collecting and reporting, was like a carnival bear now, broken and dumb, an Intelligence beast, our own. And by late 1967, while it went humping and stalking all over Vietnam the Tet Offensive was already so much incoming."[222] By 1967, the government had sold out the army.

A rock and roll prose does not disallow a literary bent. "Once it was all locked in place, Khe Sanh became like the planted jar in Wallace Stevens' poem. It took dominion everywhere."[223] In another respect, Herr knows the Vietnam War spurred an entirely different vocabulary-one was wasted, not killed; men suffered from acute environmental reaction, not shell shock; the men were grunts, not GIs; the enemy and even the South Vietnamese were slopes. While this need for a distinctive vocabulary helped separate the two wars, most of the Vietnam designations were forms of degradation not only for the enemy but also for one's own side. In this way, Herr decentered English as a form of communication. Since "wasting" means turning that individual to garbage, the central historical word of killing someone or putting him to death is insufficient for what occurred. By putting someone to death in a real battle, one defined a recognizable terrain; one located the individual's death in an historical context, where death is part of battle. By "wasting," one relocated death into garbage and devalues life to such an extent it becomes, literally, waste matter, and, by implication, shit. A vocabulary such as this helps to deconstruct a war-decentering it from its primary function of winning ground, pushing back an enemy, taking his towns and cities, and capturing large numbers of soldiers and arms, until he must call it quits. None of this worked in Vietnam.

Westmoreland's war of attrition, as Herr and others readily show, moved the war into unrecognizable areas. As Neil Sheehan reveals in his massive book on John Paul Vann and the war,[224] the Vietnam conflict kept moving away from "war" into terrain Americans could not penetrate. This was an act of military deconstruction, made especially intense by the fact the enemy could blend in with the friendlies. The Viet Cong and the North Vietnam Regulars, by merging with the indigenous population, had so relocated the terms of war that they were fighting one kind of conflict, the Americans another. It went beyond guerrilla warfare into a shapeless mass-and this alone distinguishes it from previous wars and alters the fiction that will reflect it. A decentered, relocated, shapeless war does not lend itself to a fiction that ordinarily needs solid grounding. A war whose victory depended on all the Vietnamese being killed could no longer be describable. Every Vietnam War novelist had to confront separate and distinct qualities, even while hanging on to World War II novels as examples. Let us examine some of the referents.

As we know, in the years immediately following the Second World War, an entire subgenre of the novel developed: the war and combat novel, which then appeared regularly thereafter in the 1950s and 60s, skipping (in the main) the Korean War,[225] and then trying to come to terms with the Vietnam War. The war/combat novel became for the American novelist a socio-political fiction; for at their most incisive, such novels reflect profound cultural concerns. We immediately see how they differ from Vietnam War fiction, which reflects the culture very differently, if at all-and when it does reflect anything, it is usually a certain class of men, their lack of real choice in going to war, and their fears they have been betrayed by people back home. While reflecting the larger culture, World War II novels demonstrate continuity with traditional American themes, mirroring not only contemporary society but also America itself.

Present are themes associated with an Edenic vision, pastoral as salvation, urban life as corrupt or polluted, the need to escape or run. Even a slight, but effective, novel like Harry Brown's *A Walk in the Sun* (1944)[226] reflects American cultural aspirations. The goal of one small group of men, a platoon (individuals, not large undifferentiated masses of men, but recognizable faces with recognizable needs and pasts), is to reach a farmhouse. That farmhouse "at the end of the road" is either pastoral salvation or violent death. Brown evokes the elemental nature of war, connected with the pastoral tradition: the earth, which the men hug as though their mothers; farm and farmhouse as possible mythical salvation; the silent planes, like birds, which loom up and bring instant death, only to disappear rapidly-the sudden catastrophe so familiar from American Naturalistic fiction; the road in the sun, the bright light of Italy, its heat and also its death. The farmhouse is itself in the middle of nowhere, Thoreau's cottage transformed into a desirable goal, the end of that road, but also a potential death house. It is no longer clear whether pastoral saves or destroys.

The sensibility underlying the war novel specifically has within it the strands of the social writer. A masculine world, it is not so exclusively masculine as the novel of combat. The essential element is that war novels use the military as social commentary. *From Here to Eternity*, surely one of the most exhaustive of these novels, in its prewar scenes is the "war novel" equivalent of *The Grapes of Wrath*, the army base in Hawaii substituting for the dust bowl of the Steinbeck novel. The Jones is, of course, more than that; but it is as much an atomization of the society-class, caste, upward mobility, political infighting, matters of power, controlled capitalistic systems-as of the military. Although there is no war in most of the novel, it points toward the attack on Pearl Harbor, and when the attack does come, Jones has suggested for us a military society that reflects the larger society.

The war novel, then, is not solely a subgenre of the novel, but is, in this respect, as much a part of fictional representation as the novel of manners in James, Fitzgerald, or Wharton, the novel of social disaster in Steinbeck or Dos Passos, the novel of class and caste in Dreiser and Lewis, the novel of individual dislocation in Wolfe, Norris, or even Hemingway. What the war provided was a huge arena for all the social and political energies of the novelists.

Politics were not at all ignored in the 1940s and 50s, but were frequently incorporated into the war (not combat) novel. This type of fiction has no parallel in the Vietnam War, where a social or even political dimension was virtually impossible to introduce.

The combat novel-*The Thin Red Line* and *Whistle*, *The Naked and the Dead*, some background scenes in *The Gallery*-is more exclusive, and it is far more masculine. While it would be possible for a woman to write a war novel-*Guard of Honor*, for example, is within a woman's range of experience-it is unlikely a woman would write a novel of combat, *unless* as purely an act of imagination, perhaps the way Crane and Stendhal invented battle scenes. Even so, theirs are perspectives on battle, rather than purely battle. This stress is important, for the novel of combat has within it the same kind of masculine preoccupations that we find in western and gangster novels; combat legitimizes the killing, yet many rules of conduct still hold true. Further, the absence of women in the combat novel-as against the war novel-except for an occasional hooker or waif-decentralizes it as a social construct. One reason the Vietnam War novel is so lacking in social context is that women, again except as prostitutes (and, therefore, voiceless), are missing. There obviously can be no meaningful social comment when representatives from half the population are absent.

The novel of combat is essentially a subgenre of the war novel, not the main thing. The war novel sweeps, the combat novel focuses. Only indirectly can it mirror the culture: for its violence is legalized, and its special conditions create a special kind of man and response. It carries over very little; it *is*. Despite its focus on battle situations, the combat novel becomes an intensely individual thing. For behind the war focus is the testing out of the individual: not the winning of the battle or the war, but the individual's victory over himself. Because of that focus on self, Americans are particularly fine combat novelists. In this respect, Vietnam War novels are directly descended from the combat fictions of World War II, not from the war novel generally. In the Vietnam War, victories were amorphous and had little significance beyond body counts. The sense of winning or losing was really in terms of dead; as noted above, land was hardly the issue. The individual's ability to survive within such a war became a mark of his self-ness, his care in foreseeing difficulties, and, of course, the sheer good luck involved in all combat situations. The resonance of the Vietnam War novel, like its combat predecessor, derives from that mixture of fear and courage called up in the individual soldier.

In the combat segments of Mailer's *The Naked and The Dead*, we find the best parts of the novel-and these scenes could in the main be transposed into the Vietnam War. From these combat scenes, we observe both the strengths and limitations of Mailer's world: in the male's response to challenge. Physical courage in the face of fear becomes the way a man can measure not only himself but also the quality of life. By way of bravery, the individual breaks through historical restriction. By positioning himself in the Cooper and Hemingway tradition, Mailer fixed his field of vision, forced himself to repeat, and often led himself into blind alleys, except in his "Vietnam" novel, where everything coheres.

Writers of combat fiction-in both wars-are happiest when they can bring the placid, rather stodgy American soldier up against a situation in which he becomes a killer, rapist, brutal wielder of power. The idea in Mailer, Jones, and others is to find that means by which the American soldier can be "awakened" to the primitive elements lying beneath, to what the Indian once meant to the Puritan and then to the pioneer. The experience in combat also has reference to a religious awakening, to being touched; it has elements, in our fiction, of revivalism, the sense of doom in the sermons of ministers of the Great Awakening, of religious apocalypse. Combat, which may confer swift death, also means a kind of quickened life. We are not in the presence of the Greek tragic sense of violence and death, which leads, ultimately, to a reckoning with the gods. For the American, there is no reckoning; violence establishes a purity with its own rules, its own field of force. When an American soldier reaches beneath his unfocused history toward the elemental or primitive force, he is reaching toward the vitality that identifies him as American. This held for the Second World War.[227]

In the Vietnam War, that clean, primitive feeling was ambiguous, shadowy, not definable; because the enemy was unclear, the war unexplained, the people back home not behind it, the distinction between native population and soldier blurred. When the enemy is not in uniform and may be a sweet-looking ten-year-old, then the American soldier cannot feel that violence has a cleansing effect. Quite the contrary. As Vietnam War novels repeatedly show, all the fun has gone out of killing. There is no resonance of a job well done, although there may be revenge for the death of one's buddy. But revenge is not the same as knowing that killing the enemy and winning a piece of land is a victory; there were few such victories in the later war.

Further, the presence of so many novels depicting the Vietnam War as a nightmarish memory, extending well into the postwar years, suggests how the idea of victory has been tarnished by the very nature of the experience trying to achieve that victory. Philip Caputo's *Indian Country*, in 1987,[228] and Tim O'Brien's *In the Lake of the Woods*, in 1994,[229] are the dominant novels here; describing in great detail how the war hovers long after the war has ended. More on that later. Another novel in this growing subgenre- especially now that the Veteran's Administration has recognized post-traumatic stress disorder as an illness-is Rod Kane's strong *Veteran's Day*, in 1990.[230] Not until Veteran's Day in 1982, when the Vietnam War Memorial in Washington is in place, does Rod Kane, the writer and also the main character in the drama, make some peace with his memories, nightmares, terrors. Only then can he comprehend how his warrior spirit in the earlier place has compromised and positioned every aspect of his life as a civilian. For him, writing provides a therapeutic outlet, although Kane the character does not live long to enjoy it. So unlike the way action is presented in World War II fiction, here combat is relegated to memory, presentness to pastness; memory, nightmare, and the rest are not significant in the earlier novel, since the war can somehow be reconciled with something positive. In Kane's world, while the character dies, the writer continues-and writing, the word, the reliving of events serve as much as do Alcoholics Anonymous and therapy at a Veteran's Hospital.

Like Mark Helprin in his more expansive and more fully-wrought *A Soldier of the Great War*, Kane is wrenched and torn by the way lives are disrupted by the war, and then destroyed. He does not see death as the enemy; he does see the loss of the future as the evil done by war. When he throws in his medals along with the other discarded medals from the war, at a Washington rally, he is destroying the past-as *that past* has destroyed his future, has destroyed the future of so many.

Ron Kovic's better-known *Born on the Fourth of July*, in 1976,[231] a notable American anniversary, was one of the first to use the past as a destructive force against the future. Inasmuch as Kovic returned from the war a paraplegic, his physical condition is a reminder of what pastness can do; but his anger goes further. For in his Vietnam experience, he sees all the corruption of life, even when men performed heroically, even nobly; and in that corruption lay the doom of his life, the fate or destiny that would return him a paraplegic. In one respect, this should, also, have been the message of Lewis B. Puller, Jr. in *Fortunate Son* (1991),[232] a biographical memoir. As the son of Chesty Puller, a legendary marine hero, Lewis Jr. was in a sense doomed to serve in Vietnam, doomed to bear whatever militarily came his way-and his response should have been to question a fate which gave him little choice. Instead, he wrote this book, honoring the father, equivocating on the war, presenting himself less a victim than as a man choosing, in the process winning the Pulitzer Prize for biography, and then committing suicide as he spiraled into alcoholism, drug dependency, loss of wife and children, and all the rest. Memory should have done him in, but he resists it, and he destroys himself. Kovic, on the other hand, survives, listens to the patriotic fervor of those who did not experience combat, and turns against the war that paralyzed him.

He recognizes that his sacrifice has been for nothing, and in some strange way that perception of the war-as one orderly tells him, he can shove the Vietnam War up his ass-allows him to continue. In resistance and opposition, he finds some way to vent his anger against memory. In fictional terms, as we move toward the more fully-fashioned *Indian Country*, we find in Larry Heinemann's *Paco's Story* (1986)[233] still another "memory novel" of a soldier, Paco, who carries Vietnam back to America and finds he cannot handle his past. He takes a job as a dishwasher at a greasy spoon, swallows painkillers for his wounds, listens in fury to the owner of the greasy spoon about his World War II adventures, spies on a girl who is also spying on him, all of it incoherent and inherently self-destructive. He has no future, only that past which erupts into chaos. So, too, in Joe Klein's nonfictional "novel" *Payback: Five Marines After Vietnam*, in 1984:[234] still another part of this "combat recollected" not in tranquility but in rage, anger, and opposition.

Indian Country, however, gives one of the fullest expressions to the memory-combat novel. All efforts by Christian Starkmann ("strong man," with obvious allegorical connotations as Christian Everyman) to lead a normal life in the Indian country of Michigan's Upper Peninsula are thwarted by his memories of Vietnam. In the Peninsula, he has removed himself as far as possible from the jungles of Vietnam where, he feels, he failed his men and himself-a failure that led directly to the death of one of his men-but even the Peninsula cannot save him. He fouls up his job as a forest ranger, and he runs afoul of the good wife in a marriage devastated by his memories. He is so stressed out that his behavior becomes increasingly bizarre and uncontrollable; and he only finds peace, or redemption, when he confesses to the Indian father of the dead soldier that he, Christian, was responsible for the death. Implied in this rather sentimentalized redemptive act is the fact that America betrayed Starkmann, that only by returning to basics deep in the past and deep in forest and natural lore is there any possibility of expiation and normalization. Otherwise, the war continues in the lives of men like Christian-strong man though he be-and, as well, in the American unconscious. The war has burned holes that only Indian country-the real America-can save. We may reject the sentimentality and softness of the resolution, but still see it as a metaphor of how the country must respond: that only in our most profound sense of ourselves, which we must plumb far from all the corruptive influences of Washington, politicians, and government itself, can we discover the redemptive power which will exorcise the nightmares.

Together with those other fictions and nonfictions that shape a subgenre of the combat novel, this book serves notice that the Vietnam War novel has carved out a different role from that of the World War II novel. Combat is nearly always present in this subgenre, but combat is only the catalyst, not the main arena; these books strive for a field of vision extending beyond the battle or the war. They seek to invest the entire country with a kind of collective guilt, or if not guilt then responsibility to remember. And beyond that, beyond remembering, lies expiation, the possibility of redemption which comes with recognition of who the soldiers were, what they had to do, and how they were abandoned in the country's consciousness once their tour of duty ended.

But beyond even that is an implicit criticism of government itself: those who pushed for the war, those who expanded it, those who lied to make the war seem viable, those who deceived and intrigued for reasons of career, those who became rich over it, and, finally, the large majority who having once supported the war as a patriotic duty wanted to forget it even existed. In effect, most of the country is involved in these acts of nightmarish memory; and here the Vietnam War novel has carved out its own space.

To drive home this point, we have *In the Lake of the Woods*, Tim O'Brien's 1994 novel of post-traumatic stress disorder writ large for Vietnam vets. Here, John Wade doesn't fight the war; he fights the memory of the war. Memories, especially of the My Lai massacre, dog Wade throughout his career as a rising politician, until public revelations of his role in the war undermine his primary run for the Senate. He is, also, a magician, a man who works with mirrors and for whom illusions can often close out the reality of what he has done-killed innocent people in the action which made Lieutenant Calley infamous. The narrative zigzags between past and present, the war of decades ago now immediate, as though some Proustian moment had activated memory that carries with it an incandescent intensity.

Unlike World War II fiction, *In the Lake of the Woods* does not focus on a war but on pastness; Wade dreams, suffers repeated nightmares, and cannot fully function once his self-torture is activated. His wife, Kathy, who must allay her own demons, finally walks away from their cabin in the Lake of the Woods and vanishes. Wade joins in the search, until he, too, disappears in the vast network of lakes of northern Minnesota.

In the army, Wade has been called the Sorcerer, capable as he is of Houdini-like tricks. But even as Sorcerer-a modern-day Merlin- he cannot make the memories lessen or abate; and his fear from the 60s carries over into the 80s and 90s. Despite the presence of an Eden-like countryside, the land which promises redemption-as we saw in Caputo's *Indian Country*-cannot alleviate the pain Wade experiences. The earthly paradise, a dispossessed Eden, is poisoned by memories of the war. In a way, all this is further connected to Caputo's 1983 novel, *DelCorso's Gallery*,[235] in which photography (the "gallery" of war pictures) reflects a reality DelCorso cannot confront in his life. Wade uses mirrors as a means of evasion; DelCorso uses cameras. But the goal is the same: to displace reality into either magic or images. Similarly, in O'Brien's 1990 *The Things They Carried*,[236] the materials of the war-the "things they carried"- cannot disguise what lies behind, the soldier himself and the evil spirits he cannot exorcise. Materials serve only temporary displacement. In still another "memory novel," Rod Kane's *Veteran's Day*, Kane as both character and writer, as we have seen, finds himself haunted by demons-until, in 1982, on Veteran's Day, he can exorcise them at the Vietnam War Memorial in Washington D. C.

In its insistence on holding our experience, the Vietnam venture has something of the extension of the European Thirty Years War or even the Hundred Years War. There is little peace, little redemption, although the War Memorial has helped; and in several cases, even the presence of Edenic space cannot alleviate the pain, anguish, and sense of abandonment. But such fiction goes further, because it implies that the entire war venture, whether at the time politically valid or not, was based on abandonment, triage, victimization. Redemption when it does come only arrives when the veteran recognizes he has lived through his victimization and he can emerge a person once again. For Wade in *In The Lake of the Woods*, that moment cannot ever come, since he chooses to merge with the lakes and woods, an idyllic setting which does nothing to lessen his self-destruction. The war goes on and on, and kills and kills.

In a particularly trenchant passage, in a generally incisive book, Richard Slotkin in *Gunfighter Nation*[237] points out how the American Western has isolated the saloon as the equivalent of the jungle clearing in, chiefly, Vietnam War novels. "Like the jungle clearing in the war film, the saloon is a space we leave only when danger threatens, or to accomplish some brief mission. And like the jungle clearing, the saloon's enclosure is threatened by powerful forces."[238] Slotkin also points out that the saloon enclosure is a theater, that its actions "could easily be transferred to a proscenium setting."[239] Similarly, the same could be said of the jungle setting- it is theater of a particularly brutal kind, and *its* proscenium is the clearing between the soldiers' line and where the enemy begins. But this formulation does not take into account the psychological and emotional dimension; it is merely a physical image. The subgenre we have been discussing enters a different kind of theater, and a different proscenium, one that lies within an area that becomes part of memory and cannot be exorcised by a shootout. Film has yet to reproduce this phenomenon.

As for the novel of combat, it clearly connects the American experience in war to that in detective and western fiction. It brings back the sole frontier remaining to us and provides an alternative to a bourgeois society. Of equal importance is the fact that the novel of combat removed the writer from ideological concerns, placing him in an elemental area that both transcends and falls beneath politics. This was, and is, obviously important for the American novelist, who is traditionally uncomfortable with ideological materials. Not unexpectedly, much Vietnam War fiction-even in the subgenre of "memory"-is heavy on combat, even though feelings about war could no longer be clean, pure, or elevating.

Just as musical comedy, not opera, became a distinctive American musical tradition, so the novel of combat, rather than the socially-oriented fiction associated with the continent, became a distinctive American form. In combat, the American was, in a sense, returned to that time when he was created in the wilderness Zion of the Puritans, or, even more, in the Adamic wilderness of earliest man. This was the time before Eve, or else Eve was not yet wife. There were no children, no responsibilities except to other men, and there is the camaraderie of a fellow world, untouched by the feminizing world, which, seemingly desirable, is so feared. This is the vision James Jones has, and he captures it in parts of *The Thin Red Line*, but misses it altogether in his final novel, *Whistle*, which was intended to bring together all these aspects of the American mentality.

Even spatially, the combat novel is a sympathetic form. For space in combat is measured in the proximity to enemy fire, which is death, and the distance between it and oneself, which is salvation. When the soldier closes with the enemy-the very mis-en-scène of the Vietnam War novel-caught in that transcendent experience that results from company spirit, he exposes his body in order to salvage his soul. If he can remain distant from the enemy, space represents rewards existing in a limitless world beyond. In that "beyond," there lies the spatial fantasy of insatiable women, a bottomless well of booze, uncomplicated pleasures. One final form of space is connected to a third kind of distancing, that linked to the "good wound," which places one far away from combat, in a rest cure, R. & R. or results in one being shipped home-which is the best distancing of all.

The combat novel is constantly dealing with matters of space, the characteristic American theme of escape, flight, on-the-road experiences. But in combat, space is linked to more than fleeing-although one may turn and run, as happened in the Korean War when the Chinese swept in; more often, one must measure space carefully. In the Vietnam War novel, the spatial dimension becomes even more ambiguous, however. For even as the men peered into the leafery and trees seeking the enemy, they also had to be intense about the ground, where pongis and other terrible instruments of torture and death lurked. In that instance, the soldier was caught in both far and near space: with death both in the far and close distance, with death underfoot. Mines were, of course, a danger in any war, but in Vietnam they became even far more immediate than, for example, in Pacific island hopping or in fighting one's way across Europe.

In temporal terms, the other side of the spatial universe, the novel of combat establishes short bursts of action,[240] with periods of exhaustion and rest intervening. The rapidity of battle is in contradistinction to the long drawn-out sequences necessary for the social novel, as well as for the war novel. There, scenes must occur over weeks and months, even years; in combat, minutes, or, at most, hours, on patrol. The purpose of combat, pure American in this respect, is expenditure of a lifetime of energy in a short burst that determines whether one lives or dies. In the social and war novel, preparation for action is longer, and there may be several opportunities or choices, unless the deck is marked. Yet even when the individual's fate is determined, the downfall, if it comes, is not precipitous, but serpentine. For the postwar novelist, the war had created a different sense of speeded-up time.

In one area, however, we find an enormous overlap between

Vietnam War novels and those of the earlier conflict. Except for *Looking for Cacciato* and new modes of language in parts of *Dispatches*, the novels of both wars are singularly lacking in experimental or modernist modes. The one exception in the Second World War is John Horne Burns's *The Gallery* (1947), which is much underrated, caught as it was alongside *The Naked and the Dead*, *From Here to Eternity*, *The Young Lions*, and *Catch-22*, to mention the most obvious popular successes; novels, incidentally, which translated readily into films. To back up for a moment, *The Naked and the Dead* poses its problems and resolutions within traditionally Naturalistic terms. Conventionally, the focus was man versus machine, or fate; man at the mercy of a neutral nature-Thomas Hardy's neutral-malevolent nature-or subverted by forces he cannot understand, or conquer; man as the butt of whatever lies in store for him, or ruled by ideologies he cannot penetrate. Victory, if it comes, is the result of blunders, chance, even misadventure, Tolstoyan in this respect. All this Mailer encapsulated on the island of Anopopei, and it takes heroism out of the war, locating results not in the individual but the group. Yet the American drive for the single self must assert itself regardless of group fate; so Mailer, despite the constraints, drives frantically toward individual expression. The problems begin.

These problems do not destroy the Mailer novel or the war and combat novel of either war; but they do point up how the genre is itself impervious to change, except for the very occasional anomaly. It is true that war establishes its own universe of relationships and sensations, different from those in civilian life. Men are transformed into semi-mechanical objects by fear and desire for survival. Physically, the soldier hugs the earth, tries to become smaller, a less inviting target; this is instinctual, and yet it homogenizes all men in action; disallowing individualization of response. Superior officers and the general command, in conjunction with the hidden enemy, have otherwise placed a wall around individual need and desire. Only the men's sensations can still respond, and these are severely circumscribed. The men hunker down in their foxholes, so that they lose almost all human qualities as they become analogous to animals and insects-the instinct to survive is so powerful few distinctions exist across the organic world. Within this frame of reference, *all* war experiences, as Crane and Stendhal recognized, are essentially the same, all wars comparable. Nowhere more than in the Vietnam War novel is this illustrated, since these novels do not involve the air force* or the navy, but the army and the marines, grunts who become interchangeable with each other under combat conditions.

Another matter, not directly related to technical innovation, but not completely cut off from it, is the question of intellectual distinction. Except perhaps for *The Gallery*-which combines both technical and intellectual qualities-the combat and war novels leave mind elsewhere. If intellect is signaled, as in Heller's *Catch-22*, we are reminded of it by its absence. Officers are categorized by their stupidity, the men by their lust or greed. Intellect is excluded because it would interfere with the military effort, which is, by civilian definition, senseless or ludicrous. How we won the war is usually attributed to circumstance, as it is in the Mailer novel; and has nothing to do with ideas, conceptual thinking, planning, or intelligence. Social or political issues that intertwine with war or combat are eschewed, or else are considered as so far out as to be part of a world untouched by the military. In this formulation, with mind or intellect missing, the men are in the grip of some force or element-whether in combat situations or not-over which individual will is futile. They are puppets in a plan which, more often than not, will turn out to be stupid and/or wasteful. Those "wasted" are not just the enemy, but also our own side-because of the stupidity of commanders.

Mailer's attempts to introduce intellect into *The Naked and the Dead* turn out to be among the sadder passages of the novel. Part of the problem lay in his plan. As he stated in *Advertisements*

---

*　An exception is Robert Mason's *Chickenhawk*, where Huey helicopters are the main predators.

for Myself, he wanted to write a war novel. And yet he avoided the theatre of war, in Europe, where issues were thickly textured, for the one in the Far East, which was relatively straightforward. All of this, as we explore it, has considerable relevance for Vietnam War novels, since, as part of a Pacific or an Asian strategy, the writers find themselves leached of ideas. In one sense, the ideological and political background to the Vietnam War is quite relevant. The French experience in Indo-China and America's response to the division of Vietnam and to a peace treaty are political issues of the highest importance. But they are completely absent in the novels about the war. All background, ideas, ideology, historical factors, French losses, American errors, mistakes of both judgment and omission are notably missing. As a consequence, combat narratives occur in an historical vacuum and, even worse, in an intellectual-ideological vacuum; as if fighting were taking place somewhere off the planet between natives and imperial American troops struck down by chance.

In the Pacific War of World War II, the ideological underpinning was almost completely lacking. Also, since Japan had attacked us, and Germany did not, the pro-Pacific argument focused on matters of national survival, revenge, honor. Supporters of the Pacific War tended to be from less urban states, from smaller towns and cities (the disproportionate source of Vietnam grunts), more conservative elements in the country, for whom MacArthur was a hero. Anti-Roosevelt forces saw his German priority as simply another sellout to Big Eastern interests. Anti-Japanese feeling on racial grounds ran high, also-a carryover into the Vietnam War, where the response of the grunts was almost entirely racial (not only color, but size, fighting ability, indifference to life). While the German soldier received grudging admiration, as did the German war machine, the Japanese was ridiculed personally as bucktoothed, squat, bandy-legged, little more than a savage. Jones's combat scenes in *The Thin Red Line* reflect this sense of the enemy.

The German war was of another kind, supported by urbanites, professionals, those politically committed (as against those who valued patriotism above all), and those who tended to find liberal solutions more satisfactory than conservative ones. In the Vietnam War, those people, the liberals, found themselves opposing the war altogether; whereas in World War II they tended to favor fighting the Germans first. These are more or less traditional divisions in American life and thought, and it is not unusual to find them reflected in wartime attitudes. For those who would support the primacy of the Japanese war, we need look no further than characters in novels by John O'Hara, John Marquand, and James Gould Cozzens, all of them concerned with small-town values.

In *The Naked and the Dead*, accordingly, Mailer reaped incoherence, not coherence, in his effort to infuse ideology into the war and combat novel; or, to put it another way, he tried to transform a combat novel into a war novel. He made another move, in the flashbacks, that is inevitable in novels of both wars: to offer a representative group, one Jew, one Southern Anglo-Saxon, one Pole, one Hispanic, one Italian, then in the later conflict one or two blacks. The advantages are obvious: to create in the squad or company a mosaic of America; the disadvantages are equally obvious, in that each member becomes a stereotype of his race, color, or ethnic group. When the flashbacks and forward-moving narrative fail to cohere, it is as though we had two separate groups, men existing in past history and men existing in the present, on patrol. In a related way, the long dialogues between Hearn and Cummings further clog rather than clarify the narrative. Yet Mailer needs them all to make his point: General Cummings's reactionary view, typical here of Pacific War advocates, Captain Hearn's liberalism, more suited to the European war, and Sergeant Croft's stress on pure survival, the ultimate in lower-class (stereotypical) ethics. Only the Croft segments work once the novel moves into its action phase; the rest sinks of its own weight.

This, then, poses the dilemma for war and combat novelists, for both wars, but particularly for the later one. Many of these novels read exceptionally well, with brilliant passages of combat writing, extraordinary descriptions of men about to enter into roles for which no amount of training can prepare them. But they are intellectually flaccid; their tensions undermined by the unsophisticated presentation the genre calls for. With the possible exception of *The Gallery*, the novelist was unable to incorporate into his very structure the ideological base of Remarque's *All Quiet on the Western Front*. Vietnam War novelists are particularly trapped in this dilemma: inevitably, they must move toward the firefight, the scene where men are tested, wounded, and die; toward that battle which never shapes up but which declines into sniper attacks or other disguised actions. They are forever narrowing down, limiting individual will, restricting their field of emotional and intellectual movement. Built into their kind of combat novel are boundaries of what they can do but cannot go beyond.

Once again, Mailer is archetypical. Although he handles the patrol expertly-within a Hardyesque sense of the individual dwarfed by immensity of landscape, by a universal fate-the conventionality of his approach to a scene partially vitiates it beyond the physical fact. Related problems are his uncompelling characters: their lives, their mode of speech, the level of their ideas. Mailer's need-and here we must include nearly all war and combat writers from both conflicts, but especially the Vietnam conflict-was to present, as noted, a cross-section of soldiers. A Jew is sensitive and perhaps not physically up to the demands made on him, the Italian will keep his prayer beads nearby, the Irishman will drink and curse but have a heart of gold, the Hispanic will be light on his toes, a perfect point man, the black in the Vietnam War novel will be from the ghetto, street smart, the tough white Southerner will have left a trail of failures behind him, so that the army becomes his last chance, and so on through the stereotypes in which we think about people. This stereotyping becomes more obvious in the later conflict because most of the soldiers portrayed derived from a lower economic class-tending to be uneducated, or semi-literate, unaware of anything outside their immediate world, caught up by bits and pieces of pop culture. The novelist, who is more sophisticated, has little room in which to maneuver. If it's music, it's rock and roll; it it's reading matter, it's girlie magazines; if it's talk, it's about getting laid.

In the Mailer, Sergeant Croft is such an important creation since he embodies qualities that become part of the "army man" in both this war and in the Vietnam conflict. He spills over into Warden (however humanized) of Jones's *From Here to Eternity*; he then reappears in Welsh, in *The Thin Red Line*, a figure associated with the Depression and the type classified as the lower-class misfit whose sole hope lies in army values. The Croft figure then surfaces twenty or more years later in the squad or company leader in Vietnam, and even in the film versions of the combat novel, such as Stanley Kubrick's *Full Metal Jacket* and Oliver Stone's *Platoon*, or in imitations of *The Thin Red Line* such as *Hamburger Hill*, a film of almost unrelieved combat.

One element, which makes the Croft figure and his successors so compelling, is his attempt to break free of history; and yet, at the same time, fit into an organization that insists on historical tradition, order, precedence. In this figure, we have a straining against the very elements that make it possible for him to survive. He is not, however, like Jones's Prewitt, also a misfit trying to carve out an existence in the army-Prewitt succumbs to the artist in him and vacillates when he should be rocklike. Someone like Croft yearns for Being, as against Nothingness, which he brushes and almost emulates in his nihilism. Croft and his successors attempt to transcend "being" to achieve pure Being, and yet run up against the Heideggerian paradox that "being" in its temporality restrains "Being," which lies outside of time. That play of ordinary restraints rebelling against the impossible was not only an important factor in Mailer and *his* development but also an emblem of what occurs in the war and, particularly, the combat novel. Not surprisingly, Croft is free of ideology. He moves physically and emotionally, those aspects of himself that he can control; ideology is for him meaningless, since it derives from beyond his own dictates.

When we move up to the Vietnam War novel, we recognize

that any textured sense of a political organization implicit in the army cannot be duplicated. Several writers attempted such a portrayal, but fell short; not for lack of talent, but because the war itself and its organization did not lend themselves to this kind of description. This inability to suggest a larger historical element, an important dimensional quality, makes nearly all Vietnam War novels isolated phenomena as fictional works; offshoots of the combat novel of World War II but even more restricted. James Webb's *Fields of Fire*[241] (1978) attempts some political dimensions in the figure of a young man from Harvard, Goodrich, who is called Senator by the men in his company. Goodrich becomes something of a spokesman for Webb's sense of the war, although, unlike Croft and Welsh, he is not a good soldier, certainly not the ideal. He is quite the opposite, but then that is Webb's point: the man who seems a misfit comes to honor the war because it was what his country presented him with. But Goodrich is being forced to bear too much weight, the upper class figure who, by reaching across to the lower classes fighting the war, becomes a "traitor" to his own class, which resists and demonstrates against the conflict. Goodrich, accordingly, while not the perfect or ideal military man is nevertheless a man who responds to his country's need when his own class "betrays" it.* The issues here are momentous, but within the confines of a combat novel like *Fields of Fire*, they are reductionist and simplistic, however fine the writing, however compelling the firefights.

Patterns work back and forth. Essential to the combat novel is the love of violence. Croft, for example, in the Mailer novel, enjoys killing Japanese the way a hunter enjoys a turkey shoot. If we update his situation to our present urban scene, we find comparable combat stagings in the drug wars, in the struggle for turf, in the competition for customers (also a body count); and in these wars,

---

* *Fields of Fire* carries with it a whiff of Herman Wouk's *The Caine Mutiny* (1951), in which the "intellectual" is attacked while patriotism and obedience to authority (the captain, the state) take precedence over individual values.

we find killers, like the Lurps, in Herr's description, who have entered the urban jungle, never to emerge alive. Yet strong as Croft is as a character and a creation that embodies the military, he is caught in a restrictive form. As observed his is ultimately a Naturalistic figure-all response to inner and outer challenges, almost programmed in his reactions, very much a man working through a personal fate or destiny, a man himself. The limitations of this for the war and combat novel are apparent.

One novel, which does break from conventional forms and, like *Going After Cacciato* later, attempts a freer sense of the war, is Burns's *The Gallery* (1947).[242] With varying degrees of success, Burns tried to find techniques equivalent to war; and his effort there locates the intellectual content of the novel, not, as in Mailer, in sophomoric political discussions. One caveat we must keep in mind is whether or not Burns's achievement in *The Gallery* could be replicated in the Vietnam War novel; that is, whether or not that type of war would permit such daring-although in the two O'Brien novels (*Going After Cacciato* and *If I Die in a Combat Zone*),[243] there is such an effort.

The Gallery is about the fierce war in Europe and North Africa, but has only one combat scene. The war is reflected, or refracted, in scenes of men trying to relieve the fatigue, anxiety, and fear of combat. There is, in fact, almost no war except what can be mirrored in the men's destructive means of relaxation-drink, gay and straight bars, intense staring, forms of madness which allow withdrawal and isolation of self. Burns's method reflects Nietzsche's paradoxical formulation that letting go is unnatural, antithetical to our temperament, even when it apparently relaxes us. In our leisure, we demonstrate our true insanity.

The means for Burns's formulation is the vast Galleria Umberto Primo in Naples, a temple of glass, which is a fitting emblem of the reflected pleasure soldiers, seek. In Mailer, the long sections on the patrol working behind Japanese lines preempt the shape of the novel, giving it a snakelike, episodic quality with its own tensions and dialectic; but with no structural reference to the earlier political episodes. In Burns, the dominant symbolic shape of the crystal gallery, whose glass has been shattered by Allied bombers, gives him a literal container for the novel, a pleasure dome, a sacred place where black masses occur; yet also a church that offers salvation and life but is, like war itself, a magnet for destruction, doom, and death. That shattered dome becomes, in *Going After Cacciato*, the sought-after Paris; a sacred place which can only be reached after unbearable obstacles.

With this reverse image of the war as his symbolic form, Burns had an integrative shape, something lacking in most other war and combat novels. Within it, he located two kinds of material; first, the nine "Portraits," which enfold the novel, beginning and ending it. Intermixed with these are eight "Promenades," five of which do not take place in the Galleria or even in Naples, but assume a kind of North African equivalent. They are first-person narratives that are supposed to bring together the Portraits of war with the recording consciousness of the novelist-narrator. The aim, one assumes, was to integrate the external aspects, the Portraits, with the internal elements, the Promenades; further, there was the need to achieve geographical integration, Italy and North Africa. In the final three Promenades, the recording consciousness moves from Algiers to Naples, so that external and internal intertwine.

Burns employed what was essentially the idea of the Greek chorus, a commentary on the main action. But the commentary, since it is modernist, is oblique to the Portraits, where the war lies. The effect of the Promenades, or commentaries by an I-narrator, is cumulative, not at all a direct relationship to the Portraits before or after them. The commentaries tend to be affirmative of human values, but then even the Portraits, although they may end in frustration or death, contain some affirmation. Overall, the key image is the Galleria, which is life and death, affirmation and negation, heaven for some, nightmare for others. If the galleria reflects the war and, ultimately, all life, then it is everything we are; as Moby Dick's whiteness mirrors those who challenge him. The Promenades all finally point toward the Galleria, and the

Portraits are all, somehow, contained by it, through meetings, deals, and other interchanges.

The rising arch of *The Gallery* comes with the episode called "Guilia," the seventh Portrait. In this episode and those in its immediate vicinity, Burns attempts to discover coordinates for life. In this novel, there are a society and a culture which exist and must be appealed to if civilization is to continue. The war, in other words, is embedded in a value system, which we may call society, a culture, a world-all the elements that by the nature of things are missing in the Vietnam War novel. Beyond the combat scenes, there is nothing, really nothing, for the American soldier. There is, of course, a strong and powerful culture in Vietnam predating the founding of America itself, but that culture is closed to the American. In fact, that culture is the very thing the American is dedicated to denying. In this war mission, his aim is to Americanize the culture-make the Vietnamese into "friendlies" who fight like Americans, think like Americans, eventually live like Americans, if we prevail.

Whereas Mailer pushed everything into a call for power-what we find in pure combat novels, and nowhere more than in the later conflict-Burns tried to discover where real feeling begins in a wartime situation; where sexual relief amidst fear and danger is not merely a blind force, not merely a display of power, but has individual choice behind it. Burns recognized that power obtains and obtains absolutely when one element is the conqueror and the other the defeated. Yet he is concerned in the novel with finding a mode of existence that, while accommodating the urgency of power, is also something else, varietal, as some plants are intermediary between deciduous and evergreen. Still further, he tried to move beyond that destructive naturalism which appears to grip every war novel and, of course, the novel of combat. Since war, its terrain, its power are all external forces which become fate or destiny for the individual, it appears that all life is sucked toward some black hole one can never understand. In this formulation, which Burns resists, individual will is always given over to something larger, which evitably controls him. Accordingly, we get a lopsided view of society, in which will and choice are struck down without even being given a chance; and with that, culture itself is denied.

The 1950s bore this out. A period of deadening ennui in national politics, a waste land of ideas, a good deal of outright deception on the political level with terror tactics indulged in by both parties, it nevertheless became the matrix of development for many who tried to effect radical change in the decade following. The point of this is that the Burns novel, the Mailer, Shaw, and Wouk novels to some limited extent, the Jones somewhat more helped give us some perspective not only on the 1940s but also on the 50s to come. One of the functions of the war novel, as against the combat novel, is its prophetic qualities. The society encapsulated in the novel is linked to the larger society, to later decades, not only to the past. By contrast, the Vietnam War novel dips away from the whole toward a fragment, the war zones themselves, the fight for survival, the Naturalism implicit in man against jungle and unseen enemy, against traps, mines, sharpened and poisoned bamboo sticks, and the rest. The immediacy is so immense-and inescapable-it pre-empts all else.

No one more than the novelist of war is caught in a bind. If he stresses the overall power of the war and its commanders, then we as readers lose interest in individuals; or else we have no ultimate reason for caring. If, on the other hand, he emphasizes individuals, then he is being unfaithful to what war is and what its values of dehumanization are. In a sense, this problem is endemic to the American novel as a whole. It is the "catch" of our fiction; the perpetual trap, theme, dance of death. Heller's frenetic comedy in *Catch 22* was an effort to break from this; turning the war into metaphor was one means of avoiding either/or. If the writer makes his characters dance, they are less likely to be doomed by technology. Pynchon works similar ploys in novels that are reflections of war fictions. But when all is said and done, Heller's novel is not about war or combat; it is a political novel of sorts, a book about society and culture, about organizations and how they operate. The war is merely a backdrop for an attack on exploitational capitalism and on the organizational monsters it creates to perpetuate itself.

Heller's most successful follower, in the war/combat genre, is Tim O'Brien, with *Going After Cacciato* and *If I Die in a Combat Zone*. In the latter, a very brief novel, O'Brien's narrator goes to Vietnam knowing it was a bad and wrong war. Although he never alters that point of view, he recalls Socrates, facing death, and his statement that he could have left the country, but stayed and was, therefore, obligated to follow its rules. It is a good theoretical argument, but insufficient for acting upon. In this use, he does achieve some distance on the mindless nature of the war, but he also shows his indebtedness to Mailer's *The Naked and the Dead* and those long dialogues between Hearn and Cummings over the nature of a desirable society. O'Brien also emulates Heller, especially in a scene in which nonexistent combat is created to fulfill a required job. On the night radio watch, the soldiers create nonexistent coordinates followed by a bombing of a nonexistent target; or call for a nonexistent ambush, followed by a nonexistent situation report. Through such devices, O'Brien does catch some sense of the war, but he lacks an overall structural concept for the novel-what he was able to provide in *Going After Cacciato*, with the search there joining both inner and outer worlds.

With few exceptions, then, the novelists of the Vietnam War, however talented-and most are-were caught in circumstances which disallowed the larger shaping of fiction that would have justified their intense depiction of war and combat. It takes a nonfiction work like Neil Sheehan's *A Bright Shining Lie* to create that broader sense of an entire society which lies behind the American war effort; and while Sheehan presses forward with his protagonist-John Paul Vann, a character as close to fiction as to nonfiction-he creates contexts for his main figure which the purely fiction writers seem unable to do because of the nature of the war. Another factor, noted above, is that Vietnam War novels are relatively brief. None of our novelists has attempted an inclusive novel, a Mega-novel, in which Vietnam and America are linked. As a result, the novel reflects some isolated phenomenon to which bodies are fed, as though into an extraterrestrial killing machine. In this respect, the model for most Vietnam combat fiction is James Jones's *The Thin Red Line*, which eschews all effort at inclusiveness; whose lyricism comes not from language, ideas, or thoughts, but from the rhythms of life and death in a killing zone. The men simply *are*; combat simply *is*. Here is the archetype of Vietnam War novel, a novel of combat not of war and the culture that produced it. In this form, we have an enclosed space (a jungle area, a bivouac, a perimeter to defend, a killing zone, a suspect village), a restricted cast of characters, an equally limited area of maneuver, no meaningful society or ideology, only stark tensions and anxieties, mainly fear-and into this we pour the brutality of an unseen enemy. The only course is intensity, not breadth; survival, not the larger frame of reference. In this, our Vietnam War novelists have performed superbly; as cultural critics, they are constrained by circumstances.

If we move afield, we do catch a whiff of that larger sense if we include a fiction that is neither war nor combat, Robert Olen Butler's *A Good Scent from a Strange Mountain* (1992).[244] These fifteen stories are all narrated from the perspective of the Vietnamese, a herculean effort by an American writer who is not ethnically Vietnamese. One question, which demands an answer, is whether or not Butler was "stealing" another's culture for the sake of his own literary career; whether his work is simply another version of the minstrel show in which blacks are portrayed by whites in blackface.

Put in more immediate critical terms, is he colonizing another ethnic group? Is he displaying typical white hegemony over the Vietnamese and appropriating their experience in order to vaunt the more dominating culture? The answer to these questions on all counts is No. Butler is not appropriating the "Asian" experience, as though all such experience were equal; he is, in fact singularizing the Vietnamese situation during and after the war, and doing so without patronizing, condescending, or dominating. To argue otherwise is to suggest that only Vietnamese (not even the more generalized "Asians") should write about Vietnam; only white Americans can write about other white Americans, and so on. While there is a movement toward this exclusivity among Asians, as well as having existed for many years in the black community, little of it matters when a work comes along that seems authentic. For that kind of authenticity is a literary achievement independent of its source.*

There are enough stories in this volume to make that judgment. Butler reinforces his case with "Love," which originally appeared in *Writer's Forum* and becomes the centerpiece for the entire collection. The voice is authoritative, beginning: "I was once able to bring fire from heaven."[245] This is a massive trope inasmuch as it reveals the power of the Vietnamese man in his own country, backed by American help, as opposed to the displaced, dispirited Vietnamese man in the country of his savior, America. The politics of the South and North in Vietnam are muted by the human condition which Butler explores-for that "fire" the narrator can bring from heaven is linked to American firepower which, as a spy, he calls in on the Vietcong. In all other ways, the narrator is a wimp, as he describes himself; but with American backing, he has the illusion of the strength of Prometheus. His position is equally precarious. To dilute the political implications of the story, Butler shows how the narrator uses that "fire" from American planes and guns against those Vietnamese men who try to seduce his beautiful wife, and here South Vietnamese and Vietcong are, equally, the enemy.

Once in America, however, the narrator, now living near the Mississippi River, close to New Orleans, is shorn of his firepower; and his beautiful wife remains the object of attention. His own

---

* For a fuller account of these developments, see Garrett Hongo's introduction to *Under Western Eyes: Personal Essays from Asian America* (1995). Hongo roams through several of the controversies that have gained momentum in the Asian-American literary community, mainly questions of social significance of the work versus aesthetic, historical, and personal perspectives.

manhood diminished, he counts on Vietnamese men in this country being "beaten down," but one does emerge as a distinct threat; and the remainder of "Love" is given over to the ways in which the narrator humiliates himself in order to hold on to his wife, relying, eventually, on voodoo. In some contorted way, it works, and the narrator, at the end, although himself hospitalized, has tamed his wife and driven off her persistent suitor and lover.

The value of the story lies in its modulations: this is not an "Asian" story but a Vietnamese one, particularized by the war experience and by the divided aims which developed from dislocation. Butler has managed to internalize the war into a gender culture of the narrator; so that the voodoo or magic he finally uses in America is not that different from the magic which he himself was brought up to believe in and which the American reinforced with their firepower from the air. Magic, in fact, is never distant from any of the stories: the magic of the past, the ghosts and phantoms of ancestors, the recurrences of history, the dislocations which turn all reality into hallucinatory experiences. Unlike the purely American perspective on war and combat in Vietnam, there is relatively little war in the Butler stories; but there is cultural grounding, almost all from the South Vietnamese side, from those who settled in Louisiana, in and around New Orleans.

One of the few stories with "war" in both background and foreground is "The American Couple," and here war is carried on between an American and a South Vietnamese former combatant in the resort town of Puerto Vallarta, Mexico. There, two couples meet, the result of each wife having won the vacation trip at a game show; and after the husbands seem to bond, they become increasingly estranged, until they work through the war, only this time with rocks. Here, the South Vietnamese takes out his anger at the American presence, even though at one time they were on the same side. In this way, Butler blunts the distinction between North and South: Vietnamese identify with each other despite their once deadly opposition, whereas Americans remain the enemy. With Butler's view from the other side of the mountain, the Vietnam perspective is now beginning to pass into American fictional forms: not only a "good scent from a strange mountain," but the scent of a culture which, having failed to understand, we tried to crush. The ghosts and phantoms, however, remain.

CHAPTER SEVEN

BLACKS-WOMEN-JEWISH WRITERS: RACIAL, ETHNIC, AND GENDER SEPARATION— A LOOK BACK AND FORWARD

Black, women, and Jewish writers are doomed to be grouped together as a postwar phenomenon in American fiction. In other areas of endeavor-social, economic, theoretical-the grouping has fallen apart of its own ill-design. One does not speak of black economics, or female social thought, or Jewish theory-even though Hitler once spoke of Jewish physics. And in other literary genres, in drama and poetry, for example, one looks in vain for such groupings, although one heard, for a brief time, of black theatre and a black poetic voice. In fiction, however, the phenomenon persists of such inclusive groupings; and in part this chapter will demonstrate both the weakness of a fictional gathering together of "black, women, Jewish" and the misleading nature of the terms themselves.

A relevant question arises why there should have been groups in the first place. It began, of course, in our interest in minority and ethnic cultures and subcultures after World War II. Yet while blacks are a large minority and Jews a small one, women are not; blacks are not ethnics, however, since in many instances they represent, next to Native Americans, the very oldest Americans; Jews are ethnics (a clouded issue); but clearly women as a gender grouping are not. The fit is already misleading, in terms of both larger and individual groupings. Another source of the groupings came when blacks, women, and Jews, liberated by the war, began to publish in larger numbers, or at least appeared to dominate the literary scene. Novels by Jewish writers coincided with the end of the war, with Bellow and Mailer, a little later Malamud, Roth, Heller, Doctorow, and others. Blacks were represented in the 50s, with Ellison and Baldwin, a little earlier by Wright; and then in the 60s abundantly with John Williams, Toni Morrison, Toni Cade Bambara, more Baldwin, and several essayists, Cleaver, Baldwin, Ellison.

Female writers (mainly white) did create a grouping of their own as a spate of novels directly concerned with the reverberations of the women's liberation movement appeared, all within a few years of each other, beginning in the late 60s. This was a legitimate grouping, for a short period of time, when novels by Oates (whose *them* in 1969 was the most distinctive), Jong, Alice Walker, Rossner, Alther, Diane Johnson, Lois Gould, and Toni Morrison all appeared within less than a ten-year period.

But if female writers briefly did have a common subject, black authors did not. For example, nearly all the white female authors in this five-year span commonly wrote about separation, divorce, creating an independent life for themselves. Blacks, male or female, hardly agreed among themselves. Some like Baldwin pursued intensely personal, even intimate, themes, often of one's sexual preferences; others like Morrison and Alice Walker dealt with questions of female identity and emergence amidst black social and political needs. Still others like Ishmael Reed broke with use of standard English to attempt a kind of bebop language which would pass for "black English,"[246] but which was really a language he forged for his kind of parody. Alice Walker, in her immensely popular *The Color Purple*, attempted a middle ground between standard and "black" English. That, too, was some approximate American language.

Among Jewish writers, the divisions are even greater-calling into question not only the validity of grouping Jews with blacks and women, but the valorization of such a term as "Jewish writers." What Mark Shechner says about Jews fits blacks and women: the Jewish novel's "note of suppressed grief, its mood of rejection, its plangency, and brooding is founded upon and sanctioned by the alienations that stand behind it."[247] What makes this Jewish? As Jews, what do Mailer and Joseph Heller have in common either with each other or with Malamud? And what meaning does the Jewish novel have even for Malamud when he writes *A New Life* (1961), based distinctly on profoundly American pastoral themes, or *The Natural* (1952), which is an archetypal American story of magic, Faust, and baseball?

Heller's distinctive novel is *Catch-22* (1961), and yet except for a kind of New York humor associated with standup comics who plied the Catskill circuit, there is little "Jewish" about it. Heller's next novel after *Catch-22*, *Something Happened* (1974), was concerned with a gentile family. Mailer's identification as part of the Jewish group defies description, since neither in subject matter nor language usage does he suggest any such background. He has had about as much relationship to Jews as O. J. Simpson had to blacks. Even Philip Roth, in what is often called the quintessential Jewish work, his collection of stories, *Goodbye Columbus* (1959), is concerned more with clashes of class and caste than with Jewishness. The key story catches the flavor of suburban life after World War II, that quality of posing, upward mobility, ostentatious country club climbing, which here happens to be Jewish. It has its roots in John O'Hara, no Jew, he. And it is played off in class and caste terms against the city poor of Newark who also happen to be Jewish.

Perhaps Mailer's finest fiction is *Why Are We in Vietnam?* (1967), which is about Texas, Lyndon Johnson, and the great white gentile establishment. Only Bellow, Roth, and Malamud continued to write about Jews, but, as we shall note later, in terms which made their subjects America and Americans rather than solely Jews and Judaism. Although Malamud among these writers comes closest to providing some religious aura, their most distinctive fiction does not involve practicing Jews, nor Jewish practices, nor much Yiddish and even less Hebrew. Their characters-even in *The Assistant*-are secularized, worldly Jews worried about conscience, guilt, things of the spirit. In fact, one of their favorite themes, as we have already observed in Roth, is the need of the younger generation to pull away from the older generation's notions of Jewishness. Such literary creations are part of a struggle representing not race or religion, or the Old World, but America, American themes, American temptations.

The vision of all these writers, whatever their individual emphasis, is the matter of America. The language they write in, except for occasional elements of dialect that recall Yiddish or black rural/inner city life, is American English-what used to be called regional; and that fact alone pre-empts other distinctions. If we accept that a common language, with minor divergences, draws blacks, Jews, and women together as writers, then distinctions based on color, sex, ethnic affiliation, or religious become secondary, or extraneous. Furthermore, not only language binds them, but a common American heritage-despite the fact that for many Jewish writers ancestors came, mainly, from Eastern Europe. Their history, as a result of schooling, is American history and civics, and their aspirations, reinforced by public school, are part of that upward mobility we associate with American life. Moreover, their literary and cultural antecedents are Thoreau and Emerson, and large elements of Poe, Hawthorne, Melville, Cooper, Wharton, and other classic American writers.

Mark Shechner writes that up to 1939 for the American writer and intellectual [white, male, Jewish] the country that counted most was Russia. As he says in *After the Revolution: Studies in the Contemporary Jewish-American Imagination*, ". . . it was the course of events in Russia, not in Warsaw or Auschwitz or Israel or even America, that left the deepest impression on these writers and even brought them to awareness of themselves as a generation, which might be called, for neatness' sake, the class of 1939."[248] Yet this ended abruptly with the end of the Second World War-if anything, Russia completely vanished for our writers and they Americanized, mainstreamed for the most part. Russia, the Spanish Civil War, the Hitler-Stalin pact of 1939, the Moscow trials, the Soviet attack on Finland, Finland's siding with the Nazis, and related histories all came to mean little or nothing. They made their priority American life, American culture, American society-including those who had grown up in immigrant homes where Yiddish was spoken. Their politics wobbled from radical to liberal to neoconservative, all home-grown. There was, in fact, except in Roth, little interest in European Jews, those who survived as well as those who were murdered. Even Israel has only limited meaning for most Jewish writers in their fictions. Perhaps Cynthia Ozick is our exception here.

Saul Bellow, James Baldwin, and Joyce Carol Oates may appear to live on different planets, from each other, but once we get past obvious superficial differences, they share an America. If we line up *The Adventures of Augie March* (1953), *Go Tell It on the Mountain* (1953), and *them* (1969), we have in each instance not a Jewish, black, or female novel, but an American version of the *Bildungsroman*. Each is writing about growing up; each is catching that particular experience against an inner city background; and each is using a standard language-however stretched-to hang his and her thesis on. Baldwin's novel seems immersed in the black church, but when the tone is not elegiac or religious, the usage is standard American English; and when Bellow is not falling into quasi-Yiddishness for comic effect, the language is Chicago American.

What, then, remains of our categories? A meaningful question to ask is to see what certain writers are responding to in American life; then to follow that up with a further question on how their particular situation, as a Jew, black, or woman, has helped to shape their response. In asking that question and attempting an answer, we must avoid the usual significations: that blacks are mainly socially and politically responsive, eager to demonstrate their disaffection from mainstream America; that Jews are caught between rejection of gentile values and a desire to assimilate and to be accepted and acceptable;[249] that women novelists are concerned only with establishing their own values apart from a patriarchy which has made them secondary citizens and repressed human beings. In such stereotyping, a black writer is always black, even when he or she is being himself; a Jewish writer must have a hidden agenda of American anti-Semitism and hostility somewhere; and women writers must be seeking the joys of matriarchy, the pleasures of independence and liberation.

Once we reject such classifications and recognize that all are categories of the genus *American writer*, based on language, history, literary antecedents, and common aspirations, we can make distinctions. Blacks, women, and Jews *are indeed different* from white gentile American males in their experience and in their perception of and response to that experience. The white American male, mainly Protestant, has, in fact, produced quite a different kind of fiction: what I have elsewhere in this book called the Mega-Novel; that novel like *Gravity's Rainbow, The Recognitions, J R, The Sotweed Factor, Letters,* and *Women and Men* which takes on not a segment of America but America itself. In their hands, the Mega-Novel-which projects seeming infinitude-attempts to capture the whole; it is the closest we have to a holistic product, the *War and Peace, Bleak House,* and *Ulysses* of our generation. Blacks, Jews and women writers tend to be more compartmentalized, going not after the whole thing but a segment. Some of the novelists like Bellow and Oates may seem voracious for experience, but ultimately they do narrow down. What is their development, what are they after, how do they define themselves, what do they consider *their* world?

But before we tackle these admittedly thorny questions, we

wonder about naming. How do we name or tag writers? Is a female American of Jewish background, like Cynthia Ozick, labeled a Russian-Jewish, female American writer? Is Alice Walker an African-American writer, a black writer, a black female writer, and further variations? Or is she simply or not, an American writer, born here and writing in American English? Is Ralph Ellison an African-American when he himself cited white male classic authors-Dostoievsky and Conrad-as major influences on him? Is Mario Puzo, born here, an Italian-American writer? Do we always identify someone as male or female? or gay? or bisexual? or a trans-sexual? Is Joyce Carol Oates identified as a female, white, Anglo-Saxon, straight American writer? Or merely American? Or merely a writer? Do we always add color; so that black is black, white is white, Latino may be brown, or so on? If blacks identify with their African heritage, as they have every right to do, do we label every other American writer with his or her heritage? I am myself a white, male, straight, Russian-American Jewish author; as are Bellow, Roth, Heller, and legions of others. That most of us have no liking for or connection to our Russian background is beside the point if we are so labeled. Yet we forgo the long designation and return to "an American writer." We are back to square one. Toni Morrison is an American author-it can be that simple![250]

For black and Jewish writers, the Second World War was a liberating period, and the postwar era, for several reasons, saw an outpouring of such voices. Women writers in large numbers and writing about a focused experience came later, when Simone de Beauvoir's *The Second Sex* and then its American epigone, *The Feminine Mystique*, began to take hold in the 60s. For many male writers who had served in the armed forces, the experience with foreign cultures, the subsequent attendance at universities on the G. I. Bill, the growing acquaintanceship with French and German writers, the growth of interest in Modernism in literature, music, and art all helped fuel a fiction which broke with the less sophisticated, more issue-oriented novel of the 30s. Another factor is that the "classic" writers were getting old, or had died, or were losing their grip: Wolfe, Fitzgerald, Steinbeck, Hemingway, Faulkner. The latter three were very much alive, and their presence great; but the perception was that their best work was behind them, and this perception proved liberating. This context for the new, different, and liberating helped Bellow, then Malamud, Roth, Heller, and others; also to a lesser but still real extent black writers. Some like Ellison, Baldwin, and John Williams were affected as much by foreign literature as by Richard Wright and more direct black sources in the church and community. Women writers like Carson McCullers and Flannery O'Connor-perhaps the two most distinctive female voices of the 40s and 50s[251]-were of course less directly influenced by the war and its aftermath; but they felt the presence of Faulkner, who brought into American fiction the innovations of Joyce, Eliot, and others. Within this context of general creative activity, novelists-our particular groups and others of every stripe and variety-began to emerge. In poetry, also, there was a virtual renaissance as a consequence of the influence of Whitman, William Carlos Williams, and their distinct American voices: in Lowell and Stevens, in the group known as the Beats, in Plath, Sexton, and Berryman, those who came to be known as confessional poets. Many of these were women, while still other female poets such as Elizabeth Bishop and Louise Bogan wrote within mainly traditional forms. But whatever the designation and the ultimate type of voice, in whatever medium, the arts flourished; and the surge carried into Jewish, black, and female novelists. We must be careful not to separate them from the more general energies nourishing the arts.

 The first novels that can be called "Jewish" in the broadest possible sense are Bellow's first two, *Dangling Man* (1994) and *The Victim* (1947), especially the latter. What creates the Jewish connection in the first novel is the Biblical name of the protagonist, Joseph, which also links him to Kafka's Joseph; his relationship to a whole group of schlemiels, fools, or passive individuals (Singer's Gimpel, Bellow's own Tommy Wilhelm and Moses Herzog,

Malamud's Fixer and Levin, Friedman's Stern), whose sole strength lies in their marginality; the use of a symbolic title which suggests the Jewish condition as marginal, purgatorial, "dangling" between cultures and countries; and, most importantly, the internalization of all material into an undefined self-consciousness. That latter, often bordering on narcissism-not action or externalized energy-will more than anything else help define the territory which some Jewish writers have carved out; or, put another way, in that self-conscious, undefined internality, we can recognize what may be a Jewish sensibility, although it is not exclusively that.

The enormous success of J. D. Salinger's *The Catcher in the Rye* (1951) and then his saga of the Glass family *Franny and Zooey,* 19961, along with the stories "A Perfect Day for Bananafish," "Raise High the Roof Beam, Carpenter," "Seymour, An Introduction") suggests that a Jewish sensibility had arrived. But Salinger was far more concerned with mainstream America: Holden Caulfield in that novel is a Huck Finn of sorts, and Irish-Jewish Glass children partake of American counterfeit, some successful, some doomed, all haunted. Salvation seems to lie in withdrawal from America and the embrace of what Zooey calls the "Fat Lady," the kingdom of God that lies within. Jews and Jewishness are left far behind.

Implicit in the novel leaning toward a Jewish sensibility is the uneasiness men feel toward women, and the fact that nearly all relationships come to us from the male viewpoint. But we must immediately note that this is also a more general American problem. That uneasiness of men toward women can be found in writers as far from a "Jewish sensibility" as Styron, Gaddis, Barth, McElroy, Baldwin, and John Williams, whatever the differences among them. The "dangling" of the Bellow title suggests some of that discomfort; impotence and limpness lie just below the surface of every relationship. Bellow surrounds his passive, dangling self-serving men by harem-like women; and by women who, incidentally, when they refuse that role become vicious witches. There is little in between. But is that Jewish? Enter Donald Barthelme, Toni Morrison, John Updike, and legions of others, the American way.

In still another respect, Bellow helped establish the direction for what would be an outpouring by Jewish novelists of a typically American theme: that struggle within the individual as he attempts to save himself from overindulgence in self and over-regimentation within the society. In the second of two dialogues within *Dangling Man*, Joseph insists on life, not antilife, on humanity, not antihumanity; just as in the first dialogue, he recognized that the world waits to make a whore of you, if you compliantly permit it to.[252] You can only meet this with "ideal constructions," well thought-through plans that may not even work; but in the struggle, one finds definition, and perhaps even ceases to dangle.

In *The Victim*, three years later, Bellow wrote what appeared to be an intensely Jewish novel, but we find its context in the 1940s, running parallel to the war and combat novels of the period. Asa Levanthal, far more stereotypically Jewish than Joseph, gains a sense of himself only when he is hounded by guilt feelings. Kirby Allbee, a sponger, drinker, loser, and traditional gentile from a Jewish point of view, feels wronged by Leventhal. And yet he retains a hold over the latter by virtue of their common humanity, so Bellow claims. Although the nature of the hold remains vague (homoerotic: class-structured?), and we feel Leventhal is a born sufferer, rather than a man of choice or will, there is little question his life gains significance to the degree Allbee (All-be, Al-being) violates his peace of mind. The symbolic and allegorical overtones of *The Victim* suggest that it was Bellow's attempt to find an equivalent of what Mailer, Jones, and Burns were doing with the army.

Let us project that. The key polemical ideas are suffering, at one end, and one's belief in a transcendent power (by no means God, more often Emerson's transcendental self, or even the military) at the other. Man lies stretched on a rack in between, and he may gravitate in either direction, toward suffering or toward escape. But despite the Jewish intonation of the novel and the heavy reliance on the Book of Job, Bellow has assayed a form of American existentialism, at the very time it was spreading over the French literary scene and becoming a staple of the military-oriented novel. This same influence would find its way into several black writers of the 50s and 60s (Ellison, Baldwin, and Williams, earlier in Wright), and further demonstrates how labels about Jewishness and blackness simplify or distort.

The Adventures of Augie March (1953)[253] established Bellow as a major novelist at the beginning of the 50s, a position he consolidated with *Henderson the Rain King* at the end. Two novels could not be more different. Augie picks up what will be one of the chief themes of the American 50s, the counterfeiting of ideas and feelings that developed in the great economic surge characteristic of the decade. But since this is a complicated, morally textured book, it is far more than an easy response to counterfeiting-no more than Gaddis's *The Recognitions*; for it tests out how imitational life can be assimilated even as one struggles against it. Bellow transcends the Jewishness of Augie and the Einhorn family by suggesting a broadly American theme: which is that the individual will can become hostage to the very energies nourishing it. "I am an American, Chicago-born," the novel begins, recalling of course Melville's "Call Me Ishmael." Bellow was also after big game, nothing less than the American soul, and thus the title of the novel, with its picaresque, discovering quality.

Rather than writing a Jewish novel, he is biting off the entire country; for Chicago cannot contain Augie's energies, and he heads for Mexico to train the American bald eagle. In this, we have an allegory of the decade, for in that eagle Bellow sees all the ambiguities and ambivalences in Augie himself, and in America. The eagle proves cowardly when confronted by an iguana, and Augie applauds its cowardice. Ironically, there is still hope for America, as Bellow seems to side with negative capability: letting openness and drift supersede certainties.

The "black experience" of the 50s was curiously similar, in Ellison's and Baldwin's response to counterfeiting. The theme cuts through the decade, and can be associated with some female writing as well, characterizing Flannery O'Connor's stories of this period:

authentic feeling opposed to deceptive responses which are the personal equivalent of counterfeit. Ralph Ellison's *Invisible Man* in 1952[254] (although begun seven years earlier) by its concentration on counterfeiting and forgery of feelings relates to the America of Eisenhower and Nixon as much as it does to a specific black experience. Ellison connects the paralysis and enervation underlying the 1950s with typical American themes, playing off stasis against spatiality and energy. In words which might recall a Jewish grandmother cautioning assimilation, the narrator's grandfather expresses the black equivalent to his grandson: ". . . undermine 'em with grins, agree 'em to death and destruction." *Invisible Man* is several novels in its working out.

Despite Ellison's stress on an enclosed, subterranean existence-a metaphor for black experience in America-he is also concerned, as his Prologue demonstrates, with growth. His line of development is a 1950s reflection of the *Bildungsroman* tradition, in this instance of the simpleton who grows up into a realization of how the world really functions, and then, as a result of setbacks, becomes capable of acting on his own condition. Since the narrator is black, his journey has distinctive features of black experience of rejection and frustration; but his journey is not only a black one. Salinger's Holden Caulfield in a miniature way parallels Ellison's narrator: the upper-middle-class private-school white boy playing the fool, trying to be knowing, attempting to grow up in a world of counterfeiters, offering honesty to their imitations.

In another respect, *Invisible Man* while reflecting America in the 1950s yet distinguishes this experience for the black man. Harlem becomes for Ellison a metaphor for instability, disharmony, discontinuity: that is, his sense of blackness, but also extendable to Jews and women. The disarray there is synesthesiac, the intermixing and muddling of the senses, in which a seemingly stable, orderly society is riven by dissent, deception, invisible forces of subversion and adversariness. To jump to another world, Flannery O'Connor in her stories and novels was also attempting to capture a society and its subcultures as they moved on the edge of the new.

Here discontinuity awaited her protagonists; that acute break with tradition and history that threw them into a purgatory they could not control. For her, the self no longer had a mission when the new invaded. Only indulgence prevailed, and in indulgence, she perceived the betrayal of the real self. Yet her vision of self and mission is ironic, and so heavy is the deceit and counterfeit that little is what it seems. Her peacocks are symbols of perfection that have been displaced from the natural world; and in those peacocks, the very transfiguration associated with Jesus, we have our last hope. But she recognizes that they cannot last, that the lovely birds live in a dispossessed, imperfect garden, and no perfect emblem of God can survive such deception of ourselves. The matter of her fictions seems light years away from New York or Chicago Jews and from transplanted black writers; but she is commenting, like them, on the 50s, working through 50s themes.

Invisible Man shares these concerns, cuts heavily into French existential ideas of freedom, historical necessity, and individual positioning, but gives the experience the feel of black life: in the music of Louis Armstrong, the use of jazz and jazz improvisations, the location in Harlem as a distinct subculture within America. But the larger themes, of shedding one's old skin in order to express an emerging or unfolding self, is traditional American, as American as Augie March in Mexico, Holden Caulfield in his sanitarium, and O'Connor's Hazel Mote (in *Wise Blood*) in quest of heroism in a banal age.

Malamud's *The Assistant* (1957),[255] his stories in *The Magic Barrel* (1958),[256] and James Baldwin's *Go Tell It on the Mountain* (1953)[257] well accommodate 50s themes while displaying, respectively, Jewish and black experiences. *The Assistant* cuts through layers of artificial responses in order to discover what men live by. It is this exploration of how men live which energizes Malamud's work, not any formal sense of Jewish life. His historical Jewishness is connected to its ethical sense, and how that dimension of behavior can be achieved in lives that must acknowledge other impulses, whether sexual, familial, artistic, or emotional. *The*

Assistant, far more than his first novel, *The Natural*, becomes Malamud's quintessential world: a grocery store, a beaten-down owner, his assimilated daughter, the gentile stranger, the man who first seduces the daughter and then is himself seduced by Judaism. What is unique is that swirling world of post-Holocaust ethics: Jews and gentiles intermingling in universal suffering, guilt, and penance; that despair which precedes a deepening of ethical belief; the consciousness of miracles which derives from faith in something beyond the self. With this, Malamud is responding to 1950s passivity, moral and ethical ambiguity, counterfeit activities and feelings.

For all its differences of experience, Baldwin's first novel, *Go Tell It on the Mountain*, fits into this general mold. Baldwin started out with the need to "kill" the father, figuratively, literarily, and, in some instances, almost physically. His work set off a series of challenges and responses that ran through the 50s and 60s and, as the decades picked up momentum, drew in both black and Jewish writers. They were fighting over common turf. Female writers preferred to kill the mother (or husband). *Go Tell It*, to begin there, has affinities to both black and white works: Henry Roth's *Call It Sleep* (1934), Farrell's *Studs Lonigan* (1930s on), Wright's *Black boy* (1945), Delmore Schwartz's *In Dreams Begin Responsibilities* (1935), even Salinger's *The Catcher in the Rye*; later, we find Mario Puzo's *The Fortunate Pilgrim* (1964), then Philip Roth's *Goodbye, Columbus* and *Portnoy's Complaint*. An unlikely brew of novels is held together by a common bond, the American version of the *Bildungsroman*.

The basic frame is of a young man (on occasion, young woman) thrust into an atmosphere in which ethnicity or raciality creates a conflict to be worked out in addition to the usual ones of boyhood and adolescence. In the American version, the youth may not come through, for race, religion, ethnicity, paternal authority are forms of doom-as they almost are for Baldwin's John Grimes. Simple initiation into life is not for him, as he struggles through father, race, religious experiences, and his own ambiguous feelings into a kind of process, after hovering near destruction or abulia. At the end, he can say "I'm on my way,'" for he has pushed through to the other side by way of a religious experience. But what will work, at least temporarily for John Grimes as he thrashes around in the passionate embrace of the Lord, did not work for Baldwin, except in his essays. His later fiction, beginning with *Giovanni's Room* (1956) and continuing through *Another Country* (1962), *Tell Me How Long the Train's Been Gone* (1968), and *Just Above My Head* (1979), lacks the feel for language and the centeredness of *Go Tell It*. Baldwin's essays, however, provide a pivot for the development of black consciousness in the decades after the war. It all started with his literary need to cast off the influence of Richard Wright, especially *Native Son*, which Baldwin repudiated in "Many Thousands Gone," in 1951. He followed this with a 1955 piece, his well-known "Notes of a Native Son," in which he attempts to become a father, not a son, and in which he explores the possibility of the black writer treating his characters not as social victims but as distinct personalities. He was moving toward black consciousness based on individual self-expression; so that *Giovanni's Room* curiously foreshadows *Portnoy's Complaint*. We should note at this stage how typically American all this is, whether the movable pieces are black, Jewish, or, later, female.

Wright, meanwhile, was becoming an icon of black consciousness, and the black radical left reviled Baldwin. So, too, was Ellison, who was not considered sufficiently black, although *Invisible Man* would prove to be the most enduring work of the postwar black renaissance and possibly of the entire period. Eldridge Cleaver, who had emerged as an essayist of great power in *Soul on Ice*, attacked Baldwin for his alleged hatred of blackness and accused the latter of fearing Wright because of his masculinity. Cleaver cited Norman Mailer's long essay "The White Negro," in which the latter had argued for the black stud, among other things. Wright, who had died in 1960, re-entered the late 50s and the 60s as a powerful heterosexual leader; Baldwin is put down for his homosexuality; Ellison is denigrated as whitey's man. John Williams, in his trenchant *The Man Who Cried I Am* (1967), caught all this, mixing Wright, Baldwin, Malcolm X, King, and others, fathers and sons interwoven. We find strange alignments, the Jewish Mailer on the side of the more rebellious black critics, Cleaver, Addison Gayle, Killens Hoyt, all eager to resurrect Wright and dump Baldwin and Ellison. The latter now entered the fray with a defense called "The World and the Jug," in which he responded to an article by Irving Howe, called "Black Boys and Native Sons." Howe, the outsider to black life, sympathetically describes the black experience as containing unmitigated violence that makes the individual a social victim. Ellison argued that violence is not endemic, that a coherent black culture exists, that one can seek freedom within it, and, finally, that the individual can make choices-black life, accordingly, is neither trap nor prison. This was, in fact, almost the last time blacks heated up critically, and what occurred afterward was both unpleasant and unfortunate. Blacks and Jews accused each other of racial and ethnic slurs and stopped speaking to each other; and black male writers, except for John Williams, lost much of their direction. Baldwin still published, of course, having become as "black" as Cleaver could have wished, and in the process not a little anti-Semitic; Ellison struggled mightily to produce a coherent second novel and failed, but he is as revered as Wright; and black critics are cultivating their own gardens, many of them in highly endowed chairs at major universities. The prodigiously talented Ishmael Reed emerged, but for lack of a subject he stumbled and then, as we shall see, fell into a self-imposed trap. All the major issues remain.

Most Jewish novelists and all female writers kept out of the conflict, as though the conflicts among black males was a kind of individual shootout. William Styron's *The Confessions of Nat Turner* in 1967, although by a non-Jew, opened up all the old wounds and some new ones; but here the conflict is white versus black and it takes on racial overtones that create another line of argument, less literary than social. John Williams's *The Man Who Cried I Am*[258] in the same year, nicely complementing Harold Cruse's important study *The Crisis of the Negro Intellectual*, was one of the last large fictions by a black male writer; after that, for a variety of cultural reasons, the mantle was passed to black women: Toni Morrison, Toni Cade Bambara, Alice Walker, Gloria Naylor, Jamaica Kinkaid, as well as to an entire decade of white women writers who became prominent in the 70s. Williams's novel attempted to sum it all up, as a roman à clef of the main characters in the racial arena; but more so, as a kind of compendium of black fears and frustrations. Central to the argument in William's presentation is the "King Alfred" plot, a contingency plan in which the government will eliminate black leaders, dissidents, even rank and file if racial relationships get out of hand. Here, Williams presents the ultimate in white racism, in a way that contrasts with Jewish novelists and their marked avoidance of the Holocaust, Israel, even the larger role of the Jew in America. While the Jewish novelist has, in most instances, taken assimilation (not acceptance) for granted, the black novelist, Williams suggests, must recognize the rejection of the Negro even during the heady times of the civil rights movement. The novel gains much of its power from its refusal to back off from its dramatic theme: that a people can be sacrificed to strange gods if they are unaware of what others have in mind for them. Whether an actuality or a metaphor, the King Alfred plan defines how the country feels, rhetoric aside. As conspiracy themes proliferate in fiction (from Gaddis to DeLillo and Auster), "King Alfred" becomes apple pie American, not black paranoia.

No female novelist, until Toni Morrrison's *Beloved*, has picked up the passion and urgency of Williams's novel; he had tried, surely, to write the *Native Son* of the 60s, and it is, as well, something of a response to *Invisible Man*. The Jewish novels of the 60s, on the other hand, are inward-turning; moving not onto a world stage, but a personal, sexual one: Roth's *Portnoy* and Bellow's *Herzog*. Yet another novel moved into prominence in the decade, first as a cult fiction and then as a vastly popular work-Joseph Heller's *Catch 22* (1961).[259] Heller came from the Coney Island section of Brooklyn (heavily Jewish) and clearly has something of the wit we associate with Yiddish-speaking standup comedians. His first novel has the caustic, ironic, burlesque quality of Lenny Bruce, the definitive comic of the decade. Is *Catch-22*, then, a Jewish novel? Does it belong with Bellow and Roth, who are seemingly more concerned with a Jewish self-consciousness?

Linguistically, or rhetorically, it is possible to see Heller's novel as having a "Jewish" dimension, and that is in his use of litotes for comic purposes. His entire novel is an extended litotes, that form of understatement and irony in which something is expressed by way of the negative of its opposite. One never says "not many" but "not a few," creating a dialectical confusion as to how many or how few. "Catch-22" as a phrase, which has entered the language, is linked to its litotic function. For it expresses an underlying negative aspect: if you are crazy, you need not fly, but if you do not want to fly, that proves you're not crazy. The expression upsets our notions of what is, what is not, in the way a comic uses wit to express the opposite of what we ordinarily take for granted. Since what is stated differs from what is suggested, Heller has a rhetorical context for the military of the 1940s, the counterfeit of the 1950s, and the defiance of authority which would characterize America of the 1960s and thereafter. The use of language for such comic effects is very similar to the way jokes function in Yiddish and more generally in Jewish life: the litotic function prevails as the way the Jew can mock himself-the way blacks use the "dozens" as rhetoric-even while he considers himself part of a chosen people. Yossarian, the ancient Assyrian, the modern Armenian, is really a wandering New York Jewish-American. But having experienced both assimilation into and rejection of his society, he has, in many ways, not a particularly Jewish experience, but an American one.

Bellow's *Herzog*[260] is the other side of the Jewish shekel. Here we have Moses Elkanah Herzog, whose last name means duke, whose middle name makes him the father of the Biblical Samuel, and yet whose temperament mocks Mosaic leadership. Bellow turned from the extroverted Henderson, his wandering, explorative gentile, to the internalized Jew, whose activity consists of researching and writing books, penning letters to world figures, and lying on his back, Oblomov-like in his refusal to do the world's work. Although Herzog is a Jew, and suffers from Jewish guilt, he is located on ground shaped by the universal underground man, Oblomov, Ellison's Invisible Man, Camus' Meursault, Kafka's K. and Joseph K., Beckett's enervated warriors and not least Dostoievsky's. His repertory, in American fiction alone, recalls Melville and James.

While rejecting most technical aspects of modernism, Bellow has turned his protagonist into a modernist amalgam: the very suffocated sense of life which he has attacked in essays and interviews seems to be Herzog's strength. He breathes the oxygen of defeat, and he exists because others support his parasitism. Moses Herzog fleshes out Bellow's persistent theme of the eternal sufferer, and the man who, in his pain, despair, and guilt, takes on himself an ethical role. Bellow will pursue this in *Mr. Sammler's Planet* (1970),[261] where Artur Sammler, a Holocaust survivor, will try to work out the needs of the private person without forgoing reason. Bellow's withdrawal from perceived 60s and 70s anarchy and destabilization is reflected in characters who, if they could, would like to stop time; men who conclude their efforts at rationality are wasted, given the climate of disorder. Herzog becomes an American dropout.

Portnoy's Complaint (1969)[262]-for which Roth was marked as an anti-Semite by righteous Jews-is also a response to 60s turbulence, an attempt to grapple with a Jewish version of that disorder. But once again we must stress that the Jewish component in Roth has no relationship to religion, race, ethnicity, not even an historical tradition. It is, rather, the sense that one is marked, like Cain, as a Jew from birth to death; that one cannot escape a "Jewish mother," who is really the mother of all mothers; and that the Jew is always the outsider, most of all when he thinks he is gaining ground in the gentile world.[263]

Once we get past the more sensational aspects, the Roth novel is an updated *Bildungsroman*, Portnoy our own postwar Huck Finn. Alexander Portnoy must somehow escape his house beautiful to become his own person: the primal theme of growing-up fiction. In his document, which is narrated to his analyst, Dr. Spielvogel, Portnoy stresses his sexual disturbances, especially his fear of castration, which accompany shame and dread of retribution. He locates himself near Kierkegaard's Abraham and Isaac. He must, in order to discover himself, destroy the father (and mother) in himself; which is to say he must erase his Jewishness and become an American writer.

This obsessive need will play a large part in Roth's Zuckerman trilogy (and epilogue): *The Ghost Writer* (1979),[264] *Zuckerman Bound* (1981),[265] *The Anatomy Lesson* (1983),[266] and *The Prague Orgy* (1985),[267] which constitute the major work of his mid-career. There is a constant in Roth's fiction: the generational conflict which derives from younger people's desire to become American, American as exemplified by WASPs. "Goodbye, Columbus," like *Goodbye Columbus*, is an ambiguous title, but of course more than Columbus, Ohio, or Ohio State University is indicated; for Columbus is also the first part of America, as it were. To say farewell to Columbus is to sail out oneself, away from one part of America to where another is situated. The effort is to discover one's American origins, perhaps hoping to enter the gates of Eden.

Portnoy's Complaint proved a cultural turning point for the Jewish writer, writing as a Jew or not. When Portnoy makes his now famous comment about putting the "Id" back in "Yid" (and later the "oi" back in "Goy"), he is speaking metaphorically about life in America. The remark is all about dichotomies, separations, divisions, isolation-the stuff of American literature, not merely Jewish life. Roth cites *Civilization and Its Discontents*, Freud's cynical assessment of human capability as it runs afoul of its own ordering sense; for the young Alexander, "civilization" is centered on his having his way with a girl, preferably gentile. But along with this dismissal of "civilization" is an awareness of Freud's "degradation in erotic life," the condition in which sensuality is unaccompanied by tenderness, in which sex is distinct from love. Experiences are thus separated in Portnoy, who suffers from every divorce of elements Freud defined. As his namesake (Alexander) discovered, all conquest leads to the morbid realization that the remaining territory has been diminished.

In a curious way, a good deal of what Roth is getting at has significance for female novelists as well, given the obvious difference in direction of their own interests. But before moving to that decade of writers who limned the female experience, we should note the enormous contribution of Flannery O'Connor and, to a lesser extent, Carson McCullers. On one hand, O'Connor kept the voice of Faulkner going in American fiction, and, on the other, she carved out her own territory, which differs from Faulkner's. Her mixture of wit, irony, paradox, and traditional belief in the devil and God (she was a devout Roman Catholic) gave her prose a maturity that belied the young age at which much of her fiction was written. The cornerstone of her fiction derives from her Catholicism in a mainly Protestant South; from her ability to maintain her difference and uniqueness. An early and abiding influence was that of Teilhard de Chardin, whose idea of "passive diminishment" she identified with. She came to accept an affliction (lupus) which, while determined and unavoidable, was accompanied by a strengthening of will. Thus, she was a battleground of diminishment and response, the affliction leading to an achievement based on morbid personal experience. This sense of suffering and increase or compensation makes her work far more than Southern or regional, or even uniquely female, as she suggests in her essay "The Grotesque in Southern Fiction."

O'Connor established her reputation with her short stories, although her two novels (*Wise Blood*, 1952, and *The Violent Bear It Away*, 1960)[268] display her unmistakable themes: the implicit and explicit violence of those who live intensely; lines of hatred and lines of love which are almost indistinguishable; a preoccupation with baptism, damnation, redemption which comes to limn an entire society, not only believers; bizarre, possessed people whom she makes familiar and apparently "conventional." In her two volumes of stories, *A Good Man Is Hard to Find* (1954) and *Everything That Rises Must Converge* (1965),[269] O'Connor combined a concentration of theme with gem-like prose, in a kind of deconstruction of reader expectation. In the latter volume, published the year after she died of lupus, at thirty-nine, she concentrated on a number of images or symbols which lament the passage of time: the crazy hat of young Julian's mother in "Everything That Rises"; the "Artificial Nigger," an image of immense dissolution emblematic of a waste land; the artificial leg in "Good Country People"; the tattoo in "Parker's Back"; the coffin in "Judgment Day." In "the Endouring Chill," written in prose that may be the finest of the postwar era, the ill Ashbury recognizes that he will live, and he awaits the new life that will come, the old life in him being exhausted. But the new life is one of ice: "It was then that he felt the beginning of a chill, a chill so peculiar, so light, that it was like a warm ripple across a deeper sea of cold."[270]

In a generation before O'Connor, at the turn of the 1940s, Carson McCullers in *The Heart Is a Lonely Hunter* (1940)[271] and *Reflections in a Golden Eye* (1941)[272] seemed to be mining Faulkner material, but came to locate her own ground. Her point of view in her first novel, written at twenty-two, embraces the obsessive need for man to revolt against his own inner isolation, to express himself as fully as possible in a "wasteful, short-sighted society." There are stirrings here, a good twenty-five years ahead of its time, of a distinct sensibility-adumbrating those themes of liberation and independence that will limn the "female experience" of the late 1960s and for the following decade. McCullers, before the war years, found a thread on which to hang her concern for female (as well as male) existence: in the lonely, dark terrain where the individual is suspended between love and terror and must find ways to emerge. This was not, however, Flannery O'Connor's material, which, while certainly sympathetic to the female point of view, was concerned with universal qualities of salvation and redemption.

As we move toward "female fiction," we must emphasize that all three groups-women, blacks, Jews-see themselves as drifting, as out of the mainstream, even when accepted; and that from their *perceptions* of marginality, or from the real thing, they are forging a common literature. They are not separated from America-even if they would like to think so-and only occasionally from each other. Even their bitterness is deeply American; after all, the "Amer" in America means bitter.

We must, before proceeding, distinguish between "female fiction," which does not exist, and fiction based on the "female experience," which does differentiate it from fiction with male protagonists and male sensibilities. To assert that "female fiction" exists is to suggest that the human experience bifurcates into two distinct streams, one male and one female; so that fear, pity, terror, sympathy love, not to speak of language itself, are not shared commodities. Since they are, the common ground must be greater than the differences in the quality and quantity of the given experience-which is not to deny the uniqueness of that experience. What did appear in the latter part of the 1960s and well into the 70s was an avalanche of fiction by female writers, some black, some Jewish. Thus in creating groups of any kind, we must account for several black and Jewish writers in two areas, and this makes something of a muddle of categories themselves. Further, while black female novelists such as Toni Morrison and Alice Walker are concerned with black life and experiences, few female Jewish novelists-except Cynthia Ozick-write about the being Jewish at all. Many of them are indistinguishable from non-Jews in their concern with the felt experience of bondage to male values or what independence means for women who find themselves approaching Kierkegaard's sense of dread. That is, while black writers may pursue the individual experience within a black society and community (a small town, a neighborhood, even a house), Jewish writers tend to pursue more the experience of the yawning pit: what happens when women are given the opportunity to choose. At that moment, as the Danish theologian pointed out, dread begins; fear and trembling lie in choice.

One of the considerable novels of choice is by neither a black nor a Jew, but by Joyce Carol Oates, in *them* (1969, later as *Them*).[273] Yet although it is intensely about a female experience, it is also linked profoundly to American themes of breaking out and reshaping, what goes on in the *Bildungsroman*, male or female. The novel tells of how a young woman, Maureen Wendall, attempts against tremendous odds of both nature and nurture to break a destructive and self-destructive family pattern. She is, in a sense, the obverse of Clyde Griffiths in Dreiser's *An American Tragedy*. Maureen has to learn how to deal with emptiness, and her success or failure is, for Oates, a paradigm of what women must do- emptiness, for her, defines where women are. Oates demonstrates Maureen's intense hatred of the author's comfortable and secure world, and yet survival depends on her devising strategies to acquire a piece of that world: a husband (any decent man!), her own home and child, a settled and stable existence outside her murderous Wendall background. Maureen does not seek success in the larger world; she must obsessively find stability in the domestic world, where she can be liberated from the past. Her reference point seems David Copperfield. Almost alone among white female novelists, Oates observes how different "liberation" is for the lower or working class woman from what it is for those with a more fortunate start. As it must seem clear, male working class fiction offers up similar paradigms.

Toni Morrison, in *Sula* (1973), as well as in *The Bluest Eye* (1970), *Song of Solomon* (1977), and *Tar Baby* (1981), as we have observed earlier, works through many of these lower-class concerns but with the added dimension of the black woman struggling to assert herself. Unlike Alice Walker's Meridian (in *Meridian*, 1976)[274] or her Celie in *The Color Purple* (1982), who function within recognized systems, Sula breaks through all categories and insists on the same prerogatives men obtain: sexual liberation, freedom of movement, indifference to social or familial commitments. Sula disrupts every expectation the black community has for a woman, consciously damning herself in the eyes of others so as to prove to herself what a black woman can do. Morrison's point, by 1973, was not particularly new, although it was something of a radical statement for a black woman, and it foreruns the argument Michele Wallace put together in *Black Macho and the Myth of the Superwoman* (1979);[275] an attempt to do for the black woman what Betty Friedan in *The Feminine Mystique* had done, mainly, for white middle-class women.[276]

Morrison's Sula reaches back to John Williams's novel: the man "who cried I am" only now a woman. In many ways, she is responding to materials such as those in other feminine writers, but her points of reference are not solely female. However significant she makes female equality, she reacts to what is unique in the individual, to ways in which a community can hobble that individual experience and measure it against customs which, while sometimes supportive, are often destructive. The individual life, she demonstrates, often becomes more important than the social organism or even the race.

This quality also characterizes Joan Didion's fiction (*Run River*, 1963; *Play It As It Lays*, 1970; *A Book of Common Prayer*, 1977; *Democracy*, 1984) and essays (*Slouching Toward Bethlehem*, 1968; *The White Album*, 1979), which demonstrate many negative aspects of female liberation. Didion focuses on women for whom the idea of liberation and the movement itself have little significance; women who lie outside all activity and are self-serving, narcissistic, anomic. They have already gone over. Such women move in and out of senseless marriages, become involved with men they dislike, and display their neuroses like badges. The constant, for her, is the woman who cannot deal with her own life, or whose life has gone off the tracks. Yet, strangely like Morrison, she casts her net wider than female discontinuity. In her minimalist strategies, Didion picks up the anomie of an entire community and society; and her description of wasted women, while focused on the female experience, is a depiction of an enervated society, one in which all value systems have run down. Women, too, are part of entropy.

Most of the other female novelists listed below are, like their male counterparts, less society-oriented and more attuned to personal needs. The so-called "me-ism" or narcissism of the 60s and 70s is revealed in a spate of novels that appeared in the decade from the late 60s. Among them: Judith Rossner's *Looking for Mr. Goodbar* (1975), Lisa Alther's *Kinflicks* (1976), Alix Kates Shulman's *Memoirs of an ex-Prom Queen* (1972), Maureen Howard's *Before My Time* (1974), Cynthia Buchanan's *Maiden* (1972), Rossner's *Attachments* (1977), Erica Jong's *Fear of Flying* (1973), Marge Piercy's *Small Changes* (1973), and Diane Johnson's *The Shadow Knows* (1974). Added to these should be Alice Walker's *The Color Purple* (1982) and Rossner's *August* (1983). Although they differ in narrative strategies, prose styles, qualities of wit and irony, all are interconnected by common themes of female victimization, the need for women to break through stereotypes held both by men and by themselves, and the difficulty women have in functioning or emerging within an essentially patriarchal world. Several of the novels suggest resolutions based on separatism (lesbian love, female communal life, distinct communities of "safe houses"), and several chart the disasters that result from what seems an obvious good, liberation. Male 70s writers (including of course blacks and Jews), in almost equal measure, grapple with the same or similar problems: the promise of liberation measured against the disappointment of its achievement. American lives *there*!

As we survey blacks, Jews, and women writers from the heights (or depths) of the 80s and 90s, we discover some lessening in energy. Civil rights, feminism, assimilation (for Jews and women, for some blacks) have not led to richer themes. Except for Morrison, blacks have failed to produce any writer of the stature and force of Wright, Ellison, the Baldwin of the 50s and 60s, and Williams in his single 60s novel.[277] The failure of the essay in black hands is perhaps connected to this; for when the novel flourished, it was abetted by compelling nonfiction from Baldwin, Cleaver, Cruse, and others. There is little sense at this time of a distinct black fictional voice-John Edgar Widemen has become too strident, more social commentator than novelist. While this loss of voice does not mean assimilation-quite the contrary!-it suggests a crisis in black intellectual and creative force as far as the novel is concerned. Much has been made in the 90s of black intellectuals-Cornel West, Henry Louis Gates, Stephen Carter, William Julius Wilson (in sociological studies)-but a good deal of what they write is journalism; and their impact on general intellectual life, for all their energy and occasional brilliance, is minimal. What we need are not writers pecking at the edge of the establishment, but hard, ironic, nasty literary assessments of America, for which blacks are well positioned.

Jewish novelists and so-called intellectuals (Irving Howe, the *Partisan Review* crowd, the posturing neo-conservatives and their sons) have, also, more or less run their course. The Jews writing in *Commentary*, *The New Criterion*, or *Tikkun* are someone's idea of a bad joke played on an audience willing to settle for voodoo. Bellow, Roth, Heller, Mailer, Doctorow, Friedman, and others continue to publish, and a few like Heller have moved increasingly into more explicitly Jewish material (*Good as Gold*, 1979; *God Knows*, 1984; *Closing Time*, 1994); but the novelty has worn off. The larger sense of American fiction is now attuned to several difficult and less popular novelists, those I have called, in Chapter Five, Mega-Novelists: Gaddis, Pynchon, McElroy, and earlier Barth, among others. The labeling of the "Jewish novel" was faulty anyway, as we have noted, since the novels always had more of America than of Jews in them; and this with a few exceptions was also true of black fiction, despite its intensity and concentration of black life. The more recent examples, cited shortly, only reinforce how black writers have embraced American themes, whatever their protests.

As for women novelists, the surge of a distinctive voice about the female experience has not abated; but the voices have taken on other sounds and tones in writers like Ann Beattie, Mary Ann Settle, Anne Tyler, Dorothy Allison, Alice Walker, and Bobbie Ann Mason. Furthermore, a good deal of energy-for blacks, Jews, women, and others-has been going into shorter fiction; with a consequent loss of force for the novel, except for those still working in the long, Mega-Novel area. Joyce Carol Oates has herself experimented with several forms, writing a series of novels in different genres, with *Bellefleur* (1980) the most wrought. A historical novel with strong Gothic overtones, *Bellfleur* is, at the same time, a meaningful commentary on contemporary issues. With its emphasis on large emotional patterns, huge passions, life and death elements, it is the kind of broad fiction that contemporary American women have backed away from. Full of myth, legend, epic qualities, it breaks through our common categories and becomes, despite its interest in female situations, a novel about America.

If we explore these matters further: several more recent novels by black writers while seeming to strengthen a separatist position from everyone else are in actuality pure middle America, a hybridization of people and events. Although its foregrounding seems to be concerned almost solely with blacks, Charles Johnson's *Middle Passage* (1990)[278] is a packed allegory of America. Its narrator is black, a hustler named Rutherford Calhoun, but one light-skinned enough so that the racial background becomes mixed, even confused. Calhoun, in fact, in a striking racial crossover, recalls T. Coraghessan Boyle's (white) Ned Rise in *Water Music*. A petty thief, a grifter, a swindler and the like, Calhoun stows away on a ship which turns out to be involved in the slave trade; and his story is mainly about what happens in the interaction between blacks and blacks, blacks and villainous whites, and blacks and helpful, generous whites. It is, in miniature, the story of America, from the point of view of a man who straddles several worlds: color, of course, but also class and caste, legal and illegal, marginal and central. What gives the allegory its central ballast-its white whale, as it were-is the presence of the slave ship, aptly called the *Republic*.[279]

Once again in postwar literary history, we are confronted by the spectacle of a black novelist with a black protagonist-sympathetic and charismatic *because of* his penchant for thievery and grifting-

which fits into an American model of the counterfeit and the imposter. All of the elements are part of the American mosaic-and if not a mosaic, then a puzzle distinctly reflective of American life. Late in the novel Calhoun ponders his condition: "Nay, the States were hardly the sort of place a Negro would pine for, but pine for them I did. Even for *that* I was ready now after months at sea, for the strangeness and mystery of black life, even for the endless round of social obstacles and challenges and trial colored men faced every blessed day of their lives, for there were indeed triumphs, I remembered, that balanced the suffering on shore, small yet enduring things, very deep. . . ."[280]

The central trope, *the* American nightmare, is the horror of the slave ship-that ship of doom in its "middle passage"-the tale of blacks and Arabs selling blacks in Africa and whites selling blacks in America, if and when any slaves survived the passage. The "middle passage" becomes in typical American fashion a rite of passage, one that few indeed survive; so that slavery at the end of the voyage is really part of a testing that began with capture in Africa. The allegorical voyage and consequence-the *Republic* capsizes and nearly all aboard die in a mutiny or the sinking-projects forward in history to death trains to death camps, or to any of those voyages in which the dominant group attempts to enslave or kill the weaker ones. For Calhoun, all this is part of the "weird, upside-down caricature of a country called America,"[281] a land of half-breeds, a caldron of mongrels, and every other version of human points on the compass, as he puts it.

All of this is presented in standard English, as part of Calhoun's meditations. He insists, in his way, on an American story, an American narrative. Along the way, he creates several memorable white characters, including Cringle, a mate on the *Republic*, a decent man overcome by machinations, mutiny, and other conflicts, all reminiscent of the "white liberal" who cannot stem the tide of greed and foul motive. There is, also, Captain Falcon, a man of great physical presence (although dwarfish), a man who argues with reason and logic, but who believes in the deity he has stolen from the Allmuseri, the Africans now enslaved. There is Squibb, the cook, a fall-down drunk, but someone who turns out to be stalwart when needed as doctor, cook, general helper on board the stricken *Republic*. There are the Allmuseri themselves, men and women who can bond, people who seem to have a culture which the whites lack, a tribe that at moments can transcend its horrible fate.

There is, additionally, Charles Johnson's recognition that a mutiny, enslavement, a wrecked ship requires some meta-reality. This is introduced in the stolen "deity" which Captain Falcon keeps in his hold, and which, when it emerges, seems like an embodiment of Calhoun's own father. Origins, roots regained! The metaphor here is somewhat complicated, but we can unravel it, and we must emphasize it as the metaphor of America. The deity represents the magical world of the Allmuseri, but at the same time it has resonance in the life of the Americanized Calhoun. He is, however, not so Americanized he can forsake his background, his color, his connection to Africa. But he is, also, not really part of the Allmuseri culture, and the deity is a phantasmal creature for him-father and not father, deity and not deity. Thus, with this association with the "deity" so like his father, Calhoun moves in and out of his heritage and becomes a typical part of the American pattern of "mongrels and half-breeds," to use his term to characterize who we are and where we come from. Thus, the *Republic* is formed. Unfortunately, it capsizes.

More sermon than fiction, the hugely ambitious *The Chaneysville Incident* (1981)[282] by David Bradley is notable on several grounds. While it insists on the black story or narrative, it muffles any story for a white counterpart. It is, in this respect, like several Jewish novels that marginalize gentiles or blacks-one thinks of Saul Bellow's *Mr. Sammler's Planet*. The black pickpocket there is, in fact, without any story of his own; only Sammler's counts. The difference between the two writers is that Bellow has taken away the story from a marginalized character, part of a brief urban episode, and Bradley has negated any story from a major character, the psychiatrist Judith, companion of the narrator, John Washington. All her so-called stories are either dismissed or negated as trivial in the face of Washington's urgency, to let her know how slavery, post-slavery days, and continued segregation have shaped him; whereas, in effect, *nothing* has shaped her. She is not only unshaped, but merely an avatar of a psychiatrist, disembodied; she is, additionally, almost voiceless. Her experience, her education, her medical and psychological knowledge, all are run over by the juggernaut of the historian Washington, who "sings" of the truth. He is the bard not of connecting bridges-although he sticks to Judith and says he loves her-but of separation; he insists she can never hope to understand what he is getting at as he tells and retells the stories of his childhood and youth.

Bradley has performed something of a balancing trick: John Washington, an historian, is telling his stories to his analyst, who happens to be his lover; she sits or stands by almost silently while he pours out his hatred of whites, his racial stereotyping of whites, his bundle of clichés about the white world-and she, in Freudian majesty, listens, does not respond except to protest here and there, and is finally silenced by the avalanche of his insistent words. In that respect, Washington does need a therapist. But in another respect, he rejects Judith because white, culturally different, of different class and caste, because perhaps, implicitly, she is Jewish and part of the problem. Yet since in Washington's eyes, there is no resolution-black and white are separated by their distinct stories-all his efforts are doomed.

Once the reader gets past the lectures-Washington's narrative is really a set of class lectures-he is confronted by a strange bifurcation of class, gender, and caste. Although there is a relationship between Judith and John (at least it's not Martha and George) Washington, there is no ostensible basis for it, since one member is only a listening board and the other member is only mouth. The sexual encounters are awkward, as though Bradley recognized that with no rapport on the level of language and voice, there is little or no rapport elsewhere. Judith's frequent protestations of love, made in the face of Washington's silences, withdrawals, and condescension, have no significance beyond the fact that for purposes of a plot she must stick around. Who else would listen to John Washington as he pours out a good deal of recycled Faulkner, from *The Bear* and other assorted novels and stories? Surely, no black woman could serve as a listening board. The black historian needs a guilt-ridden, liberal, possibly Jewish woman (a Judith!) accustomed to listening to others' woes. The plot structure demands that a woman without a voice of her own, despite her education and supposed sophistication, hangs around a black historian so immersed in his own narcissism only *his* words count. She accepts condescension, dismissal of her intelligence, and all the rest; for Washington, she represents "white America," perhaps whiteness at its best, but a stereotypical whiteness, a docile slave to his master.

Why, then, include the Bradley novel in this chapter that purports to illuminate the black-Jewish-female novel as really part of a larger whole, the "American novel"? a chapter which undermines the idea of separate color and gender spheres and which tries to demonstrate that writers who seem separate and distinct are in reality participants in something largely American-why? The import of *The Chaneysville Incident*, withal its emphasis on black life, black culture, black stories impenetrable to the white perspective, despite all this, depends largely on a white presence, however muted. Washington, in fact, has no one to talk to unless he can speak to the rest of America; and in its presence, which is almost an absence, the white world is a huge hovering thereness. For even while dismissing that stereotypical world, John Washington cannot function without it. His stories may be alive to him, stories of his father and of his father's friend, Old Jack Crawley and his meticulous records, but they are stories which themselves remain silent until they can be offered up to a white audience. Apparently, it is not sufficient for the stories to be bottled up in documents and other records; they must be disseminated, and no less to a shrink who cannot answer back.

Accordingly, while Washington may insist that black life

remains invisible or impenetrable to white America, it is only the latter to which he can turn as a form of explanation. And explain and explain he does, in terms that are expected to play on Judith's white liberal guilt, a form of condescension which, in gender terms, is trueblood American. Male to female, superior to inferior, male with history to female who is blank slate, male with his stories to female who must listen, who professionally is a listener: Bradley incorporates the stuff of America here, both its comic and its tragic aspects. And he valorizes the white world to the degree that black life in its stories and in its telling and retelling has no further currency unless it can be communicated beyond itself, to that white world of dominance, hegemony, and, yes, racism.

By co-opting the white world for his purposes, Bradley re-emphasizes not the separation of the races, but their intermingling, their need for each other; not their impenetrability but their interdependence. What is so disagreeable about the novel is not the racial anguish which emerges-that is a given-but the tone of smugness, superiority, condescension in male to female, as if the male, because he is black and because the female is white, possesses some dominate power. Individual intelligence, sensitivity, distinct values no longer count. Let John Washington talk like this to a black woman, as noted above, and he wouldn't get very far beyond his first few self-serving "I's." Let him talk this way to another intelligent black man and he would be mocked; let him talk this way to a white man, and the latter would simply walk away. Using the gender card, Washington can assert himself, give himself the voice, and silence any opposition, even any effort at understanding. This is the stuff of middle America, from sitcoms to truck drivers.

We must be clear. The matter of Washington's recall and memory is often moving, full of the reality of a virulent racism; but the hectoring, haranguing quality of the telling dissipates the reader's sympathetic response, unless one is already converted to sermons. Since we must assume the novel is directed at an American audience made up of 9/10s whites and 1/10 blacks, it is difficult to understand why readers would listen. Judith only listens because, by some formula not apparent to the outsider, she needs to be beaten down by condescending words which leave her no space, no air, nothing for her to relate to. Unless she buys into Washington's hectoring, she comes away empty. Washington is himself tortured in the way that Faulkner's Quentin Compson is tormented, in *The Sound and the Fury*, where he kills himself, and in *Absalom, Absalom!*, where he is resurrected so that Faulkner can give further reasons why he killed himself. But Quentin does not harangue us with the poverty of the South, with its divided, virulent aims, with its conspicuous desire to fall on its own sword; he embodies all the terrible things with which a sensitive youth grows up, and he reflects a South which, despite his grotesque perception of it, is almost limitless in its potentialities. John Washington is a failed Quentin; he dips back into Faulkner's ghosts, but what he retains is not the breadth or sense of disintegration, but the sermon, the tones of a man hectoring his captive audience.

In Paule Marshall's *Brown Girl, Brownstones* (1959),[283][284] Selina's life at home, in the war between mother and father, is based on the paradigm of David Shearl and his life at home with Albert and his mother, in Henry Roth's *Call It Sleep*. The mother is strong, the leader; the husband is weak-although Albert Shearl works, and Selina's father lives in a fantasy of wealth and success he can never achieve. Although Selina is caught between her parents, as is David, she does not hate her wastrel, self-destructive father, as does David. She loves him, but admires her mother's stoicism and work ethic: the mother is the one who pulls the family through.

By casting it as generically a Bildungsroman, we can see this story of Barbados immigrants-Selina is born here-as integrated into the American scene, as part of the immigrant novel classically focused in the Henry Roth mode. This is not in any way to deny that the Barbados experience in New York is unique; that it has qualities which distinguish it from other black experience, especially that of American blacks; that it establishes its own criteria for judgment. All of that is indisputable, especially the point that

Barbadan blacks-who call themselves Bajans-have created a different culture from that, say, of American blacks, and the two groups often seem hostile to each other. Nevertheless, once this is agreed upon, it is clear that Bajan life here, that of the Boyce family, has all the makings of the typical American immigrant experience. In fact, many Bajans, both leaders and followers, say they should emulate the example of "the Jew." Rather than badmouthing Jewish upward mobility, as have several American black leaders, the Bajans imitate it: get hold of a property, rent out rooms, buy another property, rent out rooms, and so on, until one finds a better neighborhood and a good living; then educate the children for something better, until the immigrant expectation is achieved. The American way!

Along the way, Selina Boyce must cope with the usual obstacles of the first generation, with the additional factor that color creates another dimension of obstacle, although not overwhelmingly so. One of Selina's problems, however, as she grows into young womanhood is to avoid being stereotyped of "one of them." She resists being "placed." But then she is doing something quintessentially American, which is to insist on her uniqueness, her particularity or essentialism, over those who would generalize her. In this respect, even color-while serving to stigmatize her in the eyes of some-creates in her the American ideal that she can be herself, not part of an association, group, or even family.

The most compelling parts of the novel are the "American struggle" of the first generation to find its way. As in the traditional Bildungsroman, the decisions revolve as much around family as the individual. Selina Boyce must navigate between mother and father, the latter dying later in the novel when he apparently falls off a boat on the way to the islands, or possibly jumping, once his manhood has been taken from him. But, while charming, he is infantile, unable to move beyond his fantasies of a high life in America, somewhat akin to Geoffrey Wolff's duke of deception. Selina's mother, on the other hand, is narrow, rigid, very much a capitalist entrepreneur in her equation of morality and economic advancement.

But Selina is ambivalent about each, unable to join to either, cognizant that while the father has too much useless life, the mother has too much inflexibility. At stake, running through it-and another Bildungsroman feature-are houses: *where* one lives, as much as how one lives, determines status not only in the Bajan community but also in the American. But family also involves more than the struggle of mother and father for command of the household; it also concerns an older sister, who is conventional in her expectations (dull marriage, dull home, respectability); various members of the community, who provide some of the bonding Selina misses in her home; and her own expectations, those founded on family values and those which will set her apart. She is, in brief, a typical central figure in a growth or formation novel, caught as she is between sameness and difference.

Further, Paule Marshall provides a triangulation, when she introduces Selina to Clive, and the young woman must deal not only with a passive, Oblomov-like, cynical man, but with his attachment to a mother who is clearly out to control her son's every activity. When Clive succumbs to the needs of his mother (and his own), Selina has finally broken through, from his "first love" to her own interests, wherever they may lead. Having pursued a Bajan Association scholarship and having gained it through manipulation, lies, and some deceit, she rejects it and insists upon herself. She may look like a young, attractive Bajan woman, but she is all-American in her desire to succeed on her own terms. Her return at the end to the islands is, in one respect, a return to roots, but in another an assertion she can put both family, the Bajan Association, her sister's respectability, and Clive all behind her. She has emerged.

As a parallel book, Darryl Pinckney's *High Cotton* (1992)[285] is ostensibly about how to be a Negro-Black-African-American; but as subtext it is really concerned with how to grow up and be a person in America. At one point, Pinckney's unnamed narrator-an "invisible" boy and man?-tells us: "As a black who had grown up in a small, mean American city, and in a secure, protective, claustrophobic family as well, I had always looked to Bargette [a Parisian friend] for clues, for lessons about how to be a modern Negro in the great world."[286] But becoming what he calls a "modern Negro" is about growing up, becoming mature enough to secure control of his life. For much of this fictionalized memoir, the narrator is a kind of Holden Caulfield, dumping on others even as he attempts to discover who and what he is.

The clear questions are the standard ones in American fiction, and life, of identity. *Where* do I fit? *Do* I fit? *Am* I capable of growing into a responsible person? To what extent is my immature youth a permanent part of me, or to what degree can I change? What do I become when I become? Such are the questions the narrator asks of himself as he attempts to grow from the cocoon of an overprotective family, from a story-telling grandfather, from doting parents who reinforce all the silliness the narrator is capable of.

Like so many Bildungsroman-those apprenticeship-to-life fictional novels and memoirs we examined in Chapter Two-*High Cotton* is full of stories. We see this, also, in Morrison, Bradley, and in Leon Forrest's *Divine Days*-but it is not solely a black thing; think of Barth, Pynchon, Malamud, Bellow, others. It has become an American effort to recapitulate the past, or make some sense of it, or to find meaning in the present by way of the past. Pinckney does this through his grandfather, a man of such integrity, probity, and forthrightness that he is, indeed, part of a world gone under, and, as is suggested, gone under to our loss. As a black man in a racist, often murderous situation, he insisted on dignity, insisted on his rights as a man, and in many ways puts to shame the trivial acts of rebellion of his grandson, the writer.

The latter moves in worlds his grandfather could not imagine, but the grandson trivializes nearly everything he touches or is touched by. Part of the "American" dimension is that he comes to see he must reshape or transform himself; that even if his grandfather invented all his stories, they created lessons the grandson ignored. Finally, he recognizes, in true transformational terms, that "To have nothing to offer was not, after all, the best way to have nothing to lose."[287]

Pinckney's novel is obviously about how a young black man tries to come to terms with his blackness, with his relationship to the white world in which he appears to move easily, to those small slights that accumulate and become like a wall or parapet separating him from the whites around him. There could also be sexual problems, rooted in identity, which create the "gulf" between him and others, although this is so deeply buried in the text it remains speculative. Yet, withal, his effort to understand himself and to transcend his trivialities is an American effort, culled from the American language, standard English that belongs to the entire country if one chooses to use it. Pinckney's journey, with its echoes of Huck Finn's and Holden Caufield's, and others in this genre, is part of the larger quest for identity, self-recognition, and the need to emerge personally and uniquely.

What better way to close this segment than with Ishmael Reed, the literary gunslinger of the African-American world? Once again, as in his previous work, Reed's aim in *Reckless Eyeballing* (1986)[288] is to upset both expectations and point of view. In this brief novel, he takes on several of the current ideological struggles and definitely presents views which are not politically correct; views which, in fact, are aimed at particular groups: women, black women in particular, blacks in general, Jews, the entire arts establishment, and on into transgression. Ian Ball, a black playwright, is trying to find his way back from oblivion in a minefield of feminist critics who consider him a male chauvinist pig for his first play, *Suzanna*. His new play, *Reckless Eyeballing*, is supposed to redeem him in the eyes of producer Becky French and black playwright Tremonisha Smarts; but the new play also gets him into deep trouble with other black males in and around the stage, who consider Ball a sellout to both women and to the Jews.

The situation, which runs on hyper for most of the time, allows Reed some of his usual satirical commentary. It gives him a forum for black attacks on Jews and women, even while Ball protests against such attacks; and it permits him to straddle many issues-using Ball as a voice of sanity at the same time offering many arguments against sanity. Interwoven into the situation are several subplots: the murder of a Jewish producer Jim Minsk, set up and murdered by white Southerners in their revenge for Leo Frank, the Jew executed for the death of a Christian girl sixty years ago and then more recently pardoned; the play being planned by Becky French, based on Eva Braun, in which Nazi women are perceived as innocents all victimized by their men; the tale of Randy Shank, once highly placed, now a doorman raging against Jews and women, a man who attacks black women and snips off a piece of their hair; and on into tales which reveal every cultural, ethnic, and racial divide the country has experienced in the last two or more decades.

Although the perspective is clearly black-oriented, Ian Ball is himself a moderator between sides, attempting to find some middle ground between the attacks and the "truth" as blacks see it. The attacks clearly win the day and make Ball's neutrality suspect. While the views toward Jews seem balanced between attack and defense, the views toward women are bent out of shape, so that so-called radical feminists appear to be running the theatre business and, by implication, the business of the country. The attack on women is relentless, black and white, both particularized and those unknown women massed in the wings prepared to assault men, but especially black men. The imbalance (one avoids "paranoia" as a label) subverts the satire on gender relationships, on blacks and Jews, on everything associated with Jesse Jackson's "rainbow coalition." Reed is not having any part of the coalition; his is a divided, split, screaming country. But his own hobbyhorse, to ride roughshod over women who "dare," sucks the life out of the novel; and, in some ironic way, places him in the company of entire generations of white writers themselves unable to deal with women who insist on their own priorities. One need only think of Roth,

Bellow, Mailer, and several others: black and white meet on this point that the real threat to America comes from vampirish women. It's all a hoot, in Reed's treatment. Rainbow coalitions exist as a mirage, a fantasy vision. What's left?

What's left is a diffuse, ambiguous, unstable, undefined, almost rudderless America. Yet, remarkably, the black, Jewish, female response to America has been to reflect the country; there is the commonality of language and idiom. With few exceptions, all of these writers overlap in their use of the word, however much they differ from each other in stress and quality. Further: although we can note many different kinds of fiction in postwar America, our writers coalesce in their adherence to the pastoral tradition, to matters of space and spatiality, to the incoherence and discontinuity of American life, to Americans' reliance on escape and liberation as resolution of personal dilemma, to their suspicion of history and frequent rejection of historical precedent, except their own, to their deference to determinism and yet insistence that the individual must create and shape his and her own destiny. These are common grounds. Renewal, and all that suggests, creates a bond among American writers; so that inevitably any specifying categorization as black, Jew, or woman is artificial and nonbinding.

CHAPTER EIGHT

ROTH AND UPDIKE, ZUCKERMAN AND RABBIT— JEWISH AND GENTILE PERSPECTIVES OF AMERICA

The division of America into a Jewish and gentile country, illustrated by Philip Roth's Nathan Zuckerman and John Updike's Rabbit Angstrom, is reinforced by the fact both protagonists are named for differing measurements. An Angstrom is a term of miniscule measurement, and *Zuck* in German is the word for convulsive or jerky movement (although *Zuckerman* can also be sugarman). The Jewish and gentile visions, while they do overlap and do create a spectrum along which ethnic groups and races of all variety can be located, are essentially different. They move at different rates. The division indicates that despite assimilation, despite the relative success of Jews in America, despite general acceptance, and despite the gentile acquiescence to this, a fault line separates the two. And when we talk about a "gentile country," we recognize that it is white gentile, certainly as Rabbit reflects it. The very whiteness of Melville's whale, and then some.

For more than three decades, Nathan Zuckerman was Roth's

tool for devastating America; and for about forty years, from 1960, Updike has used Rabbit for his suburban rathole's view of the country. But while some form of devastation lies at the heart of both, what immense difference lies in their respective approaches! Early in *The Facts*, purportedly an autobiography, but more fictionalized than factualized, Roth speaks of his relationship to America-he is addressing Zuckerman:

> Though I knew that we were tolerated and accepted as well-in publicized individual cases, even specially esteemed-and though I never doubted that this country was mine (and New Jersey and Newark as well), I was not unaware of the power to intimidate that emanated from the highest and lowest reaches of gentile America.[289]

What Roth sees as racial and ethnic differences, Updike and Rabbit view as class, and class, of course, can be overcome: one makes money and joins the rest of America. It's not that simple! Zuckerman, however, or any of Roth's other surrogate figures, makes money, becomes famous or infamous and remains ethnically an outsider; part of America and yet somehow marginal. It is this split which Roth pursues; so that a "Jewish America" differs from the rest because even with toleration, Jews remain "the other." And even when this is not true, it remains the perception.[290]

Where does Zuckerman come from? Roth explains, in *The Facts*, that after *Portnoy's Complaint* there was the inevitable uproar, much of it generated by Jewish groups and by distorted reviews, as we saw not least in the American Jewish Committee's *Commentary*, where politics spreads like a virus into all its reviewing. From the turmoil which ensued in Roth's life and his despair about his reputation, he created Nathan Zuckerman. Ostensibly, Zuckerman was to be an alter ego, another self, a partner in dialogue, but gradually he became Roth's voice for a widening range of views, not the least the relationship of American Jews and gentiles and, collaterally, the relationship of American Jews to Israel. Zuckerman, however, became only one of Roth's surrogates, for we must add Kepesch, Tarnapol, and other clones and offshoots. Allowing for minor distinctions, they are all the same in their function: voices which shape Roth's exploration of the strange, bizarre, exhilarating but depressing sense of the American Jew in his (and her) second or even third generation.

Along the way, Roth curiously defines the country; in this respect, he probes far more deeply than Updike, who also tries to limn the country, from Rabbit's point of view. Roth positions Zuckerman as introspective, a reader, a teacher at times, a writer, even a thinker. Updike's Rabbit is visceral, thoughtless or heedless, intent on bodily pleasures without regard for ideas beyond the ones given by the mass media, and unable to break from a limited national, no less world, view. This, too, is a sense of the country, but it skims the top.

Added to the brew is Rabbit's financial success, despite his mindlessness; and Zuckerman's disastrous personal twists and turns, his breakdowns, physical and otherwise, his inability to function, his periods of paranoia. While the two do not appear to share a level playing field, each lives with illusions about his self, his progress, his achievements. And each defines himself in an inability to relate to women beyond the physical; their distaste for women runs parallel to their appetite for female orifices. In this, they are, in the American tradition, just good old boys.

But differences often overwhelm similarities. Despite Roth's penchant for revealing Zuckerman's inner life, he is intent on hiding. The Jew seeks special nooks and crannies, or disguises; even as he reveals something, he slips away. Rabbit, on the other hand, opens up, embraces the country, reveals who and what he is, finds no satisfaction in secreting himself away. He cannot tolerate a solitary existence. Roth, however, stashes it all away in the closet, even when he exposes the most outrageous behavior. When Updike chooses to be outrageous, he displays Rabbit; there is no subterfuge, no subtext, no inner life that might get away. With Roth, it is all deception, the attempt to sneak away in the night behind voices, alter egos, surrogates, fantasies.

Roth pours on the commentaries, not to open up Zuckerman or his surrogates, but to bury them beneath layers. To discover Zuckerman, one must penetrate a palimpsest, requiring a hermeneutics or exegesis we usually associate with Biblical texts. Somewhere underneath lies the "real" Zuckerman-find him if you can, through layers of his own deception, through layers of Roth's commentaries, like a series of switchbacks on a mountain road. Rabbit, however, is *there*, yawningly open for all to see, and so empty we fear his guts might just spill out. In this, we have very different cultures, cultures that derive, we can say, from the way the Jew and the gentile view themselves and, by implication, from their relationship to the country.

Our assumption is that Roth is our novelist of interiors, Updike of exteriors. Neither is fully consistent here, but in the main the point holds; and it extends to the way they carve up the country. It is simplistic to say that while Zuckerman writes books, Rabbit sells cars-but that distinction cannot be ignored. Zuckerman is a subversive creature, not only for Jews but also for all Americans who feel insecure in their positioning of themselves; Rabbit has little self-doubt or doubt about the country, except his hatred of those who would subvert it. He is personally unfulfilled because material things, even women, leave him dissatisfied. His is the dissatisfaction of the unexamined life; Zuckerman's is the dissatisfaction of the examined life.

For Roth, or for Zuckerman, the text always has its opposite; contraries can be as significant as stated purposes. For Updike and Rabbit, the text *is*. In the 8000-word finale to *The Facts*, Roth uses Zuckerman to comment on his, Roth's fictionalized autobiography.[291] This commentary includes remarks by Zuckerman's fourth wife, the Englishwoman Maria; and the combined comments are perhaps the most brilliant part of what is otherwise an often cloying and self-indulgent narrative.

Zuckerman addresses Roth in what is analogous to a standup Catskill comic's mischief making. "Don't publish," he warns, "you are far better off writing about me than 'accurately' reporting your own life."[292] He argues that Roth makes a fictional world far "more exciting than the world it comes out of,"[293] which is another way of saying that Roth's world cannot be trusted to possess any certainty; the only certainty is the fictional world Zuckerman represents as a mirror of Roth's own crises. He questions Roth's motives in nearly every area, but especially in the writer's presentation of wife Josie and their morbid marriage. Instead of Josie destroying Roth's life, as *The Facts* presents it, possibly Roth chose Josie out of an anger which only a poor choice could assuage.

But *The Facts* only substantiates what we already learned in *The Counterlife*, published two years previously, in 1986. Here the relationships are varied, but ultimately they focus on Nathan and Maria, the Englishwoman whom the former has weaned away from a psychologically abusive English husband. Among the ins and outs of Nathan's effort to negotiate the state of being Jewish first in the State of Israel and then in England, he presents himself as a "performing self." The Jew is a performing self, we glean by inference: not only Nathan but all Jews. Expose them to any kind of alien situation, in which normal people go "over the edge," and Jews begin their unique kind of theater. "That I have instead [of a single self] is a variety of impersonations I can do, and not only of myself-a troupe of players that I have internalized a permanent company of actors that I can call upon when a self is required, an ever-evolving stock of pieces and parts that forms my repertoire.... I am a theater and nothing more than a theater."[294] This would later be echoed in *Sabbath's Theater*.

Maria-what else would Nathan's gentile companion and then (fourth) wife be called?-has argued quite persuasively for the single self, the life that is identified with pastoral. The pastoral life includes acceptance, not performance; amiability, not argumentation; she wants to avoid collision, clash, reproach, "urgent meaning." For her, it is not necessary for Nathan to be Jewish all the time, or to think of Jewishness in every situation, until he draws the confrontation which convinces him all gentiles harbor anti-Semitic feelings, especially among the British.

As against her "pastoral," Nathan offers circumcision, not because he believes in its religious significance but because it separates "us" from "them." Circumcision in some way hooks up to performance, in that both bring us out of an ideal world or fantasy into the so-called real world: circumcision is the (boy) infant's introduction into the "here," from the "not there"; and once situated in the here, he enters history, which is performance-oriented. The fantasy world has been subsumed; and he learns how to play roles, how to combat a false unity. Circumcision, so to speak, activates what makes Nathan into Nathan, and that sparks the performance, the roles, the theater that so disturbs his parents and then his succession of wives.

The implications are clear. While the gentile can operate on center stage and assume he (or she) owns the world, the Jew marginally must act out roles appropriate to the situation. Although the Jew may insist he has a clear historical identity, the gentile has already subsumed him into a Christian culture, insisting that the Jew remain foreign even when the latter meets all specifications of social behavior. Even when gentile behavior does not underline anything different about the Jew, Nathan insists, the Jew inclines toward satisfying the gentile's expectations of him: thus the theater in which the non-Christian functions.

Is the Jew unique in these respects? or little different from any immigrant whose role is marginal because of religious and social differences, or distinctions of skin color? Jews are possibly unique in a Christian culture for one striking reason: Jews created the Christian God, gave Christians the Son, and then participated to one degree or another in crucifying that Son. No other group of people, no race or ethnic segment, has played such an ambiguous role and then has had to relocate itself successively in that very "enemy" environment. Every move is a paradox.

Not so for Updike and Rabbit. To move from literary to

personal, one sees them as interlinked. Updike's delicate positioning of himself in support of American action in Vietnam-at a time in the summer of 1966 when most American writers were not supportive-suggests how, in his fiction, he can assume that his Rabbit "owns" the country. Although Updike came from an economically rather poor background, had suffered a serious, persistent skin ailment, and considered himself outside the mainstream, when it came to Vietnam he signed up (not for the military) but on the side of Johnson, Rusk, Bundy, and the rest; then with Nixon and Kissinger. His reasoning for support and his diagnosis of those on the other side suggest his assumption of hegemony and proprietorship. A marginal person in several respects, he did not perceive himself as marginal to "American interests," which he accepted in cold war, domino-theory terms. He saw protest against the war as mainly snobbish dismissal of Johnson by the Eastern establishment, and he viewed the New Left as out to destroy what it called Amerika, as equating the USA with Nazi Germany. Such attitudes underpin the jejune politics of the Rabbit books, blurring differences between Angstrom and Updike.

With the same candor, Updike boasts of masturbating a female friend in the back seat of a car while his wife sits contentedly in the front; and the witlessness there carries over into his witlessness about the war. His inability to deal with the political aspect of the war reinforces his shadowy idea that writers really don't know what they are talking about when they express political opinions; the assumption being that politicians do.

Yet going beyond that is the assumption of hegemony: that he, Updike, somehow speaks for America, whereas the other writers-Jews, blacks, women, in the main-did not. When he says he would rather live under Diem or Ky or Thieu, the corrupt South Vietnamese leaders, than he would under Ho Chi Minh, the North's dictator, he makes a childish stab at political ideas, since neither was the option open to Americans. He sounds like a pre-Reagan Reagan. He misinterprets what he calls the "civil fury" of the late 60s, since he sees it as the barbarians at the gate, when in reality, it was those seeking change-sometimes radical and sometimes senseless change-in areas that many thought needed correction. Updike's proprietorship-his Lutheran background, his marriage into a Unitarian family, his Christian remnants of religiosity, all- is clear: marginal in his early years, he has embraced the country as Christian, white, male; whereas Roth in his various guises recognizes that the Jew can never be that assertive about ownership. Even those on the neo-conservative right, those Jews who play ball with the bigoted Christian right, recognize some marginality, in their hanging on to Israel as the place to escape to if things ever get too hot for them and their kind.

Nathan Zuckerman is himself the product of several dramas. *Carnovsky*, his book based on Roth's own *Portnoy's Complaint,* created an atmosphere in which Roth says he needed some kind of surrogate figure. As we noted, the uproar it fomented "eventually inspired me to crystallize the public feud into a drama of internal family dissension that's the backbone of the Zuckerman series. . . ."[295] Nathan gave Roth the opportunity to run wild, to try out every variation on the contemporary Jew, whether in America or Israel, even in England and then in Prague. In each place, Nathan becomes the magnet and lightning rod for Roth's fantasies about the Jew as victim, as sacrificial lamb, the Jew as hated object, the Jew as the sole source of wit, satire, realism, the Jew as seducer of gentile women, the Jew who continues to crucify the Son, the Jew as antichrist. In brief, Nathan provided Roth with theater.

Yet we must not stop there. For in several dialogues in which Nathan is the subject, Roth raises substantial psychological questions about the unreality of being a Jew-an issue of particular significance when his protagonist visits Israel in *The Counterlife.* But it is equally significant-this question of the Jew's reality-when Nathan visits E. I. Lonoff in *The Ghost Writer.* In two very different novels, the matters converge; for in *The Counterlife* Nathan attempts to resolve his unreality by taking on an Israeli persona and fails, and in *The Ghost Writer,* he comes to Lonoff in the New England woods-Thoreau territory-and finds that the writer named Emanuel Isidore Lonoff is more gentile than Jew. The sole way Nathan can valorize his Jewishness amidst this bosky setting is by conjuring up Anne Frank, reincarnated, as it were, in Amy Bellette, Lonoff's assistant, and more. To validate his own unreal Jewishness, Nathan must regroup: he must bypass Lonoff, with his assimilated pastoral existence, his gentile wife, his refined manners, and re-enter the historical process by way of an imaginatively recreated Anne Frank.

The torturous route Nathan follows here creates possibly the most artistically satisfactory of the Zuckerman books until the Nineties; less convoluted and self-circuited than the others-although not modest in its pretensions. Nathan in *The Ghost Writer* can seek himself by way of a valid historical figure, the quintessential Jewish victim who, somehow, has triumphed even in her death. As a writer, Anne Frank writes her way into Jewish history, in ways that Lonoff cannot or will not; in ways that young Nathan, still trying out as an author, is not certain he can do.

The major implication is that the Jew achieves his identity not through life or through "reality," but through fictions. . . . I was continually drawn back into the fiction I had evolved about her [Amy] and the Lonoffs while I lay in the dark study, transported by the praise and throbbing with resentment of my disapproving father. . . ."[296] The sense of a fictional self as the more real is, of course, completely at odds with the gentile vision of himself, as we find in Rabbit Angstrom. Rabbit-even his nickname-is tied to a reality rooted in solid things, fixtures or furnishings, booze, female bodies. Each *object* validates him, whereas for Nathan objects have little enough reality unless they are first fictionalized or located in a fantasy. Even once we make the distinction between a writer (Nathan) and a car dealer (Rabbit), the basic point holds: for the writer lives alone, with his thoughts, his fantasies, his paranoia-and all this is part of the Jewish experience, *whether in actuality it is valid or not.* For the car dealer, the worker, the entrepreneur, the world holds few fantasies, unless they are to achieve wealth, gain power, run off with sex-hungry women.

385

The various selves Roth carves out for himself-Zuckerman, Tarnopol, others-and the convolutions of self he imposes upon his narrators are all part of a marginalization he identifies *even as* he argues for Jewish assimilation. America is both familiar and foreign; both accepting and rejecting; both accommodating and threatening. The Jewish experience, especially when it is secular and, therefore, linked to the American experience, isolates the self, creates an invisible wall between Jew and Jew, not to speak of Jew and gentile. The great pull or fascination for Jews in America who are secular is to be (white) Protestant. But the Protestants, also, as Roth explains in *The Anatomy Lesson*, are the alcoholics, the suicides, the parents of drug-addicted kids, the divorced segment. They have their troubles, but no enemies. Only Jews have enemies, regardless of assimilation (name change, class mobility, even intermarriage). Roth can only conclude that Jews live in stories: without authentication, without validation, their identity subverted by their ambiguous positioning of themselves. To put it into fictional perspective, we can say that Jews live in a gentile culture the way Zuckerman lives in Roth's novels, as someone constantly manipulated by subtle forces that lie outside his obsessive need to control them.

But even that is too neat, too symmetrical. In questions of positioning, Nathan and Roth don't know what is in and what is out. He, Roth, lives so closely through Zuckerman that the former can have love affairs only with a character inside his fiction; that is, with Zuckerman's women. In another play on this reversal that intensifies ambiguity, Roth writes of Kafka-his guide in ethnic confusion and cross-directing-that the Czech writer used his writing to gain his experience of his father. In Roth's terms, Kafka did not start from Hermann Kafka in order to create *The Metamorphosis* and *The Trial*, but created his father from the fictional experience: he was "imposing his fable onto experience."[297]

In some curious twist of irony and paradox here, Roth has redefined the Jewish experience; it does not follow the usual coordinates, but, instead, reverses fable and experience, reverses story and real life. In this reversal, the Jew fumbles for identities-that is obvious; but further than that, the Jew somehow seeks his victimization in order to validate his view of himself as victim. Even more, the Jew needs victimization in order to shape his identity, although this would only be true for the secular Jew. As Nathan's several experiences in *The Counterlife* and elsewhere reveal, while in England he must become especially attuned to the particular brand of English anti-Semitism and its class origins; also to English anti-Israel feeling, which at the same time treats Arabs as "wogs." By tuning in to the slightest slur or reverberation, and then playing it back loud and clear, Nathan can reaffirm his Jewishness without forgoing his secularity. He can remain a Jew without Judaism; and he can reiterate his positioning of himself as marginal, sacrificial, victimized, part of those who will be killed off when the pogroms start. Such flirting with paranoia of course sends Zuckerman and/or his surrogates into severe, crippling depressions.

But there is another ingredient-there always is! Even while the Jew wishes to see himself victimized, even sacrificed, he also wants to see himself as special. From Nathan's point of view, gentiles are Jew-obsessed and are poised for moments when they can stick the stiletto into Jewish lives and aspirations. The gentile is always waiting to attack because he knows the Jew holds himself ready for it. Nathan presents a Kafkaesque situation: the Jew rails against his enemies, but seeks them out in order to valorize his particularity. Jews may not be noble-certainly Jewish family life in Zuckerman's *Carnovsky* is not noble-but as people of the word Jews are nevertheless superior. And by virtue of their specialty, they become obvious targets, so that they can assert enemies surround them. Nathan's dilemma offers him and Jews both entrapment and escape, something comparable to Roth's perception of the mole-like creature in Kafka's "The Burrow," about which he, Roth, has written eloquently. The mole is secure in its Castle Keep, but enemies abound, and one such enemy may now be moving toward it, against which the mole has only its ingenuity. This is the Jewish situation for Roth in his Nathan Zuckerman guise.

For Updike, all the conventions of American fiction, and thought, are available, a whiff of the gentile sense of hegemony when it comes to traditional strategies. Eden-the Garden-the Earthy Paradise-the pastoral belongs to the gentile. Almost halfway through *Rabbit, Run,* Angstrom as gardener gives Updike the opportunity to locate his protagonist in a central American theme: the ability of the Garden to rejuvenate and, if not that, then to provide contrast. The Garden belongs to the gentile, not to the Jew, although its origins are the Hebrew Bible. When a Jewish writer does enter Eden, or does experience expulsion from it, the tone is ironic, sarcastic, an exaggerated trope, as though a lost foreigner had wandered in. For the gentile, the Garden can be taken for granted as salvational; and if not attainable-as, say, for Fitzgerald's Gatsby-it is nevertheless a potential goal just beyond one's exertions to reach and enter it.

Furthermore, for Harry "Rabbit" Angstrom, there is no need for him to identify himself outside of what he is; his slime is *his* slime, his discontent *his*, his anger at his decline no one else's. He does not align himself with any contemporary group, or see himself in opposition to that group. He moves as though he has only himself to account for. He is not an upholder or a traducer of Christian values; what he traduces is only himself. His decline from a small town basketball player to the demonstrator of kitchen utensils happens to him in isolation from whatever happens to others. Unlike Nathan, he is not in any respect held to a standard set by outsiders, or internally set as though he had assimilated the values of others. No one judges Harry outside of the immediate acts he commits: abandonment of pregnant wife, aimless wanderings in the sexual arena, a loss of respect and self-respect, a directionless early life when memories of his playing days are his sole support. When he lives on memory, history is *his*.

Updike capitalizes on gentile stereotypes: like Gatsby, all those dreams gone sour. Rabbit's best days are behind him, the so-called decline of the Wasp overrun by minorities and counter-culturists; his wife is alcoholic and so spaced out she allows their baby girl to drown in the bath water; he himself moves from wife to other women, seeking solace in heavy, fleshy bodies as objects, in sexual acts which, while momentarily gratifying, create resentment; he has no interest in news, books, the larger culture; he leads an almost completely unexamined life, separate from the world of ideas, art, and the like. This *is* the stereotype, the boorish Anglo-Saxon white male, and yet Updike makes him representative.

The unexamined life is the most stereotypical of all of Rabbit's characteristics, and clearly his demarcation from Roth's vision of life in America, which is all introspection. Rabbit acts out; Nathan and his kind act in. Although we should not make too much of a jacket photo, the one for Updike's *Rabbit Redux* (1971) shows the author as tennis player: open short-sleeved sports shirt, striped shorts, sneakers-tennis! His presentation of himself is another gentile stereotype, the George Bush model-one cannot conceive of Nathan Zuckerman or Roth photographed on the courts or links, or paddling in white water. The various roles Updike offers Rabbit suggest how a dominant culture determines those born into it; whereas with Roth, the dominant culture always dominates and forces the protagonist to seek pockets of intense inwardness. Only in his "burrow," positioning himself like Kafka's mole, is the Jew secure; whereas the gentile can roam freely, from demonstrating kitchen utensils to printer to car dealerships to tennis courts, as the case may be. Space is his.

But this only scratches the surface. For the Jew, life is all mirrors, reflections, refractions, screenings, as we observe in *Operation Shylock*. Nathan or any of his surrogates emerges as a screen for Roth, an intermediary, part of a "gaze" phenomenon in which the original is fractured into several other selves. By making his protagonists into writers in so many of his fictions, Roth has created the Jew as living within a hall of mirrors; and by so much narrative telling and retelling-Tarnopol, for example, going over much the same material as Zuckerman-Roth has reflected the uncertainty and ambiguity of the Jewish roles he depicts. Zuckerman is writer and more than writer; he takes on the role, for Roth, of a modern-

389

day Old Testament author, keeping the score of genealogy, sources and origins, recalling bits and pieces of history, forcing himself to tell all, and then retelling it in successive volumes; so that, ultimately, he has created a kind of Hebrew gospel, the first five books of Moses, as it were. In this, he offers Jewish ways of life, Jewish anxieties, Jewish dietary and sexual practices. All of these suggest a uniqueness for the Jew, even while, paradoxically, as we have seen, he seeks assimilation, hoping to shed his uniqueness.

Only rarely, very rarely, does Roth utilize background material: that is, locating Zuckerman in a social or political setting. In this respect, the Jewish figure is separated, even isolated, from the rest of the country-unlike Rabbit, who in *Rabbit Redux* and elsewhere inveighs against everything in sight. In *My Life As a Man*,[298] structured on the writings of Peter Tarnopol, a stand-in for Zuckerman, Roth introduces the country as a whole. He does so, however, not as a way of providing social/political grounding for his protagonist but as a means of revealing the insignificance of Tarnopol's sufferings as against the civil rights movement in the South, the Kennedy assassination, the Vietnam buildup. In Part I, Tarnopol writes two stories, called "Useful Fictions," concerning Nathan Zuckerman; in Part II, Tarnopol writes an autobiographical narrative called "My True Story." It is only near the end of Part II that the country as such is recognized, and that as a means of trivializing his pain as he tries to reduce his alimony payments. The "Jewish experience" pre-empts all else. On the other hand, as Rabbit proceeds, he becomes increasingly (and very superficially) connected to the social-political landscape, mainly as an angry critic of everything the 1960s brought.

In another, related area, we can see how "home" functions for each in Roth's and Updike's stereotypes. For Roth and his protagonists, "home" is safe, settled, secure, and impossible to live in. The old place in Newark, or the equivalent, becomes what Nathan must rebel against, but it is also a sacred place, where right and wrong, among other values, are clearly demarked. His rebellion is, in fact, measurable only in terms of "anti-home"; his books, which cast ridicule on home and family, are acts of hostility to a place that remains, somehow, sacrosanct. For Updike's Rabbit, home is turmoil. He moves from home to outside-cars and other women's places-and in none of these is there refuge. The value structure Roth associates with home is absent from Updike; the homes of Rabbit and wife Janice seethe with tension, hostility, anger, malfunction. He dreads home, as does Nathan, but Rabbit's dread is of a place that lacks coherence; whereas Nathan's dread derives from his fear he may be sucked into conformity and coherence. He needs his incoherence to survive; Rabbit tries futilely to find refuge.

The quite different values here tell us a good deal about a Jewish America and a gentile one. Nathan can't bear the respectability of his home and must seek alternatives, whereas Rabbit cannot bear to take responsibility for having destroyed his. He finds wife Janice stupid, is turned against her for her heavy drinking, and hates her for having shaped a trap for both. She sinks further and further into incoherence until she lets their baby daughter drown in the bath water-clearly an emblem of America and its children in incoherent families. She neglects their son, Nelson, and although Rabbit seems devoted to the boy, he doesn't have a clue as to what is going on in Nelson-the payback for this will come later.

The confusion of Rabbit's life-and the kinds of women he picks for sex, based mainly on the plumpness of their asses-plays itself out into a kind of vision of how America is recreating itself. For the incoherence Rabbit senses in his life is also the growing incoherence of the country; as *he perceives it* in the late 1960s, the country has fallen into the hands of anarchists, perverts, druggies, murderers, lazy minorities, militant blacks. For Nathan, however, the turbulence of his relationships, especially with his odiferous wives (in his perception of them), has no linkage with the fortunes of the country. Nathan may be falling apart as the result of dreadful choices in sexual partners, but the country seems to holding up through the terrible 60s, the bottomed-out 70s, the destructive 80s, and the incoherent 90s. Once again, we see the Jew "separated" from the country, even as Nathan pursues gentile women in his desire to conquer them, all this somehow the emblem of a country which does not exist for him.

Yet there are paradoxes. We can, in fact, say that the deeper the association Updike makes between Rabbit's dysfunction and the chaos of the country, the less able he is to shape his material; whereas the deeper Nathan's malfunction and isolation from events, the more brilliant Roth becomes. In *Rabbit Redux*,[299] for example, Updike's effort to penetrate the drug and black scene (with white Jill and African-American Skeeter) misses so completely that we are tempted to re-evaluate the entire Rabbit series. The language goes wrong, the comments become too outrageous to consider, the feelings are incapable of measuring up to the words, the words to the feelings. When Skeeter talks about race, there is no dialogue, only highly unlikely hectoring, which Rabbit accepts, perhaps in some way as educational, more likely as indifference. Skeeter hectors Jill and Nelson, Rabbit's son, egging him on, in language that loses all meaning, in sentiments that fall outside of what anyone of Rabbit's limited intelligence could absorb.[300]

Fictional thrust breaks down when language ceases to mean. With no ear for how an inner-city black sounds, or how the druggie scene looks, or what Rabbit can absorb from all the ranting and raving, Updike is nevertheless excellent about car talk. The car culture seems his world: his people drive, they moon over cars, they understand the innards (Rabbit will become a successful Toyota dealer)-when an engine seizes, when the ignition is faulty. The car culture appears to be "America" itself, an example of how the country functions, although for Roth, it is an alien culture, even when cars do appear. They are merely transportation, or a means to wife Maureen's crashing death; but how they work, what goes wrong with them, how one diagnoses car problems-all the ingredients of a car culture-are not available.

In the run of the Rabbit series, Updike attempts to capture some of the curve of contemporary American history, decade by decade for the most part. In *Rabbit Redux*, for example, as the country enters the Nixon presidency, Rabbit loses his job as a linotype operator in the face of newer technologies that make him extraneous. In this context, his father, a right wing fanatic, attacks Nixon and seems to locate himself back into more liberal politics-but the contradiction or ambivalence is not pursued. Political life is *there*, but unintegrated into the narrative.

Yet there is another side to a superficial response to national and international events; there is the quotidian response to smaller, even trivial, events that connect to our lives. In *Rabbit Is Rich*,[301] for example, Updike, through Rabbit's assumption of his father-in-law's Toyota dealership, is able to comment upon more immediate needs: the gasoline lines, the changes in automobile styles, the ways in which people spend their money, the methods by which the entrepreneur must adapt to changing circumstances, financially as well as socially. All politics becomes local. Rabbit's dealership capitalizes on smaller engines, lesser gas consumption, marketing strategies to handle the rising yen; and Rabbit has to learn the ways in which such technological matters will affect his fortunes.

For Roth and Zuckerman, no such process occurs; it is as though these ordinary, day-by-day events belong completely to the gentile world. Such details are part of their hegemony, their colonization of America; whereas Jews simply go along with whatever eventuates and concentrate on more introspective matters. The difference does not derive only from career distinctions or the distinctions between a worrier and thinker and a doer. The difference lies in varying expectations of what America is and what it offers. In some strange way-strange because Rabbit is so full of anger, hostility, and antipathy-the Updike protagonist considers himself "in." He may have left his best days on the high school basketball courts and he may have experienced a series of disasters, including an ill-suited, alcoholic wife, a dead infant, and more, but he can always come back.

For Zuckerman or those like him, poor choices result not in

expansiveness of girth and spirit, but in mental and physical illness, the need for intense therapy, the sense that all life is slipping away. In a self-destructive pattern that Roth never fully justifies or explains, his protagonists choose women who will undermine them, in fact make it almost impossible for them to function. The consequence is that the male protagonists succumb to doubt, anxiety, finally to deep depression and nervous breakdown, to loss of function as person and writer. Roth's protagonists set out to conquer gentile women as a means of empowerment-as a means of entering forbidden territory-and then find the mechanism by which they can destroy themselves.

The Jew-always *the Jew*-possesses the power to succeed, but also has absorbed the power that destroys: for each element of God, there is a dose of Satan. It is as though the Jew has to be sacrificed after he opts for success. The discipline that drives ambition breaks down almost completely when it comes to personal matters, especially sexual needs. While Updike's Rabbit thinks almost constantly of sex, his life is not undermined by it; whereas for Roth, it is a symbol of Jewish failure, of one's inability to be whole. Sex with gentile women is satanic and Faustian precisely because it is the key to rebellion and empowerment.

Wholeness is not the issue for Rabbit; momentary indulgence seems more his mode. Rabbit *is* sex-obsessed-one thinks of many scenes, but in particular in *Rabbit Is Rich*, when he cruises his host's bathroom and bedroom looking for sights and smells of his hostess's sexual areas; but he does not endow sex with some kind of sacred function. The woman's crotch is not a holy place, but mainly hair, crevices, and a dark hole. His interest in oral and, on occasion, anal sex does not indicate a desire to penetrate to the mysteries of the universe. He looks for variety, satisfaction, the moment. For every Roth protagonist who seeks wholeness and justification through sex, Rabbit offers ejaculation into one hole or another as sufficient satisfaction.

The distinction is critical for ways in which the Jew and gentile look not only at sex-that is significant enough-but also at sex as an emblem of the country in which Jews and gentiles perceive very different roles. In fact, the sex itself is not that different. Both focus on oral sex as the ultimate satisfaction, but the occasional anal and "eating" do not destabilize the main arena: vaginal sex, old-fashioned stuff. Roth uses tying, Updike has a urination scene (in *Rabbit Is Rich*); but these are "specials," not the norm. The norm is socially sanctioned penetration, with oral as the ultimate lubricant. In this, Jew and gentile seem agreed.

On little else, however, do they agree. The women are themselves quite different. Updike has Rabbit encounter rather unappetizing women, who become attractive to the degree they become sexual creatures, and these women hold their ground against the rather rabbity Angstrom. Updike likes the women for their staunchness, but also for their haunches and orifices. Roth, however, presents more attractive women (greater range, more intellect, some striving)-except for the ones Zuckerman and Kepesch marry, virtually the same woman-and proceeds to make them very unpleasant. There is such hostility to women that otherwise attractive ones become unacceptable because they demand something of their own lives. Women-as Jewish mothers, as gentile lovers-are the enemy in Roth; for Updike, they are receptacles, less threatening. Roth's protagonists expect to be bitten off when they enter the woman's orifices (making oral sex a kind of death-defying act); Updike's Rabbit expects pleasure. Furthermore, sex for the latter is unthinking, part of the flow and rhythm of his life; whereas for Zuckerman and his kind, it is a constant interruption of his real life, which is reading, writing, pretending to be intellectual.

What conclusions can we draw from this? Zuckerman, or his surrogates, aims high and low-the society-based mistress and the lower class self-destructive wife. He cannot find a median area, and even when he does, with his English wife, he finds grounds for dismissing her. Part of his hostility is that since the women are gentiles, he needs to convince them of his superiority, run them into confusion, and conquer them, in the process disgracing himself. Such women bring him back to what he cannot accept: the Jew as a marginal figure, even if he conquers an English class-ridden, anti-Semitic society. Rabbit has no such problems: he seeks women in the middle range, occasionally, as with Ruth, hitting the lower end. For the most part, however, he aims not at social class but at variously shaped holes.

Roth seeks forbidden fruit-another example of how the Jew feels so marginalized he can break out only by succumbing to temptation; and then as a consequence he is cast out from the Garden (from Roth's New Jersey, for example, the Garden State). Updike reveals no such worries. Except in his absurd flirtation with 60s counterculture, Rabbit never connects to anyone outside his circle. He yearns after neighbors, friends' wives, daughter-in-law, casual pickups. A seemingly destructive marriage, to Janice Springer, settles down after her long affair with Charlie Stravros, who works in her father's Toyota dealership. Some wife-swapping and other indiscretions crop up here and there, but they become a "couple." The one unforgivable transgression comes with his one-night stand with his daughter-in-law, Pru; but that, too, is explained away because Rabbit is near death. It is his final sexual performance before he plays himself out on a basketball court, on the run from wife and family: he ends as he begins, and it will kill him.

What is astonishing is how much sludge both writers generate in order to keep their sexual circus going. Updike, for one, superficially piles on contemporary detail, from social, economic, and political events, in order to provide some substance for Rabbit, who is, all in all, of little weight except poundage. The long segments on historical detail, disasters, planes blowing up (Lockerbie, for example), terrorists, foreign policy moves-all seemingly culled from the daily newspapers-are supposed to ground Rabbit in a time and place.

As observed before, Roth rarely alludes to any external matters. His sludge concerns the repetition of basically the same story, told often wittily and with occasional insight into a self-destructive character he nevertheless does not fully reveal. He fails to measure, for example, reader response to characters who have long since exhausted whatever they had to offer. What remains of significance is not sex, but self-destructiveness, not how "normal" people fall into rabbit holes. It is the question of "fit." Rabbit has a place in history; he is, for Updike, the average sensual postwar American. His active years are precisely those which fit into the changes America experiences; and he responds with all the prejudices, anger, hostility, bigotry, and sense of helplessness that characterize, we are made to feel, the typical white American male. Rabbit comes to tentative terms with many of his prejudices-blacks, for example-but he remains edgy, unhappy with developments he believes are squeezing him, unable to bend sufficiently to have a functional family or personal life. He is, as they say, average.

For Roth, quite the opposite is true. Although his Jewish protagonists are American, they could be living out their lives in any landscape. They are fighting not American battles, but struggles based on Freud, on European forms of angst.[302] They are, in all but superficial behavior, back at Bergstrasse 19, in Vienna, at the turn of the century, analysands of the founder of it all.

Both writers present a dismal America. Rabbit's rise into the middle class is a jejune experience. His values are mainly drift; his intellectual conceptions, at best, illogical; his physical prowess the chief source of his identity. The country is mismanaged at every point, he feels, except for the Vietnam War, which, like his creator, Rabbit supports as the American thing to do. His ignorance of fathering linked to Janice's ignorance of mothering turns their son Nelson into a swindler, fraud, and drug addict. This is one unhappy, dysfunctional family-Updike's sense of an America reshaping itself in the postwar years. This gloomy scenario is unrelieved by humor or wit, and is underscored by an emphasis on sex, possessions, objects. Updike locates his own social and political views as part of Rabbit's confusion; but he skims surfaces. For by choosing Harry "Rabbit" Angstrom, the Swedish-American, as his protagonist, he filters his America through someone with little or no understanding of himself. Is this his archetypal white gentile American?

Roth moves his Jew and Jewish world into far more intelligent areas, but areas which disallow wholeness. Emerson's injunction that life should consist of good days is transformed into the pursuit of moments that eventually prove ruinous. Roth has penetrated more deeply than Updike into angst, dread, failure and the other Freudian or existential imperatives which are the other side of "success in America"; but his protagonists until the Nineties over a long stretch of time remain the same person incapable of growth or learning. His Jew, in the long run, remains as standardized as Updike's gentile; in some freakish way, neither changes shape, develops, or expands; and both agonize over lost chances. Expelled from Eden, they wander directionless. What seems at first like a very different Jewish and gentile America turns out to be a frustrating, disappointing, self-destructive experience for both. The liberal, angst-ridden Jew and the angry, conservative gentile represent not complete halves of the American experience, but incompletion itself; that is, America.

Just as Roth and Updike in their prime presented diverging sides of America, so do they continue to differ in their more senior years. Updike tries to preserve some of the past-aging does not mean losing the sexual urge, or the flame; whereas Roth sees age as a kind of death of hopes, illusions, ideals, and, yes, physical capabilities. Yet despite his effort to keep up his so-called Jewish material with another Bech novel and his return to a moribund Rabbit, the Nineties have not been kind to Updike. His discourses on aging and death in *Toward the End of Time* reveal the winding down, the musings of Ozymandias.

Several books are retreads, an indication of casting about-another Bech novel (B*ech at Bay*, in 1998), the novella *Rabbit Remembered* (in *Licks of Love*, 2000), a reach into *Hamlet* for *Gertrude and Claudius* (in 2000), that lament for aging in *Toward the End of Time* (in 1997). Added to this are *Brazil* (in 1994) and *In the Beauty of the Lilies* (in 1998), and we note a loss of direction and a general need to reach back. Some of the prose still sparkles, but as we read, for example, *Toward the End of Time* and *Rabbit*

Remembered, we find writing merely to scintillate, passages Updike can negotiate like a trained pianist, the kind of arpeggio riff associated with an Updike production.

The Bech books were always formulaic, an inevitable outcome given that the episodes were published separately, mainly in *The New Yorker*. The first, *Bech: A Book*,[303] a misnomer, is an accumulation of set pieces in which Bech, as a still vibrant Jewish writer, is invited to tour abroad, in Russia, Bulgaria, Rumania, London, later Israel, and, in this country, Cape Cod. As a man passing through marriages-he has, recalling Rabbit, left one and will enter a second in *Bech Is Back*[304]-Bech free-lances, a Jewish Valentino.

Updike's immediate need was to find some common ground with the burst of Jewish writers in the Fifties and Sixties, although several of the Jewish writers-Mailer and Heller, for starters-did not write about Jewish subjects. Bech is given stereotypical Jewish features-the nose, curly hair-no Cary Grant, he (even though Grant was at least half-Jewish). As Bech ages, down to *Bech at Bay*[305] in the Nineties, he is clearly one of civilization's discontents. But what is Jewish about him? Has Updike really written a parallel version of Rabbit Angstrom? Bech may be a satirical version of the so-called "Jewish writer," but a good part of his Jewishness derives from the fact that people recognize him as a Jew. He fits Sartre's definition of a Jew as someone who is considered Jewish, but there is little else that indicates Updike has gotten into his skin, or perhaps even tried to. When we compare, or contrast, him with Nathan Zuckerman, we note the large divide-Bech is acting, Nathan *is*. And as Bech ages, he becomes even more "the writer," a general or all-purpose universal writer in decline. At sixty-eight in *Bech at Bay*, the end of the trilogy, he is being applauded for work he can no longer do, the fate of the American writer for whom there are few second acts. When he wins the Nobel Prize-as a candidate who has squeezed through the controversies over worthier candidates-the act is more wishful thinking on Updike's part, however playful the wish, than it is a validation of Bech's work.

One of the best episodes in *Bech at Bay*, which, incidentally, has nothing to do with him as a Jewish writer, is the fourth, "Bech Noir." Here, he pursues the critics and reviewers who slammed his books, and Updike comes alive. It is not only the actual murders which Bech performs that revitalize him, but the venom he generates toward those who have given him adverse reviews, "even a single mild phrase of qualification or reservation within a favorable, indeed an adoring notice."[306] He screams for "murderous satisfaction," to get back finally at those who misunderstand, judge, patter on, possibly hardly read the books under review. His only recourse is to eliminate the parasites. Camp, tongue in cheek, satire and parody, all, take second place here to real feeling, real hatred, even as Bech evolves more clearly into an "American," not "Jewish," writer.

As in the final *Bech*, in *Toward the End of Time*,[307] death is everywhere. Updike has become immersed in final things-Biblical, natural, human, his main character a sixty-six-year-old man living in a future time (2020), having survived a Chinese-American nuclear war which, having devastated the country, had established new rules for life. Yet Ben Turnbull, while counting the months and years to death, as his body deteriorates, refuses to surrender and still desires an active sex life. The sex, however, as we know from earlier Updike novels, rarely goes beyond the woman servicing the man; the orgasm is the male's provenance.

What complicates Updike's desire to say something meaningful about the end of things is his penchant for adolescent sexual fantasies. No relationship between a man and a woman can overcome the sexual desire the man feels. Every encounter is a competition. Enough is never enough, and, once again, the game is some form of conquest, indicating to the male the penis is always victorious. In several respects, *Toward the End of Time* does suggest some wise contexts for an aging man, including his need to maintain sexual viability even while performance wanes; but an aging Updike has lost his balance. In sexual matters, he is not wise; throbbing overwhelms understatement. He may want to emulate Yeats's old man raging against impotence, but when the character Ben ogles his daughter-in-law, then fondles and licks a fourteen-year-old girl of the streets, and becomes enraptured over a thuggish whore while his wife is away, then he gives away the store; his more mature observations on aging in a pitiless, anarchic world are wasted.

More death in *Rabbit Remembered*,[308] since Rabbit Angstrom is indeed dead. Updike does not resurrect him, but his family: wife Janice and her new husband, Ronnie Harrison; son Nelson, now separated from wife Pru; and a long lost half-sister of Nelson's, a daughter of Rabbit from a fling many years ago. Despite some excellent passages that fit the end of the century malaise and sense of death, *Rabbit Remembered* is a tired effort. Updike is trying to ride out the years, and surely not writing out of any sense of urgency. There is little intrinsically wrong with the novella, but the cast of characters is insipid-Janice was never compelling, little more than orifices; Nelson is not striking, whether wired or not; a marginal figure like Ronnie is less than palatable, flat and boring; and the new face on the block, the half-sister Annabelle is never clearly focused.

Updike, in fact, was tired of the characters long before Rabbit died, and his plotting of the final books in the series depended heavily on a very superficial treatment of current events. In this volume, we find comments on Clinton's morality or lack of it, family arguments on his Presidency, and a few jokes about blow jobs. Updike still seems fascinated by fellatio, a fascination he shares with Norman Mailer and Philip Roth, in fact one of the few things they have in common. But while Roth often writes sexually about less than compelling people, his witty take creates contexts; whereas Updike, except for occasional phrases that strike hard, there is no wit, little irony, nothing to validate characters who are less than compelling. Yet with him, nearly everything depends on character. Not that his characters are often merely semi-literate, it is that even at their own level of discourse they do not generate any verve or vibration. Their dependence on sexual sensibility is delimiting, purposeless, focused only on orifices. Updike's brief disquisition on Ronnie Harrison's big flat dick is of no more interest than Ronnie himself.

Clearly, the 1990s have not been kind to Updike. While he has moved wildly over the landscape seeking book topics, there is little awareness of a deeper attitude toward America. Those jacket photos of the author as golfer or tennis player suggest a real satisfaction with the country, and that would itself subvert any serious novelist. His characters take an either/or approach-as in their assessment of Clinton; there is little context for real social or political issues because the characters are so narrowed by their failure to read and their lack of knowledge. They could still be meaningful, like Quoyle in Proulx's *The Shipping News*, but their humanity does not resonate. They remain cardboard figures: the conservative rich man, the egalitarian outsider, the do-nothing, know-nothing housewife. In these later novels, Updike reveals insufficient pathology to make offbeat characters compelling, little or no psychological probing, unoriginal even stereotypical ideas, and inability to contextualize current events as more than filler. As for his presentation of gentile life in small-town Pennsylvania, it now seems lusterless, not even suitable for satire, like later O'Hara.

While Updike has added little to his view of America in the Nineties, Roth has published five novels that add a great deal. Although both writers are well into their sixties-an especially anxious time for most American novelists-Roth has not lost, but gained, energy and a greater intensity. His theme, if we read intertextually, is not only self but also identity, which he presents so insistently that we wonder what in the decade drove him so passionately. Certain personal experiences might be cited-his by-pass surgery, his profound depression from prescription drugs, the death of his father, the subject of *Patrimony*-but even if these episodes are granted, the answer must lie more in his sense of America. The theme of identity is of course insistent in most American literature, but Roth goes after it in so many ways and with such compulsion that we must view it as cultural as well as personal.

The theme for Roth in his five novels (*Operation Shylock*, 1993;[309] *Sabbath's Theater*, 1995;[310] *American Pastoral*, 1997;[311] *I Married a Communist*, 1998;[293] *The Human Stain*, 2000[313]) appears to be the theme of the Nineties. Amidst consumerism and growing financial security, the postmodern American wonders obviously who and what he or she is, in ways that differ from previous generations. Globalization, superpower supremacy and hegemony, compulsive consumerism often indistinguishable from conspicuous consumption, prosperity for perhaps three-quarters of the population (and few regrets for those less opportunistic or fortunate), the American, despite lip service to spirituality and religious belief, is more secular than ever. The question arising from such contradictions is what Roth offers up: how to make the disrupted, divided self whole. Find the whole self, Roth commands, like some secular Jeremiah ordering a set of beliefs. Yet even as he demands this, Roth divines only fragmented elements, and no more than in *Operation Shylock*. Just as his own failing heart was rebuilt, although the fragments will never regain completion, so he attempts to find the whole self, even as it fragments hopelessly into shards.

As is by now familiar, the figure seeking identity is Nathan Zuckerman, the wandering Jew of Roth's imagination, but Jewishness is not the only mark of identity in these last five novels. Roth bleeds off into black life (in *The Human Stain*), then into questions of fathers and sons (or daughters in *American Pastoral*), and still further into even, for him, what it means to be a Jew. But nowhere more than in *Operation Shylock* does he focus on the hallucinatory question of self-identity. And where is it more hallucinatory than in Israel, where every kind of conflict is enhanced? Roth finds there not only religious fervor versus secular complacence, but questions of guilt, justice, and fairness, need for survival: questions that dig deep into every crevice as Jews face both internal and external threat.

He catches this during the trial of Ivan Demjanjuk, the Ukrainian guard allegedly known as Ivan the Terrible for his hideous role in a Nazi death camp. The question for this Ivan is whether or not he is the Ivan identified by survivors in an Israeli court as Ivan the Terrible; but there is also the question of who he is, the father of a son who believes implicitly in his father's innocence, insisting that the Israelis have the wrong man. Involved in this question of identity-in which Nathan reaches across to link himself to the son who desperately wants to believe in his father-are matters of forged papers, altered photographs, rewritten documents, and all the tricks and strategies used either to disguise a person's identity or to reveal him.

But such lines of identity are carried much further. The main line comes with a man posing as the real Philip Roth, as someone who has, as it were, taken over his substance and shadow. Capitalizing on Roth the writer's fame in Israel (where Yeshiva students pour over *Goodbye, Columbus* to discover how American Jews live), the fake Roth tries to reverse Zionism. This fake Roth, labeled Pipik (or bellybutton), tries to further his scheme which he feels is implicit in Roth's attitude toward Jews-to have Jews re-emigrate from Israel back to Europe, where they belong, a procedure called Diasporism. Pipik asserts that he has spoken to Lech Walesa, who says Poland is eager to welcome back its Jews, once a thriving part of Poland's culture. The Ashkenazi Jews will re-emigrate to their original homeland, and the Sephardic or North African Jews will remain, in order to settle differences with the Arabs. Otherwise, Pipik warns, the Jews have settled in an area that will doom them: either they will be overwhelmed by the hostile Arab population, or they will have to use nuclear power and thus shame themselves before the rest of the world.

What makes Pipik viable for the real Roth is that the former's plan for Diasporism can be extracted from the writer's view of Jews and their continued alienation wherever they live; Pipik's view is that Jews really belong in Europe, which will welcome them with open arms. Of course, the writer Roth has great fun with this, with the Jew-lover Walesa waiting at the border with candies and flowers to hail the incoming Yids. But the Pipik parallel identity goes much further, because Roth becomes involved with what he believes is the Israeli Mossad and a Polish-American nurse who is loyal to Pipik even as she seduces Roth. The result is a maelstrom of cross linked loyalties, a sea of dubious identities, a checkerboard of unmatched desires, all pulled together by the madness that is at the heart of both Nathan and Israel.

This is not the end. The confusion is furthered by the case of Jonathan Pollard, the American convicted of spying for Israel and communicating valuable secret American data. Pollard is considered, by some, as a "son" of Israel, and this consideration enhances the father-son paralleling. In the distance, as far back as the Biblical story, is another father-son relationship, of Abraham and Isaac; here, Nathan sees not the happy end of the tale, but the one both Kierkegaard and Kafka posit, that even after the ram is substituted for his son, Abraham goes ahead to sacrifice Isaac, as God originally ordered him to. So all sons are sacrificed, so all parallels to the double Nathan.

The emphasis on identity, and the subject of sacrifice, may not seem appropriate for the 1990s; but they do suggest a different culture from one based on prosperity and good times for all. By questioning what it means to be a Jew, Roth returns to "Eli the Fanatic" (mentioned in *Operation Shylock* by two Israeli youngsters studying it in school), questioning what it means to be a Jew in America, and by implication what it means to be "different," even while one pursues sameness. *Operation Shylock* and the rest of Roth's work in the Nineties are a return, a circling back, a re-asking of the same questions, only now in more mature and complicated terms. What might seem paranoia in Nathan is reality: the siege of the Jew by innumerable enemies, those without but also those within.

The reverberations for the decade are palpable, since, by implication, Roth suggests that what happens to the Jew in Israel is an emblem of discordant identity in America-and even if we do not accept a parallel, the point remains. We must not forget that most American Jews derive from the same stock as the Ashkenazis of the Diaspora. Additionally, in still another parallel, Roth is in Israel to interview Aharon Appelfeld, who as a child wandered Eastern Europe and survived; but Apter, still another survivor Nathan meets, is a broken man. More parallels, perhaps-questions of identity, questions of Jewish experience, questions, inevitably, of what makes a man, Jewish or otherwise.

Meanwhile, Roth has himself posed as one Roget, taking the name of the thesaurus man, and is, accordingly, an imposter in a world of imposters and counterfeiters. At the end of the decade, which coincides with the end of the century, imposters are running free. Parallels are so numerous they become virtual realities, and the real is smothered by the counterfeit. Disguise is all, whether by name or in person. Dissembling is the only way for political man. The uncertainties of self Roth feels and which he attributes to the culture itself come together here in expressions of alternate selves going wild.

In *The Human Stain*, for example, Coleman Silk, a black man, poses as something very different, until a misunderstanding over a word trips him up, accused by black students of racism. The word is "spook," which Silk used to mean a ghost or phantom, for students who never showed in his class, but which black students took to demean blacks in general. The mistaken sense of a word is a form of doubling, since its real meaning is lost as its racial meaning is imposed; as it did recently when the word "niggardly" was held against the speaker as a racist term, the doubling of the "N" word in the mistaken view. In *The Human Stain*, the double meaning of a word is an extension of the paralleling in *Operation Shylock*, as are the uses of imposturing in Silk's presentation of himself as not-black. The ultimate question is one of identity, Roth's theme for the Nineties.

Even *American Pastoral* fits well here. The smooth path of "Swede" Levov is really one filled with impending doom; for even as he lives the so-called American dream (thus the ironic title of Roth's book), a landmine in the form of a 1960s rebellious daughter awaits him. Similarly, in *Sabbath's Theater*, while the terms are different, the puppet master, Mickey Sabbath, whose fingers are his career, reaches an impasse, as his future collapses, his present fades, and the past takes over. As he declines physically, he must, in some way, re-define himself or else perish. Even as he sinks and sees death on one side-he composes his own monument with words "Destroyer of Morals, ensnarer of Youth, Uxoricide, Suicide"-he also comes to accept life as a way to continue to hate. At the last moment, he reinvents his identity-to turn the last years of the decade into hate! No Updike solution, this.

CHAPTER NINE

THE FICTIONAL NINETIES: GOING WHERE?

What is happening in American fiction in the 90s is perhaps a happier occasion than what has happened in American life during this decade, despite relative prosperity. However addled *that* is, our millennium fictions are varied, contradictory, argumentative, critical, subversive, parodic, and not at all sympathetic to the culture at large. Furthermore, the infusion of literary ideas and forms from Chicano (Latino), Asian-American, and Native American writers is beginning to make a difference not only in the ways we view our culture but in language itself. Somewhat like what occurred in post-colonial English literature with work by Rushdie, Desai, Mukherjee, Naipaul, Soyinka, and others-with their reshaping of the language from the point of view of the former colonies-something comparable is beginning to occur in American fiction. The dominant voice remains those whose ancestors came to this country generations ago, whether by choice or forcibly; but the newer voices are creating fresh dimensions to American fiction, from point of view and technique to language.

Overall, however, it is difficult to see who we are and where we are going: whatever quandary the country is in, the literature reflects it as ambiguity, uncertainty, and confusion. The end of the century generates its own kind of feeling, a certain desperation and ennui; some desire, but downgraded, depressed; some wish, unconscious or not, to celebrate a death without exactly dying. Closing down, closing out, closing up-adverbial-prepositions linked to "closing" all point in the same direction and indicate the funereal final years. The authors in several instances are themselves aging, but these are not "golden years"; rather, they confront the negatives of the country with the despair of writers moving toward a personal closing time.

Even a bountiful America would have trouble holding its own against the demise of the century. But if our writers agree on anything-and here we include most of the newer voices deriving from minority cultures in this country-it is that America despite economic prosperity is not bountiful; and if it ever was-perhaps in the 50s and 60s-it has buried its talent. We are, for better or worse, perceived as at the end of things; the yo-yo elections of the decade surely reinforce that, as an electorate switches sides in an effort to find surer ground. With no clear goals, our writers no less than the electorate shift, change, reshape, without any definitive end in sight. It is not that everyone has given up-most, in fact, continue to swim optimistically in the destructive element-but that no direction or grounding is apparent. Our novelists have not yet peeked around the corner to see what lies in the distance, so preoccupied are they with moving rapidly so as to be able to stand still. While many have come to bury America-once again, like its politicians-we must ask if they have caught up with enough of the country to be certain of their ambitious efforts. Is there sufficient America in their fictions to validate a burial, not to say renewal or resurrection? What, first, do we need literarily before we can say what we have and how far we have gone?

America in the 80s and 90s *has needed great satirists*. Except in great sweeping satirical thrusts, it is impossible to capture the sense of the country. One thinks of Donald Barthelme having lived and been able to put together a large novel based on his devastating satirical premises; but perhaps Barthelme was only able to do this in short takes. The very nature of his talent and of the country preempted the long satire, in the genre of a Swift, Rabelais, or Dickens. We need a *Bleak House* for our times, or else a *Gargantuan and Pantegruel*, or a *Gulliver's Travels*, even a Voltairean *Candide*. Perhaps the most accessible would be a large, Dickens-like novel that has a central symbol or emblem which characterizes a country so sunk into divisions and subcultures it is no longer identifiable except by its geography and, perhaps, its military. The satirist must plumb the unacceptable, perhaps see that what American needs is a good war to pull it together. Military action and the rhetoric accompanying it-the media hyperbole-can create unity, however. The satirist must somehow create that unifying trope which does what *Catch 22* did in the 60s, or some of Barth, Gaddis, Pynchon in that decade and in the 70s. The satire must have breadth as well as pungency. It cannot particularize, or *only* particularize, but should spread, venomously, across the entire land. At the end of this chapter we ask if *Underworld*, *Infinite Jest*, and *Mason & Dixon* fulfill this role.

Realism as such cannot do the job. The older generation tried that, but it is now exhausted.[314] We require big nasty books to pursue a holistic vision, even if the emphasis is on the end of things. America generated great emblematic novels in the past, *Moby-Dick*, *The Scarlet Letter*, *The Great Gatsby*, *An American Tragedy*, *Absalom, Absalom!* as obvious examples. They were not satires, but conditions have changed, and very possibly only satire can capture the country now. The obscenities of our leadership, the incompetence at all levels of the people we vote into office, the inability of those who serve to get beyond partisan bickering, the economic hopelessness in which perhaps a quarter of the population lives, the precariousness of those who consider themselves middle class and, therefore, safe, the disproportions in earning power between those who produce little and those who labor to produce something, the permeating of a drug culture through both big cities and small towns, the lack of meaningful work for large numbers of those who have diligently prepared themselves, the social abandonment of those who cannot make it in American terms-these are all palpable, and they are not even the main arena for which the satirist is needed.

What is required is somewhat different, in which issues as such are bypassed, in which overarching emblems capture the perception of slide, decline, downfall, depression-*even if* such perceptions are exaggerated or inaccurate. The decade of this second millennium is ending in a quagmire, as the recognition builds that nothing is resolvable, whatever the issue, whatever the problem. There *are* solutions, but none of them can seemingly work amidst democratic institutions and a mythical belief in free markets. We are, after all, familiar with some problem solvers, this one for AIDS: William Buckley, who has had a regular public events program on Public Television, subsidized by contributors, suggested that one way to handle the AIDS crisis was to tattoo all gay men on the butt. While this would be a boon for the tattoo industry, it in some ways conflicted with one or other of the Ten Amendments, although Buckley and his supporters did not appear to know which ones.

But the satirist cannot become involved even in such compelling solutions-there are always political wags and standup comics ready with resolutions to individual problems. What are needed are big nasty books to pursue a vision: perhaps someone sick/paranoid/witty enough-we have Kafka in mind- to pursue a vision through his/her pathology, and-once again like Kafka-to make it representative. Wit is so important because it is so lacking in the larger world, except unintentionally whenever a so-called wise man vents. A counterfeit, artificial, superficially glazed culture needs more than television personalities to convey pathologies; it needs written words, a permanent part of the record. Some of that sense of America is beginning to appear in our 90s writers: in the vision of a society parodied, satirized, mocked. While it is sad America is presented that way, the satirical or mocking mode reveals the devotion these writers feel for the country they hope to subvert or nudge into real change.

What more appropriate place to try to locate the 90s than in Thomas Pynchon's *Vineland* (1990)![315] This novel about life in California is a mixed piece for his audience. Connecting the 1960s to the later 1980s, and suggestive of the 90s, *Vineland* contains all the Pynchon offerings: hilarious riffs (with Hawaii as the center of one of the best), weird undefinable characters (except by California standards), weird, undefinable situations (unless set within a deeper counterculture than most of us had ever recognized), a point of view which turns weirdos into sympathetic people, a plot line which features a series of searches, a deep inner mystery buried somewhere within material which may never reveal it. There are conspiracies, plots within plots, paranoia, rioting, terrorism, and all the other ingredients of a middle class culture. This carries us back in an arc to Pynchon's auspicious debut with *V.* in 1963. Like *V.* and to a large extent *The Crying of Lot 49.* but less so with *Gravity's Rainbow*, Pynchon uses rapid cuts, filmic techniques of near montage, ellipses which disallow reader ease, techniques in which the main elements are lacunae, aporias, ellipses, and similar methods which underscore uncertainty, unreliability, ambiguity, even inaccessibility.

The base of *Vineland* is still the Pynchon world of disinformation, misinformation, a perversion of knowledge and data. This "dis" or "mis" derives from the world of popular culture, especially film and television, which has permeated the government and become an integral part of the bureaucracy. The world of the 1960s has carried over, so that the elements we associate with that decade-the whole range of counterculture-rebounds into the 80s and 90s. As with all of Pynchon's previous novels, *Vineland* creates a particular landscape, clearly a post-postmodern America, which in this case uses California as an emblem of the crazy, bizarre subcultures that have overtaken the country. These subcultures-Thanatoids (those who are death-oriented), the Tubal people (those governed by television viewing), surfers (a catch-all for outlaw groups) various gangs like the Bud Warriors and the Ambassadors, the Bodhi Pizza Temple (for those who combine love of pizza with Buddhism), and the Hawaii 5-0 afficionados are, once linked, the dominant culture. What was once considered mainstream cannot any longer be defined, or even discovered.

The television personality Zoyd Wheeler's daughter Prairie in her search for her mother, Frenesi, lurches from one group to another, never touching anything so commonplace as townspeople, workers, local or state authorities, police, any regulatory agencies. Her quest takes her though the detritus of a country (state) so atomized that no group or segment has any contact with any other. There is a villain, Brock Vond, a terrestrial Darth Vader, a secret government agent, but also someone with whom Frenesi is having a relationship. Vond is the ultimate insider, apparently a man who works all sides of a situation, without loyalty or honor. He seems to represent the FBI, the investigative people whom we recall from earlier Pynchon fiction and, before that, from William Burroughs' Thought Police, ultimately the Exterminators. Although there is a need to kill Vond, he is also part of the Frenesi world, something her daughter Prairie cannot understand. She repeatedly questions DL, a tough female motorcyclist she meets who knows Frenesi, about why her mother, a 60s bomb-throwing rebel, would cohabitate with the sleezy Vond.

This query, incidentally, sets off a good part of the book, and it features dispersed, seemingly disconnected narrators. DL's story breaks off into several tributaries, as though the sole way to return to Vond and Frenesi-the inevitable goal-is by way of dispersement. Pynchon suggests the impossibility of communicating directly; so that information, such as it is, comes through several voices, each with his or her own twist and turn. And when the information finally arrives, it has been bent out of shape. That we learn to take for granted. What it means is that language is itself subjected to the same distortions we associate with physical objects; language has its curves, its gravity, its relativities dependent on angles of perception and mysterious, well-disguised laws. Unless we recognize that it is subject to the laws of physics, we ignore a huge change taking place not only in literature but also in the contextual world.

Pynchon's effort to send up several voices, each with bits and pieces of information about Vond's and Frenesi's activities, fits a condition that the computer is making possible, the creation of a "hypertext." Robert Coover has given an excellent description of this phenomenon:

> . . . unlike print text [which moves in linear fashion], hypertext provides multiple paths between text segments, now called "lexias" in a borrowing from the pre-hypertextual but prescient Roland Barthes [from his *S/Z*, a reading of Balzac's *Sarrasine*]. With its web of linked lexias, its network of alternate routes (as opposed to print's fixed unidirectional page-turning) hypertext presents a radically divergent technology interactive and polyvocal, favoring a plurality of discourses over definitive utterances and freeing the reader and writer from domination by the author.[316]

In this configuration, writer and reader become secret sharers. Having become special conspirators in the working out of the text, they are able to "read" it in ways not provided by the author. In certain respects, the reader helps the text, and then decodes it according to his own subjectivity. The author recedes, as though contained in disappearing Chinese boxes. There is the sense of the death of the old, as if the end of the century has brought with it the death of the traditional text.

Pynchon is not, of course, the first to try this method, and *Vineland* is not the debut of a new type of fiction. But it is one of the most determined efforts to turn what was once the linear mode into a labyrinth. The maze is achieved through looping, rhythmic patterns which take over narrative itself, a layering of characters and events so that each seems to assimilate the other, an effort to make information an accretion rather than definitive, giving the reader sufficient material so that he or she can "make" the novel. In the process, "novel" is redefined. Yet while such innovation, although necessary to keep an art form from dying, is welcome, experimentation is not in itself better; it may fail to gain us much, even as we recognize that it takes many such experiments or innovations before the writer hits upon something that does work. *Vineland* works to the extent that we as readers are willing to flirt with mutational forms to validate the novel.

One way in which hypertext proves an important innovation is in its ability to question conventions which do seem outmoded as ways of capturing the contemporary American experience. With so many forms of information battering us and so much distortion and misinformation, we have become, so to speak, sorting machines with a hypertext printout. That on-time ability to put segments together into a coherent whole has become increasingly difficult; our minds and ideas-except perhaps for professional philosophers-are taken over by segmented material, to the degree the hypertext has become a form of thinking. Everything loops back upon itself or describes a discrete pattern; linear elements can no longer be perceived. All this is true not only as we contemplate words and text, but political, social, and other broad ideas. Hypertext as Pynchon is trying to work it through here-or as Gaddis does in *Carpenter's Gothic* and *A Frolic of His Own*-may not be the wave of the future, since novels or narratives or fictions will have to be sold on disks, not as printed books.[317] The taste for this will, obviously, be somewhat limited; but with computers becoming so standard in schools, it is quite possible that hypertexts will eventually become the "books" of the future. We are already putting "books" in quotation marks.

Pynchon's method, which intersects some of what occurs in hypertext, is to let individual stories, whether Prairie's, or DL's, or the inset one of Frenesi and Vond, proliferate into substories and those, in turn, into further substories. The principle is one of diffusion, as though one were using gas rather than words. The actual narrative line is slender, almost inconsequential; everything depends on manipulation, angulation, articulation, the multiplication of voices and subnarratives. The object is not primarily to confuse the reader-although that is not to be discounted-but to create a labyrinth or maze as the context in which the characters move. As 1960s people caught by an updated narrative, they are perceived through a scrim: foggy, confused, ambiguous, uncertain, full of yo-yoing, even going from film to reality. The idea is to go beyond unsettlement into distortion of time and space; and the rapidity of the activity-including a rock and roll prose-is to turn conspiracy into a contemporary metaphor.

Several of the struggles are in part comic turns, but also indications of a social condition so far out of control that the country itself seems imploded. Brock Vond, the villainous government agent, is constantly horny over Frenesi, the would-be bomber. "When Frenesi came into the picture, interest perked up. Here was entertainment-a federal prosecutor carrying the torch for some third-generation lefty who's likely've bombed the Statue of Liberty if she could."[318] The woman seeking Frenesi, on behalf of her daughter Prairie, is also a mixture, attractive but butch, seductive and deadly, with the killer's ability to inflict the "Chinese Three Ways, Dim Ching, Dim Hsuen, and Dim Mak, with its Nine Fatal Blows, as well as the Tenth and Eleventh, which are never spoken of."[319] Through this knowledge, she could give people heart attacks without touching them; she could make them fall from high places; or else, through creating guilt, make them commit *seppuku*, or ritual suicide. Her abilities include "a grab bag of strategies excluded from the Kumi-Uchi, or official ninja combat system, such as the Enraged Sparrow, the Hidden Foot, the Nosepicking of Death, and the truly unspeakable *Gojira no Chimpira*."[320]

DL (Daryl Louise) learns this from Inoshiro Sensei, although some of the techniques will make sense only ten years down the line. What all this signifies is a pursuit that is both life and death, an effort to bring together daughter and mother in an ironic, mocking, parodic prose. The use of Japanese-as in T. Coreghessan Boyle's *East Is East*-is both comic and an indication of how Japanese words and techniques can become all-powerful images. By exaggerating the power of Japanese, the writers convey a kind of magic, giving DL special powers that are extrasensory; so that Japan and Japanese are viewed as having reached a level not achievable by Americans. It is an exaggerated impression, a comedic perception, but it does communicate an end-of-the-century destiny.

With its chases and Japanese strategies; its search of daughter for mother, and conspiracies in which Brock Vond is a perpetual villain; its movement into Vineland, supposedly a land of milk and honey; its emphasis on Tubal people, on television as the driving energy of our culture; its shifting back and forth between film and life; its attempt to blend the reality and the fantasy of America so that it is unclear whether we live in one or the other; its denigration of all public figures (in one indicator, Woody Allen will play the Young Kissinger in the movies); its effort to show the resilience of the counterculture now in the 80s, so that counterculture *becomes* culture; its frequent shift of characters and scenes; its lack of a continuous or linear narrative; its attempt to fit into hypertext, or brief segments without beginning, middle, or end-in all of these as well as in other manifestations, one wonders where Pynchon is heading overall. Never an "easy" writer, he is here at his most compacted, his most frenetic and frantic, his most manipulative of what is now recognized as Pynchon prose.

Toward what end? Do we learn something about the American experience? Pynchon carries over Mucho Maas from *The Crying of Lot 49*; here Mucho is very successful, a "music business biggie" connected to Indolent Records, but also stoned, spaced out, insulated against realities. This linkage with the earlier novel suggests that Pynchon sees continuity in American life, although the continuum suggests a dubious progress, more likely a loose dispersion of energy, morality, and language itself. He perceives that the breakup of elements which characterized the 60s, that fragmentation-whether home, sex, work, whatever-has become the dominant force in American life, to the extent that normal life, or what passes for it, is no longer "normal." All is discrete, distinct, separated, insulated, and isolated. The fragmentation of America, with Vineland as metaphor for the country, suggests that we have not aligned what we are with the way we speak about ourselves.

Even for those who live conventionally, the tube has made them into Tubal people; and while such conventional people appear to re-enact traditional scenarios, they are, in actuality, acting out elements which are new forms of life-abbreviated, fantasy-filled, ambiguous about the division between fantasy and reality, uncertain of present roles and future identities. *Vineland*, for believers and non-believers serves as a guide to that kind of world. It is a fine introduction to the 90s.

Joseph Heller's *Closing Time* (1994)[321] superficially seems on a different course from *Vineland*; yet the two connect as part of the "death of" a century, the end of a social compact, the loss of both great and small expectations. Although *Closing Time* might appear to be too cynical and depressing for most Americans, it does manifest the 80s and 90s. Suggesting the policies of the Reagan-Bush years, Heller's paradigm is Wagner's Ring cycle, recycled for American social and political life. Gold is, of course, the goal. As in Wagner, whoever has it gains power; whoever loses it, sinks. And in Heller's example, those who have lost power-that is, lack money-have lost themselves. At their most pitiful, they are the denizens of the inferno-like New York Port Authority Bus Terminal.

What Heller has attempted is something quite complicated: to provide a successor to *Catch-22*, his iconical novel of the more immediate postwar era; to create continuity with the characters in that novel, especially John Yossarian, Milo Minderbinder, and the Chaplain, not to speak of several minor figures; to find some metaphor or trope for the last decades of the century, as the military had been his trope for mid-century; and, finally, to attempt some deconstruction of the industrial-military complex without too much sermonizing.

The structural context for this, then, becomes Wagner's Ring, in which greed, avidity for power, and limitless ambition and self-serving all lead to the demise of Wotan's kingdom, the destruction not only of his dream but also of nearly all individuals whom he touches. Wagner's *Götterdämmerung* is the perfect background music for the climactic Donald Trump-like wedding party held in the Port Authority Bus Terminal, the permanent home of the homeless, the weak, the addicted, the perverted, and the temporary home of their counterparts among the revelers. As the place is sanitized for the society wedding, the clash of cultures is apparent, but only Yossarian seems clear as to what is occurring: that he is witnessing something terminal. He comments that the music, in the last segment of Wagner's Ring, is "peaceful, sweet, melodic, erotic, and certainly climactic and final."[322] It fits well into the scene of "closing time" where people mindlessly engage in revelry as caught on Yossarian's television monitor. And it is, he recognizes, closing time for him. He realizes, in this vast, sprawling fictional history of the postwar years, that only memory is left, Proustian moments of long, sweeping memory spots. The rest is detritus.

Not unusual is the presence of so much memory in the writers of the late 80s and 90s. And while there is some nostalgia in these memories-Heller's for Coney Island and its creator, Tilyou-nostalgia is not the key; closing out, closing down, closing up are. What prevails is memory as an escape from an unacceptable present. In Tim O'Brien's most recent novel, *In the Lake of the Woods* (1994), as we have observed in so much fiction which touches on the Vietnam War, memories of the war dominate the present; so that veterans live not the war, but their memories of it, screened, as it were, and they survive only through some kind of exorcism. Heller's use of memory is consistent with this: the Second World War was there as bonding, as romantic adventure, as a definitive moment. Once that passed and civilian life took over, there was only the industrial-military complex, which promised great rewards to those who could adapt themselves to it.

Yossarian, among others adapts; and he cashes in mercilessly on ventures-the stealth bomber, for example-that he knows are chimaeras. Heller's humor depends on the fact Yossarian hates nearly every attachment, every friendship, every business of professional connection, all the while deriving capital from them, whether women he can boff or the social-political world which pays him well for doing almost nothing. He has learned how the system works, as earlier he had learned how to survive in the military. Survival, not ethics, morality, legality, commitment, is all.

In those interstices lies the humor. Unlike the one-liners which dominated in *Catch-22*, in *Closing Time* Heller aims at longer riffs, at a narrative which subdivides into several pursuits, many of them cynically amusing, most of them targeted on those who would rule us. The most obvious is the man in the White House, with the understated code-name "The little prick"-whose chief occupation is playing in the game room and working over one particular game, Triage. From the White House point of view, Triage is the ultimate game: based on those who will be saved when nuclear warfare is unleashed. The government does not need the downfall of the Soviet empire and the end of nuclear confrontation to hang tough on possible nuclear warfare. There will always be an enemy, for that is the way the country's resources are mobilized and ethical-moral questions are resolved. Dr. Strangelove appears, of course-the inevitable figure in a system based on Triage.

But the chief beneficiary of Triage will be Milo Minderbinder, the survivor of a war in which he outfitted the men with all the luxuries the army could not supply. Milo is now interwoven with every aspect of the system that pays off in threats, intimidation, bribery, overcharging, overselling. As the quintessential insider, his philosophy is solely buy and sell; for Heller, he represents the way the country functions, with "the little prick" in the White House and Milo hoodwinking a willing defense department. Everything is a deal; everything can be bargained for, or away. This is Reagan's, Bush's, and Quayle's America, although it has continued in the 90s under Clinton. As Yossarian ages throughout the novel, coming close to seventy-one as the book closes in on present time, he, too, blows with the winds of greed.

He has withdrawn from nearly all feeling, knowing that for himself it is transitory. He does worry about one son in particular, Michael, who moves unsteadily among job opportunities; his other children, in the distance, are in various stages of disconnection to any society or community. Yossarian is confronted by ruins. The world around him that began so hopefully with his airforce missions in World War Two has now wound down, even as he expects to die from ailments the doctors cannot as yet discover.

To emphasize that winding down, that road toward death, Heller has divided the narrative into three major parts: Yossarian himself, then Samuel Singer and Lew Rabinowitz. Each has had a decent life, but when we encounter them in present time, they are floating free in their downward spiral toward deterioration and death. They, too, go back to the war and to marriages that were fulfilling-although now they are alone, directionless, slowly nodding off into meaninglessness. Even Yossarian's sexual adventures-described in adolescent terms, tits and ass stuff-only make sense against a background of postponing the inevitable, the aging process, the loss of sexual energy, the loss, finally, of all will to live. The wedding near the end in the Port Authority Bus Terminal, seemingly a celebration, is really the final state in the "twilight of the gods." For even as caviar and champagne flow, the Bus Terminal sends off its death message. Far below, in its depths, where hell reigns, the dogs of war and destruction and disease and fear are barking out their message.

What Heller has attempted, on the Wagner model of the fall of the gods, is not a sequel to *Catch-22* but a deconstruction of the world left behind when Yossarian paddled to Sweden at the end. It has, if anything, deteriorated even further than one could have conceived, through inept leadership, inept attempts at solutions, ineptitude from high to low; so that the sole alternative is to opt out. Yossarian's position is not nihilistic-that would be too positive!- but survival on any terms in a world which seems at every level intent on killing the individual. His apparent indifference to suffering is belied by the fact he sees it everywhere, and charts it, so he can retreat from it. The line between making it and falling through has narrowed. The experience of the city streets reveals such decrepitude of the body politic or any sense of social comity that the perceptive man withdraws into indifference, self-serving, and greed. This is, all in all, what Heller leaves us with, far less than even Wagner who saw (Christian) "love" as the answer to greed.

But there is, in the late 80s and 90s, no chance for love, except for money or power. Like the gods, it too has fallen. Despite the obscenities, the adolescent sexual fantasies, and the depression that accompanies aging, Heller's is a morality tale: cynical, ironic, caustic and, finally, a perception-true or not-of what he sees as *his* America. It is Swiftian. The end!

A different kind of entry in the death sweepstakes is David Markson's *Wittgenstein's Mistress* (1988),[323] a kind of exotic primer for end-of-the-century fiction. Markson has conceived a strategy to deconstruct the novel entirely, through the elimination of narrative, or of what the reader expects narrative to be. Instead of conventional narrative, he uses the random thoughts of a near mad, or mad, female who has been a painter and now lives on and off in various museums. She is in Markson's special sense a collector-someone who is trying to gather together what has been lost. Her meanderings, often little more than a line or two, underscore her mission, which is to collect the garbage of her thoughts, both personal and more broadly cultural, as the last retrieval system of our civilization. It is as though she has lived through a nuclear blast and must gather whatever wits she has left.

The point of the title is to reveal the limitations of language to express what we think: to indicate the break between thought and expression, so that in some way we become Wittgenstein's "mistress." Like Wittgenstein, Markson is interested in the silences, in the ineffable, what falls between the words. Interstices and pauses have as much significance as words themselves. The strategy of the novel is the testing out of the limits of language, the implication being that "old language" no longer defines new experience. How can words, in fact, express the near madness of the female narrator? How can words express experiences that lie between conscious and unconscious-that is, experiences that may or may not have taken place?

Since Wittgenstein put value on the ineffable, on what could not be put into words, then the female narrator becomes his "mistress" in her effort to express what lies between madness and sanity. This median line, the "between," is, in effect, the substance of the novel, or what was once prose narrative. Markson has deconstructed not only narrative, but meaning itself, placing "meaning" in those areas which Wittgenstein used to underlie his theory of what words can and cannot do.

Yet even though the mind cannot quite grapple with the words to express its thoughts, there is still continuity of cultural and historical data. They can be wrapped around each other in some ethereal area beyond history and beyond rationality or consciousness. Markson shows how data and historical events become connected *in the mind*, so that their meaning is removed from any objective status and relocated in the subjective mind reviewing or considering them. In this way, history is itself a function of the mind: thus, the question of Wittgenstein's "mistress," of how the philosopher saw language as unable to handle the real questions which lie between subjectivity and objectivity, between the thing in itself and the language one employs to describe it.

Some of this can become quite witty, especially when Markson recreates a family visit by the Agamemnon and Clytemnestra clans-going off to meet aunt Helen, with Uncle Menelaus there. "Daddy murdered our sister to raise wind for his silly ships, being what any person in her right mind must surely imagine that Electra and Orestes would have thought. Mommy murdered our daddy, being all that they think in the plays instead."[324] That is, who knows? This comic riff goes beyond momentary wit to the heart of the problem: how does language, when extended to its logical possibilities, deal with a situation in which language is secondary to the event?

In several inventive ways, Markson has created a prototypical fiction for the late 80s and the 90s. Deeply indebted to William

Gaddis's fiction, to several French predecessors, especially Michel Butor, and to the minimalism of Donald Barthelme and others, he has divined the split in which language no longer connects. And he sees that this is not only a personal and social event, but a larger political one as well. People speak, but no one communicates; no one comprehends the message, only the words. Markson is tapping key areas of 80s and 90s confusion: not simply that we cannot believe anything we hear, but, more significantly, that we *do* believe what we hear and it has little or no connection to events, real thought, or even to ourselves. The parable of Plato's cave, in which so-called reality is observed as reflected on the wall, not in itself, is exceeded now by a "reality" which is completely disconnected from what we think we believe. We don't only live with shadows of the truth; we live with the certainty that the shadows are the truth. Markson's novel insists on how dangerous knowledge has become, because we really don't recognize what knowledge is, so perverted and distorted has discourse become, so lacking in logical dialogue have we found ourselves. Wittgenstein's "mistress," beyond its innovative strategies, is a cautionary tale.

Like Markson and other end-of-the-century writers, Steve Erickson, in his *Tours of the Black Clock* (1989),[325] is trying to find some way of communicating meaning in a period when definition of self or culture was almost impossible to discern.[326] In *Tours*, he establishes a middle area of consciousness in place of certainties or stabilities. Pynchon calls him a "nocturnal" writer, which means more than that he comes at us from out of the darkness. He is a "shrouded" writer: little is clear, all is suggestive, all seems supported by myth and legend, or a dream world. The emblem of that dream world is an image firmly implanted in the text of Marc sailing back and forth while running a ferry service from the mainland to Davenhall Island, an image perhaps of the Flying Dutchman, the legendary wanderer. For fifteen years, Marc does not set foot on the island, but plies the waters and sleeps on the boat. His voyage is always the same, shrouded in fog and foggy waters; until a monster, or what passes for it, comes out of the deep, in the form of Banning Jainlight.

Like Don DeLillo, Erickson shapes unusual scenes. He defies realism, eschews surrealism, rejects normalizing narrative. "I build my own house that defies architecture,"[327] says Banning, whose job at one time is writing porn fiction for high-up Nazis, culminating with Hitler. "I've compelled the landscape of history to readjust to my visions. I've done it from a blind spot where no one sees me yet my presence cannot go unacknowledged."[328] Erickson strives mightily to create, in effect, an anti-realism, even to the point of denying historical data. In one sequence, Jainlight, the pornographer, whisks an eighty-year-old Hitler out of Europe to Mexico and then America. There, Hitler dies, and Banning returns to Davenhall Island, where at the beginning of the novel he is already dead.

There is also the mysterious Dania, as Erickson moves from character to character, like pieces on a chessboard subject to almost infinite possibilities. If fluidity is the method, then even sex takes place in some middle area, often occurring in dreams, fantasies, or in areas of consciousness that both register and fail to register. Erickson creates "another" world, not so much of pure mysticism as of inexplicability, in which "writing" allows him to break free not only of narrative but of history. Writing is all imagination, all process and reprocessing, seemingly logic-less. Time, as in Pynchon, seems "against" whatever the expected and ordinary happen to be.

Withal, a good deal of architecture underlies this book, but on Erickson's terms. Marc's ferry plying the waters between mainland and island serves, in its way, as a narrative line, a container for events held in suspension. There is symmetry here, since the ferry journey provides not only form but also dream and fantasy. Within that frame, Erickson posits Germany's conquest of Europe and parts of America, an experience within this middle area of consciousness. Some of it runs on too long, such as the episode when Banning attacks, both verbally and physically, a senile Hitler, the man for whom he wrote his most artful porno stories. But even here, within something with little resonance, we are reminded of what brings the two men together, pornography, while in the near background Marc's ferry emerges from the fog, ever moving back and forth, itself a kind of joining together of unlikely elements.

Erickson's use of fog and fantasy, of a nocturnal vision, is somehow equated to Markson's experimentation with language. Neither is concerned with clarification, but with finding the equivalent of societal fog, political darkness, self-mystification. Their America *is* recognizable, but not as an objective entity; rather, as a disconnected, dark, visioning place where everything and anything can happen, and does.

A very different kind of world in which anything can happen characterizes a novel, which received an almost unanimous negative press, Brett Easton Ellis's *American Psycho*, in 1991.[329] The excruciating violence–which does not seem so anomalous after the last two films by Quentin Tarantino, the darling of the critics, or given the people whom lawyers Kunstler and Cochran chose to defend–blinded many reviewers to the cultural weight of the Ellis novel, and to the point of vantage he had taken in regard to his protagonist. In its physical details, the novel is disgusting; but there is also a context for the depraved acts committed by a stockbroker named Patrick Bateman. What Ellis has done-and what has been misunderstood-is the way in which he reflects the extremes of the 80s and how that extremism has entered into mainstream American behavior,

Bateman is well-placed and well-dressed-"costumed" is closer to actuality. His is a consumer society that knows only one thing: triage for the weak and the powerless. Whether the weak are the homeless or women, they are the prey of those who feel empowered: white males, with first-rate educations and financial positions to match. By day, Bateman is a stockbroker with a prestigious firm, by night a psychopathic killer. His victims, mainly women, are from the underclass: the homeless, whores, escort girls, but also bums, blacks, taxi drivers, even cops.

Ellis does not delve into Bateman's psychological makeup; there is no attempt to explain why he does what he does. Ellis, in fact, has purposely eschewed explanation in order to accentuate Bateman's role as an almost automatic individual working through what society expects of him. He is, in this respect, supposed to be a killer; for the way in which the society continues to function is through its empowered groups subjecting-killing-triaging those who have fallen behind. The book, accordingly, is a violent trope for the 80s and thereafter, and especially for what we have seen in the 1994 national election: a virtual political triaging of those who are disempowered, disadvantaged, or helpless.

The novel, then, is both a reflection of the last decade and a futuristic preview of the 90s: reflecting how a narcissistic, sociopathic younger generation-one thinks of Robert chambers and his killing of Jennifer Levin, or, on the upper scale, several members of the Kennedy clan-having entered the yuppie market with values that preclude introspection, social conscience, anything but immediate gratification. One thinks of the barrage of talk shows-Ellis uses the Patty Winters show as a kind of Geraldo's or Maury Povich's-in which immediate gratification bonds both audience and those who bare their souls (and much else). Incest, mother-son-in-law affairs, sisters stealing each other's husbands, or brothers each other's wives, and all the variations: these are part of that world Ellis is invading. It is not extreme, but mainstream, part of multiculturalism. The foods, the Zagat Guide to New York City restaurants, the fashions, the boutiques, the accessories, all the material accoutrements lovingly described in the novel are part of this quest for immediacy, for unthinking selfness. The society indulges such extreme consumerism-part of the power of this white male world lies in its ability to sustain the end of the marketplace-that the leitmotif is a cocaine habit, abetted by the use of a platinum American Express card for transfer of cocaine to nose.

From this to murder, dismemberment, bloody dissection, and torture, is simply to follow the trail. The body is of particular interest: women must have hard bodies and big breasts; one's face is cared for with facial creams, the hair with special tonics, the teeth with constant flossing and expensive mouth washes; nails, body toning, massages, mud baths, facials-these traditional services for women are now the prerogative of men, part of the narcissistic pattern which separates those who have made it from those who haven't.

For his violence, Bateman uses the stock weapons of choice: a serrated knife (to scoop out eyes, a Rambo knife), a gun with a silencer (with an Uzi in his locker, mob weapons), and, also, his teeth-since Jeffrey Dahmer and Hannibal Lector, cannibalism is in. Bateman is more than serial killer, more than Ted Bundy, the Republican boy next door; for his blood lust requires mutilation of the most brutal kind. The excess is so excessive that the reader may wonder if the sociopath is Bateman or the author. Even the author's genteel photograph on the back cover serves as a kind of montage with Bateman, or what we imagine he looks like. But Bateman serves a social-political function usually denied the sociopath and psychopath. He and his friends warn the street people to get jobs, or else face death; they mock their hunger and need for help; they are designated as trash, because of their powerlessness. Blacks and Jews are subject to either physical or verbal attack; women, as observed above, are natural prey-weak, hanger-on, dependent, and easily seduced by Bateman's clothes, jewelry, accessories, and smooth manner.

When Bateman tries to confess what he is doing, to Harold Carnes, first on the message machine, then more personally, he is not believed. Such excesses are expected of the amused, witty young man; his grisly confession is considered a put-on, part of the fraternity boy aspect of the stockbroker culture. No one will listen. *Everything* is possible-what Ellis attempted to communicate once before in the rather anemic *Less Than Zero*. Here, he has made a fictional statement about a future time, which is also a reflection of the present: where the 80s and 90s combine into a nightmarish urban scene. Whereas once the best and brightest from the Ivy League suckered us into the Vietnam War, now they are, in effect, Patrick Bateman, symbols of a society gone over into another kind of death culture. As fiction, what works best for the Ellis novel is its reach into possibility, a dystopia, its horrific violence treated as commonplaces, its portrait of a consumer society gone mad on clothes and accessories, its depiction of an urban place (for which read the country at large) sunk into a death struggle between the empowered and the powerless. Like politics, it's all about triage.

On the "down" side, William T. Vollman's "deconstructive novel" *Whores for Gloria* (1992)[330] complements the Ellis. It consists of brief episodes in which a Vietnam veteran, Jimmy, living in the Tenderloin District of San Francisco on a government check, seeks Gloria, the epitome of the whore whom he has idealized into the perfect woman. Vollman's novel, in which both male and female whores partake of Jimmy's search, moves in and out fantasy, alternately scummy and idyllic. The veteran's world consists of alcohol, drugs, transvestites, degraded women. But the point of the book is never naturalistic or realistic portrayal; rather, it is part of the deceptive vision characteristic of the 90s, the blurring of lines between appearance and reality, between actual and fantasy.

Distinctions are no longer plausible, for distinctions suggest conviction; shades of behavior are more significant than definitive action. Behavior is deconstructed, as though the country were no longer visible. Withal its degradation, *Whores for Gloria* fits into the larger picture as a signifier: that the millennium is ending with the confusion of realms, that brief indeterminate bytes are almost the sole way the writer can express himself. The holistic view of the more immediate postwar writers is now impossible; all is shades, short hauls, degrees, approximations, fantasies. At the end of the novel, Vollman appends statistics on the Tenderloin and a glossary of terms, notes on prostitutes, transvestites, street prices for hair, sex, and other things, prices for lesbian sex, plus interviews. The "factual" material is, of course, a way of anchoring the novel in a realistic frame of reference, even as the text itself is linked to a fantasy world, to find the perfect woman amidst all the debris and detritus of human nature in the Tenderloin.

Wanna buy? Decepticon or Transformer
Half and Half
Hubba
Ho
Flatbacking
Lock of hair
Double date[331]

The "death of" century, the novel, the culture, the country itself would not be complete without consideration of fiction by more mainstream writers, Joyce Carol Oates, John Edgar Wideman, E. L. Doctorow or Walter Abish with *Eclipse Fever*. All of these have combined "the end of" with counterfeit, the deceptive, the struggles merely to remain human against the onslaught of age, political warfare, acceleration of horrific crimes, loss of community, inevitably loss of a society. We have already probed this argument in other writers, Don DeLillo, Paul Auster, Cormac McCarthy, William Gaddis, and Toni Morrison. It cannot be chance that so many writers are trapped in equations that do not factor out. In the face of an obdurate culture that cannot be categorized, the strategy has been to chart its demise, or else the demise of an America the more immediate postwar generation thought it knew. This is, of course, the stuff of any end-of-the-century literature, but it goes further, because it refuses to see the end as the beginning of the beginning; there is nothing transformational about its sense of demise, no Nietzschean nihilism that leads to a resurrection. William Gass's multimedia *The Tunnel* (1995) only reinforces the need to conceal and deceive as means of reflecting death of the self. Gass has even turned Auschwitz into a verb: ". . . we auschwitz along on our merry way."[332] While the motivation for this is clear, this grammatical transgression only cheapens both self and death, while it does fit the egregious usage we have come to expect.

Further, we can add to these "death" novels something parallel in the culture, nonfiction books that are permeated by terminality, or completely focused on it: some narcissistically like Styron's

Darkness Visible-beloved by the critics for its "honesty"; or else the more objective book on death, *How We Die: Reflections on Life's Final Chapter* by Sherwin B. Noland; the numerous back-and-forth arguments concerning Prozac, salvation or doom for those suicidally depressed; or the movement toward doctor-assisted suicide for the terminally ill; and, obviously, the daily newspapers with their reports of more young people than older ones dying, through AIDS, violence, and suicide. Instead of death taking a holiday as the country looks forward to a new start, it has defined the culture.

Eclipse Fever (1991)[333] continues Abish's concern with disintegrating cultures so evident in his masterpiece, *How German Is It*. There, lies, deceptions, disguise, counterfeit, and perverse strategies cover up the complicity of nearly all Germans in their Nazi past; here, in the later novel, the various agents of what should be high culture are as corrupt in their ways as the average German who refused to recognize his and her guilt, or at least recognize his and her history. There is, seemingly, no cure for such ills. It is the end of civilized life, an eclipse.

A different set of coordinates is evident in John Edgar Wideman's *Philadelphia Fire* (1990),[334] but the theme is present: how all reasonable (and unreasonable) life ends, here, in an apocalyptic fire. The factual basis for the Wideman novel is the conflagration that destroyed a block of houses in Philadelphia-when the white police chief with the black mayor's approval dropped a bomb on the Afro-American cult group called Move. Despite brevity, the novel has the advantage of reach, but the disadvantage of preachiness, an increasing trait in Wideman's work. While there is truth in every position Wideman takes-as there was in his earlier *Brothers and Keepers*-there also exists a rift in his argument. He calls for black leadership, he rightfully insists upon it; and yet when it is in the offing here, disaster occurs. The black leader is perceived as no better than the white, as, in fact, doing the white man's dirty work. A racial chasm opens here.[335]

But intermixed in what occurs with black leadership as well as without it is Wideman's plaint for his son, imprisoned for stabbing to death his roommate at camp-although the particulars of the crime are not revealed. But extrapolating from his son's crime, Wideman sees an intellectual and moral corruption in the culture; for his son is not being treated as mentally incompetent but as a common criminal. In the novel, this aspect is dramatized in the narrator Cudjoe's search for the small boy, Simba, who escaped the Move bombing. To find Simba-Wideman's son, *The Tempest*'s Caliban, and all the other young victims-is to recover black life.

Much of this returns us to *Brothers and Keepers*, where a related argument was applied to Wideman's brother, incarcerated for life for complicity in murder. Once again, Wideman rages at the society, the culture, the moral vacuity into which his brother, and his son, were sucked. Yet as mentioned in *Brothers and Keepers*, the brother came from a solid home, a devoted family, not a dysfunctional or disadvantaged background; being black meant experiencing racism, but that hardly explains the situation. Most blacks do not fall into crime, no less murder. Similarly, the mental illness of Wideman's son, given the success of the Wideman family, cannot be fobbed off on the culture, on racism, or somehow on the society. Surely, signs were there before the son stabbed his campmate to death.

Nevertheless, the strength of *Philadelphia Fire* lies in Wideman's raising of these issues, and in his linkage of his son's plight with the bombing of the Move quarter. An irrational impulse lies deeply problematically in the society, unresolvable, impossible perhaps to interpret, no less comprehend. The difficulty of understanding how these events occur leads to Wideman's extended examination of Shakespeare's *The Tempest*, whose Caliban is now the darling of the politically correct. Caliban is hailed as the heroic figure who tried to prevent the colonists from taking his island (in 1992, read this as the Native Americans fending off Columbus and his plunderers); and his craziness, or his Hamletic playacting, is the result of his loss of heritage. Caliban has asserted himself into history as his own man, in this reading, only to be baffled by whites who imperially take over his island.

Yet Wideman's strengths are best revealed in his depiction of the bomb drop and the search for Simba; somewhat less so in his discussion of his son's plight, despite the obvious pain; far less so in his use of Caliban, preachy, selective, and reductive. Caliban is victim, no question of that; but *The Tempest* must be fitted into a broader context, about art, salvation, and regeneration. Overall, Wideman's goal is to mesh these three "stories" into a single narrative, all implying the end of things, the fall of mankind, the suspicion that resurrection may not take place. The inevitable aim is to make sure that such a horrible and inexplicable act as the dropping of the bomb on Move should not recur, a point about social reality worth making, of course, but one that creates sermons. Make the white reader suffer the pain caused by the black mayor!

We should heed Wideman, but his polemics, however powerful, lead to no resolution. Hectoring turns off. A created work, as we know, succeeds to the extent it can sweep up particulars into a broader artistic statement, such as in *Invisible Man*. Anger, as Wideman points out, is a healthy response to the terrible inequities that rule in the world of race; but anger by itself, just as race by itself, does not link all irrational impulses. As a writer, he opens up the dialogue-as he did in *Brothers and Keepers*-but a created resolution (not a social or political one) is not forthcoming. That would, of course, be another kind of novel.

Joyce Carol Oates, in *Because It Is Bitter, and Because It Is My Heart* (1991),[336] has perhaps discovered a leading emblem for the 1990s, vomiting. Food is a form of death, and vomiting is in part an indicator of a terminally-minded culture. Her book is full of puking individuals who for differing reasons upchuck at many stages of their lives. As life goes sour on them, the need to vomit is compelling, although there is always the hope of renewal. Vomiting does have the sense one is eliminating foul matter in order to move on with one's life, cleansed, purified, regenerated. But the act is also foul, an emblem of the individual coughing up his or her guts, letting most foul substances disgorge, in what is an unnatural process, separate from and distinct form other more accepted forms of elimination. The process also suggests anorexia and bulimia, two areas of pathology which have struck middle class girls and young women in the main: those who have turned off from sex, food, and their bodies; or have so detested themselves they grow (with food) and then contract (with vomiting), changing their shape, creating a refracted, self-deceptive beauty. Theirs is a culture of death, with little chance of resurrection.

Anorexia and bulimia are, in fact, excellent and compelling emblems of the last two decades, if we stretch our imagination a little. In one, there is restriction, hatred of self, uncertainty of one's identity, the desire to change oneself through paring off, a form of isolation, wrapping oneself in an artificial mystery, choosing shadows over light. In the other, bulimia, there is the desire to reshape oneself through excess, but to be so ambivalent about excess as to wish to divest oneself of it through self-abuse. In both we find pathologies about abundance; thus their middle class status. There is little or no ease in what one has, but an uncertainty that translates into self-destructive behavior, forcing recognition by others that one requires help to survive. While the analogy with America in the 80s and 90s is hardly congruent, the aptness of the twin emblems should not be lost. Uncertainty surely underlies both.

Oates's young woman, here Iris Courtney, is her reprise of *them*, the late 60s novel that serves as the archetype of her work. Her view of family life is nearly always of a dysfunctional group that, on the surface, seems to be working.[337] The Courtneys pose as a golden couple when, in fact, they are falling apart: he through gambling and a personality of lies, deception, and disguise which recalls Geoffrey Wolff's Duke, in *the Duke of Deception*; she, almost the stereotypical small-town beauty-located near Lake Ontario in northern New York State-who slides into alcoholism and other forms of self-destruction. Lost in their narcissistic pursuit of fun is their daughter, Iris, the flower-like name belying her rough adolescence, daughter of Duke (yes, Duke Courtney) and Persia, the exotic-sounding names belying their grubbiness. Iris's inner life is penetrated by only one other person: when she is a young teenager, she is trapped by a local thug named Little Red Garlock and is saved by a young black youth, Jinx Fairchild. In saving her, Jinx kills Little Red, bonding him and Iris is a secret she caries with her into adulthood. The bonding extends further: for her, the couple that murders together must love together, although that is not the way it works out. She never forgets Jinx, but gets on with her life, whereas his is suddenly blighted.

Yet another emblem of the novel, and particularly pertinent for the 90s when racial relationships have so soured, is the black-white "romance" that never comes off. Once Iris feels bonded to Jinx through their crime, blacks fascinate her: they become the forbidden object of attraction and repulsion. As her parents sink, Iris descends ever deeper into her own inner life, lying to protect where she comes from, who she is, what her life might have been. The secret bond with Jinx is overwhelming, and it is not chance that such a bond should cut across racial lines. Whomever she meets, she measures against Jinx, now on a downward spiral after a badly broken ankle dooms his college basketball hopes, an act that may have been self-destructive. In the years after the murder of Little Red, Iris and Jinx rarely meet, but their relationship depends not on crossing paths but on interests which, once shared, are now skewed: the emblem of race in this country. Jinx's hold on Iris is only broken in what seems a formulaic scene, in which Iris is seized by a group of black teen thugs and manhandled and humiliated, but not raped. Once this occurs, the black becomes for her an object of fear, and she is, now, ready to make her move with a white boy friend, heading into marriage.

The sympathy she once felt for blacks is broken by a new cycle of fear, and that, too, appears pointed. We should not read this as Oates's perception; it is a created experience, the way Iris perceives herself and her thorny past. In this respect, the brutal manhandling which stops just short of rape breaks her bond with Jinx, who has joined the army as a means of avoiding a personal life that is always on the edge; and it foretells how separated black and white become: he will defend her, so to speak, as a military man, and she will fear him, as someone associated with a skin color that has led to her brutalization.

Yet the major emblem still remains food and drink-that eating and imbibing which create the tension between anorexia and bulimia, with alcoholism factored in. Although Iris must overcome an unstable parental background, a waste-land-like environment, and her own conflicted feelings about blacks and sexuality, in the larger sense she must come to terms with food and drink. In this area, Oates has caught something in the American psyche: not its obsession with food itself, but a concern with assimilation, absorption, digestion, elimination. The process is deep within the individual and society; how one fares is the subtext of how food is handled and how one eats, whether as nourishment or as enemy to be upchucked. The body is also part of that subtext-how does one perceive oneself? Iris falters, almost sinks, as she wonders about her body, as she protects it against invasion and penetration, whether by black manhandlers or white boyfriends. She shields her body-possibly as a response to her mother's easy way with hers; but more likely because she sees her body as part of what she can shape or reshape herself. Food, then, becomes part of the chain of survival, not as nourishment, but as perception.

Food, however, does not stand alone, nor does it stand only with race. It is, somehow, allied to death. Death runs through the novel as a motif, since it occurs on the first page, when Little Red Garlock's body is discovered in the river, with his head smashed. The opening vignettes are all death-oriented: in small-town life, in family disintegration, in individual and social abulia. Yet, as we have observed, death is never distant from food and drink, with their unnatural elimination, with the equation of beauty, somehow, with anorexia and bulimia. In several of her later novels, Oates has reduced significant elements to fundamentals; she has moved life and death closer together, so that we must see this as commentary, however indirectly, on America in its closing years of the decade. Iris does achieve success of sorts-she has graduated from college and she will make an interesting marriage to a high achieving young man; but her life has been strewn with deathlike phenomena, moribund images, a disintegrating family, murder itself, plus forbidden yearnings for sex.

Iris has come through all the subtexts of American life-those elements which poke beneath the surface of seemingly placid small town life. Her journey is part of what Michael Lesey described in *Wisconsin Death Trip*, his account of mayhem in a small Wisconsin town of another era. *Because It Is Bitter* links up with another Oates novel, in 1987, *You Must Remember This*;[338] in fact, her last few novels all seem part of a sequential series. Although characters change, certain primordial situations remain constant. In the earlier novel, the setting is a grim upstate New York town called Port Oriskany; the parents are, as expected, less than adequate, with the mother neurasthenic. The family slowly disintegrates, with the sisters of the main character, Enid, going off into unacceptable activities, living with unacceptable men; a brother is badly wounded in the Korean War. As a consequence of these failures-no parental reinforcement, no social skills supported, few options for future achievement-Enid falls in with her half-uncle Felix, her father's half-brother.

Enid comes through, as do nearly all of Oates's protagonists, but they have been broken figures along the way. There is a feminist message here, buried amidst the debris. But it barely makes it through: for the dominating dimension is small-town Eden-Like surface as against small-town realities, blood, food, pathology, violence. If America is disintegrating, it is rural as much as urban. And in *American Appetites* (1989),[339] there is not only the small town, there is, once again, the emphasis on food; for the main female character, Glynnis McCullough, is a cookbook writer and prides herself on the brilliance of her kitchen. Oates lovingly describes the kitchen, its orderliness, its array of timesaving devices, its strategic organization of materials and utensils. She also lovingly describes some of the foods which come from that kitchen, not only the recipes for the cookbooks, but also for regular family meals; and when Glynnis dies, her sullen daughter, Bianca, recovers from her own pathologies by trying to maintain the kitchen and cookbook tradition. Furthermore, the McCulloughs entertain a great deal and are, of course, known for their table, their wines, the lavishness of their presentation and the tastiness of the carefully prepared courses. If sex and death are the text, then food is, once again, the subtext; ever-present as an emblem of plenty in America, but also as a distorting shield.

The double or triple sense of the title-appetites for sex as well as food, appetites for certain forms of artificial or distorted life, appetites that can never be fulfilled-suggests how food is deceptive as well as temporarily satisfactory. Food leads us to believe in bounty; the McCullough home is a virtual daily Thanksgiving. But behind the meals, the lavish dinner parties, the satisfying courses and fine wines is a society which considers food as a binding element in lives which are not merely morally empty, but overflowing with trivialities, deceptions, secrets, boredom. Here, in this Oates novel, everyone has plenty of money, fine homes, solid cars and gold-plated careers; but it is American emptiness as well as appetites that prevails. This is not an original idea, but what is original about the presentation is the use of food and its aura as a way of demonstrating the emptiness, as a way of making it immanent. Food is in some ways power, but not quite; it is in some ways sex, but not quite; it is, more than either, the trope of an abundant country. The men here hold commanding positions, roles in American intellectual leadership-which must identify with food because it has little else with which to cohere. Eat, vomit; drink, upchuck. The country is balanced between anorexia and bulimia, a social more than culinary statement.

E. L. Doctorow's *The Waterworks* (1994),[340] with its return to an earlier time in New York City, would seem, on its face, not to be a novel about our own 90s, but perhaps more about the 1890s. But playing through are many of our familiar themes of 1990s life. In his way, the novelist is saying something about our century's end, although elliptically and tangentially. The novel is a detective story of sorts, a sociological exploration of old New York City in another respect. The main narrator, McIlvaine, a newspaper editor, is seeking his star reporter, Martin Pemberton, who has suddenly vanished. The major thrust of the novel comes with this pursuit through New York's under and overworld: seedy bars and alleys and streets, as well as the police, the medical profession, the family of Pemberton's wealthy and villainous father, August, and like elements.

At one level this is a quest for identity, a parallel volume to Doctorow's highly compelling *World's Fair*. Instead of 1939 and the fair, we encounter post-Civil war New York, when it was held in thrall to the Tweed Ring, to Boss Tweed, when corruption sifted into every crevice of city life. This can also be perceived as a morality story-something always close to Doctorow's way of working; in that he displays the way big cities run, whether post-Civil War or contemporary New York, for whom this is a cautionary tale. Doctorow is fascinated with how the underclass lives,[341] how it is defeated or frustrated by machinations at the top (by August Pemberton, for example, who continues to deal in slaves even after slavery is abolished). Disease, crime, sewage, rot, corruption: these are the legacy of the city, and, as in *Billy Bathgate*, they also convey its energies, its vitality, and its refusal to go under. Class considerations, of course, are never distant: whereas the poorer lower and working classes are hit hardest by the corruption, the others live in their cocooned enclaves.

But Doctorow, it becomes clear, goes further than any of this, compelling though this might be by itself. He wants to ascertain where something as mighty as Truth lies, whether it can be ascertained, how it can be gotten at through layers of narrative. Is there a *true* text, a *true* narrative? Can we rely on anything? Is all relative, or are there absolutes? Can we penetrate layers of narrative, all established to obfuscate and deceive? McIlvaine is the funnel through which everything passes, but within his narrative are several others. As the pace quickens in the search for Martin Pemberton, so does the mystery, the cover-up, the failure to find clues, the layering of experiences that distorts and disguises. While no one seems to *know*, the possibility exists that everyone is covering up. We are, however we look at it, in the world of the 1990s, where deception, the counterfeit, the obscure have overtaken the realm of information, the search for definition, finally, the pursuit of any kind of truth. In some curious way, Doctorow has moved into Pynchon territory: to uncover the truth beneath a tidal wave of lies, hypocrisies, and outright deceptions. Only fiction can penetrate the shadows.

In this strange, labyrinthine novel-the narrative conveys tunneling-much more compellingly than the tunnel in William Gass's new novel-Dr Sartorius is Doctorow's most dichotomous creation. In his coldhearted, scientific approach to life, he recalls Conrad's Kurtz, or someone even darker, Dr. Mengele. Doctorow, by way of Martin Pemberton, writes:

> What you must understand about Sartorius is that he was never committed to one therapy, he made corrections constantly, he was truly disinterested, and as ruthlessly critical of his own ideas as of others'. He sought out what was aberrant in brains and bodies, as if the secrets of living beings could be more easily exposed there. Normality obstructed the scientific vision, it suggested a self-assurance of form that life had no right to claim. But where existence was afflicted and grotesque, it announced itself as the truly unreasoning thing it is. He regularly examined people who made their living from their deformity.[342]

Dr. Sartorius is implacable and inexorable. "He kept going! That is the point-he kept going. . . through, beyond. . . sanity, whatever that is."[343] McIlvaine characterizes men like Sartorius as elusive, invisible, "dead men or men indeterminately alive," men hidden away, "Barricaded in their own created realms behind the thick walls of the brownstones of New York."[344] One sees them only in the shadows, and when they speak, they do so in the voice of others. They are "powerful, absent men" who hide away in the crevices of language, as only names in the newspapers. For such men, again like Sartorius an ironically reworked *Sartor Resartus*, Carlyle's caustic tailoring of mankind), the rest of mankind is not human, but scientific artifacts. We may be, the rest of us, strung out like waves, of all kinds and lengths, which we ourselves cannot see or feel or hear; and yet these invisible, barricaded men control the waves.

The struggle in *The Waterworks* between human elements and scientific or experimental efforts is an old one; but by layering it among narrators, by contextualizing it within the city's history, and by giving it various voices, Doctorow has complicated the process. Sartorius may be Mengele revived, McIlvaine may represent questing humanity, August Pemberton may stand for runaway capitalism, and his son, Martin, the desire to find the father; all of these ring as traditional subjects, but Doctorow proposes bigger game. To uncover, to move behind the disguises, to penetrate the counterfeit and to identify the artifice, all, bring the novel well into the 90s quest for some meaning or definition in which the sole reality seems subcultures, subtexts, and subversion.

Before charting different writers with different agendas-Latinos, Native-Americans, Asian-Americans-one "novel" remains which creates difficulties not only for the reader but also for anyone who wants to see what the 90s have become. *The Tunnel* (1995), a true end-of-the-century book, is as problematic for the reader as it must have been for the author, William Gass. It takes nihilism to a new level, and it puts to shame those other 90s books which perceive the country as having surrendered its promise. But one of the major problems with *The Tunnel*-and there are several-is that its nihilism fits no pattern: it is not Nietzschean, it is not Sartrean, it is not what we associate with any other form of negativism in American and Western fiction. It is purely death without resurrection. The tracking of the main character, William Frederick Kohler, takes place against the most nihilistic period in Western history, the Nazi era. Kohler has written a revisionist study called *Guilt and Innocence in Hitler's Germany*. His aim, as he states it, was to remove "some of the armour, the glamour, of Evil. It small e's it. It shakes a little sugar on the shit. It dares to see a bit of the okay in our great bugaboche. Inexcusable. Slander our saints, if you will, but please leave our Satan undefiled by any virtue, his successes inexplicable by any standard."[345]

What all this means is that he wants to put the Hitler regime and Germany itself, in a new context, one in which Jews, Gypsies, and homosexuals more or less sought their own victimization. Kohler "cobbles history," as he put it; but that is somewhat ironical since the cobbler's name recalls household bathroom products, made by the Kohler company and translates as "charcoal burner." The author is himself not far from toilet humor. Is the book, then, a giant put on? Is it an effort to discredit all history? Does Gass use his unsavory, incoherent narrator as a way of creating a text that lies outside history? Is all received information to be dismissed as part of the prejudice and bigotry of the historian, i. e. Kohler, a bathroom man? Most of all, is there any meaning besides the form itself of the book? Is meaning all presentation? And this leads to the question, why should we call this a novel, when it is meditation, therapy, multi-media pictorials, geometric arrangements, and other strategies more from advertising, television publicity, and mass marketing than anything usually associated with the novel? Finally, we must ask ourselves if the novel genre itself is so broad, so inclusive, so expansive that it can include all prose, even prose so clearly therapeutic rather than shaped? Many of these questions remain problematic, part of the paradoxes of *The Tunnel*.

At one level at least, for the reader, the novel is a disaster. There is almost no receptor for this-pages simply obscured with over-printing, blurring, obfuscation of every kind. The book is, to use a golf analogy, one dog trap after another. Why should anyone read it? It is a meditation of such self-enclosed narcissism as to redefine the word, and can only be perceived as the work of a man so prepared to die that he would be happy to take the century with him. The narrator himself, Kohler, is so unappetizing, so full of hatred of Jews, blacks, women, minorities of every ethnic and racial background that his calling card is the only thing authentic about him:

Dr. Kohler
Nazi
By appointment

"Nazi" comes in a different, more artistic typeface.

If the reader wants a death-oriented book to close out the 90s, then *The Tunnel* is it. That it is the product of thirty years of Gass's life in fiction[346] suggests possibly how self-indulgence can create a text his publishers might have hesitated to publish, since the book could not possibly communicate; or if it did communicate, its message was so hateful it created not merely confusion but a nauseated turning away. Another hateful book Ellis's *American Psycho*, was a spoof, a pathological hoot; *The Tunnel* is not. But such a harsh criticism is not the whole story. The real significance of the book does not lie only in its attempt to throw a different spin on Nazism, on German history, or on American views of the Holocaust. Its importance lies in its very self-indulgence, its narcissism, its sense of denial, its use of tortured, pathological reasoning, its distrust of history and memory and the past, its need to restructure and revise so as to wipe out all sense of guilt, its desire to assert personality above reason and logic. Kohler worships his mentor, Magus Tabor (Mad Meg, the name a gender crossover), founder of the Party of Disappointed People (PdP), the party for outcasts, nihilists, deniers, close in some ways to the pathology of those caught up in conspiratorial theories. The entire book, in fact, can be read as the expression that everything in American life and thought is conspiratorial. Yet Kohler's feeling of oppression is so clearly part of personal deficit, not the country, that any social and political significance is lost. This, too, makes the book a 90s guide.

Regular refrains in insistent black type-inserted doggerel verses-provide a drumbeat of anti-Semitism which puts Kohler into the company of those who see conspirators in all non-white activity, those who cannot abide Jews for their success in America, and who compensate for their own failure with hatred. The emphasis on the Jewish cock, circumcised, with the red tip protruding ominously, reinforces Kohler's own futile sexuality, his sexual fear even while he seems obsessed with it. He fears, also, that the Jew is getting greater pleasure, that he can penetrate further. With these beliefs and comments everpresent to torment him, Kohler constructs a tunnel from his house basement-an emblem, perhaps, of his need to hide such commentary, to hide himself, to avoid his wife, to escape from a self he cannot abide. The tunnel is also connected to his need to escape history, to write a novel that relies completely on a self shaped without moral or ethical considerations.

In some bizarre way, he hopes that this novel and the tunnel he is digging at great expense to his comfort will be ways into himself. But as it turns out, the tunnel is simply another failure. He does meditate about himself, his childhood, parents, marriage and wife, and the rest; but he is left with chaos. If we wanted a more negative, hateful denial of self and country than this, we would have to rummage through writers like Céline; even Nietzsche seems a yea-sayer in comparison. If these are the 80s and 90s, Gass implies, then we have not only struck out, we have abandoned the game. The question of course remains to what degree Kohler expresses Gass, or Gass Kohler; but then the text only offers one reader's speculation: that while in some ways they are far apart, in many others they are not. Here is a writer offering himself up as a sacrifice, a martyr to what we have become. Bring on your heavy guns to assail me, but the rot is systemic.[347]

This brings us around to whether we read *The Tunnel* as a novel, as autobiography, or even as biography-what we found also with Harold Brodkey's *The Runaway Soul*. The answer is that the Gass book is a mutational form, the proof, in his eyes, that there are no genres, there is no content, there are no absolutes, there is only the text. Caveat, lector.

If we seek equal doses of manic and depressive behavior, Stanley Elkin's "Her Sense of Timing"[348] is still another meeting ground of a 90s sensibility ground in final things, the juxtaposition of impotence, food, and death. A badly handicapped near sixty-year-old academic is abandoned by his middle-aged wife on the eve of an annual party they give for his graduate students. Jack Schiff is almost helpless, and much of the novella is given over to the mechanical and electrical devices he depends upon to move around and to help him if he falls. Also, a good deal is given over to his eliminatory processes, especially urination. Pissing is only equaled by eating-the body as Schiff conceives it is the conduit for insipid food turning into bodily waste (no pleasure in between) in a corrupted physical assembly line.

Schiff's indifference to food is tested when his students insist upon holding the party despite his wife's departure and further insist on bringing over all the food-pasta, salad, quiches, and other typical graduate student fodder. Meanwhile, he longs for the wife he tortured, and yet he feels unable to call off the annual celebration when one graduate student in particular takes over. The annual party turns into a drunken bacchanalia, with food, drink, and other matter strewn around the house; and with Schiff's Stair-Glide destroyed by students overloading it as a kind of amusement park ride, he is made helpless. Deposited by student bearers to his second-floor bedroom, he depends now completely on the rescue system he has just had installed. The novella ends with his having recognized what his answering system tells callers: that he can't come to the phone right away. He's fallen.

Elkin's tale is of a man who has wound down. A political geographer by profession, he has spent his adult life carving out boundaries. The novella, ultimately, is about borders and boundaries: the constrained, limited boundaries of Schiff's existence, now that he has been abandoned by a much put-upon wife and then by the graduate students as they move on to the next party. He has indeed "fallen," fallen out of life, fallen out of self-respect, fallen from whatever position he once held, fallen in sexual terms-still interested but impotent. As Elkin's own condition worsened and made him increasingly handicapped, he writes about "closing up" or "closing down" from the inside; and what he says accommodates perfectly the sense of the decade's end. Or, as he might have said, how even the less than mighty have fallen!

There are antidotes to despairing negativism. If we juxtapose Latino, Native-American, Asian-American, and similar fiction to that of native old-timers we observe a difference. Whereas their older colleagues in the postwar era have little or no hope of positive adjustment, the hyphenated writers still see in their institutions, their myths, their traditions, and their history some sense of vitality and energy, some sense of optimism and an awareness of how to survive. It is not the Latino writers-those who have come through many kinds of deprivation-who have given up on the country, but the so-called mainstream crowd which sees the country ending with the century.

First, some background: For Latino and Hispanic-Americans, assimilation has been different from what it was for Jews, Italians, and others. That is because Hispanics live closer to homelands (the islands, other land masses) and experience a steady influx of Spanish-speaking people from Puerto Rico, Mexico, and Central America. For other immigrant groups, there was a definite break since the homelands were so far, and immigration essentially fell into defined periods and then more of less ended. There was, also, little or no going back. Italians on the whole did not return to Italy, Jews did not return to Russia or Poland.[349] As for the Irish, they already had the language, and once anti-Irish hatred lessened, they could assimilate. Hispanics are confronted with relatives and friends coming through, renewing and revitalizing the old culture and keeping the language fresh. The "other world" traditions do not die out and end. They are Americans with a difference, most of all Asian-Americans, or darker Latinos and Native-Americans. While this makes assimilation less than immediate and may create profound individual difficulties, there is a positive side, in that legends and histories can energize a literature. These voices are very much of the 80s and 90s.

As for the settled older group, it is in their sixties and seventies or older; and its sense of "closing time" is never far from end-of-the-century closing time. These are millennium writers, so to speak, apocalyptic even. This entrenched, established group-but not the hyphenated writers-helps define the decade as it moves into its final phases: the sense of drift akin to entropy, an awareness that the postwar era has indeed ended; the conviction that history despite prosperity has played a tremendous joke on American expectations; and, most of all, the firm belief that no place exists where one may look for help, salvation, even direction. All plans have failed, all ideas have frittered away their energy; all desire for direction has been exhausted. All goals become personal ones. There is more than drift in this analysis: there is that apocalyptic whiff, without the religious sense of disaster looming, except for those who predict Armageddon. It is more than T. S. Eliot's assumption that we are going out in a whimper-even that jejune prediction is too definite. Unable to believe in anything, we are, according to our mainstream writers, going out in disarray, although no one can foresee just how it will occur. Indefiniteness is the fictional model, a personal as well as social scenario.

Yet there is another side, a fairly complicated one, since this side looks back as well as at the present. As we hear in other voices, in other accents attempting to define the 90s or at least provide some fictional blueprint for the decade, we note how pervasive is the heritage of William Faulkner; and if not Faulkner himself, then the "magical realism: which so many Latino writers have equated with his work and which has reinforced their own views of fiction. For the latter-and I am citing only writers in English-Cristina Garcia in her *Dreaming in Cuban* (1992) is a Latino updating of Faulkner's *As I Lay Dying*. But before examining such fiction, we can see that even for the non-Latino and other non-hyphenated writers, Faulkner still remains a huge presence down to the end of the century: not only as the creator of a world but also as an experimenter with techniques and narrative strategies that American fiction has thoroughly absorbed.

Overall, what Faulkner provided, whatever the degree of presence, was an *opening up*, a liberation from narrow realism and naturalism, of the American novel. If we measure his work against that of the other large writers of the 1920s-Hemingway, Fitzgerald, Dos Passos, Anderson, Dreiser, Lewis, Wharton-Faulkner (perhaps along with a more scattered Gertrude Stein) remains as the sole American writer who infused native traditions with Modernistic practices from abroad. This "opening up," in fact, is precisely what became so dangerous; for American writers separated into those won over by the methods of Modernism and those who have resisted for almost the entire length of their careers.

As for the latter: since writers such as Bellow, Roth, Styron, Oates, Malamud, Ellison (to a lesser degree), Mailer, Updike have rejected the inroads of full Modernism and have crafted their work outside its verbal and narrative demands, postwar American fiction has undergone a curious cultural division in the Western world. America is almost the sole country where the *dominant novel* in terms of popular recognition and exportability has been antithetical to Modernism. What this suggests, further, is the sharp division within the American cultural scene where forces of anti-Modernism (virtually the entire literary establishment, reviewers, mainstream critics, etc.) confront those who have absorbed the lessons of writers like Joyce, Eliot, Stein, Pound, Kafka, Woolf. Since Faulkner has himself been such a huge presence in contemporary writers from other countries, we recognize the paradox.[350]

Nowhere more than in our more recent Latino-American writers is this paradox underscored. For these writers are clearly indebted to novelists such as Marquez, Fuentes, Llosa, Donoso,

Borges, Cortázar, all writers in Spanish who themselves owe a heavy debt to Faulkner (as well as to Joyce). Thus, part of American fiction in the 80s and 90s is being shaped and reshaped by those- I have in mind Cristina Garcia, Rudolfo Anaya, Sandra Cisneros, Julia Alvarez-who have felt the presence of a strong Latin-American Modernism, which in turn has experienced a strong Faulknerian presence: the so-called magical realism. This development, in magical realism, extends from innovative uses of language and strategical moves with character and narrative to the sense of place and to the mystery of place, even to the invention of place, roughly equivalent to Faulkner's Yoknapatawpha. Although the Latino-American writers work in English, their Spanish-American roots are evident; and through these roots, their awareness of Faulkner either first-or second-hand as part of a large common heritage. Again roughly speaking, Faulkner's South is *the South* whether south of the border or not; part of a self-defined place which exists because writers have invented it as much as discovered it.

Strikingly, while the Latino-American short story tends to fall into naturalistic-realistic patterns, longer fiction moves toward the edges, into mysticism, magical forces, magic itself, a floating sense of place, and narrative dislocation and discontinuity. In one of the best of this kind, *Dreaming in Cuban* by Cristina Garcia, in 1992,[351] some of the magical dimension is conveyed through the *santeria* cult in Cuba; but the novel as a whole goes well beyond that, into the hallucinatory world of Cuban-Americans and their Americanized children. What makes the Garcia novel so compelling is her ability to move fluidly between worlds: not just ethnic groups, but worlds of alternating reason and mysticism. She finds narrative transitions that move the reader both in and out of a "normally" functioning culture. Through a variety of means-*santeria* episodes, a character's almost fatal burning of her husband, his ghostly presence when his children later visit him, sudden temporal shifts to before and after the Castro revolution, use of another character's letters to her former lover, mad sequences which float from the matriarch Celia to her daughter Felicia, all, provide a

449

kaleidoscope of paralleling, opposing, contradictory, complementary experiences.

The theme is a form of madness, which results from alienation and isolation, from the clash of cultures and political systems, from languages which drift in and out of each other, from tensions between old religion (*santeria* and its secret, cultish rites) and the more antiseptic forms in mainland America. Political allegiances, as Celia discovers, do not lead to satisfaction. For even though she is fervent about the Lider, Castro, her life splinters. Another daughter, Lourdes, lives in New York and is just as fervently anti-Castro; Lourdes' daughter, Pilar, thinks all political thought and talk is bull, while she is herself trapped between cultures and is taking on the worst of American popular tastes. The result is a phantasmagoria, wreckage, splits and divisions; and the narrative method is shaped to mirror the disintegration and corruption of self. As individuals seek some singular identity, they cannot escape the swirl around them, a swirl that Garcia captures in the foggy, muddy, hallucinatory method that fits not only Cuban-Americans, but also the 90s as a whole. And behind it all is not only Marquez and Fuentes, but also Faulkner and his acute sense of a splintered, Janus-faced culture.

Garcia has a central trope for the novel, in the form of an island where "tides arrange the borders." This gives her at least "the illusion of change, of possibility."[352] This image comes into particular focus when near the end of the novel, with Lourdes and Pilar on a visit to Cuba, hundreds of Cubans rush the Peruvian Embassy to escape the island. The crowds are "tides"; the island is being reshaped; and within it all the people, as well as the island, are being recreated. Into what?-no one can answer; but the Garcia novel reflects the disillusionment, the chaos of lives spread across island and mainland. The body of water between does not allow a bridge or tunnel; it is a hellish Styx.

Garcia is only one of several such writers caught in a Faulknerian, Latino-American spin, in which all value systems have come unglued and one must grasp whatever there is, without knowing what it is to grasp. All systems must be measured against what was old or abandoned, or no longer viable in the new world. Although the focus may be somewhat different, we observe a similar point in Rudolfo Anaya's popular *Bless Me, Ultima* (1972, paper reprint in 1994)[353] and Sandra Cisneros's lesser-known *The House on Mango Street* (1989, paperback in 1991).[354] Even though the Anaya novel takes place in New Mexico, there is little enough of the "new"; one feels the pressure of Chicano culture infiltrating from Mexico into the Anglo world. And it is a culture quite in contradistinction to that Anglo world. If Jesus is the God of the Anglos, then Ultima with her *curandera* magical cures is the savior of the Chicanos. But the difference goes further: for the world of magic is at the heart of the Anaya novel, a magic that is completely lost in the Anglo world.

This is more than a replay of the magical realism of Marquez and Llosa, or of Faulkner-although it is that, also—but rather, a sense that the Anglo world has flattened out, homogenized, become abstracted through loss of beliefs. This is not religion so much as tradition, memory, even history, and it is definitely not Lawrentian "blood consciousness," which has a certain racism and fascism at its root. It is the feeling that invisible forces play as large a role in our lives as the visible ones; and that invisible forces can be called up not by leaders, statesmen or the rich, but by someone in touch with vitality, energy, and curative elements. All of it is fantasy, but, according to these writers, it is fantasy that is sadly lacking in much mainstream Anglo fiction.

Latino writers like Anaya are, of course, not alone in this. The Native-Americans, Louise Erdrich and Leslie Silko, have also crossed the line from "realism" to "magicalism." In Erdrich's *The Beet Queen* (1986),[355] for example, there are several scenes in which magical moments occur, and they seem integrated into the narrative form that is itself fragmented among several voices. The Rashomon-like effect allows individual voices to emerge, not as something "actual," but as voices that come from inner areas that may or may not be objectively validated. As in some deconstructed artifact, Erdrich keeps moving the center of her novel; and this functions to open the magical option. Early on, there is a crossover between realism and magical moments when the child Mary, new to Argus, North Dakota, and to her school-and, therefore, disoriented-slides into an ice formation which then takes on the image of Jesus, although to Mary it appears to take on the image of her brother Karl.

Such magical or hallucinatory moments energize the novel, which flags somewhat in the middle sections once the young people achieve adulthood and live out their years ordinarily. What does count, however, is how Erdrich has infused a family novel-and we should emphasize that Latino and Native Americans are engaged, often, in the family novel that the serious Anglo novel finds problematic-with sparkling moments when nothing seems real, when strange forces appear to be permeating the atmosphere, when growing up is itself a form of magical imposition of elements from both within and without. There are sparks. And even when for the reader such "sparks" do not always resonate, there is enormous energy here, when instability might be the expectation.

As for the family itself, Erdrich creates a group that hardly fits the nuclear notion of familial arrangements. It is, like so many others in this genre, extended, and extended into somewhat bizarre linkages. The various voices belong to Mary Adare, the chief survivor; Sita Kozka, her cousin, daughter of Mary's aunt with whom she goes to live when her mother abandons her; Karl, Mary's bisexual brother, who marries Mary's friend Celestine James and has a child with her; Wallace Pfef, with whom Karl has sex now and then, a big man in the world of Argus, North Dakota; and Dot, the child of Celestine and Karl.

The final voice is that of Dot, mixed Indian blood from her heritage, also "mixed" in another sense as daughter of the bisexual Karl. Dot is wild, grungy, a hoodlum, seemingly a lost girl, full of anger and hostility, aware of slights, and yet alive and energized-part of that "other" or "beyond" element in an Erdrich novel even when relationships are tentative and hateful. Dot becomes the beet queen, but only because her father's sometimes sexual partner,

Wallace, fixes the vote. Dot rages, but somehow becomes human in her rage; just as Mary and Sita, her cousin, have raged with each other, come close in fact to murder, and yet have bonded. The range of emotional life is extended in some Lawrentian sense, from the usual and expected into areas where murder, suicide, and other forms of violence are never distant; and yet such emotional extremes, which nourish the magicalism of the novel, lead to a certain human blend.

Similarities exist with Anaya's novel *Bless Me, Ultima*, especially in the liberating force of the "other," the world outside rational discourse. Such opening up comes in the presence of Ultima, whose name as the "last one," the Omega, provides the scope and range of the novel. She is indeed the last or final one; her life and death underscore what is possible. As people dream, fantasize, create phantom worlds, Ultima is the sole one who can bring about "cures." Working her magic through herbs, ordinary objects, and fetishes, she can create a universe of justice where injustice routinely rules. She represents a broad definition of "soul," which goes beyond being saved into areas of social and political fairness, evening out of class and caste imbalance, adjustments of social wrongs that mark people out as perpetual victims.

Strikingly, nearly all these instances of magic and magical moments have social or political resonance. Magic derives from the common people or from the deprived, and its evocation is a way the victimized can get back their dignity or their loss of position. They use magic as a way of retribution, but even more as a means of creating some social equity. Done out of their rightful inheritance by an authoritarian leader, a corrupt landowner, a brutal patriarchal figure, the people use magic as a way of settling scores and carving out, however narrow, their own destinies. Ultima serves in this process, but she is also part of a larger group of *curanderas* who serve generally as watchdogs on an unjust society; and society from the Latino or Native-American point of view is always unjust. The title, then, of the Anaya novel is thickly textured; for "Bless Me" not only has the usual connotation of save my soul, but also my body, my spirit, my being in a society or community which would deny me what I am or could be. Magical realism, such as it is, works in many ways.

Anaya's *Alburquerque* (1992)[356] is a far more ambitious book than *Bless Me, Ultima*, so ambitious that it has trouble cohering. While it is about individuals, it also attempts to suck them into a mayoral election that will define the future of the city (presented in its old spelling). It attempts to define the challenges facing Chicanos and their culture-how to maintain the old traditions while confronted with the glistening new; but it spreads itself over several generation over illegitimacy and mixed parenting, over ownership of water rights, over city and pueblo life, over honest and dishonest politicians. Yet constant with its Latino origin is the theme of racial mixing and the mysteries and traditions behind the blending of black and white, Hispanic and Anglo.

Abrán Gonzales does not know who his father is, although he learns about his mother before she dies. He has been brought up by a Chicano couple in Albuquerque. The reader knows well, though, that his father is Ben Chavez, a close friend, and the man who having impregnated Cynthia, Abrán's mother, kept it a secret since it was a "shameful" coupling, she being upper-class Caucasian, he Chicano. So Abrán is mixed, as are several other characters.

The book works out best at the level of how the races are blended and how race shades off into "new" ethnic groupings. The shading, while creating racial animosity and hostility, nevertheless has become a fact of Latino life; and it carries both its burdens and virtues into American life that still resists color-oriented race mixing. In few other contemporary writers, except perhaps Asian-Americans, has this degree of racial blending been emphasized; surely not in African-Americans, nor in Native-Americans. The coupling produces a race of Americans which falls outside all clear definition, and that is the point; America, at least here, in this part of the country, has become a "new" race and calls for new traditions, memories, definitions. The Latino novel, as in the Anaya, does not call for a multi-cultural society; it announces that it has arrived. America, against its will, is being redefined.

Sandra Cisneros's *The House on Mango Street* moves in and out of these themes, although it lacks the pure "magic" of *santeria* or a *curandera*.[357] Here it is a magical house that saves, saves Esperanza (Hope) Cordero (Lamb). For her, Chicago slums are the trap that captures her spirit and snares her soul, eventually destroys her body. She is doubly and triply victimized, as a woman, by her lower class status, and by her race, caught as she is amidst racial animosity. She fits into no category which permits a pathway to success or even clear identity, since given all these negatives, she must struggle to remain alive, not to move ahead. Yet it is the house-aptly named on a fruit-fertility street-where she can clear away something she can call her own and survive on her terms, insofar as the neighborhood, the city, and, by implication, the country will allow her to survive.

Cisneros deconstructs the novel by creating Hispanic life, or elements of it, in very brief chapters, linked only by the voice of Esperanza. But while the method suggests constriction, the ground covered is quite broad, from crime to witch doctors, from men who die or simply vanish to those who plod on in the face of terrible odds. The sole anchor or rock on which this life is built, according to the voice, is the house itself. But the house is also something Esperanza needs to leave behind, for it is not hers, and it does not represent the kind of house she wants.

By leaving Mango Street-without denying that she always belongs to the street-she can come of age; and gaining another house is a rite of passage of sorts. But she has to avoid the passage made by many of her street friends, who use marriage as a means of escaping, only to find themselves imprisoned in another kind of house and street. For the Latino girl or young woman-as for female immigrants of an earlier era-the obstacles are enormous; in nearly every case where she seeks an example, she finds a woman entrapped-as Esperanza's own mother is. With a fine voice, two languages, and brains, the latter recognizes that her fate is Mango Street, a fate her daughter is desperate to avoid. America lies out there, but her quest is doubly difficult, inasmuch as she must seek America without forsaking Mango Street itself. All the old problems for the American remain: to become different even as one does not betray oneself, to hold to the old traditions and memories even as they no longer fully matter.

Bharati Mukherjee, an Indian from Calcutta transported to Canada and then the United States, has caught what seems to be intrinsic to the hyphenated Americans writing in the 80s and 90s. She speaks of the dilemma of those who experience a duality-Latinos, Asians, Natives-in their dealings with America. Such writers recognize that on one hand they are dispossessed, on the other not quite assimilable. For them that dual existence means they must reject minimalism (in which they would be chilled out) and strive for maximalism-that strategy which pits one kind or history (magic, mystery, and spirit) against the reality of America. For Mukherjee, that American reality must, ultimately, be the subject of the hyphenated- but as we see, it is not quite attainable. The "old," which she cites as "hokey concoctions" consisting of family memories and brief visits to ancestral villages, is a dead end.

Native-Americans, the other "Indians," would dispute her. In an early forerunner of the hyphenated genre, N. Scott Momaday in the 1968 novel, *House Made of Dawn*, explored the dual worlds of a young American Indian, Abel. The "old" was traditional, the world of fathers, memories, ceremonies; the "new" is beguiling: sexual experiences, indulgences, liberation of sorts.[358] This is, in brief, the confrontation, and it is not easily reconcilable, as we see in Leslie Marmon Silko's *Ceremony* in 1977[359] and her *Almanac of the Dead*, in 1991.[360] Although *Ceremony* derives from 1977, it fits well into the 90s scene, inasmuch as it accommodates well the politically correct context which has overwhelmed one sector of American culture. Yet the Silko book at the same time goes beyond political correctness; it becomes a valid way of looking at American life in the last two decades from the perspective of someone who belongs to two worlds and not quite to either.

Tayo, a Native-American, has fought in World War II, seen the worst mankind can do, and, having survived as a Japanese prisoner, returns to America a vegetable, having lost those closest to him. His condition is closer to what we find in Vietnam War literature than in Second World War fiction; but his post-traumatic stress disorder leaves him-as it did so many survivors of the later war-self-destructive and destructive. He is a ticking bomb, mainly in his denial of life, just another "drunken Indian," as he perceives himself and others view him. But slowly he comes into touch with himself through "ceremonies" (of the title), those Native rites that bring him back to roots and to something meaningful.

The ceremonies are holistic, in fact, and he comes to recognize that Japanese voices link with Laguna voices. When he sees that Los Alamos is on land taken from the Pueblo Indians, he "arrives at the point of convergence," wherein all voices are connected. Friends Josiah and Rocky and their lives, their line of cultures and worlds, all, are linked. "From that time on," Silko writes, "human beings were one clan, united by the fate the destroyers planned for all of them, for all living things; united by a circle of death that devoured people in cities twelve thousand miles away, victims who had never known these mesas, who had never seen the delicate colors of the rocks which boiled up their slaughter."[361] With this convergence of cultures and worlds, Tayo is on his way to recovery. He sees a pattern in the world that establishes the opposition between those voices (ceremonial) that save and those (mainly in the white world) that destroy.

This is an advocacy novel, but its chief component for the 80s and 90s is its plaint that we are destroying ourselves. These are not New Age ceremonies, not the mumbo-jumbo of Iron John, but the ancient ceremonies revived for those who need restoratives. These are not the ancient rites and traditions that infuse D. H. Lawrence's *The Plumed Serpent*, where ceremonies are merely a façade for a new fascistic order. In the Native-American version, the modern world kills, while ceremonies can possibly restore. With death, destruction, and modern life linked, salvation takes the form of returning to the older ways, eschewing the new and modern, and fitting oneself not into a new skin but into a former skin, which awaits the individual prepared to try it on.

A complicated version of old and new occurs in a strong first novel by Ron Querry. *The Death of Bernadette Lefthand* (1993);[362] complicated because while the old might appear to offer some grounding for the contemporary Native-American, the practical world is inexorable and it dooms. *Bernadette Lefthand* confronts the life of Apaches and Navajos on their reservation with the traditions and conventions carried over from past Indian life: reverence for mysteries: witchcraft, demons, exorcism. Ron Querry expertly molds one type of life to the other, so that the richness of the past is always contrasted with the seediness and sense of defeat for most Indians in the present. His method becomes, in this somewhat ironic way, typically American: Eden lost, Eden partially regained through traditional ceremonies, and then the realities-the murder of Bernadette Lefthand, the most beautiful young woman anyone has ever seen.

Her beauty is in one sense her downfall, adding to the allegorical dimension of the novel: that the losers of the Native-American world must make their mark by slashing the lovely face of someone who manages to straddle both Indian and white culture. Everything that appears optimistic or uplifting turns out to self-destruct. Querry narrates his story mainly from the point of view of Bernadette's sister, Gracie, after the murder; but he also includes an external commentary from Starr, a dissolute white woman with keen interest in Indian affairs, and one who foresees the doom awaiting Bernadette, the doom of anyone, in fact, caught between the two cultures.

Unlike most other novels in this vein-including those by white authors-Querry's offers only a modified ceremonial salvation. For while once the ceremonies functioned for older Native Americans, they have little validity for the younger generation. For them,

America is doom! A caustic commentator might say that that was pre-casino!

On the surface, the Asian-American experience seems concerned with fairly narrow matters, individual identity but not larger American issues; yet identity becomes a trope which allows for some larger generalities. What is the role of the individual whose skin color, racial mixture, un-American-sounding name are unique in American society? Earlier, masses of immigrants were white, however darkish their skin; their racial background tended to be settled; they derived from a geographical location that was identifiable. For Asian-Americans, everything seems out of synch: looks and skin color, possibly language confusions, racial mixtures that are hard to explain,[363] an older generation that remains linguistically isolated, expectations that clash with older ways. These are the concerns of all immigrants, only here more intensely. While stories of most of these writers focus on the incompatibility of their own lives with a dominant American culture, they are really talking about large sectors of the country. For a "dominant" culture is only a partial perception, and these Asian-Americans are not so much the anomaly they perceive themselves as being, as they are part of the shift in American demographics and culture.

Aside from the more well-recognized and received writers, such as Amy Tan, Diane Chang, Jose Garcia Villa (Filipino), Maxine Hong Kingston, and Bharati Mukherjee, most are concerned with victimization as their story. While describing their lives as Japanese, Chinese, Korean, Philippine, South Asian, they are also concerned, in a more general way, with their inability to penetrate what they still see as a dominant culture: white, mainstream, Christian, dysfamilial. Like Native-Americans and Latinos, they are caught between traditional mores and what seems the freer dominant culture, in this respect replicating earlier immigrant novels in which generational struggles reflected tradition versus individual emergence.

Frequently, as in David Wong Louie's "Pangs of Love," the

pull from family members creates enormous dilemmas, or else establishes pitfalls for the young person in an America where family is disposable. Or as in Shawn Wong's "Eye Contact," from *American Knees*,[364] the manner of meeting another Asian, when one is half white and half Asian, becomes a metaphysical journey into the nature of identity and, ultimately of being. The various shades of being, half this, half that, whether the Asian half is Korean, Japanese, or Chinese-and then the permutations which occur with the "other," the potential mate-consume all the air in the relationship, make it tentative at best, finally impossible.

One has expectations from every direction, which obviously cannot be met, on either side; understanding is itself out of the question since the other's "location" is not identifiable. These are variations on the old immigrant experiences, but also different because of color and culture: much more virulent and subtle than, say, the differences between Eastern European and German Jews, often based on class, or northern and southern Italians, also class. The subtleties for Asians lie in thousands of years of condescension and hatred for the "other": the ethnic pecking order in which all the Asian nationalities prioritize their own place, as in the ongoing war between Chinese and Japanese culture, and the interpositioning of World War II in which the Japanese committed genocide wherever they went, especially in China, Korea, and Singapore. All of these carry a very different cultural freight. Comparably, any effort to seek linkages among Asian groups is tentative, since so many histories clash: Vietnamese and Chinese, Japanese and Chinese and Korean, Cambodian and Vietnamese. With history balkanizing memory and tradition, even the more general fact of Asian identity is a chimaera. While American schools attempt to homogenize discordant groups, neighborhoods, parents, and ethnic traditions keep them separate.

For example, with Japanese-Americans, the defining moment in their experience is Kafkaesque, quite different from what Koreans (whom we fought), Chinese (whom we fought in the Korean War), and Filipinos (our allies, but a colonial protectorate) have experienced. The defining Kafkaesque moment for the Japanese-American writer is the detention or concentration camp, the large-scale movement of Japanese-American citizens from their homes into refugee or displacement camps at the start of World War II. This is the central trope in the life and memory of their grandparents, parents, or, in some instances, themselves. David Mura, in "Fictive Fragments of a Father and Son," captures the moment:

> One day, K. steps out of his door to find a notice: he must report to the authorities. Who are the authorities? He does not know, only that he must report to them. When he reports to them, they give him a number, tell him to come back tomorrow. When he comes back the next day, he is taken by bus to a train and then by train to a place with others who have been given numbers and notices. He realizes he has been imprisoned. He is no longer singular, no longer private. The communal beds, shower stalls and toilets only confirm this, as do the barbed wire and rifle towers with guards. What is his crime? He is K. That is his crime.[365]

He adds: "My father's name was originally Katsuji Uyemura. Then Tom Katsuji Uyeumura. Then Tom Katsuji Mura. Then Tom K. Mura." He asks: "What is the job of the son of K.? To forgive his crime? To try him again?"[366]

Yet we would be remiss to see this as solely a Japanese experience. It colors all Asians-because of their "difference," the mystique surrounding their perceived separation, their seemingly inexplicable cultural traditions and ceremonies. They remain foreign, "other," people unlike any others, and, therefore, those who can be detained in camps as so-called subverters of the very America they have embraced.

As a consequence, Asian-American fiction seems in a transitional period: preoccupied with questions of identity and the dilemmas attendant upon living in a white American culture,

461

but not yet concerned sufficiently with larger questions which go beyond the Asian community into America as an entity. We do not find as yet any searching Asian-American-or Latino-fiction equivalent to our Mega-Novels, which probe the very soul of the country. There is, however, an expanding genre of "Growing Up" fictionalized memoirs, which extend from personal to more general pain and anguish, which say something about America and its children, America and its poor, America and its underclasses. Yet, in the main, Asians seem isolated in their world, even when the writers are second and third generation Americans. They have yet by the middle 90s to emerge fully into the chaos that lies outside of their sense of internal chaos.

Despite the infusion of energy from ethnic groups, the most insistent voice in late 80s and 90s fiction is one of grief and grieving. It is as though the writers had all read Freud's "Mourning and Melancholia" and, having bypassed mourning, headed directly into melancholia. As we have observed, end-of-the-century exhaustion is an insufficient explanation, although the idea of a society or country "running down" is not to be discounted. More than that, however, is needed to interpret the depression of the writers, their loss of sparkle, their effort to delineate a minimal life, or even death, as text and subtext of their fictions. What we have, we must assume, is a perception of a reality based not only on the passing of an era, but also on profound uncertainties. Nearly all institutions, the state, the government, the very idea of society present instability. Lack of confidence in *everything* underscores the perception; and what is more, there is no hope of meaningful change. The stock market is up, the unemployment rate is down, the mid-decade economy seems strong, the United States is the indisputable leader of the free world, nearly all markers (except the leadership) seem positive-and yet none of this seems to bear on the general pessimism of our writers. Do they inhabit a different country?

May we posit a kind of mass melancholia? This is what Freud described: "The distinguishing mental features of melancholia are a profoundly painful defection, abrogation of interest in the outside world, loss of capacity to love, inhibiting of all activity, and a lowering of the self-regarding feelings to a degree that finds utterance in self-reproaches and self-revilings, and culminates in a delusional expectation of punishment."[367] The "delusional expectation" Freud speaks of can be translated into the many death images our writers have projected: death of self, death of century, implied death of all social-community life, death of state as we have known it. Melancholia, if our writers are correct, has spread throughout the land like a plague.

Yet any explanation, even one based on mass uncertainties, is inadequate unless we tie explanation to expectation. We may be suffering melancholia because we either expected too much or we misread the markers on which expectations were based, or both. We were bamboozled by success, progress, economic gain; we felt re-entry into Eden was possibly imminent. In any event, we had thought highly of ourselves at mid-century, and we assumed that solutions to problems personal and social were at hand. Letdown was inevitable. Even the less liberal of our writers threw off Calvinistic restraints on expectation and embraced, not the damnation of the soul, but the salvation of the body; and the more liberal believed in traditional reason, common sense, and a pragmatic, benevolent government. It was, all in all, a chimaera; if not that, an outright hoax, with the Vietnam War the pivotal point. Payment came near the century's end, with disdain, withdrawal, denial, depression, and melancholia. Nothing seemed simple; nothing was. The writers were turning from solutions and offering, instead, closure. Real closure, death without resurrection!

What better way to end a decade on the dissonances and paradoxes of American life than with *Galatea 2.2*[368] by Richard Powers, whose name has already surfaced several times in this book? *Galatea 2.2* helps establish the culture we have come from and darkly foreshadows where we are going; and with its large doses of mourning and melancholia, it also fits into the crater-like, yawning crevices characteristic of the contemporary experience. It is a summation, if such a thing is possible, of several defining elements: the cultural battle, now intensified, between scientific knowledge and literary or spiritual quests; the conflicts implicit in language itself, our language(s) as triumphant in suggesting but deficient in communicating; the unresolvable opposition between things (matter, possessions, goods) and ideas (the shape of the self, the individual quest for respect); the ongoing struggle among personality types, really a struggle to define whose country it is-those who can adapt to both work and play, those misfits who fall outside all systems, and those somewhere in between who wander directionless. The novel becomes an ominous sounding board for the Nineties, mainly because it reveals all the abysses.

Galatea, we recall, is the statue of a maiden carved in ivory by Pygmalion, who falls in love with it, and it is then given life by Aphrodite (or Venus). This is Powers's primary use of the name. But in Ovid, Galatea is a sea-nymph (daughter of Nereus and Doris), who loves Acis. Polyphemus, a Cyclops and son of Poseidon, is jealous of Acis and crushes him under a rock. His blood gushes out and becomes, through Galatea, the river Acis, at the foot of Mt. Aetna. This, too, figures in Powers's novel, although more obliquely. The numbers "2.2" are a program, for Galatea here is nothing less than a super-computer, named Helen. Helen, also, is a name of some resonance, calling up the beautiful "witch" whose loveliness and seductiveness made men go to war over her. And now to the computer, Pygmalion's "get" and Polyphemus's "revenge."

As a super-computer, Helen has an outreach of almost unlimited capability. This is, of course, its seductive power, its infinite possibilities, and its attraction for the decade of the 90s. As greater levels of infinitude open up, the more mysterious Helen becomes, even when she balks or becomes confused at the information fed her. As we move headlong into a computer culture, with modems and webs, internets and artificial intelligence, we have discovered new spatial arenas, the new frontiers of cyberspace,[369] and beyond that languages which put at risk our easy assumptions of what words mean or point to. Our entire culture is recreating itself in the insides of a machine that is almost human in its possibilities; a machine which, if programmed with the right touch (an artistic gesture there), will yield hitherto undiscovered territory. Helen raises ultimate questions, one of them being where life ends (or begins) and the computer ends or begins.

The narrator himself (Powers) falls under the obsessive power of the computer maven Philip Lentz, who has the idea of making the computer into a thinking element that can handle the multiple meanings of Great Books, especially poetry with its ambiguous meanings. Lentz's idea is to hook up a huge computer with thousands of subsidiaries, until through neural networks, the New Age Helen will have the interpretive intelligence of a "great reader."

Running parallel to this quest, in which Richard Powers becomes enthralled by Lentz's obsession, is his periodic effort to retrieve his own past, in the affair with C., a ten-year affair with his former student, which took them to the Netherlands. In this parallel movement but caught in different chronologies, Powers learned another language, Dutch, in much the same way that he and Lentz are trying to program Helen to learn another language. Powers's relationship with C-nearly all relationships are dehumanized to initials-is undermined by her quest to self-destruct, the opposite of Helen's effort to succeed. Since C. cannot stand achievement, she becomes displaced by Helen, who has an understanding that Powers comes to respect and accept. Helen, of course, is still artificial; she needs more, more human cynicism.

> ... What she needed, in order to forgive our race and live here in peace, was faith's flip side. She needed to hear about that animal fastened to a soul that, for the first time, allowed the creature to see through soul's parasite eyes how terrified it was, how forsaken. I needed to tell her that miraculous banality, how body stumbled by selection onto the stricken celestial, how it taught itself to twig time and what lay beyond time.[370]

What Helen cannot understand, yet, what "hung her up was divinity doing itself in with tire irons."[371]

But Powers's achievement in bringing together a computer and the ironic realities of human life goes further. He has created a prose that is just off center, as the above passage suggests: "soul's parasite yes," "stumbled by selection onto the stricken celestial," "to twig time." The edginess and unevenness of the prose suggests an uncertainty which the text of the novel supports. Coming near the end of the century, Powers must measure man's achievement against machines, a David and Goliath shootout. In the common view, of course, machines have pre-empted human lives, created corpses, strewn them around, and abandoned them to the vultures. Helen has the capacity to do this-to transform the finest expression of the human race, its multi-leveled poetry, into a digitalized "comprehension"; so that the very poetry of the poetry is mechanized. In this view, Powers would be part of the Luddite generation: those who observe machines as destructive and who find they must destroy them before they are themselves destroyed.

But this is not his point at all. He is far more cynical, less idealistic, more attuned to the failure of human endeavors. For he sees in Helen the potentiality for getting to the bottom of human feeling and fear; its propensity to learn, to accumulate capacity, and then to destroy itself. Helen, somehow, needs not to be discarded or subverted but to be upgraded until it can enter fully into the bilious human condition. To paraphrase the specious reasoning of the gun lobby, machines don't kill, people kill; which is another way of saying that Helen, or the Galatea of the title, once programmed with 2.2, has a life of her own. And it is not common sense to struggle against her, but to continue to recreate her until she is, finally, given life by Aphrodite, or gushes like Acis. This is one way to end the century, in indeterminate territory between bang and whimper.

THREE MEGAS, AND THE MILLENNIUM

Don DeLillo's *Underworld* (1997)[372] comes close to being an all-inclusive novel for the Nineties. It starts on October 3, 1951, with the shot heard round the world, Bobby Thomson's home run in the ninth inning that gave the New York Giants the victory over the Brooklyn Dodgers in the pennant playoff. The ball Thomson hit becomes perhaps the most famous baseball in history, and the way it moves through America and touches a multitude of people forms the spine of DeLillo's book. He traverses vast distances, but so does that single shot, that ball, that day, that event, making it a day people remember the way they recall where they were when John F. Kennedy was shot. The two shots, at some point, become interchangeable, one killing the President, the other killing the Dodgers and their fans' hopes. In one sequence, in fact, some people distantly touched by the Thomson shot watch the Zagruder tape, speeded up, slow-motioned, played at regular speed in which Kennedy's head is blown apart, seemingly from the front (which fits the conspiracy theory). Similarly, Thomson's shot is played and replayed at different speeds in people's minds, as baseball becomes an insistent emblem of larger American life.

Yet a baseball and a shot are not the sole metaphors DeLillo hangs *Underworld* on-another is waste, or, simply, garbage. Garbage is everywhere; it appears to be the means by which our society survives. Entire civilizations are constructed on how they responded to garbage disposal, and no civilization more than America depends on waste disposal. Floating through the novel, as it did through the waterways of the world, is a garbage-laden barge of New York waste, turned away at every port and somehow indicative of how consumerism had led to waste-ism. Garbage is linked, of course, to excrement, each being what is forced out, an emblem of how a society turns matter into waste, substance into filth.

By way of narrative process with baseball and waste matter as his twin metaphors, DeLillo has continued the Mega-Novel. *Underworld* fits the model; it is both spatially and temporally adventurous, with time shifts as well as geographical changes. The novel roams the country, in different time zones, in differing years, and by the end it roams the world, in an epilogue about nuclear bombs being used in Kazakhstan to blow up the world's nuclear waste. If there were a third emblem in the novel, it would be nuclear power, its actuality and its potential. On the day Thomson hit his historical homer, the Soviets exploded a nuclear device. But the bomb, which broke the American monopoly on nuclear power, had to take second place to the demise of the Dodgers and the Giants' victory. In a way, the threading of the nuclear threat through the novel, culminating in the Epilogue, fits well into the Mega-Novel dimensions of *Underworld*: nuclear potential suggests vast space, countries warring in the heavens, and the Mega-Novel is nothing if not spatial, vast, oceanic, with no possibility of completion or resolution.

But the novel is far more than a free flowing, interrupted, often skewed narrative. There are brilliant set pieces, all continuous with DeLillo's ability to find emblematic scenes that capture the odd "underworld" as aspects of American life. Klara Sax, connected to the main character by a kind of string theory, has organized a crew which paints World War Two planes that have been decommissioned by the Air Force and given to her for refurbishment. Deep in the desert, she works to bring something inorganic and rusting back to life-to give the planes some of the grandeur they once had, and to remind the viewer that the planes, now dead on the ground, were once saviors of the American dream. DeLillo recreates this bizarre scene without sentimentality or even nostalgia, but with a hard-edged wit: that the woman, slightly off balance and not a little obsessive, yet has a grand vision. And that vision is one of the country, not to let brilliant metals decline into rust, not to make things part of a throwaway culture, not to permit everything to decline into waste. The theme of refurbishment of the old and useless is part of the waste theme; only here it is to delay waste, deep in a desert area where possibly no one cares except Klara and her motley crew.

In a later scene, which mirrors this one, DeLillo moves his main figure, Nick Shay, to Kazakhstan, described as a forlorn place, a desert, deep into nowheresville, like Klara Sax's location. In Kazakhstan, the "waste" is more sinister throwaway, nuclear matter, and it is imported from all over the world-by an organization called Tchaika (seagull, ironically recalling Chekhov), a capitalistic venture in the new Russia. Once the nuclear waste is organized, it is destroyed, seemingly, by nuclear blasts, although the implication is that even more waste is created. The blasts are underground, but as DeLillo demonstrated in *White Noise*, toxic fumes have already transformed towns and villages into horror stories of disfigured babies and children. Here, waste not only overtakes civilization, it destroys as much as weapons themselves do.

In the earliest segments, DeLillo presents a different kind of scene, one that is balletic, graceful, and witty, recalling to some degree the choreography of Jerome Robbins in *West Side Story*. Instead of gangs dancing their way toward the audience, DeLillo has a group of young black kids running to the turnstiles of the Polo Grounds, hoping to gain free entrance by jumping the turnstiles. While many try, only a few will get through, and Cotter Martin is one of them. He is the key figure, since once he is positioned in the stands, he grabs the ball Bobby Thomson has hit to win the pennant for the Giants. The ball, having become one of the most prized of collectibles, is secured by an inner-city kid, whose father-one of the few stereotypical figures in DeLillo-steals the ball and sells it for drinking money. The sneaking into the ballpark, the maneuvering for a seat, the struggle for the ball, the chase by a white man into Harlem, the father's theft of the ball-all these activities come as the consequence of a legendary event, one that grows in the American mind and in the metanarrative of the novel itself.

The seemingly skewed individual scenes gain strength because, with typical DeLillo indirection, they link up with the major lines, about waste, the making of a legend, the weirdness of American life, the psychodrama being played out in unlikely locations, in activities which enable people to go on who otherwise might not. We recognize that the sense of America lies in individual lives, not in a sum total. DeLillo has caught the Nineties, angular, bifocaled, subcultured, divisible, lacking center or core, caught in a drift that neither fervent religion, nor morality, nor discipline, nor prosperity can salvage. There is the whiff of death, as expected when a country is ending, but DeLillo suggests the death starts much earlier, not in the Nineties, but in the Fifties, the time of seeming recovery.

One way to read the Thomson homer is of course as victory under extreme circumstances, but another way is to see it as defeat at the last moment, a monumental defeat especially for a Dodger team which late in the season had a 13½-game lead over the Giants, only to blow it. That the shot heard round the world came as the Soviets set off their own shot indicates, not triumph, but a world complicated beyond redemption. In brief, predictability vanishes; triumph and defeat are intertwined.

Underworld speaks of that "other," nether world, suggested by Sergei Eisenstein's silent film *Unterwelt*, whose footage was hidden away in an East Berlin vault. Since it deals with people living in the shadows, the film is subversive of all normalizing behavior, another emblem for DeLillo of how life is being played out beneath America's bourgeois surface. *Unterwelt*, made in the Thirties, satirizes totalitarian regimes, whether Stalin's or Hitler's; Eisenstein as a revered Russian showing the "other" side of Stalinism, but using a German title to implicate a rising Hitler. Eisenstein's creatures, DeLillo writes, "humped and scuttled through the shadows, humplurched with hands dragging, and you can always convince yourself it's okay to laugh at cripples and mutants if everybody else is laughing. . . ."[373] One thinks of Döblin's *Alexanderplatz, Berlin* (1929), which, when made by Fassbinder for German television, was all shadows, underworld life, people slinking and scuttling through streets. What connection, we ask, does this have to DeLillo's main line, especially to baseball? Like so many other scenes-one involving a wall of death and a graffiti artist, the doomed young craftsman Moonman-there is a skewed, marginal linkage to waste, to a game lost as well as won, to the suggestion of entropy, a running down, a transformation of consumerism into garbage-ism. DeLillo has always been noted for creating that "other" world-the Reverend Moon traducing the sense of marriage by marrying at one time thousands of couples, or a toxic cloud upsetting a comfortable bourgeois life in a college town, or a professor of Hitler Studies at a university, an expert on German history, who does not speak German, or a vast conspiracy working to make Oswald the fall guy in the Kennedy assassination.

The Moonman, mentioned above, creates an art form out of graffiti on a wall commemorating young lives ended abruptly. Here, too, is waste, only here preserved in a memorial on an inner city wall, not to be forgotten as waste normally is. Moonman also does subway cars, not to desecrate them, but to turn them into carefully painted art objects, dressing up an underworld into something transformed. At sixteen, Moonman-Ismael Muñoz-attempts to light up with neon paint what is gloomy and otherwise lost to death and burial. The wall is permitted, but his work on the subways is obviously illegal-and yet it follows another law, that of art transforming the world's dross, even resurrecting the dead. Once again DeLillo has spread his network of skewed interests, so that Moonman is somehow a distant relative of Cotter Martin, another inner city boy who becomes alive when he grabs the soon-to-be legendary ball. Klara-Cotter-Moonman, and a horde of others, are linked in that nether world DeLillo depicts as somehow more intense and emotionally crowded than the more mundane world lying above ground. He leads us into the new century, not with a straightforward story, but with dark possibilities.

If David Foster Wallace's *Infinite Jest* (1996)[374] were to be compared to a painting, it would fit well with Jackson Pollock's "drip" work of the late 40s and early 50s, something like "Blue Poles" or "Lavender Mist: No 1" or "Full Fathom Five." In both mediums, Wallace and Pollock allow for immense free form within a plan or pattern that distinguishes random acts from a form of art. Pollock's paintings suggest everywhere and everything, a consuming hunger to include, but there is a controlling, limiting conception buried in the work; so too, Wallace's novel, more postmodern even than Pollock, purports to go everywhere, seemingly scattered like dripping paint, and yet with a controlling pattern behind it.

The fact there is control does not mean one can necessarily pinpoint it. For Wallace, the "control" often bleeds over into postmodern, or post-postmodern, an eclecticism of forms; or else a kind of deference to Gaddis and Pynchon for their wildness of vision held together by precision of language. Little of this answers the question of control in Wallace, or Pollock, and yet we keep searching. If we take Pollock first, we see a pattern in his most famous painting, "Blue Poles." Here he segments different color areas with black "poles" rising from the bottom of the canvas toward the top, without quite reaching it.

In these segmented color fields we have Pollack's wildness, as it were, a frenzy which is bounded and controlled by streaks of yellow and red, against backgrounds of color fields that look like territories seen from an airplane bomb site. The painting as a whole opens up to light and then darkens down as the eye moves across the black. What is clearly a flat surface comes alive as the viewer sweeps across and up and down-so that flatness is belied by intense movement, like so many tiny snakes moving simultaneously along the canvas.

So, too, Wallace's novel. Impossible to summarize-intentionally an artifact of tentacles and traces which cannot be retold-it is, nevertheless, like Pollock, narrated and re-narrated. "Blue Poles" is a repeat story, with each segment a reprise of a contiguous one, sameness and difference, spoken and respoken. In *Infinite Jest*, we have the story of the tennis academy, which is attached to a private school run more as a corporate entity dedicated to turning out top tennis players than to an institution of learning. In various degrees, the players, but especially Hal Incandenza-named after the computer in Stanley Kubrich's *2001*?-are on dope, with Hal detailing lovingly how he gets hold of and enjoys grass. Then we learn that Hal's family is dysfunctional in a sensational way-father disappeared, younger brother handicapped, older brother fleeing. Juxtaposed to the tennis academy is a halfway house, both AA and NA, with its cast of Pynchon-like addicts and castoffs. There is also a video, the so-called "Infinite Jest," which has obsessed those who see it, for they cannot stop watching it. Any effort, however, to sort out the major lines is discouraged, since the book works by way of flashbacks within flashbacks (Hal's father and grandfather, for example), innumerable interpolations and interruptions, narrative looping which makes much of the looping in Woolf and Joyce seem by comparison realistic and reasonable. Even helpful hints along the way, or in the extensive notes, are merely weak guidelines.

The aim, therefore, is not chiefly to sort things out-although a reader's guide to the novel would be helpful-but to try to understand how and why the novel is presented this way. One seeks metaphysical meaning more than narrative or novelistic logic. The torrential matter-recalling Gaddis's *J R* and parts of *The Recognitions*-is not only a kaleidoscope of American life and practice, but also an unsolvable, virtually impenetrable world of behavior. So many subcultures and subgroups exist parallel to each other that the country cannot be captured in any coherent way. Wallace's method is not to bring order to disorder, but to reveal disorder so broad that even the novelist's efforts to achieve some order cannot prevail.

This latter point needs development. Most fictions, even Pynchon's and Gaddis's, have a metanarrative and some resolution, although not an easy finality or the one expected in mainstream fiction. Traditionally, novels close down, even though the Mega-Novel premise is that such fictions could continue, theoretically, forever, like Scheherazade's tales. Wallace clearly breaks with that sense of finality; his disorder is of such magnitude that any effort to harness, by the author or by an outside force, is futile. The novel reads like an acid high, colors, hallucinations, improvisation, feverish images, a rush of energy and words, as in jazz, an incoherence, seemingly, that is part of dream, disorder run amuck. More than Gaddis or Pynchon, his obvious sources, Wallace permits disorder to become the norm, not as some overarching idea but as an integral part of the way people live and manage their lives. One of his favorite words is annular and variations upon it which in itself suggests forms of circularity and circuitry caught in a continuum.

Is disorder, we may ask, an adequate mode of typifying the Nineties, or does it more closely recall the Sixties, which at first sight seems to be Wallace's beat? Or should we characterize the book as an epiphenomenon, something "beyond," rather than as an element that generically fits in the novel, however broad, wide, and deep we consider that genre? Or is it part of millennial fiction, the repository of final things? As a phenomenon or millennial artifact, *Infinite Jest* becomes an exercise in language, on the order of *Ulysses* or even some of Beckett, with Wallace not forging a new language of sounds and connotations as did Joyce and Beckett, but using arcane words and technical language as if he were reinventing the ordinary lingo of ordinary speakers. He is quite witty, for example, in parodying the governmental use of acronyms. As a phenomenon, epi-or otherwise, *Infinite Jest* makes clear we cannot read in the usual way, seeking meaning from narrative and metanarrative, and all that accrues to that. We read, instead, for segments, for individual passages of wit, for bursts of sparkling and biting commentary, for ways of indulging a runaway verbal facility that has decided to call itself a novel. Once again, the parallel to Pollock's drip paintings is suitable, since they, too, are epiphenomenal-certainly a break even with the action painting, or abstract expressionism, of Rothko and others. Wallace drips words, waves of foamy words, as if from buckets; not grasping language, but letting go and evacuating.

More than Joyce or Beckett, more appropriate might be Rabelais, his explosive exuberance, his bursts of inspired prose, his ability to get beyond the ordinary and to make exaggeration seem normal. Gargantuan and Pantegruel are larger than life, and so is the voice-not the characters-in *Infinite Jest*. As we see in the following passage, Wallace impresses us as so volcanic and oceanic that words on the page, the page itself, the novel as form are all inadequate for him to express himself. At the AA and NA center:

> ... Of one local underground stelliform offshoot from the Bob Hope-worshipping Rastafarians who smoked enormous doobsters and wove their Negroid hair into clusters of wet cigars like the Rastafarians but instead of Rastafarians these post Rastas worshipped the Infant [as part of a cult] and every New Year donned tie-dyed parkas and cardboard snowshoes and ventured northward, trailing smoke, past the walls and fans of Checkpoint Pongo into the former areas of VT and NH [we are in a future time], seeking *The Infant* they called it, as if there were only One, and toting paraphernalia a cultish ritual referred to in oblique tones only as *Propitiating the Infant*, whole posses of these stelliform pot-head reggae-swaying Infant-cultists disappearing forever off the human race's radar every winter, never heard or smelled again, regarded by fellow cultists as martyrs and/or lambs, possibly too addled by blimp-sized doobsters to find their way back out of the Concavity [the area north of Boston] and freezing to death, or enswarmed by herds of feral pets, or shot by property-value-conscious insects, or... (face plum-colored, finally breathing) worse.[375]

Not the reinventer of words like Joyce, Pound, or Beckett, Wallace is the accumulator of the detritus of our postward civilization. He knows well where myths and cults meet as shams. His discontent falls well outside any theorizing, whether Marx or Freud or any anti-or pro-; rather, it accrues from a desire to capture it *all* in its foulness, foolishness, and its humanity. Segments are headed by the parodic "Year of the Depend Adult Undergarment," a sendup of advertising. Wallace seems much more at home with the rehab centers than he does with the tennis academy, which often reads like a stretch. He digs into the rehabilitated Gately more than he can encompass Hal and his dysfunctional family. For Wallace, dafiness trumps malfunction. His deployment of the several steps toward rehab at the AA and NA center are brilliantly depicted as embodied in Gately, an ungainly, huge, mess of a man; and the other messes such as Lenz and Green who show up at the center are similarly treated with a depth of humanity that is lacking when Wallace comes to tennis.

The juxtaposition of the two centers, tennis and rehab, are not symmetrical. Wallace uses every particular case as a comic riff to move on to the edges and margins of tragic lives and their stories. The idea is sweep, the ingathering of a large number of lives: the athletes at the tennis academy, the addicts at the rehab center, marginal figures of every type of degradation: psychopaths, sociopaths, reinvented creatures, poseurs, confidence men and women, figures in high position, the homeless and depraved. The possibilities include the discrete, maniacal detail the last few decades have thrown at us. History is furious: Wallace moves into nuclear waste, for example-like DeLillo, he is a big garbage man-and has picked up all the devastation that tests have incurred, going back to testing in the 1950s. This is an America caught up by a myriad of contradictions that lie just below the mean point of American bourgeois life, and especially in the comfortable Nineties.

Nothing, apparently, is what it seems, and this is the world the novelist gets at. The tennis academy, for one, is superficially a sign of American health and productivity, its players often winners in national tournaments and emblems of health. But beneath that surface, the archeologist Wallace digs, and what he discovers is distinctly another America. Hal smokes grass whenever he can find the moment; others drink themselves into oblivion; still others are more inventive and commit suicide; some barely make it onto the court, so caught up as they are in psychological problems. The academy, we come to recognize, is a twin of the rehab center; while it does not directly rehabilitate, it provides a patina of conformity (its own "steps") and so-called sane living-the discipline of landing a ball in a particular spot on a court-over what is really just another snake pit.

Wallace often strives too hard to penetrate that patina, so that the riffs, both short and long, get further and further away from anything compelling. As in the following: "Lenz [at the AA center] tells Green how once he was at a Halloween party where a hydrocephalic woman wore a necklace made of dead gulls."[376] Or shortly before that, the rat story with Lenz as principal.[377] Or just before that, the riff about the cleaning woman who is almost electrocuted when she touches a hot knob intended for someone else.[378] There are dozens of such examples. Wallace never saw an eruption he didn't like; he never saw an objectionable act he didn't want to reproduce. Puke and vomit are never sufficient; excrement, saliva, blood, semen, vaginal discharge, menstrual blood are intermixed into the lives of the characters, especially, of course, those in and around the rehab centers. The reach toward comedy frequently overreaches.

When Wallace strains too hard for comedic effect, the humor becomes sophomoric. A segment on beds, for example, about halfway through *Infinite Jest* misses both as comedy and as an element linked to Wallace's larger plans. It fits only as disorder, but of a kind that does not validate the seven or eight thousand words expended on it. The making of beds, the taking apart of beds, with mattresses turning to sponges and jelly, accompanied by failed maneuvers to discard parts fails not only as comedy but heads nowhere, a digression for the sake of digression. Such segments, while not fulfilling any comic or dramatic function, recur like fraternity house humor, riffs out of control. Yet they persist as part of Wallace's emphasis on vaguary, disorder, the mayhem of everyday life, a kind of existential absurdity and randomness.

It is clear that even as we dismiss some hijinks Wallace's paradigm was one of inclusion. Exclusion would mean selection, and while of course he is selecting, he must give the appearance of all-ness, in a postmodern version of Thomas Wolfe's obsession with consuming everything by way of words. Wallace, in fact, recalls Wolfe, as a hungry artist (not a hunger artist) whose appetite is so unfulfilled he must keep going. Since he cannot forgo the opportunity to tell a story, *Infinite Jest* can be viewed less as "novel"-however defined-than as a sequence of short stories or riffs, or unleashed verbal segments. These stories attempt, like Wolfe, to encompass America, particularly its underside and its more horrific failures. While people in higher places are ridiculed-Wallace's social sympathies are evident-those with disabilities and personal weaknesses (alcohol, drugs, crimes) are treated with sympathy and even empathy. America is kaleidoscopic, impenetrable, indescribable, divisible into miniscule elements, segmented and hierarchical. *Infinite Jest* reflects everything America tries to disguise in its presentation of itself as the world's supreme victor. The world's greatest, here, is imploding into segments which do not mesh, do not function, do not cohere, and which, each in its way, is a form of disease (from tennis to heroin). Discontented is this civilization, and, in many instances, beyond repair. Wallace has the last word:

> ... The last rotating sight [for Gately] was the chinks coming back through the door, holding big shiny squares of the room. As the floor wafted up and C's [Bobby C., a thuggish addict] grip finally gave, the last thing Gately saw was an Oriental bearing down with the held square and he looked into the square and saw clearly a reflection of his own big square pale head with its eyes closing as the floor finally pounced. And when he came back to, he was on his back on the beach in the freezing sand, and it was raining out of a low sky, and the tide was way out.[379]

Way out!

Thomas Pynchon's *Mason & Dixon* (1997)[380] is based on journeys by two Englishmen, first to Sumatra, then to St. Helena and the Cape of Good Hope, finally to the New World, where they surveyed and drew the line dividing North from South, the so-named Mason-Dixon line. Journeys are at their most fundamental "stories," and so the Pynchon novel is about stories; maybe not "about" stories, but stories themselves. If we posit the contents of the novel this way, we can see continuity with his previous fiction, whether the stories making up *Vineland* or those in his earlier work, especially the story segments accumulated in *Gravity's Rainbow*. As in all Mega-Novels, they can go on indefinitely, as Pynchon recognizes:

> As all History must converge to Opera, in the Italian Style, however, their Tale as Commemorated might have to proceed a bit more hopefully. Suppose that Mason and Dixon and their Line cross Ohio after all, and continue West by the customary ten-minute increments–each installment of the Story finding the Party advanc'd into yet another set of lives, another Difficulty to be resolv'd before it can move on again. Behind, in pursuit, his arrangements undone, pride wounded, comes Sir William Johnson, play'd as a Lunatick Irishman, riding with a cadre of close Indian Friends,–somehow, as if enacting a discarded draft of Zeno's Paradox, never quite successful in attacking even the rearmost of the Party's stragglers, who remain ever just out of range. Yet at any time, we are led to believe, the Pursuers *may* catch up, and compel the Surveyors, to return behind the Warrior Path.[381]

Once we locate Pynchon in stories, we can understand what made him take up a pseudo eighteenth-century dialogue and narrative for *Mason & Dixon*. For just as he had used a California hip and be-bop style for *Vineland* and *The Crying of Lot 49*, or a more scientifically-oriented style for *Gravity's Rainbow*, so here, in *Mason & Dixon*, we have a manner, a style, a linguistics, so to speak, that approximates what may have been eighteenth-century speech. Slang and literary mannerisms intermix.

Of course, this is not really eighteenth-century speech. It is Pynchon speech, what we have become accustomed to from *V.* on. Pynchon speech always has an edge of irony and wit, and here it is aided by the use of capital letters for most nouns, as in the Germanic fashion. Ordinary nouns are not capitalized, as we see at the beginning of Chapter 30; "day" remains small-lettered, as is "rule" and several others. Others, however stand out.

> Upon the day appointed, pursuant to the Chancery Decision, the Commissioner of both Provinces, with Remembrancer and Correspondents, attended by a Thronglet of Children out of School, Sailors, Irishmen, and other Citizens exempt from or disobedient to the humorless role of Clock-Time here, all go trouping down to Cedar Street and House in Question, to establish the north Wall officially as the southernmost Point of Philadelphia. Fifteen Miles South of this, to the width of a Red Publick Hair or R. P. H. will the West Line [the Mason-Dixon line] run.[382]

Capitalization has its ambiguities, since it makes things not only more visible but also more pronounced when they might have been swallowed up. The word "Thronglet" is one such instance: a word hardly in ordinary usage that by virtue of being capitalized becomes part of a witty undertext to the passage. We may, in fact, see capitalization as a form of wit, because it turns the ordinary into seeming significant, the small into the large; and it disorders the page, since the reader, unless perusing a German text, does not expect nouns to appear like advertising.

Although Pynchon touches on many of the historical events which pass before the surveyors' eyes–slavery, colonial domination, acts of revenge and sadism, all varieties of high and low life–he is more interested in getting the feel of the culture of pre-Revolutionary America than of purely historical contexts. The multiplicity of personal narratives recalls the picaresque fictions of the eighteenth century and earlier, which in their extended, elongated nature seem distant forerunners of the Mega-Novel itself. The picaresque–the novels of Tobias Smollett are perhaps most recognizable–depended on the proliferation of stories resulting from the adventures of a roguish or socially marginal protagonist as he (on occasion, she) makes his way from village to village. Often the rogue or picaro may be more idealistic and naïve than purely roguish, as, for example, in the seventeenth-century forerunner of the genre, Don Quixote. But whatever his precise makeup, the genre depended on the piling on of adventures, both agreeable and disagreeable; so that the fiction itself could be extended as long as the author wished to prolong his work: almost to infinity, if he so wished, like *Gil Blas*.

Pynchon's novel, which has its own rogue in the adventurous and less disciplined Mason, is cut from the same genre as these old picaresque fictions. Historical veracity in them gives way to a cultural bias, really part of what is currently the new academic craze, cultural studies. Here, the artifacts of the period become the way to view it, rather than the purely historical events underpinning the era. Another way of thinking about it is to see the period as a sequence of objects and materials, what we may call an object culture. Here we enter into inns and taverns, and brothels, listen to the conversation, almost taste the drinks and eat the food, and then enter typical homes, with their furnishings, their artifacts, and their utensils. This is a world painterly as well as writerly–the interiors of Chardin and Vermeer, the images of Dickens.

Although Mason and Dixon are associated with outdoor work– surveying and probing the skies–a surprising part of the book is devoted to interiors. The idea is to delineate how people lived as much as how they worked and succeeded or failed. But there is more: the emphasis on interiors gives Pynchon the opportunity to tell his stories, since once inside inns or taverns, and homes, Mason and Dixon are exposed to the full blast of eccentrics, unbalanced and creepy people so reminiscent of Pynchon's earlier work. It is rewarding to see in *Mason & Dixon*, which appears such a singular effort, as part of a larger mosaic which Pynchon is creating, going back to *V.* in the early Sixties and continuing into the millennium. The crazy crew in *V.* has reappeared in the latest novel not as "crazies" but as bizarre participants in the making of *Mason & Dixon* and in the two surveyors-astronomers, themselves on a crazy mission amidst savages, both white and red.

That mosaic fits into Pynchon's plan not only to establish his view of America–as in *Vineland* and *The Crying of Lot 49*, in which California emblemizes the country–but to recreate it through skewed cultural contextualization in *Mason & Dixon*. Here his subject is chicanery and hypocrisy, whereas earlier it was counterfeiting, deception at another level. Hypocrisy is revealed in the acts of the Founding Fathers, in the suggestion by George Washington himself that Mason and Dixon can make money on the side while they are on their mission to draw a border between North and South. In this and related ways, Pynchon has created a revisionist history, not the history of schoolbooks and talking television heads, but the narrative of how people in edgy situations really behaved. There are no heroes, unless we consider Mason and Dixon themselves as heroes for undergoing the dangers they do to carry out their royal orders. But surrounding them are villains, colonialists, grifters, brothel owners, settlers with hungry eyes, slave owners, parlor tricksters (Benny Franklin–better known as Benjamin Franklin), and so on through one forger of reality after another. The contemporary scene could not be far behind–we somehow expect Oedipa's man of all seasons, Mucho Maas, to reappear suddenly.

An additional factor, a geometric one, underlies the narrative. Mason and Dixon set out to draw the line that separates parts of the still colonial America, to draw as close as possible a straight line, a boundary of sorts which will become the separation between two very different cultures. Yet as against that so-called straight line is a tale with a story–a third-person story related in a first-person voice–that is nothing if not digressive. The two men are there to create order, while the narrative they are in is all disorder, entanglements and convolutions. Further, we find triangulation, because both the orderly and disorderly material is caught in that first-person narrative which suggests order but is voiced by someone who is anything but that. Reliability is not his ticket. This, too, is traditional Pynchon territory, that dialectic between order and disorder which breaks down into chaos or mayhem, or between a so-called civilization (laws, institutions, organizations) and a not too different savagery. Even Mason, with his wild ways, and Dixon, with his more straightjacket style, fit into this paradigm which follows from *V.* through the author's entire career.

Just as Pynchon has reinvented the eighteenth-century novel, so he has reinvented Mason and Dixon and their journey or quest into what was then the heart of America. This is not the historical surveyor and astronomer, but the pair who can fit into a phantasmogoric Pynchon scenario, in which "Snow-balls have flown their Arcs"; so that from the first line we feel we are back in some earlier version of *Gravity's Rainbow*. Rockets there, snowballs here, and curving, questing measurers arcing around the world from England to America. They and their journeys arc and curve and rainbow even as they are dedicated to a straight line, leading eight yards wide into the heart of the dark West.

NOTES

INTRODUCTION

[1] In *Mason & Dixon*, Pynchon intermixes eighteenth-century vernacular stylistics with contemporary hip.

[2] Tom Wolfe has been most insistent on pushing traditional realism, and while he is not a force in the novel, he does broadcast his views in ways to make himself heard loud and clear, most recently in *Hooking Up* (New York: Farrar, Straus and Giroux, 2000), the chapter called "The Three Stooges." One problem with Wolfe, however, is that among contemporary novelists he has read the wrong books (see page 165 for some of his favorites). Even among an earlier generation, he lists Realists and Naturalists and includes Faulkner, who hardly belongs with Dreiser, Lewis, Wharton, Hurston, or Hemingway and Fitzgerald. His hasty historical analysis of the tradition of Realism is sophomoric, unworthy of a Yale Ph.D. A more extensive response to contemporary Realism and what it means comes in my Chapter 4, "The New Realism." For a more considered analysis than Wolfe's of the term, see George Levine's *The Realistic Imagination* (Chicago: University of Chicago Press, 1981). Also, some of the following are helpful: Fredric Jameson, *Marxism and Form*; Harry Levin, *The Gates of Horn*; Northrop Frye, *Fables of Identity*; Richard Stang, *The Theory of the Novel in England: 1850-1870*; Terry Eagleton, *Criticism and Ideology*; Leo Bersani, *A Future for Astyanax*. Most of these books

disagree with each other, but all manifest a far more broad theory of Realism than exists in Wolfe's simplistic efforts at definition. (More on this and Wolfe in Chapter 4.)

CHAPTER ONE

[3] *Stop Time* (New York: Viking, 1967)
[4] *Ibid.*, p. 59.
[5] *Ibid.*
[6] *The Invention of Solitude* (New York: Sun, 1982).
[7] *Selected Letters of Stéphane Mallarmé*, ed. & trans. by Rosemary Lloyd (Chicago: University of Chicago Press, 1988), p. 77.
[8] *The Invention of Solitude*, p. 6.
[9] *Ibid.*, p. 17.
[10] *Ibid.*, p. 18.
[11] *Ibid.*, p. 24
[12] *A Hole in the World* (New York: Touchstone Books, 1991; publ. 1990 by Simon & Schuster).
[13] *Ibid.*, p. 155.
[14] *Ibid.*
[15] *Brothers and Keepers* (New York: Viking Penguin, 1984). Some data to keep in mind: whereas blacks are 12% of the American population, they make up 44% of prison inmates. America, incidentally, incarcerates ten times the rate of Western European nations and Japan, indicating that many imprisonments are the consequence of poor defense lawyering, a rabid desire to punish minority offenders, a disproportionate number punished for non-violent drug offenses, and related reasons, not the least outright racism. From 1980 to 1990, the prison population doubled; and after that, even as violent crime decreased, imprisonment climbed.
[16] *Shot in the Heart* (New York: Doubleday, 1994).
[17] A sample passage (pp. 106-107): "Now that my father was sober [after a bad fall and being warned that alcohol would kill him] all the time, he was also meaner and more violent.

Bessie [the mother] had long been the object of his anger, but for the next few years, their bouts became nightmarish and brutal. My brother recalls: 'I don't think we ever went two weeks during that time without some sort of wild, fist-banging fights. Many times I saw Mom with black eyes and a horribly swollen face. Man, she looked like she had been in a prizefight sometimes, battered and bruised, her lips all swollen. I saw that so many times. He would just really pound on her.'"

[18] *An Orphan in History* (New York: Doubleday, 1982).

[19] *Lovesong: Becoming a Jew* (New York: Arcade, 1991; publ. 1988 by Little, Brown).

[20] *Ibid.*, see the entire Chapter 6.

[21] *The Duke of Deception: Memories of My Father* (New York: Penguin, 1986; publ. In 1979 by Random House).

[22] *Ibid.*, p. 118. As we can expect, Wolff is aware of Delmore Schwartz's autobiographical short story "In Dreams Begin Responsibilities," in which he tries to forewarn his parents not to marry and to have him as a son.

[23] *This Boy's Life* (New York: Atlantic Monthly Press, 1989). The title recalls the official Boy Scout's magazine, *Boy's Life*.

[24] *Ibid.*, p. 105.

[25] As we see in many other memoirs not covered here: most notably in the hugely successful Frank McCourt's *Angela's Ashes* and *'Tis*, but also in Adam Hochschild's *Half the Way Home*, Samuel R. Delaney's *The Motion of Light in the Water*, Ari L. Goldman's *The Search for God at Harvard*, Carl Bernstein's *Loyalties*, Annie Dillard's *An American Childhood*, Jonathan Yardley's *Our Kind of People: The Story of an American Family*, Mary Gordon's *The Shadow Man* (with its parallels to *The Invention of Solitude* and *The Duke of Deception*), Shirley Abbott's *The Bookmaker's Daughter*, Clark Blaise's *I Had a Father*, Brent Staples' *Parallel Time*, and James Carroll's *An American Requiem*.

[26] *This Boy's Life*, p. 213.

[27] *A Boy's Own Story* (New York: Plume, 1982)
[28] *Ibid.*, p. 218.
[29] *Ibid.*, p. 82.
[28] *Home Before Dark* (Boston: Houghton Mifflin, 1984).
[29] *Half the Way Home* (New York: Viking, 1986). The Hochschild reveals that great wealth and privilege do not substitute for other values, mainly emotional and supportive. Here, wealth means the child can be fobbed off and isolated as much as a child from sparer or more brutal surroundings. This aspect has not been sufficiently examined even in a memoir as sensitive as this one.
[30] *Home Before Dark*, p. 218.
[31] *Ibid.*, p. 214.
[32] *Ibid.*, p. 174.
[33] *Ibid.*
[34] *Ibid.*, p. 127
[35] *Lost in Translation* (New York: Penguin, 1989).
[36] *Ibid.*, p. 164.
[37] *Ibid.*, p. 248.
[38] *Ibid.*, p. 187.
[39] *Ibid.*, p. 196.
[40] *Growing Up* (New York: Plume, 1982).
[41] *Family Installments* (New York: Morrow, 1982).
[42] *Ibid.*, p. 120.
[43] *Ibid.*, p. 142.
[44] *Ibid.*
[45] *World's Fair* (New York: Ballantine, 1985).
[46] *Ibid.*, p. 150.
[47] *Ibid.*, p. 152.
[48] *Ibid.*, p. 348.

CHAPTER TWO

[49] *White Noise* (New York: Penguin, 1986; publ. by Viking Penguin, 1985).

[50] *Players* (New York: Vintage, 1989; publ. by Knopf, 1977), p. 104.
[51] *Mao II* (New York: Penguin, 1992; publ by Viking Penguin, 1991).
[52] *Ibid.*, p. 16.
[53] *White Noise*, p. 326.
[54] *Ibid.*
[55] *Mao II*, p. 140.
[56] *Ibid.*, p. 141.
[57] *Ibid.* He also travels away from his books. "Bill is at the height of his fame. Ask me why. Because he hasn't published in years and years and years. . . . It's the years since that made him big. Bill gained celebrity by doing nothing. The world caught up. . . . Bill gets bigger as his distance from the scene deepens.'" (p.52)
[58] *White Noise*, p. 51.
[59] *Ibid.*, p. 147.
[60] *Ibid.*, p. 150. With AIDS as backdrop, consider Murray's comment: Modern death "has a life independent of us. It is growing in prestige and dimension. It has a sweep it never had before. . . . We've never been so close to it, so familiar with its habits and attitudes." (p. 150)
[61] *Ibid.*, p. 26.
[62] *Libra* (New York: Penguin, 1989; publ. by Viking Penguin, 1988), p. 370.
[63] *Ibid.*, p. 440.
[64] *The Motion of Light in Water* (New York: Plume, 1988), p. 126.
[65] *Ibid.*
[66] All three published by Sun & Moon Press, Los Angeles.
[67] From *City of Glass*, where the passage not only says nothing, it denies whatever might be content: "Like most people, Quinn knew almost nothing about crime. He had never murdered anyone, had never stolen anything, and he did not know anyone who had. He had never been inside a police station, had never met a private detective, had never spoken to a criminal.

... What interested him about the stories he wrote was not their relation to the world but their relation to other stories. Even before he became William Wilson, Quinn had been a devoted reader of mystery novels. He knew that most of them were poorly written, that most could not stand up to even the vaguest sort of examination, but still, it was the form that appealed to him. . . . (p. 14) Auster's prose often builds by way of its negatives, his denial of content, his negative response to the way we expect things to work. The Mallarméan presence, the existential abyss.

[68] For this, Auster spins off Hawthorne and lands on Henry James, his "The Real Right Thing," in which a young writer is enlisted by the widow to write a biography of his friend, a writer just three months dead.

[69] *Leviathan* (New York: Viking Penguin, 1992).

[70] *Water Music* (New York: Penguin, 1983, publ. by Little, Brown, 1981), p. 3.

[71] *Descent of Man: Stories* (New York: Penguin, 1987; publ. by Little, Brown, 1979), p. 3.

[72] *World's End*, p. 22.

[73] *Water Music*, p. 234.

[74] *East Is East* (New York: Penguin, 1991; publ. by Viking Penguin, 1990).

[75] *Ibid.*, p. 50.

[76] *Blood Meridian* (subtitled *The Evening Redness in the West*; New York: Vintage, 1992; publ by Random House in 1985).

[77] *Ibid.*, p. 57.

[78] *All the Pretty Horses* (New York: Vintage, 1993; publ. by Knopf in 1992), p. 232.

[79] *Ibid.*, p. 161.

[80] *Ibid.* The near or real nihilism of men is juxtaposed to equine energy, something close to a stereotypical man-ruined world opposed to natural splendor, saved only by the prose.

[81] *Suttree* (New York: Vintage, 1986; publ. by Random House in 1979).

[82] *Blood Meridian*, p. 249.
[83] *The Crossing* (New York: Knopf, 1994).
[84] *Ibid.*, p. 186.
[85] *Ibid.*, p. 379.
[86] *Ibid.*, p. 143.
[87] *Cities of the Plain* (New York: Knopf, 1998).
[88] *Ibid.*, p. 195.
[89] *Ibid.*, p. 285.
[90] Possibly Morrison uses "Seven days" here as she says she used National Suicide Day in *Sula* as "metaphors; summonings; rhetorical gestures of triumph, despair, and closure dependent on the acceptance of the associative language of dread and love that accompanies blackness. . . ." Such categories might include "water, flight, war, birth, religion, and so on, that make up the writer's kit." Morrison, *Playing in the Dark: Whiteness and the Literary Imagination* (New York: Vintage, 1993; publ. by Harvard University Press in 1992), p. x.
[91] Henry Louis Gates, who is rapidly losing his standing as a serious critic in his rush to cheer on, has created a kind of literary monster in Morrison, while ostensibly praising her. By analogizing her to everyone from Duke Ellington and Maria Callas to Faulkner, Marquez, and Virginia Woolf, Gates has created meaningless comparisons. Because she calls a book *Jazz*, she is not Duke Ellington; because she sings, she is not Maria Callas (nor Luciano Pavorotti); because she displays technical mastery, she is not Faulkner or Woolf or Marquez. These are all different orders of being, and Gates traduces them by linking them in this offhand, blurb-y manner.

Also, several analyses of Morrison's work and of the cultural contexts in which she wrote have appeared, notably Houston A. Baker Jr.'s *Workings of the Spirit: The Poetics of Afro-American Women's Writing* (1991) and just before that, Henry Louis Gates Jr.'s *The Signifying Monkey: A Theory of African-American Literary Criticism* (in 1988). It is unfortunate that in his discussion of Morrison's work Baker failed to include *Beloved*, since that novel challenged several reference points outside of what Baker calls Afro-American female writers' "expressivity." As we see, *Beloved* is concerned as much with telling as with what is told; so that the transmission of information becomes *the* information. What we come to know of origins, history, genealogy, memory itself is communicated by the way in which we learn of these things. Baker's expressivity or "expressive empowerment" for such writers involves a sharp sense of place, time, the measurement of oneself against other spatial dimensions, and some blending of that with "telling," however possible, would be of interest.

As for other Morrison works, his following statement captures her concerns: "Interiority and the frontier of violation coalesce in the accessible body of the African woman," a means of expressiveness. But it seems to me that Baker's theory of the devastation capitalism wrought for the poor black-for example, Shadrack in *Sula*, in World War One-is only partially true if we apply this theory to *Beloved*. Here, while there is no question of the exploitation of the poor black in slavery and beyond, there is also the "matter" of the novel itself, which is the communication of past deeds into memory and how memory has shaped and reshaped our sense of history. Criticism of capitalism works well as long as it does not pre-empt what the totality of the novel suggests, or neglects the means by which the novel comes to us.

Gate's book does not directly discuss Morrison. It is more a theory of Afro-American literature which, if we wish, can be rewardingly applied to her work. Gates locates the peculiar black vernacular in two traditions, the Esu (a trickster, a messenger in Yoruba tradition) and the Signifying Monkey, also a trickster dominant in Afro-American culture. In Gates's formulation, Esu "serves as a figure for the nature and function of interpretation and double-voiced utterance"; whereas the Signifying Monkey "serves as the figure-of-figures, as the trope in which are encoded several other peculiarly black rhetorical tropes." Each explores the uses of language as it reshapes itself into literature.

For Gates, the two tricksters' traditions pre-empt other kinds of criticism of Afro-American literature, giving it a kind of exclusivity and shielding it from being swallowed by the so-called Western tradition. What is a splendid tool for the criticism of Afro-American literature, however, should not block out the essential Americanism of this writing. The trickster in American fiction may not be Esu or the signifying Monkey, but there is no lack of imposters and confidence men. While Gates may say that Ralph Ellison created texts that are double-voiced and also "modes of figuration lifted from the black vernacular tradition," he cannot ignore the several non-Afro-American writers who draw on vernaculars, both black and white. In *Terrible Honesty: Mongrel Manhattan in the 1920s* (1995), Ann Douglas demonstrates that black and white intertwined culturally in the Twenties; that both drew on each other's vernacular; and that what resulted was a peculiarly American product, what she calls variously "Aframerica" and "Aframericans." None of this denies that original, distinctive, particular elements exist in one group and not in another; but it does insist that while not everyone comes to the same table, nearly everyone eats some of the dishes.

At several points, Gates does caution against exclusivity, saying that anyone "who analyzes black literature must do so as a comparativist, by definition, because our canonical texts have complex double formal antecedents, the Western and the black." Then in a Bloomian recognition of literary traditions lying within other traditions, he writes that "all texts Signify upon other texts, in motivated and unmotivated ways." Thus, to move from Morrison to Alice Walker, whom he does write about, Gates points out her indebtedness to Zora Neale Hurston, especially Walker's use of the epistolary style, a form which goes back beyond Hurston to the eighteenth century. What emphasizes the "black" element is Walker's open expression of indebtedness to "antecedent and descendant texts." This is, for Gates, how a black text "Signifies" other texts, mainly through use of rhetorical strategies. But we should repeat that those strategies are indeed comparativist, and in most instances broadly American. (See, also, my Chapter Seven for a fuller discussion of these very points.)

Two other books, although not concerned with Morrison directly, present views of Afro-American literature which bear on all contemporary black writers, not least Morrison. In *Modernism and the Harlem Renaissance* (1987), Houston A. Baker, Jr. argues persuasively that modernism as a movement was not merely white nor relegated to writers like Joyce, Eliot, Pound, and artists like Picasso; but can be used to describe Afro-American creative work. He writes: "After surveying the limitations of this traditional scheme [based on Continental modernism], I suggest that the analysis of discursive strategies that I designate 'the mastery of form' and 'the deformation of mastery' produces more accurate and culturally enriching interpretations of the *sound* and *soundings* of Afro-American modernism than do traditional methods. Out of personal reflection, then, comes a set of formulations on expressive modernism and the manner of speaking (or *sounding*) 'modern' in Afro-America." Using such methods, Baker proceeds to "recode" the Harlem Renaissance. The relevance of Morrison comes if we apply such strategies of analysis to her work, to see where she succeeds in the tradition of Afro-American modernism or where she moves into something else (more mainstream white Americanism, feminism and questions of gender).

The second book is in some ways a companion volume to Baker's, *Vicious Modernism: Black Harlem and the Literary Imagination* (1990) by James De Jongh. Taking his title from a poem by Amiri Baraka/LeRoi Jones, De Jongh locates our sense of the new and the modern as deriving in part from "the idea of Harlem." Although Morrison is not a factor in this book, there is the sense that she is part of a continuing tradition; and

De Jongh's study suggests to us, as did Baker's books, that she and her work can be recast, without our losing sight of her essential "Americanism."

[92] *Beloved* (New York: Knopf, 1987), p. 148.
[93] *Jazz* (New York: Plume, 1993; publ. by Knopf in 1992).
[94] *Paradise* (New York: Knopf, 1998).
[95] *Ibid.*, p. 308.

CHAPTER THREE

[96] Following my *American Fictions: 1940-1980*, Tom LeClair has isolated several Mega-Novels or Mega-Texts, in his *The Art of Excess: Mastery in Contemporary American Fiction* (1989). His rationale was much the same as mine in the earlier book and, now, in the present study: "I have written *The Art of Excess* because the elephant-like (or whale-like) novel has, over the last twenty years, been increasingly relegated to the status of white elephant while moths are praised as butterflies. If the large book is not better than the small one, the massive novel-if profoundly informed, inventively crafted, and cunningly rhetorical-can have greater cultural significance, more authority to contest the powers in which literature exists. Most expressions of culture are designed to be consumed and forgotten. Masterworks lodge, oftentimes unpleasantly, in the memory. They judge us, our minds and memories and membership in American life." (p. 2)

Although I think LeClair is unduly optimistic about the long reach of these Mega-Novels-they, too, become marginally consumed and forgotten-his point is well taken for those academics who wish to keep the idea of literature alive. As for critics, we know what a beating many of the Mega-Novels took on first publication. In 1980, Alfred Kazin looked around and found, in his essay "American Writing Now," that our talented novelists do not exercise influence, that they are part of drift. Gaddis, Pynchon, Barth, for starters, meant little to him. And Benjamin DeMott in his own neglect of what was being written in the larger forms looked back on big novels of the 1920s, *An American Tragedy, The Sound and the Fury*, among others, and lamented that our time does not produce anything near their equal. To isolate Faulkner alone in the 20s or 30s, we see that nearly all the establishment critics-Fadiman, Kazin, Geismar-found his work incomprehensible. *Absalom, Absalom!*, for one, was lambasted as the indulgence of a Southern freak. A rich man has as much chance of passing through the eye of a needle as a Mega-Novel has of becoming "lodged" in our collective unconscious.

[97] For those unfamiliar with McElroy's work, I discuss in *American Fictions: 1940-1980* all of the books prior to *Women and Men*. Another survey of the earlier fiction comes in Tony Tanner's *Scenes of Nature, Signs of Men* (1987), the chapter called "Toward an Ultimate Topography: the Work of Joseph McElroy." Unusually for an English reader, Tanner immediately saw the originality of McElroy's work and, while noting the difficulty, did not retreat in midcult distaste.

Quite appropriate to any discussion of McElroy's work and especially *Women and Men* would have been Charles Caramello's *Silverless Mirrors* had he chosen to include that writer or book in his analysis of "Book, Self & Postmodern American Fiction" (Tallahassee: Florida State University, 1983). Caramello's point is that "silverless" mirrored texts do not permit a reflection of self or world, as opposed to a silvered mirror, which does reflect. As texts, he explains, "they have turned their reflecting planes inward and have further skewed these planes, by incorporating a metalinguistic discourse on that turning." (p. 52) They do reflect other texts, however, and they do fulfill a postmodern role of disallowing both expressiveness and mimetic reality. In McElroy's case, the phrase is particularly apt because so much of his work relies on interactions, as planes, lines, colors in a painting. Those "planes" indicated by

Caramello could be a Cubist conception, a geometry which expresses whatever the reader or viewer brings to it.
[98] Reported in the *New York Times* (January 12, 1995).
[99] *Women and Men* (New York: Knopf, 1987), p. 41.
[100] In a letter to me (dated February 21, 1987), McElroy points out how I missed the speaker or voice, in segments called "Alias, Missing Conversation" and "OPENING IN THE VOID (smile)." I was cheered that these were the only two I had misread!
[101] *Letters to a Young Poet* (New York: Norton, 1964), p. 64. Rilke continues: ". . . everything in us withdraws, a stillness comes, and the new, which no one knows, stands in the midst of it and is silent." (p. 64)
[102] *Women and Men*, p. 187.
[103] *Ibid.*, p. 380.
[104] *Harlot's Ghost* (New York: Random House, 1991).
[105] *Ibid.*, P. 14. There is more, parodic or straight talk? "Lovemaking with Kittredge was-I use the word once more-a sacrament. I am not at ease trying to speak of it. . . . there was ceremony to embracing Kittredge." (p. 19)
[106] *Ibid.*, p. 173.
[107] *Ibid.*, p. 159.
[108] *Ibid.*, p. 160.
[109] *The Runaway Soul* (New York: Farrar, Straus & Giroux, 1991).
[110] *Ibid.*, p. 198. That emptiness, that awareness of the "hole" in oneself, justifies the "runaway soul." Most reviewers passed over this, charging that the narcissism had no definition or initiative.
[111] *Ibid.*, p. 225.
[112] *Ibid.*, p. 226.
[113] *Ibid.*
[114] *Ibid.*, p. 597.
[115] *Ibid.*, p. 58.
[116] *Ibid.*, p. 32.
[117] *Ibid.*

[118] *Ibid.*, p. 739.
[119] *Ibid.*, p. 736.
[120] *Ibid.*, p. 828.
[121] *Ibid.*
[122] *Ibid.*, p. 819.
[123] *Ibid.*
[124] One is tempted to apply Nietzsche's now clichéd warning, that what doesn't kill me makes me stronger.
[125] *The Runaway Soul*, p. 504.
[126] *Ibid.*, p. 510.
[127] *Ibid.*
[128] *Ibid.*, p. 526.
[129] *Ibid.*, p. 34.
[130] *Ibid.*, p. 330.
[131] *Ibid.*
[132] *Ibid.*
[133] *A Frolic of His Own* (New York: Simon & Schuster's Poseidon Press, 1994).
[134] *Ibid.*, p. 11.
[135] *Ibid.*, p. 341. "tin trivial," also p. 341.
[136] *Ibid.*, p. 422.
[137] *Ibid.*, p. 42.
[138] *Ibid.*, p.37.
[139] *Ibid.*, p. 398.
[140] *Ibid.*
[141] Pronomial blurring is characteristic of several Mega-Novels, and, of course, not only them. We find it in Pynchon, DeLillo (especially in *Underworld*), in *Infinite Jest* (where Wallace makes it thematic), and in previous Gaddis novels. McElroy in *Women and Men*, as we have observed, fudges it even further, so that pronomial usage passes from grammar into metaphysics.
[142] *A Frolic of His Own*, p. 23. Also, the following quotation.
[143] *Darconville's Cat* (New York: Doubleday, 1981).
[144] *The Gold Bug Variations* (New York: HarperPerennial, 1992; publ. by Morrow, 1991).

[145] *Ibid.*, p. 89.
[146] *Ibid.*, p. 91.

CHAPTER FOUR

[147] Alan Wilde's *Middle Grounds: Studies in Contemporary American Fiction* (1987) is an often compelling effort to see American fiction in less than binary terms: as neither purely realistic nor experimental and innovative. He says this is necessary in order to include a good deal of writing that does not fit readily into the binary, either/or division. Wilde offers up writers like Max Apple, Thomas Berger, and Donald Barthelme as those either ignored or misrepresented. "The question to be posed here," he writes, "has to do with the chances for revitalized humanism in our postmodern age: for some tertium quid that avoids equally the moribund humanism that continues to inform the works of those writers I have chosen to call 'catatonic realists' [Didion, Beattie, Carver, and others] and the rabid antihumanism that allies so much of postmodern writing with poststructuralist theory." (p. 6) The assumption here is that those writers attuned to innovative or experimental modes lack that middle ground of humanism. Here one takes objection. It seems to me, noble as Wilde's enterprise is, one cannot discuss moral values in Barthelme-Wilde considers him a morally concerned writer-without considering the meta-real elements: irony, paradox, angulated language, innovative narrative strategies, deconstruction of traditional fictional structures, and the rest. Very possibly, the innovative writers are more deeply involved in moral questions than Wilde's middle ground examples *because* they seek more deeply involved (and profound) ways of expressing their concerns. Their intensity is embodied in their struggle to find the means to communicate concern, to indicate where humanism lies, to provide touchstones located outside platitude. Even minimalism is deeply humanistic, although from Wilde's point of view it may be a

void; for minimalism stresses not anti-humanism, but the state of life in this country which makes humanism so difficult. It comes to life from another direction, from the very direction Wilde calls "catatonic realism." Innovative language here often makes the difference.

Wilde's "midfiction" as he defines it eschews the oppositional extremes of realism and metafiction. But the point is that by the 90s, the New Realism demonstrates that opposition has lessened and that the two so-called extremes often overlap. Midfiction traffics in "limit situations" and reveals "the extraordinariness of the ordinary." It always works back to showing the moral complexities of "inhabiting a world that is itself, as 'test,' ontologically contingent and problematic." (p. 34) Yet one could argue that the metafiction Wilde objects to does something similar, although in different terms-in angulated language, in extraordinary tropes, in bizarre and unstereotypical relationships.

148 *The Ultimate Good Luck* (New York: Vintage, 1986, publ. by Houghton Mifflin, 1981). *A Piece of My Heart* appeared in 1976 (New York: Random House).
149 *Ibid.*, p. 36.
150 *Rock Springs* (New York: Atlantic Monthly Press, 1987), p. 148.
151 *The Sportswriter* (New York: Vintage, 1986).
152 *Ibid.*, p. 83.
153 *Ibid.*, p. 317.
154 *Independence Day* (New York: Knopf, 1995), p. 41.
155 *Ibid.*, p. 5.
156 *Ibid.*, p. 10.
157 *More Die of Heartbreak* (New York: Morrow, 1987).
158 *Him With His Foot in His Mouth* (1984), long stories, most of them novellas; and *A Theft* (1989), a novella.
159 *Blue River* (Boston: Houghton Mifflin, 1991).
160 *Ibid.*, p. 56.

[161] Strikingly, Canin's collection of short stories, *Emperor of the Air* (1998), is full of loose and open ends, far less concerned with cause and effect, or with resolution, even discovery. Expectations are raised, not to fulfill them, but to stretch us toward what is "out there" in the penumbra. The titular story, for example, focuses on an astronomy teacher and, accordingly, drives our assumptions skyward into the great mysteries of the universe, where Canin leaves us. In "The Year of Getting to Know Us," there is, once again, the night drive, repeated from *Blue River*, an abandoned drive that is close to suicidal; but here it remains ambiguous, part of those gray areas in life Canin suggests in stories, but realistically describes in his novel.

[162] *The Messiah of Stockholm* (New York: Knopf, 1987).

[163] *Outerbridge Reach* (New York: Ticknor & Fields, 1992).

[164] As the reader may have surmised, Hemingway lies here in the shadows of Stone's endeavor, with aspects of Faulkner not far behind. Behind both, Conrad.

[165] *Outerbridge Reach*, p. 360.

[166] In *Literal Madness* (New York: Grove Press, 1988).

[167] *Ibid.*, pp. 194-95.

[168] *Ibid.*, p. 197.

[169] *Ibid.*, p. 211.

[170] *Ibid.*, p. 319.

[171] *Ibid.*, p. 318.

[172] *Continental Divide* (New York: Ballantine, 1986; publ. by Harper in 1985).

[173] *Ibid.*, p. 324. Banks moves in and out of the old Naturalism-Realism mode in the following: ". . . it was his life, and then he traded a big part of that life for one with more promises and less control, but even so, it felt much of the time like his life, for there was still a part of it that he controlled. . . ." (p. 324)

[174] *American Psycho*, discussed in Chapter 9, is focused on this phenomenon, but because of its extraordinary violence was not read as incisive social commentary.

[175] *Black Water* (New York: Dutton, 1992).
[176] *Mezzanine* (New York: Weidenfeld & Nicolson, 1988; also published in different form in *The New Yorker*)
[177] *Room Temperature* (New York: Grove Weidenfeld, 1990). The title, of course, refers to the temperature at which a baby's bottle can be fed.
[178] *Mezzanine*, p. 21.
[179] *Ibid.*, p. 127.
[180] *Vox.*, (New York: Vintage, 1993; publ. by Random House in 1992).
[181] *U and I* (New York: Random House, 1992).
[182] *Ibid.*, p. 73. Strong passages like this are vitiated by attempts at facetiousness: "(I must have never successfully masturbated to Updike's writing, though I have to certain remembered scenes in Iris Murdoch; but someone I know says that she achieved a number of quality orgasms from *Couples* when she first read it at age thirteen.), p. 19.
[183] *The Fermata* (New York: Vintage, 1994; publ. by Random House in 1994).
[184] *Killing Mister Watson* (New York: Random House, 1990).
[185] *The Shipping News* (New York: Scribner's, 1993).
[186] *Postcards* (New York: Scribner's, 1992).

CHAPTER FIVE

[187] *Eclogues* (San Francisco: North Point Press, 1981).
[188] *Ibid.*, p. 24. Picasso is remembered: "Wine, bread, table: his Catholic childhood. Perhaps his Catholic life. Lute, guitar, mandolin: the Spanish ear, which abides life as a terrible dream made tolerable by music."
[189] "My Father Was a River," in *The Houses of Children* (New York: New Directions, 1986). p.84
[190] *Tatlin: Six Stories* (Baltimore: Johns Hopkins, 1982; publ. by Scribner's in 1974).
[191] *Da Vinci's Bicycle: Ten Stories* (Baltimore: Johns Hopkins, 1979).

Besides the often oblique prose, Davenport creates the Tatlin piece through montage, the filmic process suggesting how surreal Tatlin's project is even as it attempts to fit into Soviet realism.

[192] *In the Future Perfect* (New York: New Directions, 1977).

[193] *Minds Meet* (New York: New Directions, 1975).

[194] "The English Garden," in *In the Future Perfect*, p. 1.

[195] James Salter's "The Cinema," in *Dusk and Other Stories* (1988) contains some of the best qualities of the emptiers while also using film as a trope or metaphor for our time. Far less satiric than Donald Barthelme, Salter stresses the Hemingway line of abrupt, brief comments, sharp shifts. The model could be "Hills Like White Elephants" or "The Killers"-the author as puppetmaster who does not intrude. The point of attack in Salter is the fleeting quality of cinema and film: how the moment is defined and then, almost without notice, is gone. The successful actor Guivi is riding the crest of his career even as it is beginning to topple. The director Iles knows his film is wreckage, and he knows that Guivi is washed up. Meanwhile, the latter's unconscious life goes on, even as we observe his career winding down. Salter has achieved an epiphany of failure, and by linking it to film, to the exhibitionism and showiness of cinema, he has stretched it into a trope for our entire culture. Yet all his perceptions are suggestive, little stated. When statement is called for, Salter withdraws into lyrical expressions of shadows, blurring, indirection. He has the true emptiers' feel for the abandonment of things and the betrayal we make of our own lives and drives. This is not quite Barthelme disorientation, but it does recognize the throwaway nature of American life, encapsulated in the actor's attempt at craft, in his reach for celebrity, and in his fall from grace because he is, simply, the wrong man at this time.

[196] *Self-Help* (New York: Knopf, 1985).

[197] *Ibid.*, p. 4.

[198] *Ibid.*, p. 21.

[199] *Family Dancing: Stories* (New York: Knopf, 1985).
[200] *Airships* (New York: Vintage, 1978; publ. by Knopf in 1978.
[201] *Ibid.*, p. 24.
[202] *Ray* (New York: Penguin, 1981; publ. by Knopf in 1980).
[203] In his first novel, *Geronimo Rex* (1972), which won the Faulkner prize, Hannah incorporates jazz, both its rhythms and its improvisations, into prose; but more than that, he infuses jazz and jazz thinking into the very working of the novel. Although his protagonist is a boy growing up in Dream of Pines, Louisiana, he trails vapors of Holden Caulfield-if not a brother, then a distant cousin. Harriman Monroe is gentile, southern, not institutionalized, but romantic and violent; yet he shares with Salinger's Holden the ability to sniff out humbuggery and hypocrisy: Holden with shit detector turned up high. Hannah's America, however, unlike Salinger's, is vibrant.
[204] An exception is Philip Roth, whose work in the 90s demonstrated a remarkable sustained achievement.
[205] Even his nonfiction as recent as 1995, in *Oswald's Tale*, while ostensibly about Lee Harvey Oswald, turns out to be about Mailer, just as earlier Gary Gilmore in *The Executioner's Song* ends up as a Mailer persona.
[206] *Him with His Foot in His Mouth* (New York: Harper & Row, 1984).
[207] *A Theft* (New York: Penguin, 1989).
[208] If the Faulkner of *The Sound and the Fury* or *Absalom, Absalom!* were published today, he would meet the same incomprehension from reviewers and intelligent readers he received earlier. Emptiers face the same cultural crisis: when older forms are still being mined even as they have exhausted themselves; when, in fact, several emptiers have reached the end of their invention. There is little hope that new emptiers can find their niche-after all, who cares? And they are slowly giving up the ghost, not with their death, but with most mainstream publishers looking askance at little but corporate headquarters. Further, the huge proliferation of undergraduate and graduate

university writing programs has placed mainly traditional writing teachers in charge-that is, those who have caught the public (and university administration) eye. With publishers closing up or down, the impulse in such programs is to encourage young writers to find a publisher, not to aim for the subversion of forms, the reshaping of language, the creation of the new. This is not an attack on writing programs; they have resulted in several fine authors. But for the most part they are a conserving influence. What goes on in David Foster Wallace's *Infinite Jest* did not come from a writing program.

[209] *Democracy* (New York: Pocket Books, 1985; publ. by Simon & Schuster, 1984).

[210] *A Night at the Movies* (New York: Collier Books, 1988; publ. by Simon & Schuster in 1987).

[211] *Gerald's Party* (New York: Simon & Schuster, 1985). A sample: "At the cave mouth [sheets hung to form a cave], Teresa stood naked and frightened ('I feel so stupid,' she was complaining, trying to cover, not her breasts-which Gudrun was rouging-or her genitals, but the whitened rolls of fat on her tummy), while nearby Jim leaned over Ros's cadaver, laid out amid pilaf, cheese balls, and sliced salami on our dining room table, a butcher knife in his hand." (p. 245)

[212] *The Color Purple* (New York: Simon & Schuster, 1982).

[213] *The Terrible Twos* (New York: Avon Books, 1982). Reed is particularly good on Santa Claus: "Santa Claus is ubiquitous this year. Dolly Parton appears on the cover of *Rolling Stone* in a Santa Claus outfit; a little doll Santa Claus peeks from between her bosom lines. On the cover of *Fantasy* magazine, Santa Claus appears as a robot. United Press International reports on December 23, 1980, that the Sussex County Superior Court judge gave Leroy Scholtz permission to change his name to Santa C. Claus. . . . But all wasn't jolly for Santa Claus during 1980 Xmas. Associated Press reported on December 19, 1980, that the 125 members of the Truth Taber-

nacle Church, in Burlington, North Carolina, had decided that Christmas is the work of the devil and Santa is an imposter." (pp. 5-6)

[214] *Carpenter's Gothic* (New York: Viking, 1985).

[215] Consider Liz after a stressful phone call for her absent husband: "Silenced, the vexation in her voice surfaced in her hands back streaking While the bonnet is trimming, the face grown old, on the glass of the sampler; culling the morning's mail for Doctor Yount, Doctor Kissinger [not *that* Kissinger], Dan-Ray Adjusters, Inc. crumpled and tossed; B & C Storage, the American Cancer Society and the National Rifle Association aside unopened; a flood of glossy pages from Christian Recovery for America's People, the community college flyer's offerings unfurled in mini-courses on Stress Management, Success Through Assertiveness, Reflexology, Shiatsu, Hypnocybernetics and The Creative You; Gold Coast Florists torn open. . . ." (pp. 61-2)

[216] *Bright Lights, Big City* (New York: Vintage, 1984).

CHAPTER SIX

[217] In an interesting take on American war fiction, including novels that refer to both World War Two and the Vietnam War, John Limon (*Writing After War: American War Fiction from Realism to Postmodernism*, 1994) extends the genre considerably. He sees sports, among other things intersecting the war, citing, for example, Bernard Malamud's *The Natural* and John Updike's *The Centaur*. They are pre-Vietnam, "but taken together they illustrate the formal possibilities sport offers to Vietnam-era literature that is obsessed with the war it despairs of representing." (pp. 156-7) The football novel, obviously, has the broadest overlap with war, is, in fact, war. ". . . Vietnam as the quintessence of football-patricidal and filial, homophobic and homoerotic, Negrophile and Negrophobe, mechanical and primeval-as portrayed in all football novels

[DeLillo's *End Zone*, Dan Jenkins's *Semi-Tough*, Peter Gentry's *North Dallas Forty*, not least Mailer's *Why Are We in Vietnam?*]." Limon's book, which also includes the war culture as presented in "Women's Words," is less a study of war fiction than it is of the role war plays in our culture, a seeping, persistent presence.

[218] Robert C. Mason's *Chickenhawk* (1983) suggests that the war becomes so hallucinatory and unreal that he repeatedly refers to it as "a movie scene" or as "Something right out of the movies." The filmic dimension is often the one he relates to to preserve his sanity, much as Binx Bolling in Walker Percy's *The Moviegoer* perceived life through movies and movie celebrities, even when he knew they were misleading. Film validated what was otherwise unreal, or so commonplace as to go unobserved.

[219] *Going After Cacciato* (New York: Dell, 1979).

[220] *Dispatches* (New York: Knopf, 1977).

[221] *Ibid.*, p. 48.

[222] *Ibid.*, p. 53.

[223] *Ibid.*, p. 98.

[224] *A Bright Shining Lie* (New York: Random House, 1988).

[225] The Korean War has received possibly its best representation not in fiction but in a memoir, James Brady's *The Coldest War* (2000), combining autobiography with fictional narratives.

[226] *A Walk in the Sun* (Phila., Pa.: Blakiston, 1945)

[227] Here the Hemingway presence is palpable; and not only in war, but in bullfighting, deep sea fishing, and, frequently, in marital disputes. Hemingway spoke of grace under pressure, but much closer to his meaning was that male ability to reach deep down to probe his atavistic side. To do that was to be a man, not a wimp.

[228] *Indian Country* (New York: Harper Perennial, 1991; publ. by Bantam Books in 1987).

[229] *In the Lake of the Woods* (New York: Penguin, 1995; publ. by Viking, 1994).

[230] *Veteran's Day: A Memoir* (New York: Orion, 1990).

[231] *Born on the Fourth of July* (New York: Pocket Books, 1977; publ. by McGraw-Hill in 1976). Not to be neglected in the subgenre of memory books is Joe Haldeman's *The Forever War* (New York: Avon Books, 1977; publ by St. Martin's Press, 1977), mixing memory, Vietnam, and all wars.

[232] *Fortunate Son* (New York: Bantam Books, 1993; publ by Grove Weidenfeld, 1991).

[233] *Paco's Story* (New York: Penguin Books, 1987; publ. by Farrar, Straus & Giroux, 1986).

[234] *Payback* (New York: Knopf, 1984). See, also, *Bloods: an Oral History of the Vietnam War by Black Veterans* by Wallace Terry (New York, Ballantine Books, 1984). The best overall history of the Vietnam conflict is Marilyn Young's *The Vietnam Wars: 1945-1990* (New York: HarperCollins, 1991). The plural "wars" indicates that Young has narrated the war as part of the Cold War and domestic policies; that the Vietnam conflict extended well past the end of the war. Other estimable books on the Vietnam War are Tom Wells's *The War Within: America's Battle over Vietnam* (New York: Henry Holt, 1994) and Gabriel Kolko's *Anatomy of a War: Vietnam, the United States, and the Modern Historical Experience* (New York: Pantheon, 1985). The grandfather of all such books was William Shawcross's *Side-Show: Kissinger, Nixon and the Destruction of Cambodia* (New York: Simon & Schuster, 1977), accusing Kissinger and Nixon of waging genocide in their secret invasion and subsequent destruction of Cambodia.

[235] *DelCorso's Gallery* (New York: Holt, 1983).

[236] *The Things They Carried* (Boston: Houghton Mifflin, 1990).

[237] *Gunfighter Nation* (New York: Atheneum, 1992). Two books perfectly illustrate how the saloon in the western becomes the jungle in Vietnam War fiction: *The Expandables* by Leonard B. Scott (New York: Ballantine, 1991; publ. by Random House in 1983) and *We Were Soldiers Once. . . and Young* by Harold G. Moore and Joseph L. Galloway (New York: Random House, 1993). Both are descriptions of the battle of Ia Drang in

which 450 men from the First Cavalry landed by helicopter and were then surrounded by 2000 North Vietnamese Regulars. For a more general sense of battle zones, see *Fields of Fire* by James Webb, one of the very rare Vietnam fictions (or memoirs) that see something positive in the American involvement.

[238] *Ibid.*, p. 386.

[239] *Ibid.*, p. 387.

[240] We are reminded, once again, of the saloon image, where the gunfight is over within seconds, or at the most, minutes, with short bursts, blood flowing, quick death, and even quicker results.

[241] *Fields of Fire* (New York: Bantam Books, 1979; publ. by Prentice Hall in 1978).

[242] *The Gallery* (New York: Bantam Books, 1950; publ. by Harper & Brothers in 1947).

[243] *If I Die in a Combat Zone* (New York: Dell Laurel, 1979).

[244] *A Good Scent from a Strange Mountain* (New York: Penguin, 1993; publ. by Holt in 1992).

[245] *Ibid.*, p. 73. Complementing Butler's view from the "other side" of the mountain are the views of a Japanese and a Korean observer of the American action in Vietnam, in *Bulletin of Concerned Asian Scholars* (Vol. 32, No. 4, 25-32), an article by Richard C. Kagan called "Disarming Memories: Japanese, Korean, and American Literature on the Vietnam War." The Japanese observer asserts that American writers on the war, including many mentioned in this chapter, "lit up only the part of Vietnam they understood"; which means they presented none of the cultural or historical background of Vietnam, nothing about Asia or Asians, and what little they did know came from a few limited, often corrupted, sources. The Japanese, Takeshi Kaiko, a war correspondent, further pointed out that on the Vietnamese side, there was also little understanding of America, and much of that was stereotypical. Books were not something American soldiers carried, books which might have provided historical and cultural contexts. For ex-

ample, did the American side, soldiers, writers, leaders, ever recognize the role Buddhism played in Vietnamese intellectual and social life? Similarly, the Korean observer, Ahn Junghyo, saw America as defining the conflict in terms of economic and cultural domination, really an extension of French colonialism with a slightly different face. Inevitably, tragedy flowed from misunderstanding and ignorance.

[246] Whereas Reed attempted an approximation, June Jordan's *His Own Where*(1970) *was* written entirely in what she describes as black English.

CHAPTER SEVEN

[247] *After the Revolution: Studies in the Contemporary Jewish-American Imagination* (Bloomington: Indiana University Press, 1987), p. 10.

[248] *Ibid.*, p. 9.

[249] In the following chapter, on Roth and Updike, I touch on all these themes as we observe them fighting for their own vision of America. Yet despite their divisions into a "Jewish America" and a gentile one, what remains is the enormous overlap, so that when all is said and done there is only America itself.

[250] In his latest book of essays, *The Blue Devils of Nada* (1996), the novelist, Jazz critic, and cultural historian Albert Murray writes of how an "American tradition" pre-empts both biological (racial, ethnic) and even ideological commitments. The observation continues Murray's attack on black separatism in *The Omni-Americans*, in 1970. None of this implies that Murray is disloyal to blacks; on the contrary, he is a persistent supporter of the black contribution to and reinforcement of American values and culture; even to the extent that he can posit a black America as the "truest" America, the maker of what he calls the national character.

[251] Katherine Anne Porter was basically an earlier writer; *Ship of*

Fools (1962), while well-known, is not representative of her best work.

[252] Bellow's much later fiction, *Ravelstein*, is compelling in that his subject, the Jewish Allan Bloom, is a voracious consumer after his serious book (*The Closing of the American Mind*) makes him a fortune; he embraces that world which makes a whore of those it seduces. Bloom had been one of Bellow's closest friends at the University of Chicago, and *Ravelstein* pretends to be celebratory.

[253] *The Adventures of Augie March* (New York: Viking, 1953).

[254] *Invisible Man* (New York: Signet Books, 1960; publ. by Random House in 1952), p. 20.

[255] *The Assistant* (New York: Farrar, Straus and Cudahy, 1957).

[256] *The Magic Barrel* (New York: Farrar, Straus and Cudahy, 1958).

[257] *Go Tell It on the Mountain* (New York: Knopf, 1953).

[258] *The Man Who Cried I Am* (Boston: Little, Brown, 1967).

[259] *Catch-22* (New York: Simon & Schuster, 1961).

[260] *Herzog* (New York: Viking, 1964).

[261] *Mr. Sammler's Planet* (New York: Fawcett Books, 1971; publ. by Viking in 1970).

[262] *Portnoy's Complaint* (New York: Random House, 1969). One of the more vociferous attacks on Roth and his presentation of Jews came from *Commentary* Magazine which, under its editor Norman Podhoretz, turned all fiction into politics, here the politics of Jewishness. Podhoretz failed to see how American Portnoy and *Portnoy* are.

[263] For more on this, see Chapter Eight, "Roth and Updike."

[264] *The Ghost Writer* (New York: Farrar, Straus & Giroux, 1979).

[265] *Zuckerman Bound* (New York: Farrar, Straus & Giroux, 1981).

[266] *The Anatomy Lesson* (New York: Farrar, Straus & Giroux, 1983).

[267] *The Prague Orgy* (New York: Farrar, Straus & Giroux, 1985).

[268] *Wise Blood* and *The Violent Bear It Away*, in *3 by Flannery O'Connor* (New York: Signet Books, 1962). The third selection is *A Good Man Is Hard to Find*.

[269] See both of these in Flannery O'Connor, *The Complete Stories*

(New York: Farrar, Straus and Giroux, 1971). Also, for occasional prose, see *Mystery and Manners,* ed. by Sally and Robert Fitzgerald (New York: Farrar, Straus and Giroux, 1969). These occasional pieces reveal that O'Connor thought long and hard about the craft of fiction, in essays such as "The Fiction Writer & His Country," "The Regional Writer," "Some Aspects of the Grotesque," "The Nature and Aim of Fiction," "Catholic Novelists and Their Readers." Further, she revealed some of her deepest thoughts in her letters, selected and edited by Sally Fitzgerald in a volume called *The Habit of Being* (New York: Farrar, Straus and Giroux, 1979). Of special significance are the letters she wrote to the person she called "A."

[270] *Complete Stories,* p 382.

[271] *The Heart Is a Lonely Hunter* (Boston: Houghton Mifflin, 1940).

[272] *Reflections in a Golden Eye* (Boston: Houghton Mifflin, 1941).

[273] *them* (*Them*) (New York: Vanguard Press, 1969).

[274] *Meridian* (New York: Harcourt, Brace, 1976).

[275] *Black Macho and the Myth of the Superwoman* (New York: Warner Books, 1980; publ. in 1979).

[276] The "liberated" black woman by the 1990s has entered soap opera-literally soap operas, daytime talk shows, nighttime sitcoms, and soap opera novels like *Waiting to Exhale.*

[277] Just below we will examine the recent spate of black novelists, all accomplished, but none catching us literarily the way the earlier novelists did. Among other things, they lack rhetorical power, or else point to conclusions already reached before their novels begin.

[278] *Middle Passage* (New York: Plume Books, 1991; publ. by Atheneum in 1990).

[279] Most immediately we think of Herman Melville's *Benito Cereno.* Johnson has deconstructed and then reconfigured the color variations Melville used to reflect a deeply divided America. If anything, Johnson is more conciliatory than his nineteenth-century predecessor, who saw little hope in the black-white dichotomy.

[280] *Middle Passage*, p. 179.
[281] *Ibid.*
[282] *Chaneysville Incident* (New York: Harper & Row, 1981).
[283] But more recently reissued, as a seminal novel of a black woman.
[284] *Brown Girl, Brownstones* (New York: Feminist Press, 1981; publ. in 1959).
[285] *High Cotton* (New York: Penguin, 1993; publ. by Farrar, Straus and Giroux in 1992).
[286] *Ibid.*, p. 259.
[287] *Ibid.*, p. 306.
[288] *Reckless Eyeballing* (New York: Macmillan, 1986).

CHAPTER EIGHT

[289] *The Facts* (subtitled "A Novelist's Autobiography: New York: Penguin Books, 1989; publ. by Farrar, Straus & Giroux, 1988), p. 20. Roth continues this passage by showing how his father's employer, the Metropolitan Life, was run by gentile executives, the implication being, of course, that while they tolerated a Jew, he had no power in the company.

[290] Roth's creatures can be characterized as "non-Jewish Jews," a descriptive term first used by Isaac Deutscher. This is the Jew who retains his identification as Jew but insists on a more universalist designation: someone who does not celebrate, does not follow traditions, does not defer to history, but who, nevertheless, identifies as a Jew because he is, inexplicably, a Jew. Even if as in a few cases such Jews convert, they remain unconverted; and if they go with gentiles they become more Jewish without becoming Jews. Such are the paradoxes Roth revels in.
  Among so-called "Jewish writers," he is almost alone in focusing on the non-Jewish Jew who must define himself *against* gentiles and a gentile world. Only Bellow and Malamud come close here.

[291] "Those scenes [in *My Life As a Man* on Peter Tarnopol's mar-

riage to Maureen Johnson] represent one of the few occasions when I haven't spontaneously set out to improve on actuality in the interest of being more interesting." *Ibid.*, p. 161. The scene with Maureen is supposedly close to Roth's with wife Josie, in that both women tricked their companions into believing they were pregnant. But, of course, Roth as a novelist is incapable of not improving on the actuality, and his disclaimer is simply another way of intensifying his deception of the innocent reader into believing his "facts." Facts, factoids, what's the difference!

[292] *Ibid.*, p. 162.
[293] *Ibid.*, p. 107.
[294] *The Counterlife* (New York: Farrar, Straus & Giroux, 1986), p. 321.
[295] *The Facts*, p. 117.
[296] *The Ghost Writer* (New York: Farrar, Straus and Giroux, 1979), p. 137.
[297] *Deception* (New York: Simon and Schuster, 1990), p. 125.
[298] *My Life As a Man* (New York: Holt, Rinehart and Winston, 1974).
[299] *Rabbit Redux* (New York: Knopf, 1971).
[300] Skeeter on the Vietnam War: "I'm not one of those white liberals like that cracker Fulldull [Senator Fulbright of Arkansas, an opponent of the war] or Charlie McCarthy [Eugene McCarthy, an even more vocal opponent] a while back gave all the college queers a hard-on, think Vietnam some sort of mistake, we can fix it up once we get the cave men out of office, it is *no* mistake, right, any President comes along falls in love with it, it is lib-er-al-ism's very wang, dingdong pussy, and fruit. Those crackers been lick' their mother's ass so long they forgotten what she looks like frontwards." *Ibid.*, p. 263.
[301] *Rabbit Is Rich* (New York: Knopf, 1981).
[302] They would be quite at home in Kafka's Prague, speaking German amidst Czech-speaking nationalists, in the final days of

the Austro-Hungarian Empire under an aging and increasingly desperate Franz Joseph.
[303] *Bech: A Book* (New York: Knopf, 1970).
[304] *Bech Is Back* (New York: Knopf, 1982).
[305] *Bech at Bay* (New York: Ballantine, 1998; publ. by Knopf in 1998).
[306] *Ibid.*, p. 169. Good passages abound: "Bech found himself described in scholarly offprints as 'Early Postmodern' or 'Post-Realist' or 'Pre-Minimalist' as if, a narrowly configured ephemerid, he had been born to mate and die in a certain week of summer." (p. 158) Or, he mentions other writers' advice: Mailer says, "Ignore the cretins," and Heller wonders why he even reads "such crap." (p. 160)
[307] *Toward the End of Time* (New York: Knopf, 1997).
[308] *Rabbit Remembered*, a novella in *Licks of Love* (New York: Knopf, 2000). The remainder of the volume consists of short fictions and essays, including a recollection of Harold "Doc" Humes in "Scenes from the Fifties."
[309] *Operation Shylock* (New York: Simon & Schuster, 1992).
[310] *Sabbath's Theater* (Boston: Houghton Mifflin, 1995).
[311] *American Pastoral* (Boston: Houghton Mifflin, 1997).
[312] *I Married a Communist* (Boston: Houghton Mifflin, 1998).
[313] *The Human Stain* (Boston: Houghton Mifflin, 2000).

CHAPTER NINE

[314] As mentioned above, Tom Wolfe argues realism, and perhaps entering into Wolfe's window of opportunity would be Frederick Exley's trilogy, an effort to return to that old, old realism. Exley's devotion to professional football, to Frank Gifford (the golden New York Giant back), and to bar life in *A Fan's Notes* (1968) was a noble attempt to get at the underside of a part of American culture. Tell it from the loser's point of view, the male loser, that is. But what was charming there, if overdone (too much mea culpa), has become less charming, more ado-

lescent in *Last Notes from Home* (1988). This latter book evidences a downhill slide from the middle novel in the trilogy, *Pages from a Cold Island* (1975), for which Larry McMurtry described the author as "a kind of American Dante." Exley does lead us through the nether world, but booze, easy lays with bar pickups, and inconvenient situations hardly qualify for the *Inferno*. Dante had something else in mind. While trying to be a chronicler of our time, Exley does not "make it new"; instead, he recycles old tough guy material, the loser side of Mailer or Chandler, the little guy at heart who can, nevertheless, write. Characterizing himself not as Dantean but as a "virtually unknown and unheralded author, drunk, child abandoner, and ex-mental patient," he seems, by the 1990s, stale, Wolfe-stale. Quote is from *Last Notes from Home* (New York: Random House, 1988, p. 363).

[315] *Vineland* (Boston: Little, Brown, 1990). Not to be confused with Vinland (or Vineland, Wineland), the place in America once visited by Eric Ericsson and Norsemen in the 11th century.

[316] In the June 21, 1992, New York *Times Book Review*. Coover at one point asks some of the questions which arose with the Mega-Novel, particularly the area of closure. Coover: "How does one resolve the conflict between the reader's desire for coherence and closure and the text's desire for continuance, its fear of death? Indeed, what is closure in such an environment? If everything is middle, how do you know when you are done, either as reader or writer? If the author is free to take a story anywhere at any time and in as many directions as she or he wishes, does that not become the obligation to do so?" Such questions remain just that, questions.

[317] However, copies of these books will perhaps one day be produced in the bookstore from a single master copy and printed and sold on demand, as it is now possible with publishers on the web.

[318] *Vineland*, p. 279.

[319] *Ibid.*, p. 127.
[320] *Ibid.* For sheer dazzle, the reader is directed to page 19, where an entrepreneur named Isiah wants to construct theme parks around a chain of violence centers, complete with family activities, food courts, and gift shops. He also plans "Third World Thrills," where the visitor can show his or her survival skills against "indigenous guerrilla elements." Another idea is the "Scum of the City" center, where the visitor could blow away "Pimps, Perverts, Dope Dealers, and Muggers." A third plan is for a "Hit List center, where the visitor could shoot away at a conveyor belt of public figures he wants to waste.
[321] *Closing Time* (New York: Simon and Schuster, 1994).
[322] *Ibid.*, p. 418.
[323] *Wittgenstein's Mistress* (New York: The Dalkey Archive Press, 1988).
[324] *Ibid.*, p. 197.
[325] *Tours of the Black Clock* (New York: Poseidon Press, 1989).
[326] What he also conveys in other mid to late-80s novels: *Days Between Stations, Leap Year, Rubicon Beach.*
[327] *Ibid.*, p. 249.
[328] *Ibid.*
[329] *American Psycho* (New York: Vintage Books, 1991).
[330] *Whores for Gloria* (New York: Penguin, 1994; publ. by Pantheon in 1992).
[331] *Ibid.*, p. 153.
[332] *The Tunnel* (New York: Knopf, 1995), p. 464.
[333] *Eclipse Fever* (New York: Knopf, 1991).
[334] *Philadelphia Fire* (New York: Vintage, 1991; publ. by Holt in 1990).
[335] The narrator uses "Derridian didley-bop" as a means of condemning white hegemony over blacks; on the assumption that if moral or ethical values are all relative, then so is race. It's all up for grabs, so to speak, and there is no justice no fairness, no equality. Derrida speaks for the slave master.
[336] *Because It Is Bitter and Because It Is My Heart* (New York: Plume

Books, 1991).

[337] In her brief novel *Black Water* (1992), noted above about Mary Jo Kopechne and her misadventure with Ted Kennedy, another dysfunctional family is implicated, perhaps the most famous dysfunctional family in America, the Kennedys. A cool, religious surface disguises pathologies of every variety: extreme personal anguish, considerable alcoholism and drug usage, obsessive sexual activity, a morality that has nothing to do with Catholic observance, a view of women as servants of demanding men, and everything identified as dysfunction except perhaps wife-battering, although psychological abuse is everpresent.

[338] *You Must Remember This* (New York: Dutton, 1987).

[339] *American Appetites* (New York: Dutton, 1989).

[340] *The Waterworks* (New York: Random House, 1994).

[341] For a companion volume, see Luc Sante's *Low Life*, in 1991.

[342] *The Waterworks*, p. 199.

[343] *Ibid.*, p. 231.

[344] *Ibid.*, p. 213.

[345] *The Tunnel*, p. 155. The reader might measure this cynicism against another form in Walter Abish's *How German Is It*. The lack of a question mark in the title leaves the process open and unending; no closure there. Gass picks up from that.

[346] An amusing sidenote on the blurb business: *The Tunnel* is only Gass's second novel, after *Omensetter's Luck* in 1966. That novel was hailed by critic Richard Gilman as the single "most important work of fiction by an American of this literary generation," an amazing dismissal of Gaddis's *The Recognitions*, now a modern classic even among those who have never gotten through it; Heller's *Catch-22*, the iconic fiction of the postwar generation; Pynchon's *V.*, the beginning of the most influential novelist of his generation. This is for starters. As always, blurbs and/or reviews are part of the deception the better novelists have to cut through. *The Tunnel* has no blurb. Author's choice or no takers?

[347] Another "tunnel" appears in Richard Powers's *Prisoner's Dilemma* (1988) in the form of the father's secret project, Hobstown, a tunneling into his past. Eddie Hobson, Sr., like so many other 80s and 90s figures, heads an unstable family and must himself escape his own obsessive character by way of tape recording his memories. Only memory, caught on tape, validates his existence. Powers's comedic novel combines public and private, political and personal, social and self; but, mainly, it feeds the schizoid quality of the last decade: that need to assert the self by escaping it; that impulse to become obsessive about what seems an evasion of one's own reality.

[348] "Her Sense of Timing," in *Van Gogh's Room at Arles* (New York: Hyperion, 1993).

[349] The idea of a Jewish return to Poland is the source of fun in Philip Roth's *Operation Shylock*.

[350] Not solely from other countries, as we see with Toni Morrison. Among more recent American writers, we need only cite Dorothy Allison's *Bastard out of Carolina* as a descendant of Faulkner, surely with some intermix of Erskine Caldwell's *Tobacco Road* and *God's Little Acre*. More than anyone else, however, Allison's colorful Boatwrights, although less grasping and more beguiling, owe much of their substance and attitude to Faulkner's Snopeses. And her central adult figure, "Mama," has something of Eula Varner's magnetic heat, without herself becoming merely a "sex object." The central child figure, called "Bone," is less Faulknerian only because Allison deals directly with child abuse, here that of a stepfather for his stepdaughter from early childhood to her near teens. But even that relationship, between Bone and Daddy Glen, is presupposed in Faulkner's Eula, whose ripening figure creates lust in men when she is still a child. None of this takes away from Allison's achievement; like Faulkner's mythical Yoknapatawpha, she creates a rural place far from Eden and a time that seems eternal. Greenville County, South Carolina, produces Boatwrights, as much as Yoknapatawpha created Snopeses and Varners. Both

places and times emerge from expertness with language, the deconstruction of more traditional or expected family lines, and a sense of evolution that lies outside history.

[351] *Dreaming in Cuban* (New York: Ballantine, 1992).

[352] *Ibid.*, p. 99.

[353] *Bless Me, Ultima* (New York: Warner Books, 1994).

[354] *The House on Mango Street* (New York: Vintage, 1991).

[355] *The Beet Queen* (New York: Bantam, 1987; publ. by Holt in 1986).

[356] *Alburquerque* (New York: Warner Books, 1994; publ. by University of New Mexico Press in 1992).

[357] An Anglo version of magicalism comes in Paul Auster's *Mr. Vertigo* (1994). In a Huck Finn for our times, his protagonist, Walter, becomes Wonder Boy, who can levitate, walk on water, soar over his audience. When after excruciating headaches, Wonder Boy fails, he shapes and reshapes himself, an artist figure who can draw on magical, mysterious powers. That ultimately he will fail in his various enterprises does not subtract from what he suggests: that rational discourse, logic, science itself cannot explain the mysteries of will, determination, reshaping. Walter becomes as much an emblem of American failure as of success, but, nevertheless, he seems touched by a spirit lying just beyond achievement. That "beyond" is what the Latino Writers seem to take for granted.

Even more in the Latino-American mode is Alice Walker's *The Temple of My Familiar* (1989), a world of spirits, stretched historical dimensions, and culture clashes; but marred by an attachment to Africa that seems more ideological than real, more as adversary to American culture than as a realistic portrayal of the African scene. The Walker novel is in the broad tradition of *One Hundred Years of Solitude*, with various black lives illustrative of different periods in African and American culture: slavery, village life, worship of spirits, glimpses into a magical realm where spirit, soul, and body seem to unite. Yet Walker's celebration of African life-a continuation of *The Color*

Purple-fails to take into account that it is *history*, not the present; that, like most places which once had a way of life, it is no longer what it was and that her nostalgia for "paradise" is a form of blindness to corruptive inroads into village life and its customs. There are no more "pure" places.

[358] The so-called pleasures of "indulgence" are a mixed experience in the 80s and 90s. Fun is redefined. Popular culture has been, if anything, more negative about life in these United States than the writers and entertainers aiming at a more sophisticated audience. In that pop world, sex is painful and dangerous; it is misogynist to an alarming degree; it is often racially and ethnically offensive; it makes drugs appear more as downers than as uppers; it offers little beyond violence on the streets among home boys; it is full of rage, hostility, hatred. For rockers, rappers, and their kind, pleasure is long gone; what remains is dread, incoherence, a brief life and a violent end. No love, intimacy, relationships can exist. The temptations of that world are hardly attractive-all they offer is being with it. More likely than not, there is a gun in your future; or else AIDS, child abuse, rotten parental figures, only gangs to fall back upon, destructive streets, the hood and hoods.

[359] *Ceremony* (New York: Penguin Books, 1986; publ. by Viking in 1977).

[360] *Almanac of the Dead* (New York: Penguin Books, 1992; publ. by Simon & Schuster, 1991).

[361] *Ceremony*, p. 246.

[362] *The Death of Bernadette Lefthand* (New York: Bantam, 1995; publ. in Red Crane edition in 1993).

[363] Sigrid Nunez-as her name indicates-is a United Nations of colors and races: Chinese father, also Spanish and German in the background. The narrator in her story "Chang" is identified as Chinese, although nothing in her house is Chinese except her father, and she wants to be known as "Sue Brown," an All-American girl.

[364] Both the Louie and the Wong stories are in *Charlie Chan Is*

Dead: An Anthology of Contemporary Asian American Fiction, edited with an introduction by Jessica Hagedorn (New York: Penguin Books, 1993).

[365] "Fictive Fragments of a Father and Son," in *Charlie Chan Is Dead*, p. 357.

[366] *Ibid.*

[367] "Mourning and Melancholia," in 1917, in *Collected Papers* (New York: Basic Books, 1959).

[368] *Galatea 2.2* (New York: Farrar, Straus and Giroux, 1995).

[369] It is ironic that cyberspace derives from the idea of a helmsman (*cyber* or the Greek *kyber*) steering; that is, a human being at the helm, whereas in the modern usage the machine-like Helen is overtaking man's functions.

[370] *Ibid.*, p.320.

[371] *Ibid.*,

[372] *Underworld* (New York: Scribner, 1997).

[373] *Ibid.*, p. 430.

[374] *Infinite Jest* (Boston: Little, Brown, 1996).

[375] *Ibid.*, p. 562.

[376] *Ibid.*, p. 558.

[377] *Ibid.*, p. 538.

[378] *Ibid.*, p. 512.

[379] *Ibid.*, p. 981.

[380] *Mason & Dixon* (New York: Holt, 1997).

[381] *Ibid.*, p. 706.

[382] *Ibid.*, p. 296.

INDEX

Abbott, Shirley 66, 487
Abish, Walter 82, 273, 277, 278, 430, 431, 518
Acker, Kathy 15, 101, 226, 249-252
Allen, Woody 190, 281, 417
Allison, Dorothy 289, 363, 519
Alther, Lisa 338, 362
Alvarez, Julia 449
Anaya, Rudolfo 449, 451, 453, 454
Anderson, Sherwood 226, 448
Apple, Max 499
Auster, Paul 14, 15, 20, 25, 27, 28, 30, 31, 36, 50, 80, 84, 97, 98, 100-108, 122, 168, 203, 224, 229, 283, 353, 430, 490, 520

Baker, Houston A., Jr. 491, 492, 494, 495
Baker, Nicholson 226, 259-263
Baker, Russell 27, 62, 70-72, 98
Baldwin, James 13, 338, 341, 344, 345, 347, 349, 350-352, 362
Ball, Ian 374, 375
Bambara, Toni Cade 274, 338, 353
Banks, Russell 226, 227, 252-256, 501

Baraka, Amiri (LeRoi Jones) 494
Barth, John 13, 15, 23, 101, 121, 132, 138, 155, 156, 161, 163, 164, 170, 175, 178, 182, 273, 345, 363, 377, 410, 495
Barthelme, Donald 13, 15, 17, 23, 98, 108, 224, 225, 273, 277, 278, 280, 281, 345, 409, 424, 499, 503
Barthelme, Frederick 16, 273, 277, 279, 280, 289
Barthes, Roland 88, 414
Baudelaire, Charles 210
Beattie, Ann 16, 274, 279, 363, 499
Beckett, Samuel 281, 355, 474, 475
Bellow, Saul 13, 22, 31, 112, 122, 132, 137, 138, 157, 162, 195, 226, 240, 241, 242, 274, 285-287, 291, 338, 340-347, 353-355, 363, 366, 373, 376, 448, 511, 513
Berger, Thomas 499
Bergson, Henri 171
Bernstein, Carl 50, 203, 487
Berryman, John 344
Bersani, Leo 485
Bishop, Elizabeth 344
Blaise, Clark 487
Bly, Robert 49, 58, 234
Bogan, Louise 344
Borges, Jorge Luis 276, 278, 449
Bosch, Hieronymus 123
Boyle, T. Coraghessan 14, 16, 25, 80, 84, 108-113, 115, 116, 118-121, 364, 416
Bradley, David 23, 155, 157, 366-369, 373
Brady, James 507
Brand, Max 228
Brecht, Bertold 254
Brodkey, Harold 16, 23, 155, 157, 194-198, 200-213, 445
Brown, Harry 309, 310
Broyard, Anatole 122, 123
Bruce, Lenny 354

Buchanan, Cynthia 362
Buck, Pearl 137
Burns, John Horne 306, 321, 328-331, 346
Burroughs, William 15, 80, 183, 270, 413
Butler, Robert Olen 333-335, 509

Calvino, Italo 276
Camus, Albert 355
Canin, Ethan 226, 242, 243, 501
Caputo, Philip 300, 313, 317
Caramello, Charles 496, 497
Carlyle, Thomas 441
Carroll, James 487
Carter, Stephen 363
Carver, Raymond 15, 16, 273, 279, 280, 499
Cary, Lorene 55, 62
Cather, Willa 79, 226
Cervantes, Miguel de 101, 102, 132
Chandler, Raymond 101, 227, 516
Cheever, John 27, 50, 62-66
Cheever, Susan 27, 50, 62-66, 203
Chekhov, Anton 280, 469
Cheuse, Alan 123
Christo 146
Cisneros, Sandra 449, 451, 455
Cleaver, Eldridge 338, 351, 352, 362
Collins, Wilkie 100
Conrad, Joseph 110, 114, 116, 248, 280, 343, 440, 501
Conroy, Frank 27, 28
Cooper, James Fenimore 177, 312, 340
Coover, Robert 13, 185, 285, 289, 290, 414, 516
Cortázar, Julio 449
Cowan, Paul 27, 44-46
Cozzens, James Gould 324

Crane, Stephen 226, 311, 322
Cruse, Harold 353, 362

Darwin, Charles 110
Davenport, Guy 15-17, 271-273, 276, 277, 503
de Chardin, Teilhard 357
de Chirico, Giorgio 100
De Jongh, James 494, 495
de Sade, Marquis 251
Del Vecchio, John 300
Delaney, Samuel R. 57, 58, 99, 487
DeLillo, Don 14, 16, 17, 19, 22, 25, 78, 80-93, 95, 96, 157, 229, 275, 353, 425, 467-471, 476, 498, 507
DeMott, Benjamin 496
Derrida, Jacques 517
Desai, Anita 408
Dickens, Charles 23, 156, 211, 410, 481
Didion, Joan 128, 227, 280, 288, 289, 361, 499
Dillard, Annie 62, 67, 487
Doctorow, E L. 13, 25, 27, 62, 75-77, 291, 338, 363, 430, 438-441
Donoso, José 448
Dos Passos, John 162, 310, 448
Douglas, Ann 493
Dowell, Coleman 275-277
Dreiser, Theodore 46, 79, 226, 252, 310, 360, 448, 485
Dryden, John 114

Eagelton, Terry 485
Eliot, George 156
Eliot, T. S. 79, 137, 344, 447, 448, 494
Ellis, Brett Easton 426-429, 443

Ellison, Ralph 13, 20, 122, 138-140, 146, 295, 338, 343, 344, 347, 348, 351, 352, 355, 362, 448, 493
Emerson, Ralph Waldo 79, 163, 213, 215, 231, 340, 346, 398
Erdrich, Louise 451, 452
Erickson, Steve 424-426

Fadiman, Clifton 496
Faulkner, William 13, 46, 79, 116, 117, 120, 122-125, 127, 130, 131, 133, 137, 141, 145-147, 151, 159, 177, 222, 227, 263, 264, 267, 268, 280, 344, 357, 358, 368, 370, 447-451, 485, 491, 496, 501, 504, 519
Fielding, Henry 156
Fitzgerald, F. Scott 13, 46, 246, 248, 257, 310, 344, 388, 448, 485, 512
Ford, Richard 15, 98, 100, 226-241, 260
Forrest, Leon 373
Forster, E. M. 137
Frank, Anne 385
Freud, Sigmund 192, 356, 357, 397, 462, 463, 475
Friedan, Betty 361
Friedman, Bruce Jay 345, 363
Frye, Northrop 485
Fuentes, Carlos 448, 450

Gaddis, William 13, 14, 16, 23, 25, 80, 81, 87, 108, 121, 122, 133, 155, 156, 160, 161, 163, 178, 182, 185, 191, 194, 195, 213-222, 224, 227, 271, 285, 289, 295-297, 345, 347, 353, 363, 410, 415, 424, 430, 472, 473, 495, 498, 518
Galloway, Joseph L. 508
Garcia, Cristina 447, 449, 450, 459
Garreau, Joel 68
Gass, William 13, 158, 159, 273, 430, 440-445, 518

Gates, Henry Louis 363, 491-494
Gayle, Addison 352
Geismar, Maxwell 496
Gentry, Peter 507
Gilman, Richard 518
Gilmore, Mikal 27, 40-44
Goldman, Ari L. 487
Gordon, Mary 291, 487
Gould, Lois 338
Greene, Graham 129
Grey, Zane 228

Hackworth, Colonel David H. 300
Hagedorn, Jessica 522
Hammett, Dashiell 101, 228
Hannah, Barry 15-17, 99, 121, 283-285, 504
Hardy, Thomas 321
Hawkes, John 13, 80, 108, 121, 185, 224
Hawthorne, Nathaniel 79, 98, 102, 103, 144, 163, 177, 213, 340, 490
Heidegger, Martin 326
Heinemann, Larry 300, 315
Heller, Joseph 13, 15, 121, 271, 285, 291, 322, 331, 332, 338, 339, 343, 344, 353, 354, 363, 399, 418-422, 515, 518
Helprin, Mark 23, 155, 157, 274, 286, 314
Hemingway, Ernest 13, 46, 79, 131, 137, 184, 187, 188, 192, 226, 227, 231, 310, 312, 344, 448, 485, 501, 503, 507
Herr, Michael 300, 302, 307, 308, 328
Hijuelas, Oscar 290
Hobbes, Thomas 106
Hochschild, Adam 50, 62, 487, 488
Hoffman, Eva 27, 62, 67-70
Hogarth, William 113
Hongo, Garrett 334

Hopper, Edward 100
Howard, Maureen 362
Howe, Irving 352, 363
Hoyt, Killens 352
Hurston, Zora Neale 485, 493
Huxley, Aldous 137

James, Henry 124, 310, 355, 490
Jameson, Fredric 485
Janowitz, Tama 280, 281
Jenkins, Dan 507
Johnson, Charles 364, 366, 512
Johnson, Diane 338, 362
Jones, James 305, 310, 312, 319, 323, 326, 331, 333, 346
Jong, Erica 338, 362
Jordan, June 510
Joyce, James 76, 137, 161, 164, 167, 170, 227, 280, 344, 448, 449, 473-475, 494
Junghyo, Ahn 510

Kafka, Franz 20, 33, 34, 70, 89, 97, 98, 100, 104, 108-111, 127, 196, 207, 278, 280, 344, 355, 386, 387, 389, 405, 411, 448, 514
Kagan, Richard C. 509
Kaiko, Takeshi 509
Kandinsky, Wasily 271, 274
Kane, Rod 300, 313, 314, 317
Kant, Immanuel 261
Kazin, Alfred 495, 496
Kerouac, Jack 299
Kierkegaard, Søren 356, 359, 405
Kingston, Maxine Hong 78, 459
Kinkaid, Jamaica 353

Klein, Joe 315
Kolko, Gabriel 508
Kovic, Ron 300, 314
Kubrick, Stanley 326

L'Amour, Louis 228
Lawrence, D. H. 173, 457
Leavitt, David 282
LeClair, Tom 495
Lester, Julius 27, 46-48
Levin, Harry 485
Levine, George 485
Lewis, Sinclair 79, 137, 226, 310, 448, 485
Limon, John 506, 507
Llosa, Mario Vargas 448, 451
Lloyd, Rosemary 486
London, Jack 124, 131
Lopez, Barry 122
Louie, David Wong 459
Lowell, Robert 344

Mailer, Norman 13,15, 22, 41, 43, 80, 122, 155, 157, 161, 162, 183-194, 208, 209, 220, 251, 285, 286, 291, 305, 307, 312, 321, 322, 324-328, 330-332, 338, 339, 346, 351, 352, 363, 376, 399, 401, 448, 504, 507, 515, 516
Malamud, Bernard 13, 157, 283, 285, 338-340, 344, 345, 349, 350, 373, 448, 506, 513
Mallarmé, Stéphane 100, 106, 108, 210, 486, 490
Markson, David 422, 423, 424, 426
Marquand, John 324
Marquez, Gabriel Garcia 157, 448, 450, 451, 491
Marshall, Paule 370, 372

Mason, Bobbie Ann 274, 279, 363
Mason, Robert C. 322, 507
Matthiessen, Peter 122, 226, 263, 264
McCarthy, Cormac 80, 122-136, 227, 229, 430
McCourt, Frank 487
McCullers, Carson 285, 344, 357, 358
McElroy, Joseph 13, 15, 23, 80, 155, 157, 158, 161, 163-182, 191, 195, 220, 221, 285, 345, 363, 496-498
McInerney, Jay 280, 281, 298, 299
McMurtry, Larry 516
Melville, Herman 79, 98, 123, 124, 144, 163, 177, 183, 213, 340, 347, 355, 377, 512
Milton, John 114
Momaday, N. Scott 456
Monette, Paul 57
Moore, Harold G. 508
Moore, Lorrie 281, 282
Morrison, Toni 13, 14, 16, 20, 25, 80, 122, 136-141, 143-154, 157, 291, 293, 294, 338, 343, 345, 353, 359-362, 373, 430, 491-494, 519
Mukherjee, Bharati 408, 456, 459
Mura, David 461
Murray, Albert 489, 510

Nabokov, Vladimir 121, 278
Nader, Ralph 176
Naipaul, V. S. 408
Naylor, Gloria 353
Nietzsche, Friedrich 328, 444, 498
Noland, Sherwin B. 431
Norris, Frank 226, 310
Nunez, Sigrid 521

O'Brien, Tim 300, 305, 306, 313, 316, 317, 328, 332, 419
O'Connor, Flannery 13, 285, 344, 347, 348, 349, 357, 358, 511, 512
O'Hara, John 324, 339, 402
O'Neill, Eugene 137
Oates, Joyce Carol 13, 25, 122, 126, 132, 157, 195, 226, 227, 256-259, 274, 285, 338, 341-343, 360, 364, 430, 433-438, 448
Ovid 464
Ozick, Cynthia 226, 227, 244, 245, 341, 343, 359

Peckinpah, Sam 123
Percy, Walker 507
Picasso, Pablo 271-273, 494, 502
Piercy, Marge 362
Pinckney Darryl 372, 373, 374
Plath, Sylvia 344
Podhoretz, Norman 511
Poe, Edgar Allan 79, 98, 100, 101, 144, 223, 340
Pope, Alexander 114
Porter, Katherine Anne 510
Powers, Richard 223-225, 463-466, 519
Proulx, Annie 264, 266, 267, 402
Proust, Marcel 157, 181, 205, 260, 261
Puller, Lewis B., Jr. 314
Pynchon, Thomas 13-15, 18, 23, 25, 80, 81, 87, 104, 108, 121, 122, 138, 155, 157, 159-162, 166, 175, 178, 182, 185, 191, 195, 224, 227, 271, 285, 331, 363, 373, 410, 412-415, 417, 424, 425, 440, 472, 473, 478-483, 485, 495, 498, 518

Rabelais 410, 414
Reed, Ishmael 13, 15, 20, 122, 291, 294, 338, 352, 374-376, 505, 510

Remarque, Erich Maria 325
Rhodes, Richard 27, 33-36, 50, 203
Richardson, Samuel 156
Rivera, Edward 27, 62, 72-75, 203
Robbe-Grillet, Alain 100
Rossner, Judith 338, 362
Roth, Henry 78, 87, 350, 370
Roth, Philip 13, 14, 20, 22, 24, 50, 62, 122, 138, 157, 285, 289, 290, 338-341, 343, 344, 350, 353-357, 363, 375, 377-381, 384, 386, 389-398, 401-406, 448, 504, 510, 511, 513, 514, 519
Rushdie, Salman 87, 109, 170, 405

Sack, John 300
Salinger, J. D. 58, 78, 87, 345, 348, 350, 504
Salter, James 503
Sartre, Jean Paul 399
Schiller, Lawrence 43, 44
Schoenberg, Arnold 159
Schwartz, Delmore 60, 350, 487
Scott, Leonard B. 508
Settle, Mary Ann 363
Sexton, Anne 344
Shaw, Irwin 305, 331
Shawcross, William 508
Shechner, Mark 339, 340
Sheehan, Neil 300, 303, 308, 332
Short, Luke 228
Shulman, Alix Kates 362
Silko, Leslie Marmon 451, 456, 457
Singer, Isaac Bashevis 344
Slotkin, Richard 318
Smollett, Tobias 480
Sorrentino, Gilbert 273

Soyinka, Wole 408
Springsteen, Bruce 281
Stang, Richard 485
Staples, Brent 487
Steinbeck, John 131, 137, 310, 344
Stendhal 311, 322
Stevens, Wallace 308, 344
Stone, Oliver 92, 326
Stone, Robert 25, 227, 245-249, 300, 501
Styron, William 13, 148, 285, 345, 352, 430, 448
Swift, Jonathan 410

Tan, Amy 459
Tanner, Tony 496
Tarantino, Quentin 426
Terry, Wallace 508
Thackeray, William Makepeace 156
Theroux, Alexander 155, 157, 223
Thoreau, Henry David 79, 163, 272, 310, 340, 385
Tolstoy, Leo 156
Trotsky, Leon 276
Tyler, Anne 274, 363

Updike, John 13, 24, 157, 195, 236, 262, 263, 279, 285, 286, 345, 377-380, 382-384, 388-402, 407, 448, 502, 506, 510, 511

Van Gogh, Vincent 272, 519
Villa, Jose Garcia 459
Vollman, William T. 429
Vonnegut, Kurt 121, 285

Wade, John 316-318
Walker, Alice 13, 20, 227, 274, 286, 291, 292, 338, 343, 353, 359, 360, 362, 363, 493, 520
Walker, Keith 303
Wallace, David Foster 16, 21, 23, 157, 452, 453, 471-478, 498, 505, 508
Wallace, Michele 361
Warren, Robert Penn 123
Webb, James 300, 327, 509
Wells, H. G. 263
Wells, Tom 508
West, Cornel 363
Wharton, Edith 46, 79, 226, 252, 310, 340, 448, 485
White, Edmund 27, 50, 57-60, 203
Whitman, Walt 141, 344
Wideman, John Edgar 20, 27, 35-40, 203, 243, 291, 430-433
Wilde, Alan 499, 500
Williams, John 291, 338, 344, 345, 347, 351-353, 361, 362
Williams, Robin 16, 190, 294
Williams, William Carlos 344
Wilson, Edmund 214
Wilson, William Julius 363, 490
Wolfe, Thomas 310, 344, 477, 516
Wolfe, Tom 485, 486, 515
Wolff, Geoffrey 27, 40, 49-53, 203, 371, 434
Wolff, Tobias 16, 27, 49, 50, 53, 54, 57, 203, 274, 286, 487
Wong, Shawn 459, 460, 521
Woolf, Virginia 137, 142, 448, 473, 491
Wouk, Herman 327, 331
Wright, Richard 79, 226, 338, 344, 347, 350-352, 362

Yardley, Jonathan 62, 67, 487

RECEIVED AUG 17 2005 36.99